PARIS AND THE

M000295224

This transnational history of Paris in 1919 explores the global implications of the revolutionary crisis of French society at the end of World
War I. As the site of the peace conference Paris was a victorious capital
and a city at the center of the world, and Tyler Stovall explores these
intersections of globalization and local revolution. The book takes as
its central point the eruption of political activism in 1919, using the
events of that year to illustrate broader tensions in working-class, race,
and gender politics in Parisian, French, and ultimately global society
which fueled debates about colonial subjects and the empire. Viewing
consumerism and consumer politics as key both to the revolutionary
crisis and to new ideas about working-class identity, and arguing
against the idea that consumerism depoliticized working people, this
history of local labor movements is a study in the making of the
modern world.

TYLER STOVALL is Professor of History at the University of
California, Berkeley. He specializes in modern and contemporary
French history, in particular questions of race, colonialism and post-
colonialism, labor, and transnationalism.

NEW STUDIES IN EUROPEAN HISTORY

Edited by

PETER BALDWIN, University of California, Los Angeles
CHRISTOPHER CLARK, University of Cambridge
JAMES B. COLLINS, Georgetown University
MIA RODRÍGUEZ-SALGADO, London School of Economics and Political Science
LYNDAL ROPER, University of Oxford
TIMOTHY SNYDER, Yale University

The aim of this series in early modern and modern European history is to publish outstanding works of research, addressed to important themes across a wide geographical range, from southern and central Europe to Scandinavia and Russia, from the time of the Renaissance to the Second World War. As it develops, the series will comprise focused works of wide contextual range and intellectual ambition.

A full list of titles published in the series can be found at:
www.cambridge.org/newstudiesineuropeanhistory

PARIS AND THE SPIRIT OF 1919

Consumer Struggles, Transnationalism, and Revolution

TYLER STOVALL

University of California, Berkeley

CAMBRIDGE
UNIVERSITY PRESS

CAMBRIDGE
UNIVERSITY PRESS

University Printing House, Cambridge CB2 8BS, United Kingdom

Cambridge University Press is part of the University of Cambridge.

It furthers the University's mission by disseminating knowledge in the pursuit of
education, learning and research at the highest international levels of excellence.

www.cambridge.org
Information on this title: www.cambridge.org/9781107521230

First published 2012
First paperback edition 2015

A catalogue record for this publication is available from the British Library

Library of Congress Cataloguing in Publication data
Stovall, Tyler Edward.
Paris and the spirit of 1919 : consumer struggles, transnationalism, and revolution / Tyler Stovall.
p. cm. – (New studies in European history)
ISBN 978-1-107-01801-3 (hardback)
1. Working class – France – Paris – History – 20th century.   2. Labor movement – France –
Paris – History – 20th century   3. Popular fronts – France – Paris – History – 20th century.
4. Strikes and lockouts – France – Paris – History – 20th century.   5. Consumption
(Economics) – Social aspects – France – Paris – History – 20th century.   6. Paris (France) –
History – 20th century.   7. France – History – 1914-1940.   I. Title.   II. Series.
HD8440.P2S76 2012
944'.3610815–dc23
2011030735

ISBN 978-1-107-01801-3 Hardback
ISBN 978-1-107-52123-0 Paperback

To the Memory of
Bob Frost
(1952–2011)
Scholar, Teacher, Comrade, Best of Friends

Contents

Illustrations

Tables

Acknowledgments

Over the all-too-many years it took to bring this study from inception to completion I have been fortunate to benefit from the kind support and sage advice of colleagues, family, and friends. I would first like to thank two colleagues, Mary Louise Roberts and Laura Levine Frader, who both took valuable time out of their schedules to read and comment extensively on full drafts of this manuscript. I am indebted both to their commitment to my work and to the exemplary nature of their own. My thanks also to David Bell and Martha Hanna, whose editing of my article for *French Historical Studies* on the consumers war helped enormously in shaping my thinking on the subject. I owe a great deal of gratitude to colleagues both near and far who patiently read sections or listened to presentations of this project, including Michael Cohen, Sarah Sussman, Ted Margadant, Joby Margadant, Cathy Kudlick, Aron Rodrigue, Patricia Lorcin, Eric Weitz, Michael Vann, Joe Bohling, and Alex Toledano. I am particularly grateful to the staff of the Undergraduate Division at the University of California, Berkeley, especially Laura Demir, Jill Gerstenberger, and Paul Schwochow, for always cheerfully helping out when needed. In France I benefited enormously from the counsel of Jean-Louis Robert, who was always willing to share his encyclopedic knowledge of Parisian labor with me. Many archivists in France went out of their way to help me with my research; I would like to single out for particular mention Claude Charlot of the Archives of the Paris Prefecture of Police for his many kindnesses. I am also grateful to Dominique Taff at the Archives Nationales Section Outre-Mer for introducing me to some important materials. Funding for this project came from several sources, most notably the Committee on Research of the University of California, Santa Cruz, and the Ford Foundation Minority Postdoctoral Fellowship Program. At Cambridge University Press, I am very grateful to Michael Watson, whose support of this project never flagged. I also want to thank Chloe Howell, who shepherded me through the production process, and Caroline Howlett, who did an excellent job of copyediting this book. In addition, I am indebted to James Collins, editor of the series New Studies in European History, and to the anonymous reviewers for Cambridge University Press, whose incisive comments have made this a much better book.

Most of all, I am enormously indebted to my family: my wife Denise and my son Justin. Time and time again, my wife took up the slack on the home front, at times at the expense of her own career, in order to help me complete this book. In particular I thank her for never once complaining about how long it was taking, even though she had every reason to do so. My son showed the same boundless enthusiasm for this book he shows for most things (except vegetables and bedtime). At one point he proclaimed that when he grew up he wanted to be a French historian and a fireman. Not only did he teach me more about consumerism than I ever hoped to learn, but most of all kept my focus on the truly important things in life.

During the last year I lost two of my closest colleagues and friends, both historians of France who had an important impact on this study. The passing of Susanna Barrows came as a tragedy and a deep loss not only for me but for all those she helped train in French history at Berkeley. I was privileged to know her as a mentor, colleague, and friend, and she encouraged this project right from its very beginnings. A few months later I lost my best friend of thirty-five years, Bob Frost. Bob was simply a force of nature, a brilliant scholar, passionate and devoted teacher, and fiercely loyal friend and comrade. I do not think I will see his like again in this lifetime. I very much regret that neither Susanna nor Bob will see this finished book, but I hope in some small way it will help to preserve our memories of them.

In short, my thanks to all those whose support, collegiality, and friendship made this book possible. Many can share responsibility for its fruits, whereas I alone am accountable for its defects. I hope you will all enjoy it, if for no other reason than that you no longer have to listen to me obsess about it.

Materials in this book previously appeared in *French Historical Studies* ("The Consumers' War: Paris, 1914–1918," vol. 31/#2, Spring 2008), *Le Mouvement Social* ("Du vieux et du neuf: économie morale et militantisme ouvrier dans les luttes contre la vie chère à Paris en 1919," no. 170, January–March 1995), and *The Proceedings of the Western Society for French History* ("*Sous les toits de Paris:* The Working Class and the Paris Housing Crisis, 1914–1924," vol. 14, 1987). I thank the editors of these journals for allowing me to reproduce these materials here.

Introduction: a year like no other

Prenez garde, prenez garde	Watch out, watch out
Les sabreurs les bourgeois, les gavés	You cavalrymen, bourgeois, fat-cats
V'là la jeune garde	The youth Guard is here
V'là la jeune garde	The youth Guard is here
Qui descend sur le pavé . . .	We are taking to the streets . . .
C'est la lutte finale qui commence	It's the start of the final struggle
C'est la révolte de tous les meurt-de-faim	It's the revolt of the starved
C'est la Révolution qui s'avance	It's the Revolution on the march
C'est la bataille contre tous les coquins[1]	It's the battle against all the rogues

As a number of historians have recognized, for drama and significance the year 1919 has few parallels in the history of the modern world. William Klingaman called it "the year our world began," while Margaret MacMillan has characterized Paris in 1919 as "six months that changed the world."[2] Most recently, Anthony Read has portrayed it as "a world on fire."[3] Whereas other key dates in modern history, ranging from 1789 to 1914, 1917, 1933, 1945, and 1989 have generally marked either the beginning or the end of something, 1919 interests us precisely because of the character of those twelve months themselves, and the paths taken or not taken by historical actors during them. Like 1848 and 1968, 1919 was a year in which many things seemed up for grabs, one that seemed to offer a wide range of choices, yet at the same time underscored the limits of the possible.[4]

[1] René Michaud, *J'avais vingt ans: un jeune ouvrier au début du siècle* (Paris: Éditions syndicalistes, 1967), 105.
[2] William Klingaman, *1919: The Year Our World Began* (New York: St. Martin's Press, 1987); Margaret MacMillan, *Paris 1919: Six Months that Changed the World* (New York: Random House, 2002); David J. Mitchell, *1919: Red Mirage: Year of Desperate Rebellion* (London: Cape, 1970).
[3] Anthony Read, *A World on Fire: 1919 and the Battle with Bolshevism* (New York and London: W. W. Norton & Co., 2008).
[4] Jonathan Sperber, *The European Revolutions, 1848–1851* (New York: Cambridge University Press, 2005); Barbara and John Ehrenreich, *Long March, Short Spring: The Student Uprising at Home and*

This study considers the transformation of working-class life in Paris as a result of World War I, taking as its central point political activism in 1919. The turbulence of Paris in 1919 resembled that produced by the confluence of two or more streams into the same watery basin. The resulting white water is a spectacular but evanescent display, as the disparate streams eventually blend and flow into a routinized channel. This book argues that working-class identity in the French capital shifted in important ways, and that these shifts were especially apparent during the year after the Armistice. In particular, I contend that the war brought questions of consumerism and the state to the fore, and that racial and gender difference were of vital importance in elaborating new visions of what it meant to be a worker in the era of World War I. Central to this study is the assertion that consumerism concerns necessities as well as luxuries (and in fact a rejection of hard-and-fast distinctions between the two). Following from this, I argue that consumerism can just as easily be a radicalizing force politically as a conservative one, that the desire for goods can move people to challenge capitalism and the status quo rather than integrating them into it. As this book will show, an insurgent vision of consumer culture played a key role in the revolutionary spirit of 1919.

The war years gave a new urgency to working-class consumerism, focused overwhelmingly on basic consumer goods like food and housing; during the immediate postwar era debates about the nature of peacetime conversion and deregulation of consumer goods underscored the political character of not just consumer life but working-class identity in general. At the same time, different processes of peacetime conversion both called into question and ultimately reaffirmed the diverse and splintered character of working-class identity in Paris. More generally, insurgent consumerism and issues of difference and transnationalism underlined transitions from nineteenth-century working-class life, which emphasized narrow corporatist struggles, to a more inclusive vision of working-class community that would set the tone for the twentieth century. In the end, the instability of working-class life in 1919 highlighted themes that would henceforth loom large in the world of labor as a whole.

Those who observed such changes at the end of World War I often framed them in terms of revolution. Not only did the threat (or promise) of insurrection seem omnipresent in 1919 but the war itself seemed to have destroyed the old world without making clear what was to replace it. This

Abroad (New York: Monthly Review Press, 1969). Also like 1848 and 1968, as I shall argue, 1919 represented an era whose revolutionary hopes failed in the short term but to an important extent ultimately triumphed.

study takes as one of its central questions an exploration of why revolution seemed so imminent in the postwar era, even in a victorious nation like France. However, rather than attempt to explain why the revolutionary moment never achieved fruition, it seeks instead to illustrate how the prospect of revolution arose from and helped shape fundamental changes in working-class politics and identity. Ultimately it sees the turbulence of 1919 as a template for the uncertainties and anxieties germane to class and class society in the twentieth century.

1919 IN HISTORY

Several qualities made 1919 special. It was a year divided almost exactly between war and peace. Although students generally learn that World War I ended with the Armistice on November 11, 1918, in actual fact the belligerent nations remained in a state of war until the signing of the peace treaty at Versailles on June 28, 1919. Unlike 1945, when peace and unconditional surrender came at the same time, the first six months of 1919 in particular represented a liminal period caught between violence and diplomacy, victory and defeat. Moreover, although the guns of the Western Front had fallen silent, military struggles continued in the Balkans and most notably in the infant Soviet Union. The year 1919 thus presents an intriguing mixture of conflict and concord, a fitting beginning to a European century that would witness extremes of both.[5]

The year 1919 also represented contrasts of chronology and geography. Like World War I in general, it looked both back to the nineteenth century and forward to the twentieth. For Europeans the year underscored the collapse of empire and the widespread creation of liberal democratic nation-states.[6] One of the great paradoxes of the Peace of Versailles was its effective abolition of empire within Europe at the same time as it reinforced and extended empire overseas, thus emphasizing the racialized nature of democracy on a global scale and justifying W. E. B. Dubois' remark about the centrality of the color line to the twentieth century. At the same time it showed how such changes had to adapt to the persistence of tradition or fail. Most Europeans, even in an industrialized nation like France, lived in the countryside or in small towns, areas whose daily rhythms had little to do

---

[5] Arno Mayer, *The Politics and Diplomacy of Peacemaking* (New York: Knopf, 1967); William Keylor, ed., *The Legacy of the Great War: Peacemaking, 1919* (Boston: Houghton Mifflin, 1998).

[6] See on this point Mark Mazower, *Dark Continent: Europe's Twentieth Century* (New York: Vintage, 2000); Jay Winter, Geoffrey Parker, and Mary R. Habeck, eds., *The Great War and the Twentieth Century* (New Haven: Yale University Press, 2000).

with the pronouncements of diplomats and prime ministers.[7] A movement such as Italian fascism, like German Nazism born in 1919, demonstrated both the attractions of new forms of politics and the persistence of the old. The year 1919 also represented the first major attempts in the twentieth century to conceptualize the world as a unified whole. The leaders who gathered in Paris to make peace not only addressed wartime conflicts but also other fault lines, issues that would henceforth dominate global relations. The exclusion of the Soviets did not prevent the rivalry between democratic capitalism and state communism from assuming center stage in world politics. Similarly, the refusal of the Paris diplomats seriously to acknowledge colonial demands for self-determination only stoked the fires of anti-colonial nationalism. East vs. West, North vs. South, the tensions that would divide the world in the new century first became apparent in 1919.[8]

Above all, 1919 was a year of revolution, both actual and potential. Even more than 1968, it was the year during the twentieth century in which the overthrow of the dominant order seemed possible on a global scale.[9] Not only was the Bolshevik regime in Russia fighting for its life and calling for world revolution, but most of Europe east of the Rhine and south of the Alps seemed caught up in massive, indeed insurrectionary challenges to the political and social status quo. Even that most bourgeois of nations, Switzerland, did not seem immune from the revolutionary contagion.[10] Moreover, the spirit of revolution surfaced far beyond the bounds of Europe, unleashing massive popular movements in China, Korea, India, Mexico, and Egypt. The United States, already the world's symbol of conservative democratic capitalism, experienced major labor unrest, including a general strike in Seattle.[11] The old line from *Solidarity Forever*, "We can

[7] Arno Mayer, *The Persistence of the Old Regime* (New York: Pantheon, 1981).
[8] On the Paris peace conference see, among many studies, MacMillan, *Paris 1919*; Mayer, *Politics and Diplomacy* and *The Persistence of the Old Regime*; Keylor, *The Legacy of the Great War*. Studies of colonial questions at the peace talks have received less attention than some other issues: some interesting texts include Erez Manela, *The Wilsonian Moment: Self-Determination and the International Origins of Anticolonial Nationalism* (New York: Oxford University Press, 2007); David Fromkin, *A Peace to End All Peace: The Fall of the Ottoman Empire and the Creation of the Modern Middle East* (New York: Avon Books, 1990).
[9] In this respect it also resembles 1989, at least for the peoples of eastern Europe.
[10] In fact, Paris was chosen as the site of the peace conference in part because Switzerland seemed too unstable politically. As David Mitchell put it, "if quaint, picture-postcard Switzerland went Red, where would the rot end?" Mitchell, *1919: Red Mirage*, 67.
[11] On revolutionary movements in postwar Europe, see Roger Magraw, "Paris, 1917–1920: labour protest and popular politics," in Chris Wrigley, ed., *Challenges of Labour: Central and Western Europe, 1917–1920* (London and New York: Routledge, 1993); Charles Bertrand, ed., *Revolutionary Situations in Europe, 1917–1922: Germany, Italy, Austria-Hungary* (Montreal: Interuniversity Centre

bring to birth a new world from the ashes of the old," seemed to some an apt description of the state of Europe and the world in 1919.[12]

In choosing to focus on a single year, I have largely departed from the historians' traditional emphasis on chronology.[13] Not only do I focus for the most part on a few months, but I organize this study around major themes rather than the succession of days, weeks, and months. For some this may appear problematic: after all, if the essence of history is the study of change over time, one cannot expect to see major shifts in a mere twelve months. I do not therefore claim that this study offers a thorough accounting of the rise and fall of a major historical epoch. Nor do I argue that 1919 was a central "turning point" in history, such as the beginning of the twentieth century. I regard such arguments with some suspicion, since the concept of the turning point tends to rely on teleological narratives of history and can obscure important continuities in both popular and official mentalities and practices. Instead, I consider 1919 important because of the insights it offers into important aspects of Parisian society, culture, and politics in the early twentieth century. Some looked forward, some back, and most had relevance far beyond the Ile de France. Moreover, the focus on a single year naturally enables the historian to engage in a level of detail far greater than studies of longer periods, helping us to see events through the eyes of those who lived them, who did not know how things would turn out nor their significance for the future. In shying away from teleological narratives of the passage of time, I thus respond to and take seriously the critiques frequently leveled against the writing of History by postcolonial critics.[14] Additionally, such an approach best illustrates the often inchoate, unstable character of the times. My analysis of 1919 both focuses on the important events that happened in that year and also uses it to illustrate broader tensions in Parisian, French, and ultimately global society. Consider this study a portrait of a singular year, one full of paths taken and not taken, yet one whose scope and implications ultimately go well beyond 1919.[15]

for European Studies, 1977); James Cronin and Carmen Sirianni, eds., *Work, Community, and Power: The Experience of Labor in Europe and America, 1900–1925* (Philadelphia: Temple University Press, 1983).

[12] Stewart Bird *et al.*, *Solidarity Forever: An Oral History of the IWW* (Chicago: Lake View Press, 1985).

[13] Although this book is about 1919, not all sections focus exclusively on that year. The first chapter addresses the roots of the 1919 crisis in World War I, and those sections that rely on statistical evidence look more generally at the early postwar years, simply because of the absence of census data and other quantitative materials for that year alone. Nonetheless, this remains a study centered overwhelmingly around the year after the Armistice.

[14] Robert Young, *White Mythologies: Writing History and the West* (London and New York: Routledge, 2004).

[15] Consider for example Charles C. Mann, *1491: New Revelations of the Americas before Columbus* (New York: Vintage, 2006); Ray Huang, *1587: A Year of No Significance: The Ming Dynasty in Decline* (New Haven: Yale University Press, 1981). A huge historiography of 1968 now exists: see,

PARIS, FROM NINETEENTH TO TWENTIETH CENTURY

This study addresses the history of one city, Paris, during what was in many ways a uniquely tumultuous year. On the face of it, the French capital does not seem the most likely site for a study of revolution in 1919. A victorious nation, France did not face the same kind of political upheaval so evident elsewhere on the Continent. Russia and Germany, the two countries that would dominate the history of Europe in the twentieth century, were the battlegrounds where the fate of world revolution would be decided.[16] Moreover, as the site of the peace conference Paris stood for the forces of the global establishment, those trying to contain or eliminate Bolshevism as a threat to the new world order they hoped to create.[17] Paris, symbolic capital of revolution in the nineteenth century, seemed to have ceded this role to Petrograd and even Berlin at the start of the new era.

Yet precisely this contrast between revolutionary heritage and global powerbroker makes the French capital such an interesting place to study the revolutionary spirit of the age. Paris in 1919 represented in extreme form something common to many great cities: the close proximity of haves and have-nots, of privilege and protest.[18] No other place in the world more completely encapsulated the tensions of a world divided. Chronologically, 1919 stood exactly between the Paris Commune of 1871 and the May movement of 1968, and as we shall see social and political movements in that year bore more than a passing resemblance to both events.

Moreover, the era of World War I was an important period of transition for the French capital. In a famous essay Walter Benjamin called Paris "the capital of the nineteenth century," a symbol of urbane culture and modernity (and, he might well have added, of revolution). Yet the twentieth century would bring a new face to the city. The 1921 census would record the largest population in the city's history, over 2.9 million people. The nineteenth century had been one of dynamic population growth, as the

---

among many others, David Caute, *The Year of the Barricades: A Journey through 1968* (New York: Harper and Row, 1988); Todd Gitlin, *The Sixties: Years of Hope, Days of Rage* (New York: Bantam, 1993); Mark Kurlansky, *1968: The Year That Rocked the World* (New York: Random House, 2005).

[16] For contrasting views on the Russian Revolution see Sheila Fitzpatrick, *The Russian Revolution, 1917–1932* (Oxford University Press, 1994); and Richard Pipes, *Russia under the Bolshevik Regime: Lenin and the Birth of the Bolshevik State* (New York: Vintage, 1994).

[17] Arno Mayer, *Wilson vs. Lenin: Political Origins of the New Diplomacy* (Cleveland, OH: World Publishing Company, 1959).

[18] My ideas about the structure and politics of Paris as a great city owe much to the work of David Harvey. See his *Social Justice and the City* (London: Arnold, 1973); *Consciousness and the Urban Experience: Studies in the History and Theory of Capitalist Urbanization* (Baltimore: Johns Hopkins University Press, 1985); and *Paris, Capital of Modernity* (New York: Routledge, 2003).

number of Parisians quintupled thanks to massive immigration from the provinces and the annexation of the outer *arrondissements* in 1860. The year 1921 was a high-water mark for Paris, however: almost every succeeding census would record a population decline, both absolutely and relatively.[19] Henceforth urban growth would come almost entirely in the suburbs, which since the end of the nineteenth century had been growing at a much faster rate than the city itself. Thanks to the failure of city officials to annex the new suburban areas, as they had done with *la petite banlieue* in 1860, by the late twentieth century the overwhelming majority of "Parisians" would call the suburbs home. Paris itself would remain in large part a nineteenth-century city, to the delight of tourists and city planners, but the dynamism and the future of France's greatest urban area would lie increasingly *extra-muros*. The final destruction of the city's walls in 1919 reflected this move toward the periphery.[20]

The contrast between city and suburb was social and political as well as geographic. As a substantial body of historical literature has demonstrated, the new suburbia of the early twentieth century was overwhelmingly working class, whereas Paris itself was becoming increasingly bourgeois. In 1919 the French Socialists would score a wave of municipal victories in the suburbs of the Department of the Seine, laying the grounds for the Red Belt to come. Paris, in contrast, voted for the right and would continue to do so in most elections during the twentieth century. Whereas the city became increasingly world-famous for luxury consumption, its suburban ring displayed the nation's greatest concentration of heavy industry. One should not overemphasize this contrast: in 1919, as this study will show, large parts of Paris remained *populaire*. This is especially true of the outer *arrondissements* (districts), former suburbs annexed in 1860. Nonetheless, the outlines of the dichotomy between white city and red suburbs were already evident in 1919. As I shall argue throughout this text, this dichotomy paralleled and reflected global splits between East and West, North and South.[21]

---

[19] On the population of Paris and the Paris area see Louis Chevalier, *Laboring Classes and Dangerous Classes in Paris during the First Half of the Nineteenth Century*, translated by Frank Jellinek (Princeton University Press, 1973); Norma Evenson, *Paris: A Century of Change, 1878–1978* (New Haven: Yale University Press, 1979); Michel Huber, *La population de la France, son evolution et ses perspectives* (Paris: Hachette, 1937); Philippe Ariès, *Histoire des populations françaises et leurs attitudes devant la vie depuis le XVIIIe siècle* (Paris: Éditions du Seuil, 1948).

[20] Jean Bastié, *La croissance de la banlieue parisienne* (Paris: Presses Universitaires de France, 1964); Norma Evenson, *Paris, A Century of Change, 1878–1978* (New Haven: Yale University Press, 1979).

[21] Jean-Paul Brunet, *Saint-Denis la ville rouge: socialisme et communisme en banlieue ouvrière, 1890–1939* (Paris: Hachette, 1980); Tyler Stovall, *The Rise of the Paris Red Belt* (Berkeley: University of California Press, 1990); Annie Fourcaut, *Bobigny, banlieue rouge* (Paris: Éditions ouvrières, 1986).

For these reasons, therefore, a study of Paris in 1919 has much to contribute to our understanding of what Italian historians have called the *biennio rosso*, the revolutionary upsurge in Europe at the end of World War I. In part, this contribution takes the form of challenges to some key themes of this historiography. Many historians writing about this period have concentrated above all on explaining the failure of revolution in Europe outside Russia. They have advanced a number of plausible explanations, including the strength of bourgeois society in western and central Europe, the absence of a mass aggrieved peasantry, the splits within international socialism, and the strength of repressive state forces. Perhaps most important, scholars have argued that the fires of revolution did not spread outward from Russia because the forces of the moderate left ultimately proved too powerful. Reform, not revolution, most clearly expressed the desires of European labor, and carried the day in 1919.[22]

This study departs from such perspectives in two major respects. First, it focuses less on why France did not take the revolutionary path in 1919 and more on why the prospect of insurrection loomed so large in the first place. That is to say, it concentrates less on what did not happen, more on what actually did. The fact that a French version of the Bolshevik seizure of power was never a realistic possibility after World War I does not lessen the importance of the political and social turmoil that Paris experienced in that period, nor does it explain why so many in France hoped for such an outcome. Second, this study challenges the dichotomy between reform and revolution that has shaped so much of our understanding of the *biennio rosso*, and indeed of modern revolution in general.[23] Instead, it considers the ways in which grievances often considered reformist in fact contributed to the spirit of revolution. The sharp opposition between, say, Friedrich Ebert and Lenin did not necessarily reflect the views of many of their followers or the revolutionary potential of the era.

---

[22] Albert S. Lindemann, *The "Red Years": European Socialism versus Bolshevism, 1919–1921* (Berkeley: University of California Press, 1974); Helmut Gruber, ed., *International Communism in the Era of Lenin: A Documentary History* (Ithaca: Cornell University Press, 1967); Martin Clark, *Antonio Gramsci and the Revolution that Failed* (New Haven: Yale University Press, 1977).

[23] On the *biennio rosso* see Paolo Spriano, *The Occupation of the Factories: Italy 1920* (London: Pluto, 1975, translated by Gwyn Williams); Gwyn Williams, *Proletarian Order: Antonio Gramsci, Factory Councils, and the Origins of Italian Communism* (London: Pluto Press, 1975); Richard Bellamy and Darrow Schechter, *Gramsci and the Italian State* (New York: St. Martin's Press, 1993). On questions of reform and revolution in general, see Janet L. Polasky, *The Democratic Socialism of Emile Vandervelde: Between Reform and Revolution* (Oxford and Providence RI: Berg, 1995); Willie Thompson, *The Left in History: Revolution and Reform in Twentieth Century Politics* (London: Pluto Press, 1997).

CLASS AND IDENTITY: CONSUMERISM, DIFFERENCE, AND GLOBALIZATION

This book argues that Paris in 1919 experienced a series of crises that taken together seemed revolutionary in their potential and implications. Even if the prospect of an overthrow of the established order did not seriously exist, in contrast to much of the rest of Europe, that was not necessarily evident at the time. Many Parisians did believe that the winds of change blowing from the east could in fact reach their city and transform life there. In studying the reasons for the revolutionary climate in postwar Europe historians have generally pointed to the impact of the war and the example of the Bolshevik revolution as its main causes. This study recognizes the importance of those factors, but also argues for a more specific analysis of the reasons for revolutionary sentiment. In particular, I will consider three main themes as key to the study of political upheaval in Paris at the end of World War I: consumer politics, shifting and unstable conceptions of working-class identity, and intersections between local and global relations of power.

Consumerism, politics, and the politics of consumerism have long been recognized as major issues in the construction of modernity. In an important article Victoria de Grazia has noted that "Next to the extinction of communism, nothing has disconcerted labor historians as much as the proliferation of cultural studies about mass consumption."[24] My broad aim in undertaking this study is to bring these two scholarly traditions together. Students of consumer culture have generally characterized it as the proliferation of mass consumer goods to the extent that society as a whole is increasingly shaped around consumption.[25] This shift away from production necessarily entails the weakening of workplace-based identities in favor of those centered around material goods. The study of consumerism as a cultural formation has drawn more attention to the symbolic subtexts of consumer goods and the ways in which the diffusion of mass-produced goods has structured both individual identities and social cleavages in modern societies. If class consciousness is created at the point of production, as the dominant tradition in labor history has claimed, then surely a shift

---

[24] Victoria de Grazia, "Beyond time and money," *International Labor and Working Class History*, 43 (Spring, 1993), 24–30.

[25] The scholarly literature on the history of consumer culture is now vast. Some useful works include Neil McKendrick *et al.*, *The Birth of a Consumer Society: The Commercialization of Eighteenth-Century England* (Bloomington: Indiana University Press, 1982); Whitney Walton, *France at the Crystal Palace: Bourgeois Taste and Artisan Manufacture in the Nineteenth Century* (Berkeley: University of California Press, 1992); Leora Auslander, *Taste and Power: Furnishing Modern France* (Berkeley: University of California Press, 1996).

from production to consumption as the source of social identity must weaken such consciousness. In particular, many historians of working people in America, home to the world's leading consumer culture, have pointed to the rise of consumerism as the main explanation for the weakness of labor movements there.[26]

Questions of gender have played a key role in the challenge posed by studies of consumerism to labor history. The tradition that men produce and women consume has not only proved commonplace in modern popular culture but has also permeated much of the work on both labor history and consumerism. Many of the leading historical studies of consumerism focus on women as consumers, and explore how and why such practices have traditionally been gendered female. In particular, studies of working-class women have made the point that consumer activities are just as important to both gender and class consciousness, if not more so, than workplace concerns. Historians of consumption have also demonstrated how men's consumer patterns are central to masculine social identities. In general, histories of consumer behavior have made the point that social identities result from the interaction of a number of factors, including but by no means limited to those of class and gender.[27]

The relations between consumerism, politics, and popular culture have prompted extensive research among historians and other scholars. For example, anthropologists have made important contributions to our understanding of the ways in which commodities become repositories of meaning. One important debate has engaged what John Clarke has labeled the "pessimistic" vs. "populist" schools of thought.[28] The pessimists, most notably historians of advertising like Stuart Ewen and T. J. Jackson Lears, draw upon the perspectives of the Frankfurt School to portray consumerism as a lynchpin in the creation of capitalist cultural hegemony.[29] The

---

[26] The classic analysis of this issue is Thorstein Veblen's *Theory of the Leisure Class: An Economic Study of Institutions* (New York: Macmillan, 1899); Doug Brown, ed., *Thorstein Veblen in the Twenty First Century: A Commemoration of "The Theory of the Leisure Class," 1899–1999* (Cheltenham: Edward Elgar, 1998). See also Warren Susman, *Culture as History: The Transformation of American Society in the Twentieth Century* (New York: Pantheon, 1984).

[27] On this point see in particular the essays in Victoria de Grazia and Ellen Furlough, eds., *The Sex of Things: Gender and Consumption in Historical Perspective* (Berkeley: University of California Press, 1996).

[28] John Clarke, "Pessimism versus populism: the problematic politics of popular culture," in Richard Butsch, ed., *For Fun and Profit: The Transformation of Leisure into Consumption* (Philadelphia: Temple University Press, 1990).

[29] Stuart and Elizabeth Ewen, *Channels of Desire: Mass Images and the Shaping of American Consciousness* (New York: McGraw Hill, 1982); T. J. Jackson Lears, ed., *The Culture of Consumption: Critical Essays in American History, 1880–1980* (New York: Pantheon, 1983).

populists, including the British neo-Gramscians and historians like Roy Rosenzweig, Kathy Peiss, Dana Frank, and Lizabeth Cohen, characterize consumerism as something used by individuals and communities to carve out autonomous cultural and political spaces.[30] To a large extent such a debate resembles the question of whether a glass is half full or half empty, arising from different emphases on the production vs. the assimilation of consumer culture. Ultimately, one must transcend the domination/resistance duality to study how consumer goods both transform and are transformed by the user.[31]

In doing so, however, certain presumptions of consumer studies must also be challenged. Much of the literature has focused on the proliferation of discretionary or luxury goods, such as automobiles, or on leisure and entertainment expenses. Such an approach arises partly from a "trickle down" view of consumer behavior, seeing consumer patterns as being transferred from the aristocracy to the middle class during the Industrial Revolution, and then finally to the working class in the twentieth century. However, this perspective tends to create a questionable dichotomy between "real" needs and "false" wants, with consumerism belonging firmly to the latter sphere, and to ignore the ways in which all goods can take on symbolic and political significance. Moreover, the emphasis on discretionary consumption tends to make consumer culture irrelevant to working-class life, setting up a reductionist polarity between middle-class consumers and working-class producers. Indeed, I would argue that working-class consumption by definition excludes luxury goods; as Pierre Bourdieu has demonstrated, if such commodities are used by lower-class people they very quickly lose their luxury status. The distinction between necessities and luxuries is socially constructed, and "necessities" can vary from a loaf of bread to an automobile. As Frank Trentmann has argued, historians should

[30] Roy Rosenzweig, *Eight Hours for What We Will: Workers and Leisure in an Industrial City, 1870–1920* (New York: Cambridge University Press, 1983); Stuart Hall and Tony Jefferson, eds., *Resistance through Ritual: Youth Subcultures in Post War Britain* (London: Hutchinson, 1976); Dick Hebdige, *Subculture: The Meaning of Style* (London: Methuen, 1979); Liz Cohen, *Making a New Deal: Industrial Workers in Chicago, 1919–1939* (New York: Cambridge University Press, 1990). Feminist scholars in particular have analyzed women's relationships to consumerism. See for example, Dana Frank, *Purchasing Power: Consumer Organizing, Gender, and the Seattle Labor Movement, 1919–1929* (New York: Cambridge University Press, 1994); Victoria de Grazia, "Empowering women as citizen-consumers," and Kathy Peiss, "Making up, making over: cosmetics, consumer culture, and women's identity," both in Victoria de Grazia and Ellen Furlough, eds., *The Sex of Things: Gender and Consumption in Historical Perspective* (Berkeley: University of California Press, 1996), 275–286 and 311–336, respectively.

[31] The work of Michel de Certeau concerning the symbolism of consumption is particularly relevant here: see *The Practice of Everyday Life*, ed. Luce Giard (Minneapolis: University of Minnesota Press, 1998).

focus less on the ideology of consumerism and more on specific histories of consumption.[32]

Ultimately at issue here is the classic argument, first formulated by the theorists of the Frankfurt School, that consumerism and consumer society are fundamentally anti-democratic and reactionary, that they distract people from engaging in politics and challenging the socioeconomic status quo.[33] In recent years a number of scholars have challenged this view, arguing conflicts over consumer goods can push people into political action instead of seducing them away from it.[34] Rather than see consumerism as antithetical to citizenship, some have developed the notion of the consumer citizen, illustrating how social groups have used consumer action to become political actors. This is especially true of subaltern groups for whom traditional politics offer little recourse. Lizabeth Cohen has shown how in 1930s America women and African Americans were particularly likely to resort to consumer activism. The notion of the consumer citizen could be deployed both by elites seeking to integrate constituents into a given regime and by consumer groups asserting their own power and identity. In general, the concept of the consumer citizen underscores the idea that consumers are not passive, isolated individuals but rather political actors.[35]

The book will argue that the sharp increase in protest activities in the years immediately following the end of the war arose in large part from the politicization of consumer issues. I thus contend that, far from representing the cooptation or *embourgeoisement* of working people, in 1919 discourses around consumption became a language of protest and resistance for the workers of Paris and its suburbs. Moreover, the strident radicalism of working-class protest in 1919 derived in large part from the combination of consumer and workplace crises, producing a multifaceted (although not coordinated) challenge to capitalist hegemony. The consumer politics and

[32] Frank Trentmann, "Beyond consumerism: new historical perspectives on consumption," *Journal of Contemporary History*, 39/3 (July, 2004), 400.

[33] Max Horkheimer and Theodor Adorno, *Dialectic of Enlightenment* (London: Allen Lane, 1973); Herbert Marcuse, *One-Dimensional Man: Studies in the Ideology of Advanced Industrial Society* (Boston MA: Beacon Press, 1964). For a more recent restatement of this argument, see Zygmunt Bauman, "Exit *homo politicus*, enter *homo consumens*," in Kate Soper and Frank Trentmann, eds., *Citizenship and Consumption* (Basingstoke and New York: Palgrave Macmillan, 2008).

[34] See for example Matthew Hilton, *Consumerism in Twentieth Century Britain: The Search for a Historical Movement* (Cambridge University Press, 2003); T. H. Breen, *The Marketplace of Revolution: How Consumer Politics Shaped American Independence* (Oxford University Press, 2004).

[35] Soper and Trentmann, *Citizenship and Consumption*; Lizabeth Cohen, *A Consumer's Republic: The Politics of Mass Consumption in Postwar America* (New York: Knopf, 2003); Lisa Tiersten, *Marianne in the Market: Envisioning Consumer Society in Fin-de-Siècle France* (Berkeley: University of California Press, 2001); Erika Rappaport, *Shopping for Pleasure: Women in the Making of London's West End* (Princeton University Press, 2000).

activism of 1919, like the year as a whole, looked both backwards and forwards at the same time. In many ways they drew on the traditions of moral economy that shaped popular consumer protests until the mid nineteenth century, traditions supposedly rendered obsolete by modernization. At the same time they anticipated the new social movements of the second half of the twentieth century, offering not only an alternative to workplace organizing but also the possibility of a progressive politics that transcended class divisions. During an era when Europeans were increasingly discussing, if not yet applying, the Fordist model of increased labor discipline and mass consumption, working-class consumers in Paris posited an alternative model of consumer citizenship: instead of individuals exercising agency through buying goods, communities would exert political control over their supply and pricing.[36] In 1919, Parisian consumerism had an insurgent character that constituted a micro-politics of revolution.[37]

The politicization of consumption arose in large part from the sharp increase of state intervention in the economy during the war years. While France had never embraced economic liberalism to the same extent as Britain during the nineteenth century, and in particular had a strong tradition of governments setting the prices of basic commodities, during the Third Republic powerful voices continued to insist on the importance of keeping the economy out of the hands of politicians. Similarly, on the left the anarcho-syndicalists emphasized the separation of political and economic activism, devoting themselves entirely to the latter. The French state's intervention in the consumer economy during World War I not only called both perspectives into question but at the same time rested on solid historical precedent, most notably during the French Revolution. Once the war ended French men and women debated whether or not to continue public intervention in the consumer economy. The sharpness of this debate contributed powerfully to the revolutionary aura of 1919 and more generally emphasized the role of the state as instrument, rather than enemy, of working-class activism.

---

[36] On Fordism in Europe during the early twentieth century see Victoria de Grazia, *Irresistible Empire: America's Advance through 20th-Century Europe* (Cambridge MA: Harvard University Press, 2005); Mary Nolan, *Visions of Modernity: American Business and the Modernization of Germany* (New York: Oxford University Press, 1994).

[37] On moral economy, see E. P. Thompson, "The moral economy of the English crowd in the eighteenth century," *Past and Present*, 50 (February, 1971); Thompson, *Customs in Common* (New York: New Press, 1993). On new social movement theory, see in particular Jean Cohen, "Rethinking social movements," *Berkeley Journal of Sociology*, 28 (1983); Klaus Eder, *The New Politics of Class: Social Movements and Cultural Dynamics in Advanced Societies* (London: Sage, 1993).

Closely related to the politics of consumerism, both in this study and in the general historiography, is the nature of the working class in general. Ever since Karl Marx famously distinguished between a class of itself and a class for itself, scholars and social analysts have grappled with the question of how to define working people as a collectivity.[38] In particular, how does one understand the relationship between subjective and objective criteria, how does one balance self-identification and social definition? Led by E. P. Thompson, the new social history of the 1960s responded to such questions by emphasizing the relationship between the process of production in the workplace and the formation of working-class consciousness.[39] Since the 1980s, this view of working-class life has been challenged on several fronts. Some have criticized the tendency of social historians to neglect the politics of class, and have turned instead to an analysis of political discourses. Scholars like Patrick Joyce and Gareth Stedman Jones have looked at the language in which ideas of class are not just expressed but indeed created.[40] Another school of labor historians has sought to supplement (or in some cases replace) the traditional emphasis on the workplace with a focus on community instead, arguing that the latter provides a more comprehensive portrait of working-class life. The tendency of social historians to focus on local histories led to a host of community studies which have considered the nature of urban identities, gender, ethnicity, and other factors beyond life on the job.[41] Finally, and perhaps most importantly, scholars of difference have challenged labor historians to incorporate the experiences of women and members of ethnic and racial minority groups into narratives of working-class history. Joan Scott's pioneering work on gender and class has prompted many such reappraisals.[42] Similarly, the

---

[38] Karl Marx, *The Eighteenth Brumaire of Louis Bonaparte* (New York: International Publishers, 1963); Edward Andrew, "Class in itself and class against capital: Karl Marx and his classifiers," *Canadian Journal of Political Science/Revue canadienne de science politique*, 16/3 (September, 1983), 577–584.

[39] E. P. Thompson, *The Making of the English Working Class* (London: V. Gollancz, 1963). For an interesting overview see Geoff Eley, "Is all the world a text? From social history to the history of society two decades later," in Gabrielle M. Spiegel, ed., *Practicing History: New Directions in Historical Writing after the Linguistic Turn* (New York: Routledge, 2005).

[40] Patrick Joyce, *Visions of the People: Industrial England and the Question of Class, 1840–1914* (Cambridge University Press, 1991); Gareth Stedman Jones, *Languages of Class: Studies in English Working Class History 1832–1982* (Cambridge University Press, 1983).

[41] For one example among many, see Michael H. Frisch and Daniel J. Walkowitz, eds., *Working Class America: Essays on Labor, Community, and American Society* (Urbana: University of Illinois Press, 1982).

[42] Joan Scott, *Gender and the Politics of History* (New York: Columbia University Press, 1988); Laura L. Frader and Sonya Rose, eds., *Gender and Class in Modern Europe* (Ithaca: Cornell University Press, 1996); Laura Levine Frader, *Breadwinners and Citizens: Gender in the Making of the French Social Model* (Durham NC: Duke University Press, 2008); Stephen Brooke, "Gender and working class identity in Britain during the 1950s," *Journal of Social History*, 34/4 (Summer, 2001), 773–795.

work of David Roediger and other scholars of whiteness in America has given us a much more nuanced vision of working-class life.[43]

This study's emphasis on the political significance of working-class consumption is part of a broader insistence on the continued importance of class as a historical reality and class analysis as an approach to history. This is particularly true because a considerable body of scholarship on consumer society has portrayed it as the successor to, not a version of, class society. More generally, labor unions and the traditional Left have declined in power in Europe and especially the United States since the 1960s, at the same time as the rise of new social movements based in what has been termed identity politics, especially centering around questions of race and gender.[44] Both proponents and critics of identity politics have at times, wrongly in my view, portrayed it as an alternative to and rejection of the politics of class. Although most scholars interested in questions of difference proclaim the importance of race, gender, and class, it often seems that the third leg of this triad, identified with a traditional and suspect Marxist ideology, is more wobbly than the other two.[45]

Yet as this image suggests, without attention to all three key aspects of difference (and others besides) studies of identity lack solidity. Rather than accepting an opposition between identity and class, this study considers the politics of working-class identity. It explores the political implications of the turbulence surrounding working-class identity in 1919, seeing it as a key factor in the revolutionary tenor of the times.[46] Rather than seeing the upheavals of the 1960s as a refutation of class politics, it looks to another time when questions of class and identity led to social upheaval. Parisians in 1919 inhabited a world where divisions and hierarchies based on wealth, occupation, and living conditions not only existed but were widely commented on by people of all social ranks, and served as a key means of group identification. Certainly, class was not the only marker of identity for

[43] On whiteness see David Roediger, *The Wages of Whiteness: Race and the Making of the American Working Class* (London: Verso, 2007); Roediger, *Working toward Whiteness: How America's Immigrants Became White: The Strange Journey from Ellis Island to the Suburbs* (New York: Basic Books, 2005); Matthew Frye Jacobson, *Whiteness of a Different Color: European Immigrants and the Alchemy of Race* (Cambridge MA: Harvard University Press, 1998).

[44] Todd Gitlin, "The rise of identity politics," *Dissent* (Spring, 1993); Eric Hobsbawm, "Identity politics and the Left," in Steven Fraser and Josh Freeman, eds., *Audacious Democracy: Labor, Intellectuals, and the Social Reconstruction of America* (Boston: Houghton Mifflin, 1997).

[45] See the special issue of *International Labor and Working-Class History*, "Class and the politics of identity," 67 (Spring, 2005).

[46] As many historians have argued, working-class politics, especially before World War II, often centered around questions of identity. See Verity Burgmann, "From syndicalism to Seattle: class and the politics of identity," *International Labor and Working Class History*, 67 (Spring, 2005).

working-class Parisians, nor was it always the most important one at all times and places. But, as we shall see during this study, it did loom large in both the objective circumstances and subjective identities of many, forming the basis for a politics that at times took on an insurgent character. While greater attention to gender, race, and other social differences certainly challenges traditional portraits of working-class life, issues of class equally have the power to complicate notions of gender and racial identity. Rather than retreat from all notions of social belonging in favor of an atomized individualism, it is more useful to consider the continual interactions of different identities. Whether or not such identities can be demonstrated objectively, they retain great subjective power.

Both social history and the challenges to it have given us a far more complex and sophisticated view of the working classes than was available fifty years ago. However, in underscoring the diversity of these experiences they have inevitably raised the question: does the working class exist at all? Can one social identity truly encompass such a variety of experiences? Such difficulties have led some to deny or discount the existence of class as a meaningful social and historical category, and not just for working people. In a stimulating discussion, for example, Sarah Maza has argued that the idea of the bourgeoisie in nineteenth-century France was more a myth and a specter than a sociological reality.[47] Such work fits into a broader range of studies that focus on representation as the key to social and cultural experiences, demonstrating how identities are constituted through a range of discursive practices.[48]

In general such approaches to the study of class call for more sophisticated ways of conceptualizing it rather than abandoning it altogether. In particular, one must view class from the standpoint of both social structure and cultural identity, considering both how workers conceived of their own lives and how they appeared to others. In short, class exists as both an emic and an etic category. This study of Paris in 1919 argues that working-class identity was fundamental to the insurgent imagination, but that the nature of this identity was dynamic and in flux. More specifically, I would suggest a

[47] Sarah Maza, *The Myth of the French Bourgeoisie: An Essay on the Social Imaginary, 1750–1850* (London and Cambridge MA: Harvard University Press, 2003). One issue, of course, is whether to refer to the working "class" or the working "classes." As I hope to show, one can usefully employ both the plural and the singular here; while Parisian laborers were a very diverse population composed of many subgroups, at the same time many of them (as well as many of their observers, both friendly and hostile) identified them as a single collectivity. This certainly constituted a process of reification, yet it also helped shape class identity in this period.

[48] Lynn Hunt, ed., *The New Cultural History* (Berkeley: University of California Press, 1989); Catherine Gallagher and Stephen Greenblatt, *Practicing New Historicism* (University of Chicago Press, 2000).

parallel, if not necessarily a causal, relationship between the instability of working-class identity in Paris and the tumultuous nature of the times. The changing character of what it meant to be a Parisian worker operated on several levels. Like other great cities, more than factory towns, the French capital represented a great variety of working-class experiences, ranging from skilled artisans to semi-skilled and unskilled mass-production workers. Many Parisian workers were born elsewhere, either in the French provinces or in foreign nations, and came from a diversity of religious and ethnic backgrounds. If we seek for a general theme in Parisian working-class life, heterogeneity must take pride of place.[49]

The year 1919 both highlighted and challenged this diversity. As we have seen, the very geography of working-class life in the capital was shifting at this time; the increasing suburbanization of popular Paris called into question the very meaning of the urban experience. More specifically, 1919 witnessed massive attempts to remake the profile of the area's labor force, reversing trends necessitated by the shift to a war economy. The year after the Armistice saw the widespread exclusion of women and colonial subjects from the industrial economy, and to a certain extent from working-class life as a whole. Yet, as I shall argue in more detail later, this process only partially succeeded: one cannot put the genie back in the bottle, and the attempts to reverse the wartime transformation of Parisian labor ultimately only served to underscore how much had changed since 1914.

In addition, I shall consider working-class identity from the standpoint of spectacle. In particular, I am interested in the display of working-class identity in urban public space in 1919. Paris in that year was a city of demonstrations and parades, appealing to a variety of constituencies around a multitude of issues. Workers staged a number of street actions to proclaim their own political goals, and in the process set forth a dynamic vision of what it meant to be working class. A focus on the politics of public spectacle, and the spectacular nature of politics, as an approach to the analysis of working-class identity is especially appropriate to the study of a large city placed center stage in world affairs, one in which social identity seemed not only strikingly diverse but also constantly changing.[50]

---

[49] Lenard R. Berlanstein, *The Working People of Paris, 1871–1914* (Baltimore: Johns Hopkins University Press, 1984); Jean-Louis Robert, *Les ouvriers, la patrie et la Révolution: Paris 1914–1919* (Paris: Annales Littéraires de l'Université de Besançon/Les Belles Lettres, 1995); Michael Torigian, *Every Factory a Fortress: The French Labor Movement in the Age of Ford and Hitler* (Athens: Ohio University Press, 1999).

[50] On urban political spectacle, see Temma Kaplan, *Red City, Blue Period: Social Movements in Picasso's Barcelona* (Berkeley: University of California Press, 1992); Mary Ryan, "The American parade: representations of the nineteenth-century social order," in Lynn Hunt, ed., *The New Cultural History* (Berkeley: University of California Press, 1989).

In recent years labor historians have devoted a lot of time to globalization and studies of working-class life as a worldwide phenomenon. In part this new focus has involved increased attention to labor movements and struggles outside Europe and the United States, but more generally it has insisted on the transnational character of the working-class experience, the natural result of the global reach of capitalism. In studying working-class Paris in 1919 I found I could not avoid considering the nature of working-class identity in an international light. While Parisian workers were very conscious of being French, this very consciousness was shaped by a host of transnational factors, ranging from the war itself to the debates about immigrant and colonial labor, as well as the very prospect of world revolution. Objectively and subjectively, the world of Parisian labor in 1919 was both cloistered and cosmopolitan, both suspicious of and fundamentally conditioned by influences beyond the borders of France.[51]

Such considerations bring me to a third major theme of this study, the intersections between local and global life. For years now many historians have been proclaiming the importance of transnational history, at least rhetorically dancing on the grave of the nation-state. Both informed by and often in direct opposition to contemporary discourses of globalization, historians and many other scholars have investigated the ways in which modern life is shaped by processes and populations that transcend national boundaries.[52] Since at least the 1980s, historians of the United States have been challenging scholarly (and political) notions of American exceptionalism by examining American history in global context.[53] To take another example, scholars of diaspora dominate the field of African American studies today, exploring black populations around the world and the ways in which they do (or do not) engage with each other.[54] Students of immigration, colonial and postcolonial studies, environmentalism, and

---

[51] Marcel van der Linden, "Transnationalizing American labor history," *Journal of American History*, 86/3 (December, 1999); Michael Hanagan and Marcel van der Linden, eds., "New approaches to global labor history," special issue of *International Labor and Working Class History*, 66 (Fall, 2004).

[52] Arjun Appadurai, *Modernity at Large: Cultural Dimensions of Globalization* (Minneapolis: University of Minnesota Press, 1996); Kenneth Pomeranz, *The Great Divergence: Europe, China, and the Making of the Modern World Economy* (Princeton: Princeton University Press, 2000).

[53] On global approaches to American history, see Akira Iriye, "The internationalization of history," *American Historical Review*, 94/1 (February, 1989), 1–10; David Thelen, "The nation and beyond: transnational perspectives on United States history," *Journal of American History*, 86/3 (December, 1999), a special issue on transnationalism and American history, 965–975.

[54] See in particular Paul Gilroy, *The Black Atlantic: Modernity and Double Consciousness* (Cambridge MA: Harvard University Press, 1993); Tiffany Ruby Patterson and Robin D. G. Kelley, "Unfinished migrations: reflections on the African diaspora and the making of the modern world," *African Studies Review*, 43/1 (April, 2000), special issue on Africa's diaspora, 11–46.

international cultural and artistic movements have all argued that the key issues confronting humanity in the modern era must be grappled with on a world scale.

Much of this is not new, of course: students of world, comparative, and diplomatic history have long taken a global perspective on human events. More innovative, perhaps, is a view of the nation-state as a problem to be investigated rather than a given to be assumed, as well as increased attention to how individuals and groups construct their lived experiences outside national boundaries. This approach sees international interchanges as operating on a number of levels, not just relations between state actors. Certainly, the rise of the internet and other forms of rapid communication in our own era has undermined those boundaries and underscored the salience of transnational perspectives, yet as many historians have shown, as long as there have been nations the lives of their inhabitants have been shaped by phenomena beyond their borders. Not only have people frequently crossed those borders, as immigrants, tourists, soldiers, business travelers, or refugees, but they have absorbed ideas and influences from throughout the globe without necessarily leaving home, often without realizing it.[55] A key goal of transnational history, one that informs this study, is thus an investigation of the relations between local, national, and global events. In short, the borders between nations have their parallels within nations; like the classic armchair tourist, one can in some ways experience the world without leaving home.[56]

Postcolonial studies has also made major contributions to our understanding of articulations between global and local experiences in the modern world. Originating with Edward Said's seminal text *Orientalism*, postcolonial studies has both challenged binary oppositions between colonizer and colonized and at the same time underlined the many ways in which the colonial encounter lies at the heart of modernity.[57] For historians of France and of Europe in general, this new emphasis on colonialism has argued that metropoles and colonies interacted to create each other, rather than simply seeing the latter as created by the former; modern Europe does not just have a colonial past, but is itself a product of the colonial encounter. Moreover, postcolonial studies of Europe have focused on the rise of

---

[55] For example, most Americans are probably not aware that the Bic pen is a French product.

[56] Masao Miyoshi, "A borderless world? From colonialism to transnationalism and the decline of the nation-state," *Critical Inquiry*, 19/4 (Summer, 1993).

[57] Edward Said, *Orientalism* (New York: Vintage, 1994); Anne McClintock, *Imperial Leather: Race, Gender, and Sexuality in the Colonial Context* (New York: Routledge, 1995); Frederick Cooper, *Colonialism in Question: Theory, Knowledge, History* (Berkeley: University of California Press, 2005).

populations of colonial origin there after formal decolonization, and the ways in which their presence has created new conflicts around race, religion, and citizenship. The massive demographic and ultimately cultural shifts in the nature of European nations since 1945 (for example, today the most popular first name for newborn males in Britain is Mohammed) have given postcolonial studies a significance far beyond the world of the library and the scholarly seminar.[58]

Until recently scholars in Britain and America have devoted much more attention to postcolonial studies than those in France itself, so that Francophone postcolonial studies has developed primarily as an "Anglo-Saxon" field of inquiry.[59] This fact, along with sharply divergent perspectives on universalism vs. difference, has led many French scholars to reject postcolonial theory as inadequate and ultimately foreign.[60] Such is no longer the case. The year 2005 in particular witnessed a flowering of postcolonial analyses in France, in response to two seminal events of that year: the February 23rd law (since revoked) ordering French history teachers to interpret the nation's colonial past in the most positive light possible, and the widespread suburban disturbances of November, seen by some as France's first major postcolonial uprising. The 2005 "riots" in particular not only renewed the old tradition of insurgent Paris but reaffirmed the full-scale interpenetration of dynamics of class, race, and gender that one can glimpse in embryo during 1919. The controversy surrounding the publication that same year of the edited volume *La Fracture coloniale*, by Pascal Blanchard, Nicolas Bancel, and Sandrine Lemaire, further contributed to the sense that postcolonial studies in France had finally come of age.[61]

What does it mean to think of France as a postcolonial nation, and how should the historian deploy postcolonial concepts to understand the past? These questions have guided much of my thinking about the history of Paris in 1919, and they highlight this book's contribution to Francophone

[58] Tariq Modood and Pnina Werbner, eds., *The Politics of Multiculturalism in the New Europe: Racism, Identity, and Community* (London: Zed Books, 1997); Gilles Kepel, *Les banlieues d'Islam: naissance d'une religion en France* (Paris: Seuil, 1987); Paul Silverstein, *Algeria in France: Transpolitics, Race, and Nation* (Bloomington: Indiana University Press, 2004).

[59] Charles Forsdick and David Murphy, eds., *Postcolonial Thought in the French-Speaking World* (Liverpool University Press, 2009).

[60] Emily Apter, "French colonial studies and postcolonial theory," *SubStance*, 76–77 (1995); Pascal Bruckner, *La tyrannie de la penitence* (Paris: Grasset, 2006); Emmanuelle Sibeud, "Post-colonial et Colonial Studies: enjeux et débat," *Revue d'Histoire Moderne et Contemporaine*, 51 (2004); Nicolas Bancel and Pascal Blanchard, "From colonial to postcolonial: reflections on the colonial debate in France," in Forsdick and Murphy, *Postcolonial Thought*.

[61] Pascal Blanchard, Nicolas Bancel, and Sandrine Lemaire, eds., *La fracture coloniale: la société française au prisme de l'héritage colonial* (Paris: La Découverte, 2005).

postcolonial studies. Scholars have generally defined the concept "postcolonial" in one of two main ways: either as a method that challenges colonial binaries, or as the period after the end of formal colonial rule. I agree with those who argue that the "post" in postcolonial refers to the transcendence of colonial binaries and in particular the questioning of boundaries between metropole and colony.[62] At the same time one cannot simply dismiss chronology: the achievement of independence by Europe's colonies fundamentally redefined those boundaries. I argue here for a blend of the two approaches, considering the ways in which issues of race and colonialism appeared in 1919 that would achieve greater prominence after 1945 and the end of formal imperial rule. In other words, I see the relationship between colonial and postcolonial as a continuum rather than a sharp break. Moreover, I regard this as a postcolonial study in spite of (to a certain extent because of) the fact that it does not just or even primarily deal with issues of colonialism and racial difference. Rather, I see postcolonial factors as central to what it meant to be Parisian and French in the early twentieth century, and explore how colonial and racial difference interacted with class to shape working-class identity.

Both transnational and postcolonial issues played a major role in Paris at the end of World War I, and their interactions with local politics contributed to the revolutionary tenor of the times. In 1919 many Parisians still lived in insular communities and neighborhoods: the famed *esprit de clocher* continued to characterize the social and political life of the city. Many of the social movements that arose in Paris and its suburbs drew their strength from this localism.[63] At the same time, both the presence of the peace conference and the specter of world revolution emanating from Moscow inspired many Parisians to think in apocalyptic terms, so that global affairs and local grievances constantly interacted in 1919. Unlike many studies in transnational history, my focus here is less on encounters between peoples from different regions or on border crossings, and more on the ways in which the residents of a great city articulated their demands for local and national change within a global context.[64]

---

[62] Anne McClintock, "The angel of progress: pitfalls of the term 'post-colonialism,'" *Social Text*, 31/32 (1992).

[63] On local and neighborhood life in Paris, see Alain Faure, *Paris careme-prenant* (Paris: Hachette, 1978); Françoise Raison-Jourde, *La colonie auvergnate de Paris au XIXe siècle* (Paris: Ville de Paris, 1976); Henri Leyret, *En plein faubourg, moeurs ouvrières* (Paris: Charpentier-Fasquelle, 1895).

[64] The sociologist Roland Robertson has popularized the term "glocalization" to characterize this confluence of local and global forces. See Robertson, "Glocalization: time-space and homogeneity-heterogeneity," in Mike Featherstone, Scott Lash, and Roland Robertson, eds., *Global Modernities*

Moreover, this study views the presence and subsequent expulsion of colonial subjects as key to the uncertainty and political turmoil of the time. I argue here that one should view the era of World War I as a major landmark in the history of postcolonial France. The parallels between the exclusion of imperial laborers from the working class and the silencing of colonial demands for independence at the peace conference show how in Paris in 1919 postcolonial debates were both local and global at the same time. They underscored the fact that henceforth discourses of racial difference would play a major, if often muted, role in working-class life and French identity as a whole. The Parisian revolutionary Left certainly did not see things that way: questions of race and colonialism did not explicitly feature in their political demands and activism in 1919. However, the very uncertainty created by emerging postcolonial social fissures placed working-class radicalism in a new context.[65]

As this study will demonstrate, these three themes constantly interacted with each other, collectively producing the sense of crisis and upheaval that so distinguished Paris in 1919. Believers in the possibility of revolution at home needed only look abroad for examples, and perhaps more than any other time in its long history Paris was the stage upon which all the passions of the world seemed to unfold. In a period in which working-class identity seemed in flux, when questions of race and gender called into question its unity, consumer politics held out the promise of struggles that could bring together not only workers but many others in common cause. The counterpoint between the politics of the breadbasket and the efforts to craft a new world order underscored the politicization of everyday life key to the revolutionary impulse in 1919.

To sum up, I argue in this study that the high levels of political turmoil in Paris in 1919, which many Parisians viewed as (at least potentially) a revolutionary crisis, arose primarily from three factors: the politicization of consumerism, the unstable and changing nature of working-class identity, and the concatenation of local and global struggles. Taken together, these factors not only created political and social turmoil but also highlighted fundamental transformations of working-class life in the French capital. These

(London: Sage Publications, 1995). For an interesting application of this concept, see Jacqueline Nassy Brown, *Dropping Anchor, Setting Sail: Geographies of Race in Black Liverpool* (Princeton University Press, 2005).

[65] Alec Hargreaves, *Immigration, "Race" and Ethnicity in Contemporary France* (London and New York: Routledge, 1995); Alec Hargreaves and Mark McKinney, eds., *Post-Colonial Cultures in France* (London and New York: Routledge, 1997); Tyler Stovall and Georges Van Den Abbeele, *French Civilization and Its Discontents* (Lanham MD: Lexington Books, 2003); Herman Lebovics, *Bringing the Empire Back Home: France in the Global Age* (Durham NC: Duke University Press, 2004).

developments all took place in the context of the transition from war to peace in 1919, and the debates in many circles about how to effect that transition. In recent years a number of historians have considered the aftermaths of the twentieth century's world wars, and the ways in which the wartime spirit lingered on after hostilities ended formally. For example, Bruno Cabanes and John Horne have studied "cultural demobilization" in France after World War I, arguing that soldiers' hatred of the enemy took some time to abate.[66] In this study I consider the demobilization of the home front, arguing that what Paul Fussell has termed "the versus habit" played a major role in postwar radicalism. Moreover, I challenge the notion that France abandoned wartime state controls over the economy, portraying instead this process of ideological peacetime conversion as a contested one whose results were far from certain in 1919.

The central themes outlined above pervade this study as a whole, instead of being organized neatly into individual chapters. Yet each appears more systematically in some parts of the book than others. In general, this book departs from a straightforward chronological approach to focus on the interaction of these different themes and their manifestations in different aspects of Parisian life. The result is a text that is heterogeneous rather than homogeneous, one whose disparate character mirrors that of 1919 in general. Chapter 1 considers Parisian life during World War I, and therefore constitutes a kind of prelude to the book's central focus on 1919. It looks at the ways in which the war politicized consumerism to an unprecedented degree, and the ways in which consumer conflicts challenged the spirit of wartime unity, instead contributing to the rise of antiwar and revolutionary sentiment. Chapters 2, 3, and 4 focus on working-class identity in 1919. Chapter 2 both gives a sociological analysis of Parisian workers in the era of World War I, and considers two case studies in working-class self-representation. Chapter 3 examines how the exclusion of female and colonial labor from industry in 1919 reshaped ideas of what it meant to be a worker. Chapter 4 looks at Parisian working-class politics as public spectacle in 1919 with an analysis of working-class self-representation, exploring the ways in which issues of power, conflict, and revolution were mapped onto the streets of the city. It also considers the impact of the Paris peace negotiations on popular movements there, analyzing the impact between local and global struggles. The final two chapters of this study examine

---

[66] Bruno Cabanes, *La victoire endeuillé: la sortie de guerre des soldats français, 1918–1920* (Paris: Seuil, 2004); John Horne, "Démobilisations culturelles après la Grande Guerre," *14–18 Aujourd'hui*, 5, Éditions Noésis (May, 2002).

militant activity in Paris during 1919. Chapter 5 gives the history of consumer movements around housing and food, considering the ways in which consumerism created new forms of struggle challenging the postwar liberal status quo. Chapter 6 discusses the history of the June 1919 metalworkers' strike, detailing its revolutionary character and its basis in consumer discontent.

Finally, it is important to discuss the nature of the historical source material upon which this book rests. Like the text itself, the sources I have used are heterogeneous and vary from chapter to chapter. Some chapters, notably Chapters 1 and 5, rest heavily on police reports and other material found in state archives. Others, especially Chapters 2 and 3, make significant use of quantitative, statistical data from the French census. Throughout this study I use the Parisian press, of a variety of political tendencies, as well as memoirs and other forms of direct testimony. Moreover, much of my analysis, especially in Chapters 4 and 6, relies on secondary source material. In short, the variegated, heterogeneous character of 1919 is mirrored by, and no doubt to a certain extent created by, the variety of sources from which I have drawn my information. This may not always add up to a neat, consistently uniform portrait, but such is frequently the messiness of history. I hope this catholic approach will enhance our ability to appreciate the many perspectives offered by Parisians in 1919.

This study thus offers an in-depth view of a fascinating city at a singular moment in time, one that showcased many of the conflicts and contrasts that continue to shape our world today. At a time when thoughts of revolution seem definitely *passé*, it considers a year at the beginning of the twentieth century when the overthrow of the capitalist order seemed a likely (and for many a desirable) possibility.[67] Perhaps most important, it seeks to connect global narratives of power and authority with the gritty realities of daily and local life, taking as its subject a city renowned for both. A variety of paths intersected and paralleled each other in Paris during 1919, and together they created a uniquely turbulent era in a city that for a brief period of time truly seemed to be the capital of the world.

---

[67] The idea that revolution is obsolete has been a staple theme of conservative and neoconservative theorizing since the beginning of the Cold War. See Daniel Bell, *The End of Ideology: On The Exhaustion of Political Ideas in the Fifties: With "The Resumption of History in the New Century"* (Cambridge MA: Harvard University Press, 2000); Francis Fukuyama, *The End of History and the Last Man* (New York: Bard, 1998).

CHAPTER I

The consumers' war

Any discussion of working-class insurgency in 1919 must of course begin with World War I itself. The principal themes of postwar unrest in Paris, ranging from consumer protest to state regulation to gendered reformulations of class politics, all emerged between 1914 and 1918. Two examples illustrate this. The first comes from an editorial published in *Le Temps* at the beginning of March, 1917. Written just before the great spring crisis of wartime morale, it contrasts trenches and home front, war and consumerism:

While a relative calm reigns at the front, apart from a few surprise attacks to keep the troops in a state of readiness, at the rear the great offensive against the centers and strong points of food supply has begun. The attack lasts all day long, but is most fierce at certain hours. According to a schedule fixed in advance the imposing assault columns form up, advancing not in dispersed order, but in compact masses in a continuous torrent. They are after plunder, not prisoners. All the newspapers have their food communiqués: people seize them with as much curiosity and anxiety as the military communiqués. What instructions will they transmit to this formidable infantry of consumers? Henceforth, the public is interested not only in the movement of armies but also in the movement of foodstuffs. We now have economic strategists who comment upon and predict the food situation . . . Ah, if only we listened to them! Paris, indeed France would become the granary of the world.[1]

The second example comes from a police report on a meeting held by the Union of Trade Unions of the Department of the Seine (Union des

---

[1] "Nouveaux décors parisiens," *Le Temps*, March 1, 1917, 1. Paris was blessed with a variety of daily newspapers during the early twentieth century, which I have made use of in my research, and each had its own journalistic and ideological perspective. To put it somewhat simplistically, *Le Temps* was a classic bourgeois establishment newspaper, *Le Figaro* was similar but somewhat more mass-oriented and Right-wing, *Le Petit Parisien* appealed to a working-class audience and was essentially apolitical in tone, and *L'Humanité* was the organ of the French Socialist Party (it would become the mouthpiece of the French Communist Party after 1920). On the history of the French press see Laurent Martin, *La presse écrite en France au xxè siècle* (Paris: Libraire Générale française, 2005); Christophe Charle, *Le siècle de la presse, 1830–1939* (Paris: Seuil, 2004).

Syndicats de la Seine, USS) in December 1915 to organize around the issue
of the high cost of living (*la vie chère*). As the report notes, things quickly got
out of hand:

This meeting was intended to have a strictly private character and be reserved to
working women and men who were union members ... However, from 2:30 PM
on about 2,000 people had gathered in the main room of the Union House: non-
union members, women, girlfriends of workers (unionized or not) who had easily
gained admittance, as well as anarchists who were professionally unemployed. In
the middle of the shouting the audience proclaimed [Gabriel] Pericat (a notorious
pacifist) president of the meeting ...
    Bled, interrupted several times by women who cried out "We want peace!
Enough murders!" tried to outline the goals of the meeting, which were to allow
everyone to speak to the issues of rents and the high cost of living ... He was
followed by Luquet, who tried to give a report on the rents question ... He began
to speak about the arbitration commissions, but was very violently interrupted.
The meeting turned into an uproar, people cried out "We want to exercise our right
of recall and make the Revolution! You've betrayed the working class!" ... Luquet
left the podium disgusted ... [Next] in a period of relative calm Maxence Roldes
discussed the question of wheat and sugar in a report full of statistics. The audience
shouted out: "It's the war that has caused the rise of the price of sugar and wheat!
Therefore, let's make peace!"[2]

Both quotations blend questions of war, class, and consumerism, underlining both parallels and ruptures between the battlefield and the home
front. The struggle for food becomes a warlike maneuver, one that according to some can only be won by achieving peace. At the same time these
texts contrast and oppose war and consumerism with each other, the
precision of military campaigns set against the disorganized anger of
women, non-union workers, and the "professionally unemployed." Both
in very different ways interpret life in wartime Paris as a consumers' war.
    This chapter will explore the idea of a consumers' war in Paris, in
particular considering the ways in which the struggle for one's daily bread
illustrated and reshaped the politics of class and gender. I argue that the
transformation of working-class identity in Paris that led to the revolutionary climate of 1919 began during World War I. The experience of war
both strengthened pre-industrial notions of moral economy and at the same
time highlighted the importance of the state and the national community to
working-class life in the French capital. In particular national mobilization
for war politicized basic consumer goods like food and housing, making
them sites of class conflict that were both intensely local and national

[2] AN F7 13617, police report of December 13, 1915.

(indeed global) in character. At the same time the new role of women, in a city much of whose adult male population was absent, reshaped the very nature of working-class identity. The result was new forms of worker radicalism that would flourish in the months after the Armistice, but whose seeds took root during the war years.

More specifically, I wish to complicate the idea that the war, in particular its early years, brought an era of social peace to Paris and made class conflicts (temporarily) obsolete.[3] France entered the war in a spirit of unity known as the *Union Sacrée*, a rejection of class and other internal divisions for the sake of the national war effort. The *Union Sacrée* certainly shaped consumer culture, especially in terms of clothing. The fact that people of all classes bought basic consumer goods (if of different price and quality) meant that they could easily serve as a symbol of social and national unity. Yet at the same time, and for some of the same reasons, basic consumer goods also functioned as a space of class conflict. Charges and counter-charges about the monopolist rich, bourgeois wastefulness, the luxurious habits of workers in war industries, and the venality of both landlords and tenants flew back and forth throughout the war. Well before the crisis of the spring of 1917 anger over consumer issues had the power to call national unity and wartime resolve into question. The contested nature of wartime consumerism in Paris suggests that, rather than disappearing altogether when banished from politics and industry, ideas of class conflict remained evident in other areas of society. The struggle for one's daily bread, and other goods, thus came to represent class struggle in general.

The idea of the consumers' war both complicates and at times confirms standard notions of social cleavage in Paris 1914–1918. Everybody complained about the high cost of food and housing in particular, and demands for lower prices had a potential for cross-class alliances, or at least sympathies, that more narrowly conceived working-class movements could not achieve. Moreover, consumer movements often had a strongly nationalist tone, expressing radical discontent in a patriotic discourse that often recalled the siege of 1870 and the Paris Commune.[4] Even at their most radical, consumer movements often combined antiwar conviction with pro-French sentiment in ways not open to strikers in munitions factories. Yet at times, the consumers' war also reinforced both traditional gender roles and prewar

---

[3] See Jean-Jacques Becker and Annie Kriegel, *1914, la guerre et le mouvement ouvrier français* (Paris: Armand Colin, 1964), 376–485.

[4] During the war Parisians made frequent references to the war and crisis of 1870–1871. For example, on Christmas Eve 1914 *Le Temps* printed an article on Christmas during the siege of 1870. December 24, 1914, 3.

notions of class conflict. Both a militarization of civilian life and a radicalization of consumer behavior, the consumers' war illustrates the micro-
politics of the Parisian home front during World War I.

THE WORLD OF GOODS GOES TO WAR

The sudden outbreak of hostilities in August 1914 had an immediate and
dramatic impact on consumer life in Paris. Many Parisians responded to
the crisis by hoarding food, spurred on by memories of the bitter siege of
1870–1871. Reports from Les Halles noted shortages and sharp rises in the
prices of meat, chicken, butter, and eggs. The price of potatoes in particular
skyrocketed, forcing public authorities to step in and restrict further
increases.[5] Army purchases of foodstuffs (Illustration 1.1), as well as the
sudden requisition of many horses and trucks normally used to transport
food to the capital, explained to an important degree the sudden shortages.
Yet at the same time a gut feeling of worry about the future seized many

1.1 Requisitioned cattle, place de l'Opéra, August 1914

[5] Becker and Kriegel, *1914*; *Le Figaro*, "L'alimentation à Paris," August 7, 1914, 2; *Le Temps*, "Le prix des
denrées," August 3, 1914, 3; *Le Petit Parisien*, "Les ménageres font des provisions," August 1, 1914, 2.

Parisian shoppers, contradicting optimistic forecasts about victory by Christmas. As *L'Humanité* reported on the second day of the war:

A serious crisis has broken out in the food business.

The population has literally rushed into the food stores. It buys the maximum that can be preserved in order to constitute reserve stocks, so much so that the Prefecture of Police has been forced to assign officers in almost all neighborhoods, especially in front of Dumoy and Potin stores.

The price of dried vegetables and of pasta has gone up by 40 to 50%. Carrots are selling at 10 sous a bunch, instead of 3 sous; the price of lettuce has almost doubled.

The increase in the price of potatoes is verging on the scandalous. Prices have risen from 12 francs to 24 francs, and then – this was yesterday's price at Les Halles – to 60 francs per 100 kilos. And the potato constitutes a major part of the essential diet of the poor [emphasis in the original].[6]

The last line of this quotation makes the point that not all Parisians experienced food shortages equally, that the burden in fact fell heaviest upon the shoulders of those least able to afford it. Thus even on the second day of the war, when all of France seemed united in the spirit of the *Union Sacrée*, consumption permitted the expression of class differences.

From this position it was only a short step to denouncing price rises and shortages as the work of speculators and other economic evildoers. Pre-industrial discourses of hoarding and manipulation of food prices as a way to make money off the sufferings of the people quickly resurfaced.[7] Less than a month later another journalist for *L'Humanité* wrote:

Working people are beginning to view the wartime behavior of the bakers as excessive. At a time when, in the spirit of patriotism, all good citizens should help each other out, the bakers continue to sell bread at the price of 45 centimes per kilo. However, the wheat harvest is abundant and, thanks to the actions of certain speculators, they can buy wheat at below-market prices ...

We hope that the government will make haste to give legitimate satisfaction to consumers by lowering the price of bread.[8]

Many of the traditional themes of moral economy, such as normative community-sanctioned prices for goods and the hatred of speculators, appear in this brief quotation and would play a major role in wartime

[6] *L'Humanité*, August 2, 1914, 2
[7] E. P. Thompson, "The moral economy of the English crowd in the eighteenth century," *Past and Present*, 50 (February, 1971). See also Steven L. Kaplan, *Bread, Politics, and Political Economy in the Reign of Louis XV*, 2 vols. (The Hague: Martinus Nijhoff, 1976); H. L. Root, "Politiques frumentaires et violence collective en Europe moderne," *Annales E. S. C.*, 45/1 (January–March, 1990); Georges Rudé, "La taxation populaire de mai 1775 a Paris et dans la region parisienne," *Annales historiques de la Revolution Française*, 143 (April–June, 1956).
[8] "Le pain cher," *L'Humanité*, August 30, 1914, 2.

discourses on consumerism.[9] The appeal to patriotism strikes a new note, however. The appeal to national exigencies goes well beyond the geographically limited, community-based world of pre-industrial moral economy. Moreover, it casts an interesting light on popular conceptions of the *Union Sacrée*. Much has been made of the striking *volte-face* of the French (and European) Left from antiwar opposition to support for national mobilization in August 1914: the triumph of nationalism over revolutionary socialism has become a key theme of the history of World War I.[10] Yet, as the quotation above suggests, the two ideologies did not necessarily conflict, not even in August 1914. By embracing a traditional discourse of popular consumerism, *L'Humanité* could keep ideas of class struggle alive while at the same time wrapping them in the tricolor flag.

The fact that consumer discontent in the early weeks of the war went well beyond the working-class Left in Paris rendered this strategy all the more effective. Shoppers of all classes hoarded food and fretted about rising prices in August 1914, fearing a return of the dread days of 1870. Indignation against shopkeepers and wholesalers went well beyond the households of the poor. In short, everyone worried about adjusting to a wartime economy. As *Le Figaro* put it on August 9, "The problem of food supplies and of hygiene in Paris has been of greatest concern since the start of the war. In spite of those very rigorous steps that have been taken, the population has been very affected and troubled by the sharp increase in the cost of living. People wonder how they will make do and protect themselves against famine, illness, poverty, in short against all the scourges which accompany such a campaign."[11]

Not surprisingly, the incidents which deserve to be called the first consumer movement in wartime Paris emphasized strident patriotism, indeed xenophobia.[12] Whereas most of the popular demonstrations that

---

[9] Several scholars of early modern France have criticized the idea of moral economy, arguing that, among other things, it tends to ignore social cleavages like gender in favor of an ideal, undifferentiated notion of community. While I accept such arguments, I also contend that the idea of moral economy retains its value if one sees it as one discourse of popular activism among others, rather than as a complete world view. See Cynthia Bouton, *The Flour War: Gender, Class, and Community in Late Ancien Régime French Society* (University Park PA: Pennsylvania State University Press, 1993); William Beik, *Urban Protest in 17th Century France: The Culture of Retribution* (New York: Cambridge University Press, 1997); Reynald Abad, *Le grand marché: l'approvisionnement alimentaire de Paris sous l'ancien régime* (Paris: Fayard, 2002).

[10] Becker and Kriegel, *1914*; Merle Fainsod, *International Socialism and the World War* (New York: Octagon Books, 1966).

[11] "Comment vivra à Paris pendant la guerre," *Le Figaro*, August 9, 1914, 3.

[12] The riots of 1914 raise the question of the relationship between looting and consumer protest. The looting of stores and other commercial establishments during incidents of civil unrest can represent

1.2 Riot at a Maggi Store, Paris, August 1914

accompanied the rush to colors in Paris acclaimed the soldiers headed for the front lines, some also took the opportunity to attack those perceived as enemies of the nation. During the evening of August 2 Parisians staged attacks against a number of stores selling food and other consumer goods to residents of the capital, usually on the pretext that they were owned by Germans or Austrians. The Maggi food stores, actually owned by a Swiss family, suffered the greatest damage; rioters invaded the stores' branches throughout Paris and its suburbs during the evening (Illustration 1.2).[13] The store in the rue Richer was completely destroyed by a crowd of 300 people. One young boy, crying "Down with Germany!," seized a handful of eggs and began juggling with them, shouting "Who wants some Prussian eggs? Free today, come and get them!" He then smashed the eggs against the window and sang the *Marseillaise*.[14]

---

both a rejection of the rules of consumption and a desperate embrace of consumerism. On this point see Sabakinu Kivilu, "Pauvreté et misère: elements pour une économie politique des pillages," *Canadian Journal of African Studies*, 33/2–3 (1999), 448–482; Michael J. Rosenfeld, "Celebration, politics, selective looting and riots: a micro level study of the Bulls riot of 1992 in Chicago," *Social Problems*, 44/4 (November, 1997), 483–502.

[13] Becker and Kriegel, *1914*, 499–503. [14] "Les incidents de la soirée," *Le Figaro*, August 3, 1914, 3.

Many other stores with German-sounding names felt the wrath of the Parisian crowd that evening. A crowd of between 400 and 500 men attacked the Klein leather-goods store on the boulevard des Italiens. The rioters broke all the windows, tore down the signs, and made off with some of the merchandise. Several taverns, with names like Zimmer, Muller, Appenrodt, and Pschorr, suffered a similar fate. In one case a crowd stormed a bar, the Chope du Chatelet, simply because a German had sought refuge there from the crowd. The rioters forced their way in and demolished the interior of the establishment.

However, xenophobia did not solely explain these attacks. Rioters also targeted stores they believed were raising prices unfairly and profiteering from the crisis. Crowds attacked food stores in the nineteenth *arrondissement* and in suburban Aubervilliers in retaliation against price hikes there. In particular, stores seen as cheating departing newly mobilized soldiers were fair game for reprisals. Rioters broke into two shoe stores, in the rue de Flandre and in the boulevard de Sebastopol, accusing their owners of overcharging for the shoes they sold to the new recruits. As the Prefecture of Police observed:

More or less grave scenes have broken out this evening at diverse locations in Paris, where shopkeepers raised prices excessively on basic consumer goods. Certain stores have been the object of serious incidents; thieves have even taken advantage of the circumstances to steal considerable quantities of goods and cash.[15]

The consumer riots that broke out in Paris at war's onset thus combined patriotic hatred of the enemy with resentment of rising prices and the shopkeepers and others who raised them. They demonstrated, when the war was only a few days old, the power and volatility of consumer anger. Parisians wanted their consumer purchases to support the war effort, and refused to buy from those they viewed as enemies of the nation. Enemy aliens certainly fit this image, but so did shopkeepers making illegitimate profits off the travails of a nation struggling for its very life. In short, like the soldiers departing for the front, consumers could also do their part by fighting the enemy at home. Here again, patriotism and class resentment joined hands.

As the example of shoe stores mentioned above suggests, concerns about clothing also occupied consumers in Paris at the start of the war, but in a very different way. Like food, clothing had a long political history, in France and elsewhere. The French Revolution, combining social difference and militant political ideology, elevated the politicization of costume to an art

[15] *Ibid.*

form, defining revolutionary allegiance in terms of clothing. The sans-culottes, those who wore long pants, became the symbol of the Paris crowd and of revolutionary virtue in general.[16] In France today, disputes over the right of Muslim women to wear the veil and the burka have become flashpoints in the conflict over the postcolonial dimensions and in general the nature of contemporary French identity.[17]

At the beginning of World War I the link between politics, clothing, and the nation resurfaced dramatically. Few aspects of daily life mark the transition from peace to war more graphically than the donning of uniforms by millions of young men, and in August 1914 Parisians witnessed the almost overnight sartorial transformation of much of its adult male population. The "uniform" (in both senses) clothing of the soldier exemplified the *Union Sacrée* in visual terms: the clothing differences that still substantially demarcated social groups in Paris seemed to vanish overnight.[18] An observer looking at soldiers departing for the war would no longer see classes, but only French men.[19] Illustration 1.3 makes this point clearly. A marquise and her maid contemplate two small-scale versions of their sons in identical uniforms, the marquise commenting with some surprise how alike they look. Whereas popular discourses about food emphasized both patriotism and class distinctions, clothing seemed to show a France united in the fight for victory.[20]

The reaction of Parisian fashion to the war crisis reinforced the idea of sartorial unity. Women throughout the world looked to Paris as the center of

---

[16] Aileen Ribeiro, *Fashion in the French Revolution* (New York: Holmes and Meier, 1988); Caroline Weber, *Queen of Fashion: What Marie Antoinette Wore to the Revolution* (New York: Henry Holt, 2006); Richard Wrigely, *The Politics of Appearances: Representations of Dress in Revolutionary France* (Oxford: Berg, 2002).

[17] Joan Wallach Scott, *The Politics of the Veil* (Princeton University Press, 2007); Françoise Lorcerie, *La politisation du voile: l'affaire en France, en Europe et dans le monde* (Paris: Harmattan, 2005); Alma Lévy et al., *Des filles comme les autres: au-delà du foulard* (Paris: La Découverte, 2004). In 2010 both the French National Assembly and the Senate passed a law banning the wearing of the full-body veil, or burka, in France.

[18] On clothing and class status see Diana Crane, *Fashion and its Social Agendas: Class, Gender, and Identity in Clothing* (University of Chicago Press, 2000); Philippe Perrot, *Fashioning the Bourgeoisie: A History of Clothing in the Nineteenth Century*, translated by Richard Bienvenu (Princeton University Press, 1994).

[19] The world of military uniforms had its own hierarchies, of course, denoting rank and status in a much more rigid way than civilian fashion. I would argue, however, that in the early days of the war these distinctions were overwhelmed by the sheer mass spectacle of hundreds of thousands of men in uniform. On the history of uniforms, see Paul Fussell, *Uniforms: Why We Are What We Wear* (Boston: Houghton Mifflin, 2002); Nathan Joseph, *Uniforms and Nonuniforms: Communication through Clothing* (Westport CT: Greenwood Press, 1986); Liliane and Fred Funcken, *The First World War* (London: Ward Lake, 1974).

[20] H. Pearl Adam, *Paris Sees It Through: A Diary, 1914–1919* (New York and London: Hodder and Stoughton, 1919), 176.

1.3 "Union Sacrée"

high fashion, and the industry made a key contribution to the city's economy. Yet Parisian fashion largely shut down at the beginning of the war. To a certain extent this resulted from scarce resources needed more urgently for the war effort, but it also reflected a sense that fashion was simply too frivolous for such serious times. Both conservatives and feminists counseled women to forget about new frocks for the time being and devote their attention to supporting their menfolk under arms.[21] Another consequence of the war was a certain standardization of dress at home. H. Pearl Adam, an English woman living in Paris, noted that in the early days of the war everyone in Paris, men and women, seemed to be wearing black. The classic color of mourning, black clothing (especially for women) also harked back to the peasant's shapeless dress, an anti-fashion statement if ever there was one.[22] Women thus sacrificed bright colors and fabrics for the somber retinue of wartime solidarity.

---

[21] Margaret H. Darrow, *French Women and the First World War: War Stories of the Home Front* (Oxford and New York: Berg, 2000), 69–71; see also Valerie Steele, *Paris Fashion: A Cultural History* (New York: Oxford University Press, 1988), 237.

[22] Adam, *Paris Sees It Through*, 38. Helen Pearl Adam was an English journalist in her late thirties living in Paris when the war broke out. In addition to *Paris Sees It Through*, she also wrote widely for the British press during the early twentieth century. See Edward Martell, ed., *Who Was Who Among English and European Authors, 1931–1949* (Detroit: Gale Research Company, 1978), vol. 1 (A–F).

When fashion did revive by the end of the year, the first clothing lines betrayed a pronounced military influence; even if she wasn't a soldier, the smartly dressed consumer could at least look like one.[23]

Yet while the rush to uniform cloaked some social distinctions, it highlighted others. Most obviously, it created a world divided between soldiers and civilians, between those in uniform and those in civilian garb. At the same time, it also exemplified the sharp gender divide imposed by the war: men wore uniforms, women did not.[24] Whereas the men in Illustration 1.3 wear identical uniforms, the women remain clothed in traditional garb that underscores their social difference. Indeed, their difference forms a counterpoint to the men's uniformity that only emphasizes the latter.[25] The eclipse of the fashion industry in the initial weeks and months of the war downplayed this distinction, in the spirit of the *Union Sacrée*. But however much fashion might strive for a military look, clothing provided one of the most salient examples of the gendered character of the home front.

In the initial weeks of the war, gender shaped views of food and clothing in contrasting ways. Both were traditional women's activities, yet Parisians viewed them differently. On the one hand, commentators saw questions of food price and availability as absolutely fundamental to civilian morale and the home front, requiring immediate government intervention. On the other hand, clothing was reduced to fashion, a frivolous diversion for idle women out of step with the pressing needs of an invaded nation.[26] Consequently, whereas journalists and other social commentators acknowledged at times that housewives did most of the shopping for food, they tended to speak of the needs of consumers and the Parisian population in general rather than of women specifically. Whereas the home front was certainly a female zone, this speaks to a certain "masculinization"

[23] As Valerie Steele has noted, many of these changes in Parisian fashion had already begun before August 1914. See her discussion of the "war crinoline" of 1915 in Steele, *Paris Fashion*, 239.

[24] This of course contrasts with (and perhaps complements) the idea that civilian men in wartime France were in effect feminized. On questions of masculinity and World War I see Leonard V. Smith, "Masculinity, memory, and the French First World War novel: Henri Barbusse and Roland Dorgelès," in Frans Coetzee and Marilyn Shevin-Coetzee, eds., *Authority, Identity, and the Social History of the Great War* (Providence RI: Berghahn Books, 1995).

[25] Another important aspect of this illustration is its implicit critique of luxury for the sake of national unity. The maid is dressed as a national symbol, a kind of Marianne, and her clothing (as well as her upright, energetic poise) contrasts with the reclined position and costly garb of the marquise. In this reading, one that would surface repeatedly during the war, the *Union Sacrée* belonged above all to the people, not the elites.

[26] The idea of fashion as frivolous fits into a broader denigration of consumer issues in general as inconsequential. See Richard Bienvenu's preface to Philippe Perrot, *Fashioning the Bourgeoisie: A History of Clothing in the Nineteenth Century*, translated by Richard Bienvenu (Princeton University Press, 1994), xi.

of a classically women's issue that had received a new public importance. Most of the participants in the riots against Maggi and other food stores seem to have been young men, for example. Conversely, when commentators discussed clothing they did so mostly in terms of women, and they made it clear that this was not a vital issue. The one exception to this was the question of clothing for soldiers. As the war stabilized and it became clear that the troops might not be home in time for Christmas, Parisians began collecting winter clothes for their men at the front.[27] At least initially, therefore, the consumers' war effort inhabited a gender-neutral space, one that could not acknowledge the central role played by women.[28]

The attacks on food stores at the start of the war underscored for the public authorities the immediate need to ensure adequate food supplies and prices for Parisian consumers. However, with the signal exception of bread, municipal and national authorities did not begin addressing the price and supply of items like meat, sugar, and produce until well into the war.[29] The influence of powerful agricultural lobbies, plus the strength of free-market ideology, effectively checked regulatory moves until the food crisis worsened significantly as the war dragged on.[30] In contrast, housing became an immediate source of public concern, and remained so throughout the war. Protection from rapacious landlords and assurance of a decent place to live became a key consumer demand for Parisians. It is to this aspect of the consumers' war that we now turn our attention.

HOUSING AND THE MORATORIUM ON RENTS

At the start of the World War I Paris had long been known as one of the cities with the worst housing stock in Europe. Parisians in general paid a smaller percentage of their income for housing than their neighbors in other countries, and in return lived in places that were older, smaller, and

---

[27] *Le Petit Parisien*, September 23, 1914, 2; *L'Humanité*, November 1, 1914, 1.

[28] Historians of central Europe have addressed the issue of gender and food during World War I. See Belinda J. Davis, *Home Fires Burning: Food, Politics, and Everyday Life in World War I Berlin* (Chapel Hill: University of North Carolina Press, 2000); Maureen Healy, *Vienna and the Fall of the Hapsburg Empire: Total War and Everyday Life in World War I* (Cambridge University Press, 2004).

[29] A major reason for this was the so-called "miracle harvest" of 1914, during which French peasants managed to bring in abundant yields despite the chaos of war and mobilization. See Martha Hanna, *Your Death Would Be Mine: Paul and Marie Pireaud in the Great War* (Cambridge MA: Harvard University Press, 2006).

[30] Thierry Bonzon and Belinda Davis, "Feeding the cities," in Jay Winter and Jean-Louis Robert, *Capital Cities at War: Paris, London, Berlin, 1914–1919* (Cambridge University Press, 1997), 305–341.

generally in poorer condition.[31] However, many people in the French capital did not see this as a bargain, but instead complained about both the cost and quality of shelter. Rents had been rising steadily since the late nineteenth century: as a consequence, a sizeable renters' movement had sprung up in the Department of the Seine, couching resistance to the landlord ("le vautour") in terms of broader questions of class struggle.[32] Since not only working-class Parisians but also most middle-class residents of the city rented rather than owned their lodgings, the housing question was central to life in the capital.

The outbreak of the war immediately produced a crisis in rental housing. With the departure of thousands of Parisian men for the front, many families were left without their principal breadwinner and thus with no way to pay the rent. In addition, the rapid mobilization of men caused a sharp economic slump in the early months of the war, throwing many people out of work. Parisians in 1914 generally paid their rent on a quarterly basis, so that payments were due in early October. The prospect of landlords throwing the soldiers' families into the street *en masse* spurred the government to take rapid action. On August 14 the national government decreed a three-month moratorium on all apartments with a rent of less than 1,000 FF per year, the overwhelming majority of Parisian apartments. The moratorium also applied to all furnished rooms, the notorious *garni* which constituted the shelter of last resort for the city's poor. At the beginning of September this moratorium was extended to all Paris apartments, and landlords were prohibited from evicting tenants for non-payment of rent.[33]

The moratorium reflected the close proximity of the German armies at the start of the war and was designed largely to protect those (mostly middle- and upper-class) Parisians who temporarily fled the city before the enemy advance.[34] After the victory of the Marne the government relaxed

---

[31] On housing in modern Paris see Roger-Henri Guerrand, *Les origines du logement social en France* (Paris: Éditions ouvrières, 1967); Guerrand, *Le logement populaire en France* (Paris: École nationale supèrieure des beaux arts, 1983); Christian Topalov, *Le logement en France: histoire d'une marchandise impossible* (Paris: Presses de la Fondation nationale des science politiques, 1987); Roger Quillot and Roger-Henri Guerrand, *Cent ans d'habitat social: une utopie réaliste* (Paris: A. Michel, 1989); Anne-Louise Shapiro, *Housing the Poor of Paris* (Madison: University of Wisconsin Press, 1984); Susanna Magri, *Politique du logement et besoins en main-d'oeuvre* (Paris: Centre de sociologie urbaine, 1972).

[32] Susanna Magri, "Housing," in Winter and Robert, *Capital Cities at War.*

[33] "Les loyers," *Le Figaro*, August 28, 1914, 3; "Les loyers," *Le Figaro*, September 3, 1914, 3; *L'Humanité*, September 3, 1914, 3; "Les loyers," *L'Humanité*, September 16, 1914, 1; *Le Temps*, September 4, 1914, 1; "La question des loyers," *Le Petit Parisien*, September 10, 1914, 1, 2.

[34] The conservative *Le Figaro* interpreted this as a triumph of democracy and egalitarianism. September 3, 1914, 3.

these regulations somewhat, but its decree of January 7, 1915 (the day before quarterly rents were due), reaffirmed the rents moratorium for all units renting for less than 600 FF per year. This represented 77 percent of all housing in the city of Paris, and 84 percent of all housing in the suburbs of the Department of the Seine. Consequently, not just working Parisians but many members of the middle class as well benefited from government protection of renters.[35]

Like price controls on bread, the housing moratorium represented the government's intention to prevent consumer difficulties from spilling over into popular disaffection with the war effort and the established order in general. The hasty termination of the rents moratorium in 1871 had been a major cause of the Paris Commune, and authorities had no desire to repeat that mistake.[36] Moreover, municipal and departmental officials put pressure on the national government to ensure social peace in their cities by address-ing the housing question. Yet although the moratorium brought temporary relief for millions of Parisians, no one regarded it as a definitive solution to the problem of wartime housing. It of course infuriated landlords, who began organizing their own associations. But even tenants recognized it was only a stop-gap measure, and clamored for the government to enact a conclusive solution to the problem.

This was a long time in coming. The history of French housing policy during World War I is one of indecision and temporization. Many officials felt that housing was ultimately a matter for the market, so that anything beyond temporary moratoria would be counterproductive in the long run. Both landlords and tenants pressured their representatives to enact policies favorable to them. As a result, the government did not enact a definitive housing law until March 1918, nearly four years after the start of hostilities. Until then, the government went from one rents moratorium to the next, so that what had begun as an emergency measure gradually became the prevailing approach to housing in Paris during the war.[37]

As Susanna Magri has pointed out, the French government took so long to address the question of rents not out of idleness, but rather out of fear of the social and political consequences of intervening in the conflict between landlords and tenants. Concerns about further spurring the growth of a powerful tenants' movement led legislators to postpone addressing the issue for as long as they could. Not surprisingly, the law that they finally passed

---

[35] Magri, "Housing," 380–381.   [36] *Le Figaro*, October 14, 1914, 4.
[37] For example, an article in *Le Temps* in 1915 noted that the government had decreed eleven rents moratoria since the beginning of the war. *Le Temps*, April 18, 1915, 1.

on March 9, 1918 pleased neither side. By maintaining exemptions from payment of rent for many low- and moderate-income renters it pleased tenants and angered landlords. In contrast, the establishment of arbitration commissions which enabled landlords to claim rent payments from their tenants gratified the former and embittered the latter. Far from appeasing this hostility, the arbitration commissions themselves became the locus for increased ill-will between the two groups, helping to lay the groundwork for the upsurge of renters' activism in 1919.[38]

The basic issue was less the actions of the government than the fact that landlords and tenants conceived of themselves as two separate, opposed groups in general. What Paul Fussell famously called "the versus habit" dominated discourses around housing in wartime Paris.[39] The spirit of the *Union Sacrée* did little to restrain expressions of bitter feeling between landlords and tenants, and the conviction shared by both of being exploited and abused by each other. In the view of the tenants, the war had made their lives much more difficult, and therefore they deserved relief from crushing rent payments rather than losing their homes. Renters' advocates constantly emphasized the plight of mobilized soldiers and their families, arguing landlords (and the nation as a whole) should share their sacrifice. In this reading, the gap between tenants and landlords replicated that between the front lines and the rear. In contrast, landlords pointed to the many individuals who benefited from the moratoria and yet held good jobs with solid incomes. Municipal employees and war factory workers, both male and female, usually featured prominently in such characterizations. If tenants highlighted the difficulties of mobilized soldiers, landlords emphasized the travails of the small property owner, people who rented out one unit or even a room in their own house or apartment, for whom the absence of rent spelled disaster. For landlords in general, their defense of their rights against rapacious tenants came to symbolize a defense of all the values that France was fighting for.

Not surprisingly, war metaphors crept into discourses about the relations between landlords and tenants, making the housing question a central front in the consumers' war. Two newspaper cartoons illustrate this graphically. One, published in *L'Humanité* in October 1916, depicts a union of landlords as a massive army, characterized by standardized, almost uniform appearance and hostile gazes (Illustration 1.4). The caption reads simply "A new threatening army." The other, which appeared in *Le Petit Parisien*, shows a French soldier taking a German officer prisoner. It turns out,

[38] Magri, "Housing."   [39] Fussell, *Uniforms*.

1.4 "A new threatening army"

however, that the German is the soldier's landlord, so the soldier demands his rental receipt, or else (Illustration 1.5). Both cartoons, especially the second one, play on a certain disconnect between visual image and written word to drive home the point that the struggle between property owners and renters is a war.[40]

---

[40] *L'Humanité*, October 1, 1916, 1; *Le Petit Parisien*, December 23, 1915, 4.

— *Kamerad! Kamerad!*
— *Tiens, mon proprio!... Mes quittances, ou j' te zigouille...*

1.5 "Kamerad! Kamerad!"

In February 1915 *Le Temps*, a firm defender of property, recognized this conflict by running a series of articles expressing the perspectives of both tenants and landlords on the rents moratorium and Parisian housing situation in general. Several people wrote in, both property owners and renters, to complain about the housing situation in Paris. More often than not, they directed their anger not at public authorities but at each other. One sees this especially with the landlords, who frequently viewed their tenants as unrealistic at best, lazy and venal at worst. One landlord wrote:

I own a building with both small and large renters[41] ... Not one has paid rent, neither in October nor in January. Many of the small renters are state employees who continue to receive their entire salaries. A nurse, with a substantial clientele,

---

[41] Small renters were those paying less than 1,000 FF/year in rent, large renters those paying more than 1,000 FF/year.

earns on average 15 FF per day, but refuses to pay 50 FF, hoping to profit from the decrees. A politician, with a good position in business, refuses to pay, under the pretext that he doesn't earn anything. After the war the upswing in business will enable him to earn much more . . . Why should the landlord make a gift of housing, more than the butcher, the baker, and many others?[42]

Another writer attacked renters in even blunter terms, claiming "the bad faith of renters has today reached its apogee." S/he went on to observe, "All this sullies the French national character, which is built upon honor and correctness in public affairs. People are promised impossible things: to be housed for free, to ruin landlords. All this will come back to haunt us one day."[43]

In presenting the case of the landlords, *Le Temps* borrowed themes of hardship habitually used to depict the plight of tenants. In particular, it gave examples of landlords who were themselves mobilized soldiers, turning upon its head the logic that suggested rents must be frozen in order to protect the homes of those fighting for France:

Some small landlords are also mobilized soldiers. They counted upon their rents to maintain their families during the war. A sergeant in the territorial army, who had built small apartments renting for 400 francs, states that since he was called to the colors his wife and children have been completely destitute. The municipality has refused to aid them, because they are property owners.

The wife of a soldier, "who left courageously, like all the others," writes us a letter in a style typical of the semi-literate: "I understand . . . that all must help the *patrie* to recover. But I believe, humble woman that I am, that our politicians should be aware of the fact that the small property owners have left their wives with few resources."[44]

As the voices quoted above demonstrate, images of women were key to discourses about the rents moratorium and housing in general in wartime Paris. If the home front was a feminized space, then at its heart lay the home itself. The image of the wife, or even more so, the war widow, left without a home had tremendous power, not only because it reflected a very real dilemma for many *Parisiennes*, but also because it encapsulated much of the anxiety about the war in general. Soldiers fought to protect their families

---

[42] *Le Temps*, February 21, 1915, 1.

[43] *Ibid.* Many of the landlords in Paris were in fact small property owners, possessing one or two buildings into which they had invested their life savings. For such landlords, the prospect of large numbers of tenants not paying rent could spell disaster. This was especially true in the working-class *arrondissements* of eastern Paris. See Topalov, *Le logement en France*; Susanna Magri, "Les propriétaires, les locataires, la loi. Jalons pour une analyse sociologique des rapports de location, Paris 1850–1920," *Revue française de sociologie*, 37/3 (July–September, 1996), 407.

[44] *Ibid.*

and their nation, but if a soldier could not prevent his wife from losing their own home he could hardly consider himself victorious, no matter what the outcome of battle. Moreover, this emphasis on the soldier trying to protect his family highlights the largely passive portrayal of women in discourses on wartime housing. The home might be a woman's space, but it was a man's job to pay the rent. Consequently, both landlords and tenants used the image to women to make the point that effective housing policies really meant defending the masculinity of French soldiers, and French men in general.[45]

Not surprisingly, given the political orientation of *Le Temps*, in general it represented the viewpoint of landlords much more extensively and eloquently than that of tenants. Nonetheless, it did air some of the grievances of the latter as well. Tenants who wrote in to defend the rents moratorium did so primarily in the name of patriotism and national sacrifice, and almost always invoked the case of mobilized soldiers. From this point of view, a break on housing costs was something the nation (including landlords) owed to its soldiers. As one correspondent wrote, "Upon returning from war ... the victorious soldier will have experienced the applause of a delirious people, received the homage that comes once in a century, marched under the Arch of Triumph; this man, who will be happy to rejoin his family and resume his civilian work, will have to think about paying his landlord!"[46] Others argued that the rents moratorium was justified by the disruption of the national economy and the resultant joblessness of many Parisians at the outset of the war, noting that failing to suspend rent payments would have meant throwing innocent people into the street.[47] Finally, some tenants' defenders invoked the specter of the Commune:

Several correspondents remind us that the Commune of 1871 started with the rents question. Although such types of analysis are hardly acceptable, we have heard threats of revolution. One anonymous writer affirms that, if one must pay rent, one will see a *bonfire of the boots of Parisian landlords*. We regard such literary excesses as mere caprices, seeing them as an example of the sufferings of the people who write them [emphasis in the original].[48]

This discussion of landlords' and tenants' views in one leading newspaper gives one example of contrasting discourses on housing in wartime Paris.

---

[45] On the history of masculinity in modern France, see Robert A. Nye, *Masculinity and Male Codes of Honor in Modern France* (Oxford University Press, 1993); Anne-Marie Sohn, *"Sois un homme!": la construction de la masculinité au XIXe siècle* (Paris: Seuil, 2009); Régis Revenin and Alain Corbin, eds., *Hommes et masculinités de 1789 à nos jours: contributions à l'histoire du genre et de la sexualité en France* (Paris: Autrement, 2007); Judith Sirkus, *Sexing the Citizen: Morality and Masculinity in France, 1870–1920* (Ithaca: Cornell University Press, 2006).
[46] *Le Temps*, January 27, 1915, 1.   [47] *Ibid.*, February 19, 1915, 1.   [48] *Ibid.*, January 28, 1915, 1.

Sharply divided by who they believed was to blame for the situation, many landlords and tenants seemed at least to agree that it was bad, even desperate, and showed no signs of improving. How true was this? To what extent did images of tenants living in ease without paying rent, or being forced into the street by cruel landlords, reflect life in Paris during the war? In the years before the war housing in Paris did in fact improve in both quantity and quality, to a certain extent catching up with London and other comparable cities. The low-rent housing stock used by working people registered a relative decline in the city of Paris, partly compensated for by the expansion of working-class suburbia. By 1914, therefore, the improvements in Parisian housing seemed to come at the expense of those who could least afford to pay the increasing rents.

The war of course intensified the shortage of low-cost housing in Paris. While housing construction essentially stopped, the Paris area grew substantially during the war years, in part because of the greater concentration of war industries in the Department of the Seine.[49] This brought about an influx of workers to the area as the nation struggled to find labor for its war effort. For the rest of the war years, in fact for most of the early twentieth century, finding a place to live in Paris, especially an inexpensive one, became a daunting task. The increased popularity of the furnished room, or *garni*, indicated the intensity of the housing crisis. The use of furnished rooms, both in cheap hotels and in apartment buildings, became common in Paris shortly before the war in response to the decline of inexpensive apartments. Such rooms were small, dark (they usually had only one tiny window), and lacked bathrooms, running water, and heat.[50] The number of Parisians living in such conditions more than doubled between the end of 1914 and the end of 1918. Traditionally the *garni* represented housing of the very last resort, and had long been identified by public health specialists as a major source of urban pathologies.[51] The fact that Parisians availed

---

[49] On the growth of the Paris suburbs in this period, see Roger Bastié, *La croissance de la banlieue parisienne* (Paris: Presses Universitaires de France, 1964); Tyler Stovall, *The Rise of the Paris Red Belt* (Berkeley: University of California Press, 1990).

[50] See for example Jeanne Bouvier's description of her furnished room in a cheap Parisian hotel at the end of the nineteenth century. Jeanne Bouvier, "My memoirs; or, fifty-nine years of industrial, social, and intellectual activity by a working woman, 1876–1935," in Mark Traugott, ed., *The French Worker: Autobiographies from the Early Industrial Era* (Berkeley: University of California Press, 1993), 368.

[51] Nils Hammerstrand, "The housing problem in Paris," *Journal of the American Institute of Architects* (February, 1920), 88–89; Jacques Bertillon, *De la fréquence des principales causes de décès à Paris pendant la seconde moitié du XIXe siècle et notamment pendant la période 1886–1905* (Paris: Imprimerie Municipale, 1906).

themselves of such poor lodgings more frequently during the war underscores the depth of the housing crisis.

Housing crises usually consist of two primary aspects, shortages and rising rents. Obviously the two interact closely, the former tending to produce the latter. Yet in the case of wartime housing in Paris, they operated discursively in different ways. Dominated by concerns about the rents moratoria, public discussion of housing tended to focus upon the issue of costs: landlords arguing the moratoria gave tenants free rent, tenants arguing that rents still imposed a crushing burden upon themselves and their families. People devoted much less attention to the question of housing supply, except in the case of landlords who argued that the moratoria would produce an eventual disinvestment in Parisian residential housing, thus adversely affecting tenants in the future. In discussing who should pay for housing, it was easy to choose up sides and blame one's opponent, but the knottier question of how to increase the housing supply, especially in the absence of any solid public-sector initiatives, received much less attention.

One reason for this was the fact that discussions of housing supply tended to undermine Manichean views of the housing crisis, especially as far as tenants were concerned. Although the moratoria tended to lump the great majority of Parisian renters into a single category, in fact even working-class tenants experienced the moratoria in different ways. In particular, native or long-term residents of the area had a decided advantage over newcomers to the city. Native Parisians, especially those men employed in the armaments industry, received relatively high salaries and were able to use the moratoria to stay in lodgings they had occupied before the war. Unless they wanted to move to another apartment, the housing shortage had little effect upon them. In contrast, new arrivals from the provinces and from outside France had to seek shelter in furnished rooms and other inferior types of housing, often at higher rates. Benefiting little from the moratoria, they experienced the shortage of decent low-cost housing in full measure.[52]

The housing crisis was also gendered. Women, especially those whose husbands were in uniform, moved more often than men. Although lawmakers designed the rents moratoria specifically to help war wives and widows, in the absence of a male breadwinner many women nonetheless found it necessary to seek cheaper lodgings.[53] Women employed in the war

---

[52] Magri, "Housing."

[53] In spite of the moratorium, many women were aware of the fact that they could still be held responsible for back rent once the war ended and the moratorium was lifted, so some chose to move to less expensive housing rather than risk expulsion once the moratorium expired. *Ibid.*, 398.

industries did earn significantly more than working women before the war, as many commentators rushed to point out, but they still earned less than men, often for the same work: Laura Lee Downs has noted that women in French war plants earned roughly half as much as men.[54] However, as the war went on cheaper lodgings became harder and harder to find. Consequently for Parisian women the wartime housing experience often meant a frenzied search for a new place to live, and getting used to a definite drop in the quality of one's home once they found one. Although poor women of course suffered the most, many middle-class women with absent husbands also had to move to cheaper lodgings.[55] Some found themselves forced to resort to furnished rooms, such as the refugee from the Aisne who moved into a *garni* with her three children.[56] The various wartime moratoria on rent certainly helped some women to hang onto their homes, but they did little to aid those forced to search for new housing, especially if they were new to the Paris area.

In short, whereas the question of rents tended to highlight the unity of all renters, the question of housing supply generally undermined that unity, exposing fissures along lines of class, geography, and gender. Naturally, therefore, tenants' movements during the war focused overwhelmingly on defending the moratoria against pressure by landlords and government officials, and much less on the thornier question of creating more housing.[57] Tenants' organizations had come into existence in Paris shortly after the turn of the century. Before the war the *Union Syndicale des Locataires* had organized branches in most of the *arrondissements* of Paris, especially the fifteenth and twentieth, and was beginning to make inroads in suburbs like Clichy as well. Decidedly revolutionary, its members saw the fight against landlords as a crucial part of the class struggle in general, and advocated actions like the *déménagements à la cloche de bois*, in which tenants would move out in the middle of the night to avoid confiscation of their furniture for non-payment of rent.[58]

[54] Laura Lee Downs, *Manufacturing Inequality: Gender Division in the French and British Metalworking Industries, 1914–1939* (Ithaca: Cornell University Press, 1995), 107. See Chapter 3 for more on this point.
[55] For an example of the impact of such a move, see Simone de Beauvoir's discussion of her family's financial difficulties and move to cheaper lodgings after the war. Simone de Beauvoir, *Memoirs of a Dutiful Daughter* (New York: Harper Perennial, 2005).
[56] *Ibid.*
[57] On rent control and housing see Bertrand de Jouvenel, *No Vacancies* (New York: New York Foundation for Economic Education, 1948); Emile François Xavier Fender, *La crise du bâtiment dans la région parisienne* (Paris: Librairie du Recueil Sirey, 1935).
[58] See the reports in APP BA 1429; see also Susanna Magri, "Les locataires se syndiquent," in Quillot and Guerrand, *Cent ans d'habitat social.*

The war years saw a proliferation of renters' organizations in Paris. Already in September 1914, the Paris Prefect of Police noted their increase in the city:

On their side, renters are organizing resistance and in several *arrondissements* have already created defense groups under the sponsorship of socialist organizations or socialist elected officials. One should note that this resistance has been furthermore encouraged by soldiers on leave, who in certain neighborhoods have declared that they expect to be exonerated entirely from paying the rent that fell due during their absence.[59]

In July 1915 the SFIO created a new organization, the Federal Union of Tenants, to spearhead the struggle for renters' rights. In doing so, the Socialists argued that tenants needed a more systematic strategy and movement to counteract the power of the landlords, and therefore should rally around its new group. As an article in *L'Humanité* put it,

Incontestably, what has made the defense of renters particularly difficult, both yesterday and today, has been their state of disorganization, the absence of any links between them, in the face of landlords whose demands and abuses, helped by powerful groups, increase from day to day. There was at one point an attempt at organization, but the noisy use of them by certain personalities deformed and distorted their character. The *déménagement à la cloche de bois* may be an expedient – not always without advantages for the landlord – it cannot serve as a weapon for all renters nor a reliable defensive practice.

Here as on all other terrains, the weak need to organize themselves to counteract the power of the strong.[60]

During most of the war tenant activism operated from a position of strength. The FUT and other organizations stood four square behind the government's rents moratoria, a policy which not only conformed to their own ideas but also benefited the overwhelming majority of Parisians. Until 1918 they pursued a dual strategy. On the one hand, they pressured government officials to renew the moratorium each time that rents came due. By 1916 the FUT had taken the position of demanding full exemption from rents for all tenants during the war. On the other hand, they tried to delay the enactment of a definitive law on rents until the end of the war. Socialist legislators fought against pressure by landlords and conservatives in general to weaken protection for tenants.[61]

---

[59] Cited in Jean-Jacques Becker, *Les Français dans la grande guerre* (Paris: R. Laffont, 1980), 127.
[60] *L'Humanité*, October 18, 1915, 4.
[61] "Les logements à Paris," article by Marcel Cachin, *L'Humanité*, March 12, 1918, 1.

With the passage of the renters' law in March 1918 this second strategy came to an end. Parisian tenants' organizations quickly attacked the law, especially its provisions allowing landlords to haul refractory tenants before the arbitration commissions. The FUT in particular went on the offensive, boycotting the commissions and increasing its efforts to organize renters. The transition to a more aggressive strategy after March 1918 took place in a context of increased consumer discontent in general, paving the way for the tenants' movement of 1919.

A key aspect of this heightened consumer unrest was the issue of food. Procuring enough to eat loomed just as large in the life of Parisians as finding a place to live, and was an issue that people had to cope with on a daily basis. As we shall see, consumer activism around food had its own traditions, very different from the practices of tenants' organizers. Yet discontent over issues of both food and housing worked together to create a sense of consumer crisis during the war. Particularly after 1917, consumer anger over the prices and supplies of these two fundamental commodities contributed to the perception of France as a nation on the verge of revolution.

THE POLITICS OF FOOD IN WARTIME PARIS

Food occupied the central place in the consumers' war. The biggest category of expenses in the budgets of working-class Parisians, indeed most Parisians, food symbolized well-being, the ability to carry on with a decent life in spite of the difficulties of the times. More than any other commodity, it had to be procured and prepared on a daily basis; among other things, food shortages increased the amount of time the housewife had to devote to shopping for it. At best, food could represent a small, accessible luxury; at worst, the lack of it could encapsulate all the misery of the times and threaten one's very survival. Even though most Parisians still consumed large quantities of bread, their diet had become much more diverse than that of their parents. Daily consumption of meat had become the norm, for example, and Parisians also consumed dairy products and fresh fruit and vegetables on a regular basis. While most understood that the war and the survival of the nation required sacrifices, those involving food cut most deeply.[62]

---

[62] Peter J. Atkins *et al.*, *Food and the City in Europe since 1800* (Burlington VT: Ashgate, 2007); Frank Trentmann and Flemming Just, *Food and Conflict in Europe in the Age of the Two World Wars* (New York: Palgrave Macmillan, 2006).

Food was not just a matter of physical nourishment, of course, but also a key aspect of social and cultural life. H. Pearl Adam noted that one of the main consequences of meat shortages had to do with entertaining: middle-class Parisian families might go without meat from time to time, but they would never dream of inviting guests to a meatless supper. As one woman in mourning noted, "They've killed my husband and taken my son prisoner, but they won't make me do without meat."[63] Another British woman living in Paris, Marjorie Grant, wrote about her experiences volunteering in a soup kitchen for war refugees and soldiers in the Latin Quarter. One of her frustrations was the constant complaints of those she served about the food.

Whatever they get displeases some of the women. They want rice when macaroni is served, and cabbage when it's potatoes, and peas instead of beans, and they unitedly and heartily hate lentils. But I am getting not to mind their complaints now, and in the end they usually eat what is put before them and ask for more.[64]

For Parisians, problems with the quality and quantity of food exemplified the deteriorating quality of life for consumers in a city under siege. The very image of the besieged city traditionally carried with it ideas of starvation, and the people of Paris needed only look back to the siege of 1870 for a recent example. In comparison with those bitter days (or, for that matter, with the Occupation years of the 1940s) the city was fortunate: Parisians managed to procure enough food to meet their needs. Yet although famine did not reoccur, food prices rose sharply during the war, in some cases tripling between 1914 and 1917. Parisians also had to contend with shortages of many of their favorite foods, as well as other consumer items like tobacco. While government officials did not for the most part immediately impose price controls as they did with housing, by the end of the war most major foodstuffs had come under public regulation.

Although food issues also mirrored and shaped discourses of class in wartime Paris, they did so in a more complex way than the Manichean struggle between landlords and tenants. To be sure, ideas of hoarding, illegitimate price-fixing, and starving the people did reappear during the war. At the same time, however, different foods came to symbolize virtue and vice, noble abstention versus iniquitous luxury, and loyalty to the national cause versus wanton selfishness. Moreover, as in the case of conflicts over housing, Parisians of different classes accused each other of overindulgence and neglect of the war effort. The classic image of the

---

[63] Cited in Adam, *Paris Sees It Through*, 109
[64] Marjorie Grant, *Verdun Days in Paris* (London: W. Collins Sons, 1918), 32.

corpulent, cigar-smoking bourgeois was countered by the portrait of the
overfed, wasteful war industry worker. Discussions about food supplies and
prices thus became sites of class conflict, frequently deployed in nationalist
terms: class enemies often also became enemies of the nation at war. Finally,
discourses around food also shaped ideas of gender in wartime Paris.
Women had the overwhelming responsibility for buying food and making
the household budget stretch to fit the family's needs. At the same time, the
war brought the increased intervention of men, ranging from union activists
to government officials, in the previously feminine world of the shopping
basket.

In this section I shall focus on popular and official discourses around two
central foodstuffs in wartime Paris, bread and meat. Before doing so,
however, it makes sense to give an overview of provisioning in the French
capital. As noted above, the outbreak of the war brought an immediate crisis
of shortages, price rises, and hoarding to Parisian markets. This proved
temporary: by the end of 1914, aided by a better than expected harvest, food
supplies and prices had stabilized. Before long, however, problems began to
manifest themselves in certain sectors. Starting in October 1914, sugar
supplies became scarce, partly because the large majority of French sugar
refineries lay in occupied territory. As a result of these shortages, the price of
sugar doubled by the early months of 1915. For the rest of the war, straitened
availability and high costs made sweetening one's food a haphazard and
luxurious enterprise. Milk and other dairy products also soon became
scarce. In spite of extraordinary measures taken by public authorities, including converting Longchamps and other Paris race courses to pastureland for
transplanted provincial cows, milk was in short supply by the fall of 1915, and
the prices of butter and cheese had risen sharply by 1916. Supplies of meat also
proved inadequate, leading to regular price increases during the war.[65]

In general, the price of food rose sharply throughout the war. By the end
of 1915 increasing costs had become a matter of public concern, and
Parisians began to employ the term *la vie chère* to characterize what seemed
to be runaway inflation.[66] Although statistics vary significantly, all agree on
the same general outline. For example, Jean-Louis Robert notes that the
general cost of living in Paris rose by over 200 percent during the war; other
analyses suggest as much as 400 percent.[67] Moreover, all suggest that prices

[65] Pierre Darmon, *Vivre à Paris pendant la Grande Guerre* (Paris: Fayard, 2002), 169–172.
[66] See for example "La vie chère," *Le Figaro*, October 8, 1915, 2, or "Contre la vie chère," *L'Humanité*,
October 17, 1915, 4.
[67] Robert, *Les ouvriers, la patrie, et la Révolution*; Bonzon and Davis, "Feeding the cities"; Darmon, *Vivre
à Paris*.

rose most sharply in 1917, the period that saw the revival of strike activity and a general crisis of French morale both on the front lines and at home. In response, public authorities kept a close watch over public reactions to food-price increases, seeing them as a threat to civilian support for the war effort. Parisians' widespread grumbling over *la vie chère* did not have the same political consequences as in Russia or Germany. Nonetheless, remarks such as the following, recorded by a police agent in the boulevard Richard-Lenoir, became relatively common in Paris by the end of the war.

The housewives are complaining of the rise in the price of commodities, especially given the approach of the holidays. "It is becoming harder and harder to live," they say, "these increases result not from the cold, nor from the transportation crisis, but rather from middlemen and speculators who engage in their illicit commerce while our elected officials worry about their political matters rather than dealing with the economic crisis which is getting worse and worse."
A third woman declares: "One would believe that the government is looking for a revolution, because if you pull too hard on the rope it will break one day. This would be unfortunate for us, because we have the best intentions and suffer in silence. If we no longer have the means to survive, then let them give us back our husbands, that's all that we ask."[68]

For Parisians, especially working-class Parisians, feeding the city's people was central to the war effort as a whole.

In terms of specific commodities, let us start with bread, the great symbol of popular diets and the politics of food ever since the Revolution.[69] Bread in wartime Paris presents us with a paradox. Public authorities quickly moved to regulate bread sales, long before those of any other foodstuff, so that the price of bread hardly budged at all during the war. Supplies, of course, were another matter. Transportation problems, military requisitions, and labor shortages in bakeries combined to produce a major shortfall in bread supplies during the war. As with housing, the cap on bread prices discouraged production, leading to a notably poor wheat harvest in 1917. Bakers limited their hours and Parisian shoppers had to get used to bread lines.[70]

Bread shortages led inexorably to accusations of hoarding and speculation, and many Parisians found it tempting to blame avaricious peasants for hardships in the city. At the same time, bread became itself a symbol of

[68] APP BA 1587, report of December 23, 1917.
[69] On the history of bread in France, see Steven L. Kaplan, *The Bakers of Paris and the Bread Question, 1700–1775* (Durham NC: Duke University Press, 1996); Jean-Louis Flandrin and Massimo Montanari, eds., *Histoire de l'alimentation* (Paris: Fayard, 1996).
[70] Darmon, *Vivre à Paris*, 199–201.

social and economic difference. Not all breads were the same, and they were certainly not equal. By the early twentieth century Parisians had become accustomed to eating a wide variety of breads, ranging from the traditional black bread of the countryside to white flour loaves, not to mention an increasing amount of pastries.[71] This came to a halt with the beginning of the war, as the French government imposed a ban on so-called *pains de fantaisie*, or "specialty breads." Attempting to ensure adequate supplies of bread and to rein in price rises, public authorities decreed that only ordinary breads made largely of wheat flour should be sold.[72]

The ban on specialty breads represented a kind of *Union Sacrée* of the bakery, a policy of equality among all consumers. This spirit of national unity in the bakeshop did not last long, however; by the end of 1914 reports indicated that bakers were again selling specialty breads to eager customers. The initial ban provoked numerous protests: in a resolution on November 8, 1914, the parliamentary deputies of the Department of the Seine voted to "express the regret that, for reasons which do not seem sufficient, the population of Paris and its suburbs should be deprived of certain types of bread which it was used to buying at its bakeries."[73] In response, General Gallieni, head of the military garrison of Paris, defended the ban, arguing that the shortage of bakery workers due to wartime mobilization had forced the government to ban specialty breads so as to ensure adequate bread supplies for the population as a whole.[74]

The government responded with a compromise, allowing bakers to sell specialty breads and pastries, but by weight rather than by unit price. This proposal pleased no one: those who opposed the sale of croissants and baguettes were not convinced that they would pose any less of a threat to bread supplies, while those who supported specialty baked goods did so largely because they were more profitable, which would cease to be the case under the new system. Authorities made numerous attempts to render the system of bread pricing more supple, but the question of specialty breads

---

[71] White bread of course has long been a symbol of luxury. See Steven Kaplan, *Good Bread Is Back: A Contemporary History of French Bread, the Way It Is Made, and Those Who Make It* (Durham NC: Duke University Press, 2006).

[72] *Le Petit Parisien*, "Il faut abaisser le prix du pain et autoriser le pain de fantaisie," October 30, 1914, 2; "Les parisiens auront-ils du pain de 'fantaisie?,'" October 31, 1914, 2; *Le Temps*, "La question du pain de fantaisie," November 3, 1914, 2; *Le Petit Parisien*, "Nous ne reverrons ni les croissants! . . . ni les petits pains de fantaisie," July 9, 1915, 3.

[73] *Le Petit Parisien*, November 9, 1914, 2.

[74] *Ibid*. Bakers themselves were divided on the question. While many attacked the ban as a violation of the liberty of commerce and of their customers' rights as consumers, others (particularly representatives of small bakeries) defended it as a result of labor and material shortages. In July 1915 the Parisian bakeries syndicate voted to uphold the ban. *Le Petit Parisien*, July 9, 1915, 3.

and pastries remained a contested one until finally national authorities once again banned their manufacture and sale outright in February 1917.[75]

Did the baguette and the croissant come to symbolize class conflict and lack of commitment to the national war effort? Yes and no. Certainly, the desire for specialty baked goods was not limited to the wealthy: croissants and pastries, like cigarettes, represent the kind of small luxury that even those of modest income can indulge in, at least once in a while. At the same time, however, it was hard to avoid the conclusion that specialty breads catered primarily to the well off, and that the ban on them in contrast forced them to sacrifice for the good of the nation at war. Even those who opposed the ban at times framed their argument in class terms. *Le Petit Parisien*, for example, in attacking the idea of selling specialty bread by weight, argued that: "Specialty bread that you find in La Villette does not generally resemble that which you can obtain in rich neighborhoods. The bread they give you in poor establishments [*bouillons à bas prix*] is not like the more delicate breads served in fine restaurants."[76] As with other aspects of consumerism in wartime Paris, debates over types of bread expressed at times both consumer unity and class divisions.

Another type of basic food, meat, exemplified these conflicts more sharply. Like other foods, it came to symbolize the inequality of supply during the war.[77] Margaret Darrow has shown how middle-class consumers viewed chicken as a symbol of working-class luxury, blaming overpaid munitions workers for the high price of food in general.[78] In response, unions and socialists emphasized the difficulties of working-class families in trying to feed their families. In July 1915, for example, *L'Humanité* discussed the heavy burden of meat expenses upon workers in Paris, arguing that "They have limited the price of bread, because it is considered an indispensable foodstuff. But isn't meat just as indispensable, especially in large urban areas?"[79] Such observations were not limited to the political Left. An October 1915 article in *Le Petit Parisien* followed a working-class housewife into the market as she tried to buy food for her husband and three children on his meager salary of 40 francs a week. It showed how she was forced to turn down one type of meat after another as too expensive:

---

[75] *Le Petit Parisien*, February 20, 1917, 1.
[76] *Le Petit Parisien*, August 4, 1915, 2. See also *Le Figaro*, November 8, 1914, 2.
[77] For another perspective on the history of meat in Paris, see Sydney Watts, *Meat Matters: Butchers, Politics, and Market Culture in Eighteenth Century Paris* (Rochester NY: University of Rochester Press, 2006).
[78] Darrow, *French Women and the First World War*, 200.   [79] *L'Humanité*, July 1, 1915, 4.

Well then! No fish, no chicken, no rabbit, no roast of veal, no stew! All the same, one must eat meat from time to time, murmured the housewife – because they are starting to murmur in the marketplace. But her discontent stops there and, like last Sunday, she falls back upon a *pot-au-feu.* "It's the best bargain," the butcher confides to her.[80]

At the same time, working-class opinion tended to blame the traditional bogeymen of high food prices, rapacious butchers and food speculators.

This discourse of conflict surrounded one of the most innovative attempts to lower meat prices, importing frozen beef. As the extent of the war effort and its impact on the Paris food market became clear by the end of 1914, public authorities began to explore a number of ways to increase meat supplies and thereby lower the cost to the consumer. One project concerned importing beef from the French colony of Madagascar; some even suggested bringing Malagasy cows to France to replenish local herds.[81] By early 1915 both national and municipal officials began to focus upon trying to get Parisian consumers to eat frozen beef. A small amount of frozen meat had already been introduced into France before the war, especially mutton, but most French consumers were still used to eating freshly slaughtered beef from local cows. In deciding to import more frozen beef, principally from South America, the government focused less on the needs of Parisian consumers than on front-line soldiers. In May 1915 the Chamber of Deputies voted to authorize the War Ministry to begin importing frozen meat from France's colonies and from overseas to feed the troops. This initiative soon led to proposals to introduce *le frigo* into civilian meat markets and butcher shops; after all, if it was good enough for France's fighting men, it ought to be good enough for those they defended. As the nation's largest center of beef consumption, as well as the place where consumers complained most loudly about the high price of meat, Paris was chosen as the place to launch frozen meat.[82]

In bringing mass amounts of frozen beef to Parisian consumers, French authorities had to cope with a number of difficulties, technological and otherwise. Relatively few butchers in Paris had the freezer boxes or cellars equipped to handle and preserve frozen meat. More generally, well before

---

[80] *Le Petit Parisien*, October 24, 1915, 2.
[81] *L'Humanite*, May 6, 1915, 4; May 13, 1915, 3. One French letter writer suggested that when Malagasy natives slaughtered cattle for their hides, the leftover beef could be sent to France.
[82] *Le Petit Parisien*, "Viande fraîche et viande frigorifiée," May 31, 1915, 2; "Aux Halles, fut vendue, hier, la première viande frigorifiée; ce fut un succès," August 8, 1915, 2; *L'Humanité*, "Les conditions de l'importation des viandes frigorifiées en France," July 16, 1915, 4; "La cherté de la viande constitue un problème des plus graves," July 1, 1915, 4.

the era of electric refrigeration in private homes, many Parisian consumers regarded with suspicion the very idea of frozen meat, fearing it might be spoiled.[83] Some Parisians also disliked frozen meat out of a sense of protectionism. Frozen beef was perforce foreign beef, and some consumers simply felt that French meat must taste better. Louise Deletang, a seamstress in the fifth *arrondissement*, noted in her wartime journal her strong preference for "good French beef."

A municipal butcher shop opened on the corner, and they sell frozen meat there, half price . . . You won't see me there . . . it may be stupid, but it disgusts me, the idea that these beasts are killed a year or more ago, I would rather not eat meat at all. I've never found anything wrong with French livestock, and I won't help enrich the Argentines![84]

The issue of transportation also got mixed up with a certain amount of xenophobia. At the time only Britain possessed a significant number of ships outfitted for the transport of frozen foodstuffs. In spite of that, the French government required frozen meat to be transported to France in French ships, a move which prompted *L'Humanité* to note that this would simply increase the price of this meat once it finally got to Paris.[85]

In spite of these difficulties, Parisian butcher shops did begin to sell frozen beef in significant quantities by the late summer and fall of 1915. The political Left in particular embraced *le frigo* as a way of making meat affordable for working-class families. Consumer cooperatives, very much a part of working-class political life in the early twentieth century, took the lead in promoting frozen meat, arguing for its healthful qualities, and instructing housewives how best to prepare it.[86] An October 1915 article in *L'Humanité* trumpeted some of the first sales of frozen meat in Paris as a salvation for housewives and a victory for the working class in general.[87] Throughout 1916 the working-class press ran a series of articles touting the benefits of frozen beef. It did so with the full support of public authorities, who hoped that these erstwhile revolutionaries would help overcome

[83] As the recent movements for local food production and slow food have argued strenuously, fresh local food does in fact usually taste better and is better for you. Carlo Petrini, *Slow Food: The Case for Taste*, translated by William McCuaig (New York: Columbia Press, 2004); Michael Pollan, *The Omnivore's Dilemma: A Natural History of Four Meals* (New York: Penguin, 2007).

[84] Louise Deletang, *Journal d'une ouvrière Parisienne pendant la guerre* (Paris: Eugène Figuière, 1935), 465, diary entry of March 16, 1919.

[85] *L'Humanité*, July 16, 1915, 4; *Le Petit Parisien*, May 31, 1915, 2.

[86] Jean-Louis Robert, "Cooperatives and the labor movement in Paris during the Great War," in Patrick Fridenson, ed., *The French Home Front, 1914–1918* (Providence RI and Oxford: Berg, 1992).

[87] *L'Humanité*, October 16, 1915, 4.

popular resistance in general to this new type of food and in the bargain remove meat prices as a source of working-class discontent.

Yet while the Left's support of frozen meat may have helped convince some Parisians to try beef from South America, it did not necessarily follow that it depoliticized the issue. On the contrary, labor's backing was intimately tied to oppositional political discourses. These took two primary forms. The first depicted opponents of frozen meat as lazy, wasteful bourgeois, too concerned with their own creature comforts to bother about the welfare of the people or the nation as a whole. Drawing upon traditional stereotypes of corpulent plutocrats, it paralleled popular middle-class images of the overfed war worker. The second form, in the best traditions of moral economy, attacked speculators, middlemen, and sometimes the butchers themselves for resisting the sale of frozen meat. As an article in *L'Humanité* argued:

French consumers are beginning to understand that those who tell them that frozen meat is nothing but carrion are making fools of them. The sacred battalion of routine and of exploitation is composed of the majority of retail butchers, of the Halles brokers [*mandataires*], and *especially of the meat wholesalers at La Villette*. The first are opposed to frozen meat by habit, by stupidity, and by their frequent desire to insult their "dirty" clients. The brokers and meat wholesalers [are opposed], because frozen meat means freezers, and freezers rationally used would prevent them from speculating, from letting meat rot while consumers fret, thus abusing the honesty of both meat producers and consumers [emphasis in the original].[88]

The struggle to ensure the acceptance of frozen beef and thus to lower meat costs was not so much a question of correcting popular prejudices as it was a matter of fighting the attempts of the bourgeois and the speculator to starve the people.

The analysis of political and popular discourses around bread and meat in wartime Paris gives a nuanced portrait of the *Union Sacrée*. Both the ban on specialty breads and the promotion of frozen meat represented an attempt to forge a national consensus from below by limiting luxury food consumption and making workers' diets the standard of wartime unity. Therefore, such measures did not oppose the idea of united opposition to the Germans so much as recast it: in these readings working people became the true symbol of embattled France. In particular working-class women, embodied in the figure of the housewife seeking to feed her family, appeared as the heroines not just of the marketplace but of the nation as a whole. Yet unlike the traditional narrative of the *Union Sacrée*, consumers frequently located

[88] *L'Humanité*, October 18, 1915, 4.

the enemy at home, not on the other side of the trenches. For middle-class consumers, highly paid workers in war plants represented not only an unwelcome inversion of class hierarchies but also a luxurious standard of living unseemly for a nation at war. For working people, speculators, rapacious shopkeepers, and the wealthy in general placed profits above people, selfish desires above the national interest. By 1915, therefore, the versus habit had invaded the city's food markets, and the search for dinner had developed into the consumers' war.

All of this happened well before the crisis of civilian morale that France experienced beginning in the spring of 1917. That year brought both unprecedented increases in food prices and the renewal of strike activity by French workers, with and without the consent of their unions. As Laura Lee Downs and others have noted, the first major Parisian strikes occurred not in the war factories but in the garment industry, and women, not men, overwhelmingly executed and led them.[89] Consumer issues played a central role in the dressmakers' strikes of 1917, as they would in the metalworkers' strike of 1919. In particular, during 1917 conflicts over clothing and fashion wrote a new chapter in the history of the consumers' war.

FASHION ON STRIKE

"Is women's wear frivolous or functional?" asks historian Nancy L. Green in a major study of the garment industries in Paris and New York.[90] Like all good questions, this immediately gives rise to others. For example, is the garment industry an example of women's production or consumption? Does it represent labor or luxury, travail or taste, hardship or *haute couture*? Specifically in the context of World War I Paris, how did women's clothing, and clothing in general, figure in discourses of consumption and the idea of the consumers' war? The study of wartime attitudes toward clothing gives us another set of insights into the micro politics of consumerism and the *Union Sacrée* in Paris: if the croissant could represent everything from class arrogance to a lack of patriotism, so could the Paris frock.[91]

---

[89] Downs, *Manufacuring Inequality*; Françoise Thébaud, *La femme au temps de la guerre de 14* (Paris: Éditions Stock, 1986); Darrow, *French Women and the First World War*.

[90] Nancy L. Green, *Ready-to-Wear, Ready-to-Work: A Century of Industry and Immigrants in Paris and New York* (Durham NC: Duke University Press, 1997), 1.

[91] See Laura Casalis, ed., *Parisian Fashion, from the "Journal des dames et des modes"* (New York: Rizzoli, 1979–1980), translated by John Shepley; Mary Louise Roberts, "Samson and Delilah revisited: the politics of fashion in 1920s Paris," in Whitney Chadwick and Tirza True Latimer, eds., *The Modern Woman Revisited* (New Brunswick: Rutgers University Press, 2003).

At the same time, to a much greater extent than with food or housing, clothing and fashion represented the collision of discourses about consumption and production. Consequently, although increases in food prices lay at the root of increased civilian discontent by 1917, clothing first symbolized mass discontent with the *Union Sacrée*. Consumer issues played a central role in the dressmakers' strikes of 1917, as they would in the metalworkers' strike of 1919. In particular, the dual role of working women as both producers and consumers highlighted the relationship between these two spheres of civilian life, underscoring the centrality of consumer discontent to the rising tide of antiwar sentiment in the French capital.

These strikes also loomed large because no aspect of the Parisian economy was more important than the garment industry. In 1906, for example, the industry employed some 290,340 workers in Paris and its suburbs, more than twice the number of the next largest industry, metals. At this point the garment industry accounted for nearly two out of every five manufacturing jobs in the city. Women predominated in these jobs, increasingly supplemented by immigrants, both male and female. If its workers constituted a central sector of the Parisian economy, the products of the garment industry symbolized the genius of French art and culture. To a very important extent our concepts of modern fashion arose in nineteenth-century Paris, and by the turn of the century *haute couture* had emerged as the fashion standard-setter for wealthy women around the world. Based upon a tightly woven network of elite fashion designers, dressmakers, and department stores, the world of *haute couture* made "Paris" and "fashion" virtual synonyms during the late nineteenth and early twentieth centuries. Affluent women from Europe and the Americas would make yearly pilgrimages to the French capital to be outfitted with the latest styles, and dressmakers abroad, especially in Britain and America, soon copied the designs of the leading Parisian couturiers. The Paris clothing industry thus represented both the city's workers and its elites, not only providing work for hundreds of thousands but also underscoring the global supremacy of French taste.[92]

No other industry in France more sharply and publicly showcased this contrast between hard productive labor and elite consumerism, and this contrast would play a major role in debates over clothing and fashion in wartime Paris. Yet these distinctions were not absolute, and fashion had

---

[92] As such, it represents a prime example of the contrast between global and local in Parisian life. On the fashion industry, see Valerie Steele, *Paris Fashion*; and Crane, *Fashion and Its Social Agendas*. On questions of French style in general, see Joan de Jean, *The Essence of Style: How the French Invented High Fashion, Fine Food, Chic Cafes, Style, Sophistication, and Glamour* (New York: Free Press, 2005); Leora Auslander, *Taste and Power: Furnishing Modern France* (Berkeley: University of California Press, 1996).

broadened its appeal beyond the highest reaches of French society by World War I. Even the rarified world of *haute couture* represented a certain standardization of clothing and taste, a decline from aristocratic traditions of garments made to order. By the beginnings of the twentieth century urban working men and women had begun to diversify their clothing, to a certain extent following trends set by the industry's elite tastemakers.[93] In particular, working-class women employed outside the home were expected to dress elegantly and follow the dictates of fashion. The shop girl in the great Parisian department stores like the Bon Marché epitomized this trend, but her sisters in other branches of commerce and industry often followed suit.[94] Like food, Parisian working-class clothing had moved well beyond providing for basic needs by 1914, representing instead a range of personal and social identity choices.

As noted above, the beginning of the war virtually brought Paris' garment industry to a standstill. The specter of mass unemployment in the industry, particularly at a time when the absence of so many men at the front made women's earnings more central than ever to family economies, led public authorities to support the revival of *haute couture* by early 1915.[95] Fashion also won support as a symbol of French commercial and artistic supremacy overseas. At the same time, by bringing large numbers of women into heavy industry at much higher wages than were typical for women workers, the war created a new mass market for stylish clothing, furthering the standardization of fashion.

Yet far from underscoring a kind of *Union Sacrée* of taste, the increased elegance of lower-class Parisians became an object of resentment on the part of their social superiors. The idea that working-class women could dress with style and even luxury prompted resentment on the part of many middle-class and bourgeois people who felt their living standards squeezed by the privations of the war economy. In particular, observers attacked the opulence of the *munitionnettes*, women workers in war plants. One commentator charged that they wore diamond combs and silk stockings to work.[96] Another, writing at the end of December 1917, condemned the high wages and lavish lifestyle of both male and female workers:

---

[93] This did not begin in the *fin de siècle*: Daniel Roche has noted the existence of such standardization during the eighteenth century. Daniel Roche, *La culture des apparences: histoire du vêtement au XVIIe et XVIIIe siècles* (Paris: Fayard, 1989).

[94] Theresa McBride, "A woman's world: department stores and the evolution of women's employment, 1870–1920," *French Historical Studies*, 10 (1978), 664–683.

[95] *Le Figaro*, "Chronique de la mode," October 6, 1915, 3.

[96] Darrow, *French Women and the First World War*, 199.

The worker wastes huge amounts of money, using it to buy goods that formerly well-off people can no longer afford . . . I assure you that the immoral, dirty, and revolutionary words that one hears everywhere contrast with the insolent luxury of those who voice them. Many women workers have on their feet big boots, of blue or russet tinted leather, that because of the shortage of leather generally sell for a hundred francs.[97]

In general, the war generated a sense of unmoored social boundaries, of people misusing the opportunities it offered to transgress class and gender norms.

The revival of the Parisian garment industry by 1915 thus took place in the context of continued sharp debates about the meaning of fashion during wartime. The lives of the city's seamstresses mirrored these conflicts over clothing, and over consumer life in general. For one thing, more than any other major industry in Paris the garment industry employed a significant number of home workers, predominantly women who sewed at home on the order of dressmaking firms and department stores. The last great vestige of early modern proto-industrialization, this system relied on women working in small garret rooms, often without heat during the winter, for twelve hours a day and more. It enabled the garment industry largely to evade the provisions of the November 1892 law on women's work, which in theory restricted their labor to no more than eleven hours a day.[98] At the same time it fostered the image of the dressmaker in general as less a modern proletarian and more a traditional woman preoccupied with her sewing and her home. This worked to their advantage in the spring of 1917, because when they complained about their inadequate salaries, they were able to do so effectively as consumers, striking a chord that resonated among many Parisians far removed from the factory floor.

By 1917 the high cost of living had become a major factor in labor agitation and Parisian life as a whole. From 1915 on the term *la vie chère* became prominent in French newspapers and other accounts. Generally referring to price inflation, it overwhelmingly denoted the high cost of food and other basic consumer commodities. By 1916, for example, newspaper ads for health remedies referred to the problem of the high cost of living and the demands it placed upon the housewife trying to keep her family healthy. Women's columns in newspapers included tips on how to stretch the food

---

[97] SHAT 7 N 997, "Rapport mensuel – état moral et politique, decembre 1917 – janvier 1918." Note the conflation of consumer opulence and political radicalism, or "insolent luxury."

[98] Judith G. Coffin, *The Politics of Women's Work: The Paris Garment Trades, 1750–1915* (Princeton University Press, 1996); Clare Crowston, *Fabricating Women: The Seamstresses of Old Regime France, 1675–1791* (Durham NC: Duke University Press, 2001).

budget and to prepare nutritious meals at low cost.[99] As workers began threatening or undertaking industrial actions, they increasingly couched their demands for higher wages as a response to inflation. In particular, by late 1916 many began asking specifically for a cost of living allowance (*indemnité de vie chère*), separate from their standard wages. In August 1916 the city's tramway workers submitted a demand for a cost of living allowance, citing food prices in particular as a justification.[100] Unions and workers in public sector employment pioneered this strategy, but the precipitous rise of food prices in the spring of 1917 made it a common practice.

Not only the high cost of living but also the question of the length of the workday helped trigger the dressmakers' strikes in 1917. Seamstresses often worked long hours, especially during the busy seasons. Jeanne Bouvier mentioned in her memoirs working once for thirty-three hours at a stretch, from 8 a.m. to 5 p.m. the following day, during the 1890s.[101] By the outbreak of the war many activists in the industry were demanding *la semaine anglaise*, the English week, which gave workers Saturday afternoons off. However, proposals to enact it soon ran into a conflict between time and money. Employers generally interpreted the idea as meaning that their workers should receive less pay for less time worked. For seamstresses, the idea of paying for increased leisure held little appeal, especially in an era when the cost of living was constantly rising. Appealing for cost of living allowances thus seemed an effective way of preserving one's income while also benefiting from a shorter workday.[102]

Both long-standing grievances about the nature of work and the specific consumer difficulties caused by the war thus provoked the dressmakers' strikes of May–June 1917. They began on May 14 at the Jenny clothing firm on the Champs-Elysées. That day the management informed the 250 women who worked there that, effective immediately, they would no longer work on Saturday afternoons, for lack of orders. Consequently they would lose a half-day's salary. The women decided to go on strike, demanding their full Saturday's pay plus a cost of living allowance of 1 franc per day. They contacted their union who sent representatives to negotiate with their employers, but after the latter rejected their demands the women decided not only to continue their strike but also to expand it to other dressmaking

---

[99] *L'Humanité*, March 14, 1915, 3; *Le Temps*, August 25, 1916, 3; August 25, 1915, 4; *Le Figaro*, June 27, 1917, 3;

[100] *L'Humanité*, August 31, 1916, 2.   [101] Bouvier, "My memoirs," 373.

[102] *L'Humanité*, May 22, 1917, 2.

firms. The next day the *midinettes* held a mass meeting at the city's Bourse
du Travail and agreed that dressmakers throughout the city would go on
strike for a wage increase. Within a day women had gone on strike at several
other garment firms, raising the number of strikers to 2,000. The movement spread like wildfire throughout Paris and its suburbs, as roving bands
of pickets went from firm to firm calling upon workers to join them. Within
a week over 20,000 *midinettes* had gone on strike and Paris' garment
industry had largely ground to a halt.[103]

One of the most notable aspects of the strike was its spectacular quality,
as demonstrators took to the streets of Paris. In contrast to many industrial
actions, which remain limited to the factory, the Paris dressmakers organized a dramatic series of marches and public displays as part of their movement. Striking *midinettes* appeared throughout the city (Illustration 1.6),
both on the main boulevards of the city center and in working-class
neighborhoods as well. One group tackled the *grands boulevards*, marching

1.6 Striking *midinettes*, place Vendôme, May 18, 1917

[103] *Le Figaro*, May 27, 1917, 3; May 31, 1917, 3; *Le Petit Parisien*, May 27, 1917, 2; *L'Humanité*, May 22,
1917, 2; Yvonne Delatour, "Le travail des femmes, 1914–1918," *Francia*, 2 (1974); Downs,
Manufacturing Inequality, 136–137; Darrow, *French Women and the First World War*, 194–197.

down the rue Réamur and the rue du 4 septembre. Others invaded the rue de Belleville and the avenue de Choisy. In one notable incident, a cortége of strikers marched into the rue de la Paix, where they were serenaded by an English army band. As one newspaper noted, "These Allied warriors, who wore such gigantic fur hats, could hardly remain indifferent to the milliners."[104]

Ostensibly the strikers staged these marches to proceed to other dress-making firms and persuade their workers to join them. Yet their presence on the streets of Paris also gave their movement the feel of a public spectacle, somewhere between a fashion show and an Easter parade. As a reporter from *L'Humanité* noted:

Noon.

Along the *grands boulevards*, a long cortège advances. It is the Parisian *midinettes*, wearing corsages of lilac and lily of the valley; they run, they leap, they sing, they laugh, and yet it is neither St Catherine's day nor Lent [*Mi-Carême*]: it is a strike.[105]

Demonstrators took care to march in their finest clothes, both a concrete advertisement of their craftsmanship and an affirmation of their sense of pride and dignity. Partly this reflected the tradition of dressing up when one left the workplace, but it also served the ends of the strike. What observers saw was not a horde of dangerous revolutionaries or defeatists but instead stylish young women whose elegance symbolized all that Paris was supposed to stand for. At the same time, their very elegance drew attention to the contrast between the luxurious nature of what they produced and the miserable conditions in which they worked and lived. A parody of "ladies on strike," the strike asserted the right of working women to enjoy bourgeois fashion while at the same time it could be read as an implicit rebuke of those who enjoyed the products of *haute couture* without any concern for their producers. The strikes thus blurred and underscored class divisions at the same time. As Alice Brisset, one of the strikers, noted many years later, "the sidewalk has always been a little bit the *midinettes'* domain. In happier days, we paraded there, singing, to celebrate St Catherine's day. But now, the street belonged to us."[106]

In transforming their strike into an urban spectacle the *midinettes* succeeded in creating a very favorable impression with the Parisian public as a whole. During the early twentieth century the terrible conditions of the city's sweatshops had received a great deal of attention, so many Parisians

---

[104] "Grèves féminines: les incidents se multiplient," press clipping file on 1917 strikes, Bibliothèque Marguerite Durand.
[105] *L'Humanité*, May 16, 1917, 4.   [106] Cited in Darrow, *French Women and the First World War*, 196.

already viewed seamstresses with sympathy. The crisis of *la vie chère* during the war, and its demands upon working women in general, gave the movement the allure of a consumers' struggle, one with which most people in Paris could identify:

> Between their "employers" who don't give them enough money, and their suppliers, grocers, butchers, and other food merchants, who ask too much of them, the proletarians of the garment industry . . . are in a pitiful state. And this situation is not new. It has been going on for several months, because the increase in the cost of living didn't just happen yesterday. How these women, these young girls have been able to "hold fast" for so long during such conditions, is one of the mysteries of small daily acts of heroism on the home front.[107]

The public's benevolent view of the *midinettes'* strike contrasted notably with the widespread hostility directed against women working in war plants. Since the latter's strikes were also motivated in large part by the increased cost of living, consumer discontent does not alone explain this difference. To go on strike in an industry whose production was vital for the war effort risked national security, and commentators bitterly accused the *munitionnettes* of betraying the nation.[108] Moreover, women metalworkers received higher salaries than women in the garment industry, and as noted above had a reputation for luxurious consumption.[109] In contrast, the *midinettes* seemed to challenge luxury consumption, symbolized by the elite women who wore the products of *haute couture*. During the spring 1917 strikes, therefore, clothing became a symbol of both privation and privilege, and thus a new front in the consumers' war.

The 1917 strikes in the Paris garment industry have gone down in history as a classic women's social movement, part of a broader strike wave dominated by women workers in the munitions industry. Yet a not inconsiderable number of men joined the movement as well, and it quickly spread beyond the bounds of the clothing sector. After May 22 workers in a number of other industries began to make similar demands of their employers and to go on strike. By May 26 workers in restaurants (both waiters and waitresses), department stores, and administrative offices, as well as other branches of the clothing industry including hats, furs, rubber wear, and corsets, had gone on strike. Most, but not all, were women, and they all

---

[107] *Le Journal*, May 26, 1917, in clipping file, Bibliothèque Marguerite Durand.
[108] Darrow, *French Women and the First World War*, 194–197; Downs, *Manufacturing Inequality*, 136–137.
[109] Darrow, *French Women and the First World War*, 199–201; Thébaud, *La femme au temps de la guerre de 14*, 169–170.

made roughly the same demands: higher wages, the English week, and cost of living allowances. It was a very Parisian strike movement, touching many of the non-war-related workplaces of the capital and representing a firestorm of protest against the material privations caused by the war.[110] As such, it represented both a labor and a consumer movement, blurring the distinctions between the two.

The garment industry strikes of 1917 were also resoundingly successful. Most strikers succeeded in winning recognition of their demands for higher wages and cost of living increases, thanks in part to high wartime profits. In June 1917 the French Senate passed a law requiring the English week, granting Saturday afternoons off, for women workers in the garment industry, without loss of salary. Backers of the bill presented it as a homage to the wartime sacrifices of French women in general; some also emphasized the importance of enabling women to spend as much time at home as possible.[111]

The 1917 dressmakers' strikes present a fascinating example of intersections of class and gender in wartime Paris. They represented the first major example of working-class on-the-job activism during the war, centering on questions of income and consumption. In particular, the focus on cost of living increases illustrated an awareness that wage increases by themselves would not enable working women to provide adequately for themselves and their families, that strikers needed to address consumer issues directly. The strikes contextualized the demands of Parisian working women in an industry of global luxury, emphasizing the contrast between wealth and poverty. At the same time, they drew upon traditional stereotypes of femininity, the woman both as homemaker and as symbol of beauty, to win widespread popular support from Parisians. Finally, the very public nature of the strike laid symbolic claim to the city's boulevards, giving the capital's residents a glimpse of working women whose labor generally took place in isolation behind closed doors. In spite of a few cries of "give us back our *poilus*!" these strikes had little political or antiwar content. Yet the movement's explosive character and its ability to mobilize masses of women around issues of consumption and leisure constituted a warning signal of the dangers posed by consumer discontent. The final year and a half of the war would render that peril all too apparent.

---

[110] "La grève de la couture a fait boule de neige," *La République*, May 27, 1917, 2, in Marguerite Durand clipping file.
[111] "Le Sénat vote la semaine anglaise," *Le Petit Parisien*, June 9, 1917, 2.

THE HUNGRY YEARS: CONSUMERS AND THE STATE
IN 1917–1918

"We need a revolution in order to have something to eat!" Overheard in a bakery in the fifteenth *arrondissement*, January 1918.[112]

As historians have noted, the strikes of the spring of 1917, in Paris and throughout France, brought a rebirth of industrial militancy, a process that continued unabated in 1918 and after. Strike activity increased sharply, so that 1918 witnessed huge walkouts in war plants throughout the country, particularly affecting the Paris area and the Loire valley. The strikes not only grew in intensity but also became more politicized, increasingly featuring calls for ending the war and even revolution.[113] At the same time, the cost of basic commodities continued to rise during the last two years of the war. If we set the average food expenses of a working-class Parisian family at 100 in July 1914, those expenses had risen to 189 by October 1917, and 214 by May 1918.[114] The Parisian population as a whole continued to support the war effort, although the strain of the sacrifices required by it became ever more evident. While most continued to hope and work for victory of arms, Jules Guesde's famous character-ization of war as the mother of revolution appeared more relevant than ever.[115]

If any Parisians doubted this, they only needed to look elsewhere in war-torn Europe. The winter of 1916/1917 was a bitter one across the Continent, known as the "turnip winter" in Germany because of the food shortages that resulted. In all the belligerent countries food prices rose sharply, and inflation reduced the incomes of most citizens. The straitened economic circumstances that prompted grumbling and discontent in Paris led to revolution elsewhere. Food riots broke out in German cities at the begin-ning of the year, and in April the Social Democratic Party formally split over the war. Throughout Europe increasing numbers of workers went on strike, spurred mostly by the ravages of inflation but also at times by opposition to the war itself. On March 8, women demonstrating for bread and coal in

---

[112] APP BA 1587, report of January 8, 1918.
[113] Kathryn Amdur, *Syndicalist Legacy: Trade Unions and Politics in Two French Cities in the Era of World War I* (Urbana: University of Illinois Press, 1986).
[114] AN F 23 188; Bonzon and Davis, "Feeding the cities."
[115] Cited in Harvey Goldberg, *The Life of Jean Jaurès: A Biography of the Great French Socialist and Intellectual* (Madison: University of Wisconsin Press, 1962), 480.

Petrograd triggered a state crisis resulting in overthrow of the Tsar by the February Revolution.[116]

Increased food shortages, and rising popular discontent, prompted much more systematic government intervention in the consumer economy. During this period public authorities introduced price fixing and rationing for several basic foodstuffs, placing themselves as a result at the center of the consumers' war. As happened with its regulation of rents and housing earlier in the war, governmental management of food prices and supplies did ease the material plight of Parisian consumers but at the same time seemed to increase conflicts around food. As the state demanded more and more sacrifices, consumers posed more and more sharply the question of exactly who was (and more importantly, who was not) making these sacrifices. Moreover, by making the state the ultimate authority on food prices and the consumer economy in general to an unprecedented degree, the intervention of public authorities tended to politicize consumer discontent by making the state itself its target. It was of course a long way from anger over meat and milk prices to the radicalism of the minoritaire factions of the unions and the Socialist Party, let alone the Russian Revolution. But the increasingly public nature of food and consumer policy would render such a convergence more possible after the war ended.

By the end of 1917 the Paris police were keeping detailed daily reports on the morale of Parisians. Above all concerned with the issue of *propos séditieux*, these reports also chronicled the many dissatisfactions with daily life expressed by the local population. Usually recording conversations overheard in marketplaces, cafés, and stores, they revealed the depth of consumer discontent in the last stages of the war.[117] Housewives in particular frequently complained about the cost of food, the lack of supplies that necessitated long waits in line at food stores, and the discourteous attitudes of shopkeepers. The next day another group of housewives, gathered at a distribution center for potatoes run by the City of Paris in the Faubourg Saint-Antoine, complained that after standing in line they were told by the city employees that they had to leave because service stopped at 4 p.m.:

They protested "that they are making fun of them, that they pay a lot for potatoes that are distributed to them after a long wait, and that they are being pushed toward

---

[116] James E. Cronin, "Rethinking the legacy of labor," in James Cronin and Carmen Sirianni, eds., *Work, Community, and Power: The Experience of Labor in Europe and America, 1900–1925* (Philadelphia: Temple University Press, 1983); Chris Wrigley, ed., *Challenges of Labour: Central and Western Europe, 1917–1920* (London and New York: Routledge, 1993).

[117] See in particular APP BA 1587, APP BA 1639, SHAT 7 N 985.

revolution . . . The city employees are lucky to finish their work day at 4 p.m. while their own husbands are spending their fourth winter in the trenches."[118]

As the first incident noted above illustrates, many Parisians blamed speculators, shopkeepers, and others in the food industry for raising prices and oppressing the people. But they also frequently blamed each other. Parisian consumers often drew a direct connection between the shortages and high prices they suffered and the luxurious over-consumption of others. Bakeries frequently appeared as the sites of such resentment, as shoppers pointed to long lines of people waiting to buy pastries or cakes as an indication of public greediness. A woman in the rue St-Lazare complained that "Since we lack flour, it is shameful to see so many people in the pastry shops. I just walked by the Chavaneau pastry shop, 10, rue du Havre: fifty people at least were eating cakes there, while so many unfortunate people suffer. A war tax should be established on every cake."[119] The attempt earlier in the war to ban specialty baked goods had made them a symbol of wasteful consumption, and the failure of these attempts was a sore point for many Parisian consumers. As another person noted, in calling on the government to close all *patisseries*, "If they do not take such measures, the population will become enraged if it sees that the wealthy can compensate for the insufficiency of their bread ration by eating cakes."[120] Let them eat cake indeed!

Inequality of sacrifice affected other consumer goods as well. Workers complained that bourgeois smokers were able to get whatever tobacco was available, either because they could afford to buy specialty brands or because they had the time to wait at the distribution centers for cigarettes, only open while working people were on the job.[121] Coal was another issue: rumors circulated about wealthy bourgeois who hoarded tons of it in their basements.[122] Automobiles also became a symbol of excessive luxury, especially after the government began rationing gasoline, so that consumers could contrast the small amounts of gas available to them for their homes with the large quantities required by private cars. In one case a report observed that "The housewives are harshly criticizing the public authorities 'who make no attempt to resolve the crisis and who permit the automobiles of lazy rich people to circulate around Paris. Some have no gas, whereas others get as much of it as they want.'"[123] In another incident, a fancy car represented not only luxury and waste but immorality and venality as well.

---

[118] APP BA 1587, report of December 24, 1917.   [119] *Ibid.*, November 30, 1917.
[120] *Ibid.*, December 2, 1917.   [121] *Ibid.*, December 3, 1917.
[122] *Ibid.*, December 10, 1917. See also Conseil Municipal de Paris, *Procès-verbaux*, July 20, 1917, 635.
[123] *Ibid.*, February 27, 1918.

A luxury automobile . . . drove through the place de Clichy at 5:40 p.m., headed for the boulevard des Batignolles. An electric lamp placed in the interior enabled one to see a fairly young woman, elegantly dressed.

Passers-by murmured:

"There goes our gasoline: it is used to drive around the w[hores] of our public officials. All the while, we don't have two pennies' worth of gas at home.

That woman deserves a brick in the face, for making fun of the unfortunate."[124]

Working people weren't the only Parisians to blame their neighbors for the difficulties of consumer life at the end of the war. Many residents of the capital, often but not always from the more elite sectors of society, blamed the shortage and high price of goods on them. One report recorded conversations overheard at the Paris Stock Exchange in response to the antiwar strikes in the munitions plants of the Loire: "the personnel of the Stock Exchange, which has been reduced to bare subsistence, does not understand the spending habits of the workers, especially as far as food is concerned. They call the workers 'chicken eaters.' But it has been a long time since the restaurants frequented by the people of the Stock Exchange could serve chicken at their tables, because of its high price."[125] Soldiers on leave in the city frequently criticized the opulence of workers in war plants, contrasting their ease with their own sufferings. One soldier talking with a comrade in a café near the Gare du Nord commented "The factory workers talk about going on strike to end the war. These guys earn twenty francs a day. Since they don't have to pay rent, they can spend it on aperitifs, theatre, concerts. And they want to earn more!"[126] Another soldier commented that Parisian civilians were lazy and spent all their time in cafés, asserting that he had no desire to risk his skin for them.[127] In July 1918 the French government prepared a report on the causes of the high cost of living during the war. Among other things, the author placed the blame squarely on working-class consumerism:

I should also note the impact of the increase in working-class buying power. Everyone knows about the considerable increase in salaries given to workers in certain professions. The buying power of these workers has increased significantly. Moreover, it has been observed that they do not save their money and spend virtually everything they earn. In addition, the intelligent and benevolent measures undertaken by certain industrialists to save their workers money on basic goods (cooperatives, cooperative stores, etc.) have to a certain extent encouraged their consumption. The multiplicity of cooperatives (dairies, butcher shops, clothing stores for men and women, hats, lingerie stores, etc.) has given birth among many

[124] *Ibid.*, February 15, 1918.   [125] *Ibid.*, May 25, 1918.   [126] *Ibid.*, March 7, 1918.
[127] *Ibid.*, January 27, 1918.

workers to fictitious needs for luxury, for convenience and well-being, which too
often lead them to increase their sumptuary expenses.[128]

Finally, people from all sectors of society frequently blamed the high cost of
living on foreigners, seen as idling around in Paris and enjoying the easy life
while good French men were sent off in their place to die in the trenches. If
the war introduced a major theme of the twentieth century, the increasing
diversity of the Parisian population, it also underscored the frequently sharp
resistance to that trend.[129]

In general, the decline and collapse of the spirit of the *Union Sacrée*
merely reinforced the tendency, already evident in the early years of the war,
of many Parisians to see the process of providing food and other basic
necessities for one's household as a struggle and to view each other as
enemies to be dealt with, even conquered, in order to achieve victory in
the consumers' war.

As public authorities in France intervened ever more systematically in the
world of consumption, popular expectations of its power to allay the ravages of
la vie chère increased apace. It became the state's job not just to stop war
profiteering in basic commodities but also to enforce egalitarian modes of
consumption. Those who spent wastefully should be targeted as enemies of
the nation and their opulent habits brought to heel. Parisians especially
criticized government efforts to regulate the consumer economy that did not
treat all people equally, and complained about certain neighborhoods where
restricted commodities were widely available, or those individuals whose
contacts enabled them to get whatever they wanted. A report on conversations
overheard in a café in the place d'Italie illustrated these concerns:

In general, the restrictions have been rather badly received by the working class that
has had "under its eyes" the proof that numerous individuals obtain, thanks to their
connections or to their money, the means to evade them.
    Take for example the case of sugar: "Who are the people who, having been able
to buy a certain quantity in advance, have been able to amass a stock of it? There are
those who possess kilos and kilos of it, while the poor worker who lives from day to
day is obliged to tighten his belt."[130]

Call it the politicization of jealousy, but government calls to Parisians for
sacrifices to support the war effort often confronted the sentiment that not
all sacrificed equally.

---

[128] AN F 23 188, "La vie chère: ses causes," 7–9.
[129] APP BA 1587, reports of December 2, 1917; January 12, 1918; January 26, 1918. Pierre Darmon
emphasizes the importance of xenophobia in wartime Paris. Darmon, *Vivre à Paris*, 223–227.
[130] APP BA 1587, December 10, 1917.

During 1915 and 1916 local and national governments held to a policy of *laissez-faire* as far as most foodstuffs were concerned. Even with the impact of the war, free-market ideology remained a force to contend with, especially when it came to sectors of the economy not directly related to the war effort.[131] All this changed with the consumer crisis of 1917. The last two years of the war witnessed a sharp increase in the state's role in consumption. Public authorities pursued several different strategies to limit the price of food and other basic commodities. The most dramatic of these was food rationing. In March 1917 the national government began by rationing sugar. Coal followed in October, and in December bread itself became rationed. For all these products, Parisians received rationing cards that allocated a specific quantity of the rationed material (Illustration 1.7). The specific quantity varied according to one's individual situation: in the case of bread for example, the amount ranged from 200 grams per day to 500 for female factory workers, 600 for male factory workers.[132]

1.7 Parisians getting bread ration cards, 1918

---

[131] Bonzon and Davis, "Feeding the cities."
[132] *L'Humanité*, March 12, 1917, 2; December 2, 1917, 2; *Le Figaro*, July 25, 1917, 2; *Le Petit Parisien*, December 5, 1917, 1; January 24, 1918, 1.

Public authorities also imposed regulations on food sellers to limit consumption and thus prices. A February 1917 decree forced chocolate shops to close on Tuesdays and Wednesdays, for example, and the same month authorities limited Parisian restaurants to serving meals with no more than two courses. In April 1917 butcher shops were ordered to close at 1.30 in the afternoon. This soon gave way to the establishment of "meatless days"; at first intended just for Thursdays, they rose to two per week by the summer of 1917, and three a year later. In addition, local and state authorities also experimented with direct involvement in food distribution. The harsh winter of 1916–1917 prompted city authorities to distribute free potatoes during the cold months to about 600,000 Parisians. In March 1918 the city of Paris opened the first municipal butcher shops, selling meat at below market prices and managed by public authorities. Such "steak socialism" proved a great success, and by the end of the war twenty-five had been created, mostly in poorer neighborhoods.[133]

Like other belligerent nations during World War I, France experimented with the creation of "national" commodities, as a way of demonstrating patriotism and popular unity in the face of the enemy. Most prominent of these was the "national loaf," in part modeled on Germany's famous *Kaiserbrot*. The state had laid down standards for bread production as early as the summer of 1915. In February 1917 the national government, following upon its efforts to rein in the manufacture of specialty breads, laid down new guidelines for the bakers of France. In particular, the decree mandated that bread must be made entirely of wheat flour, and banned all other specialty breads, including croissants, brioches, and others. Moreover, it banned the sale of fresh bread in favor of *pain rassis*, ordering bakers to sell loaves no less than twelve hours after they came out of the oven.[134] This new bread, quickly dubbed the "national," the "victory," or the "French" loaf, promoted a spirit of sacrifice for the war effort.[135]

Perhaps more unusual was the effort by French authorities to promote the sale and use of the "national shoe." By increasing the demand for soldiers' boots, the war created a shortage of leather, thus sharply increasing the price of shoes. Starting in March, the Commerce ministry began negotiating with the nation's shoemakers to collaborate in the production of a national shoe, made of leather requisitioned by the government and produced at set rates by selected private manufacturers. Both houses of the legislature approved the project in July 1917, and by the end of the year the

---

[133] Conseil Municipal de Paris, *Procès-verbaux*, 1918, meeting of March 18, 1918, report 23.
[134] *Le Figaro*, February 10, 1917.   [135] Darmon, *Vivre à Paris*.

authorities established a goal of producing 450,000 pairs of economy-priced shoes every month.[136] That this was more than a little ambitious soon became clear: in November 1917, for example, the government only managed to produce 50,000 pairs, not its stated intention of 500,000.[137] The project only really gathered steam in the early months of 1918, and remained in force for the rest of the war.

Such "victory commodities," like the ban on specialty breads, represented a way of giving a concrete expression to national wartime unity at the level of basic consumer goods. They functioned both to subsidize low-income households by providing cheap alternatives for certain key commodities, and promoted an inexpensive vision of consumerism that implicitly condemned the luxurious spending habits of the wealthy as contrary to the national interest. Yet they also reflected social and political tensions in wartime Paris, not only resolving but also contributing to the consumers' war. By making working-class consumerism a national and patriotic standard, they focused class resentment and anger upon those who still desired white bread and high-fashion shoes. In August 1915, for example, *L'Humanité* published a blistering riposte to an article in *Le Temps* which attacked the idea of the national loaf as, among other things, a betrayal of French baking traditions and an imitation of "Kaiser bread" in Germany. Entitled "Defend the national loaf," the article called into question its competitors' patriotism:

But what then is the source of *Le Temp*'s rage? Where would we be if, for the duration of the war, we were deprived of specialty breads and had to eat the same bread that we give to our soldiers? One could hardly believe it ... But what most enrages our colleagues are the measures taken by the Chamber [of Deputies] to ensure that France has the wheat it needs while saving money and hindering the speculators. A bad, very bad operation, says *Le Temps* ... Freedom! Freedom of trade, freedom of imports, freedom of flour sifting will be better for everyone!

Very sweet, gentlemen. You forget that you have just demonstrated the contrary. It is your own excesses that have proven that such excesses at this time only benefit the few, while they drive the nation towards the abyss.[138]

Those who refused to support victory commodities were therefore lumped together with speculators as enemies of the nation at war.

This approach emphasized support for state attempts to equalize consumption. At the same time, however, dissatisfaction with victory commodities also translated into anger at public authorities. This dissatisfaction

[136] *Le Figaro*, December 6, 1917, 1.   [137] *L'Humanité*, November 28, 1917, 1, 2.
[138] *Ibid.*, August 10, 1915, 4.

took two general forms: discontent with the quality of victory commodities, and resentment at their unequal availability and distribution. *Le Petit Parisien* and other newspapers attacked the idea of the national loaf, among other things claiming that the health benefits of whole-wheat bread were exaggerated. Such complaints increased when a professor at the Academy of Medicine charged that eating the national loaf could cause, among other symptoms, digestive problems, gas, swelling of the mouth and lips, and abdominal pains.[139] In describing the new bread one letter writer noted, "What can you say about the bread that they are making us eat now? It has made many people sick in Paris, and some have even died from being poisoned by it!"[140]

Not surprisingly, in the fashion capital of the world the idea that sensible shoes would help win the war did not go unchallenged. A trade journal, *Leather*, attacked the idea of the national shoe, claiming it would not only impoverish many skilled cobblers but also endanger the elegance of French fashion.[141] More commonly, consumers complained that shoe stores didn't stock the national shoe, or that whenever they asked the stores didn't have their size. Many were angry both at the stores, whom they at times saw engaged in a conspiracy to "sabotage" the national shoe, and at the government for not making enough of them or for failing to distribute them equitably.[142] As with other commodities, the idea that the wealthy or well connected got more than their fair share fueled both class resentment and hostility to the public authorities. "[G]o to any store, and they will tell you that they are still waiting [for the national shoes] or they don't have your size. Most times, this is not true. In reality they reserve these shoes for friends and regular clients. Since a shoe ration card does not yet exist, they give many pairs to some to the detriment of others."[143] A mixture of resentment at privilege and irritation at the traditional Parisian *esprit de clocher*, such attitudes showed how state intervention in the consumer economy was a double-edged sword, both promoting and undermining civilian unity at the same time.

One of the most systematic efforts made by public authorities in France to equalize wartime consumption was the luxury tax. The concept of luxury

---

[139] "Le pain actuel," *Bulletin de l'Académie de Médecine*, 2 (1917), 335–348, cited in Darmon, *Vivre à Paris*, 201.

[140] SHAT 7 N 997, report of August 15–September 15, 1917.

[141] Cited in *L'Humanité*, May 6, 1917, 2. This common idea of conspiracy spoke both to the preindustrial heritage of moral economy and to ideas of total war, which warned all citizens to guard against the machinations of the enemy. On the atmosphere of paranoia in wartime Paris see Darmon, *Vivre à Paris*, 157–161.

[142] APP BA 1587, report of February 7, 1918.   [143] *Ibid.*, report of December 20, 1917.

is of course a relative one, one that changes over time, so that yesterday's luxury objects (be they white bread, automobiles, or cell phones) often become tomorrow's basic commodities.[144] During the war luxury became a symbol of waste at best, dereliction of duty at worst, frivolities out of place while the nation fought for its very existence. Moreover, many argued that the production of luxury goods limited the supply of basic commodities: more croissants equaled less bread. As *L'Humanité* argued in its defense of the national shoe, "the leather that you waste for the 'elegant man' and the 'woman with a low-necked dress' . . . raises the price of shoes for everyone, as we know very well."[145]

In response to these sentiments, the French government passed a law on December 31, 1917 imposing a 10 percent tax on objects formally classed as luxury items. These included, among others: camera equipment, personal automobiles, gold and silver jewelry, silk hats and clothes, liqueurs and aperitifs, first-edition books, Oriental carpets, and pleasure boats, as well as certain foods served in restaurants.[146]

In general, the tax does not seem to have done much to hinder luxury consumption. An investigation undertaken by *Le Petit Parisien* a few days after the start of the tax reported that proprietors of jewelry stores and high-fashion boutiques did not notice any significant decline of sales.[147] One department store, Palais de la Nouveauté, in a clever merchandising coup announced that for a few months in the fall of 1918 it would pay the tax on all luxury goods purchased there.[148]

The conservative press and members of elite social circles roundly condemned the luxury tax. It was attacked as impractical, unjust, and a danger to the livelihood of workers in the luxury trades. In an article entitled "The taste for luxury," *Le Figaro* portrayed it as an assault upon beauty, no less: "As soon as they buy [luxury goods], these lovers of precious things, of beauty, these enemies of the vulgar and the utilitarian, they . . . know that they will attract, fatally, the incomprehension, jealousy, and hatred of others."[149]

Many working-class consumers, in contrast, strongly approved of this tax on the consumption of the wealthy. Yet some also criticized the law for not

---

[144] See Philippe Perrot, *Le luxe: une richesse entre faste et confort, XVIIIe–XIXe siècle* (Paris: Seuil, 1995); Jean Castarède, *Histoire du luxe en France: des origines à nos jours* (Paris: Eyrolles, 2007); John Shovlin, *The Political Economy of Virtue: Luxury, Patriotism, and the Origins of the French Revolution* (Ithaca: Cornell University Press, 2006).
[145] *L'Humanité*, May 6, 1917, 2.   [146] *Le Figaro*, February 6, 1918, 1.
[147] *Le Petit Parisien*, "Pour la première fois hier, la taxe de luxe a joué," April 3, 1918, 2.
[148] *Le Temps*, July 31, 1918, 4.   [149] *Le Temps*, January 9, 1918, 1.

going far enough. Consumers in a café on the rue de Lyon noted that "the tax on luxury objects as usual only hurts the poor. It is incomprehensible that an automobile worth 15,000 francs is not taxed, while a bicycle worth 255 francs, used by its owner to go to work, is. Why, moreover, would a fishing pole worth 12 francs (a modest price) be subject to the tax, whereas a window shade worth 28 francs would not be at all? . . . Instead of being fixed uniformly at 10%, the tax should be progressive."[150] While not necessarily opposing the idea of the tax, the consumers of the rue de Lyon, in the old Faubourg Saint-Antoine, nonetheless viewed it as an example of the government once again favoring the wealthy.

Shortages in basic commodities and exasperation with government attempts to remedy the situation prompted some Parisians to speak in terms of revolution. This was not necessarily the revolutionary discourse of the antiwar Left. Most Parisian consumers continued to support the war effort, even if they believed that the public authorities were mishandling it, and many blamed overpaid war workers and foreigners for the sufferings of the French consumer. Talk of anger at food prices also diminished notably when Paris suffered German bombardments, as happened in the spring of 1918. Nonetheless, some felt that the situation could not last, that further declines in the standard of living would provoke a revolution. Many blamed this on government incompetence, sometimes going so far as to suggest that perhaps the authorities even wanted such a situation. As one person commented in a café on the boulevard Saint-Marcel, "The restrictions on bread are really too hard for the workers. Who knows if our leaders, despairing of finishing the war with a glorious peace, are not intentionally trying to provoke a popular movement which would give them the excuse to accept a gimcrack peace."[151] Consumer disputes that occasionally turned violent reinforced the idea that after four years of war Paris stood on a political precipice. In January an incident occurred in a tobacco shop in Montparnasse. As some 200 smokers pushed and shoved to gain entry, the shopkeeper suddenly closed the store, fearing the outbreak of violence. The waiting customers responded by trying to break in. A group of soldiers stood by watching the scene, and one said to his fellows, "Don't leave! We're about to see how civilians mount an assault against a bistro!"[152]

---

[150] APP BA 1587, report of February 10, 1918. While it was not literally true that cars weren't subject to the luxury tax, such sentiments underscored the inability of the law to appease hostility to "luxury" consumption.
[151] *Ibid.*, report of January 29, 1918.   [152] APP BA 1587, report of January 11, 1918, 9–10.

Some bourgeois Parisians also feared the outbreak of revolution in their city by the spring of 1917. The combination of increasing hardships for working people and the sumptuous displays of wealth by the *nouveaux riches* could produce political tumult. One woman, writing to a friend in New York in April 1917, informed him that "The poor are suffering too much and heartily detest the bourgeoisie. I don't know, but it seems there is a feeling of revolution in the air. One has no idea what is going to happen, and to whom."[153] Another Parisian wrote:

Life here is becoming impossible, everything is disgustingly bad, even bread, as well as the vegetables we still have. What will happen this winter? There will certainly be a revolution in Paris, and I advise you ... to close up everything and come to the countryside. It's no joke to find oneself in the middle of riots, all the more because, since this will be a revolution provoked by famine, they will pillage your house.[154]

In a similar vein, a man wrote to a relative in Brazil, "Life here is starting to be difficult, at least for the masses, because there are also people that are making fortunes, either by speculation or from military contracts. It is scandalous to see the displays of unheard-of luxuries while so many people are ruined ... Will we have a repetition of 1871? The fishers in troubled waters are already at work."[155]

For Parisians of all social classes, the idea of revolution was intimately linked with the crises of the consumer economy. Members of the bourgeoisie at times observed that the increased poverty, both relative and absolute, of the working classes caused by *la vie chère* might very well drive them to extreme measures. Some Parisians of modest means complained that the ineptitude of public attempts to regulate the consumer economy, and their failure to create a spirit of egalitarian sacrifice for the war effort, could leave them with no other choice than the barricades. Such sentiments seemed sharpest during the crisis of the spring and summer of 1917, but did not entirely disappear during the rest of the war. As both memories of the Commune and the contemporary example of the Russian Revolution demonstrated, in the right circumstances the consumers' war could turn into the consumers' revolution.

The concept of the consumers' war in wartime Paris operated on several different levels. Most obviously it worked as metaphor: Parisians could view their struggles to obtain basic consumer goods as analogous to the combat of front-line soldiers, indeed the nation's very fight for survival. It also served

---

[153] SHAT 7 N 985, "Rapport moral, Avril 1917," letter of Mme Lille to M. Keyes, 12.BA
[154] Cited in Becker, *Les Français dans la grande guerre*, 207. [155] SHAT 7 N 985, letter of July 10, 1917.

to reframe class conflict and gender politics, so that commodities became symbols of social differences and divisions. In addition, the consumers' war gave an alternative view of the *Union Sacrée*. It suggested that for many working-class Parisians in particular national unity was achieved by excluding the wealthy, not by joining with them. It implied that the enemy was at home as well as abroad; the role reserved in official discourse for spies and traitors was here extended to speculators, dishonest shopkeepers, and sometimes the bourgeoisie as a whole. It showed how the official *Union Sacrée* did not abolish class conflict but rather forced it into alternative channels shaped by pre-industrial traditions, channels that were often gendered female.

This consideration of the micro-politics of consumer behavior offers us a glimpse into how Parisians experienced World War I on a day-to-day basis, and how they made sense of this conflict. It also shows how a society negotiated major social distinctions to mount a massive war effort, and how those attempts at unity sometimes foundered or were at least interpreted differently by different types of Parisians. In addition, it suggests that consumerism remained an issue of important political significance well into the twentieth century, blending early modern notions of moral economy with modern techniques of state mobilization. Although Parisian consumer discontent did not have the dramatic impact it did in Russia, where a women's bread riot in 1917 sparked the overthrow of the Tsar, it did nonetheless loom as a major cause for concern for the French state and leaders of society in general. Ultimately, victory in the struggle against Germany would depend at least in part upon a successful resolution of the consumers' war.

In the eyes of some Parisians, especially by 1918, there was another option: revolution. Failure to meet consumer demands might very well call the legitimacy of the state into question; riots at food stores might lead to barricades and insurrection. For the people of the French capital, success in this realm was intimately linked to questions of victory and defeat in the war itself. Yet, as we shall see in the chapters that follow, the Armistice of November 11, 1918 did not bring an end to working-class discontent; quite the contrary, during 1919 it reached unprecedented levels.

The events of 1919 thus grew directly out of the politicization of consumer discontent that occurred during World War I. Ultimately many interpreted the consumers' war as a class war, so that concerns about food, shelter, and clothing reinforced the idea of class divisions and identities. In consequence, the turbulent political and social movements arose out of the broader context of Parisian working-class life during the era of

World War I, in particular the ways in which the world of the Parisian worker was reshaped by the war years. As I shall argue in the next chapter, working-class identity lay at the heart of radical working-class politics. In order to explain why the siren of revolution tempted many members of this class in 1919, one must define the Parisian working class in general. We now turn to this process of definition.

CHAPTER 2

The working class of Paris: definitions and identities

Whose victory, what kind of peace? For Parisians during 1919, still basking in the warm glow of the Armistice but anxiously awaiting the final resolution of hostilities, such questions had multiple answers. The great conflict between nations had come to an end; would it be succeeded by a war between classes in the French capital itself? In 1919 many middle-class Parisians in particular treasured the memory of the *Union Sacrée*, regarding the mounting wave of working-class radicalism with fear and anger.[1] Parisian workers often interpreted these questions very differently. Many still shared the patriotism of other French men and women, rejoicing at the national victory. At the same time, however, an increasing number also began to see the war as a victory of the bourgeoisie over the workers, and, inspired by the distant but brilliant spectacle of the Russian Revolution, to dream of returning to *la lutte finale*.[2] These two sets of working-class attitudes did not necessarily contradict each other; it was in fact the intersections between them that most effectively accounted for much popular activism in the year after the Armistice.

In the previous chapter we saw how consumer issues continued discourses of class and class conflict during World War I. This chapter will build upon those insights to explore how Parisians conceptualized class, and in particular working-class identity, in the year after the Armistice. If class was a key social

---

[1] On bourgeois fears of the working class during the war, see especially Jean-Jacques Becker, *The Great War and the French People* (New York: Berg, 1985); for the postwar period, see Jacques Girault, ed., *Sur l'implantation du Parti Communiste Français dans l'entre-deux-guerres* (Paris: Éditions Sociales, 1977); Jean-Jacques Becker and Serge Berstein, *Histoire de l'anticommunisme*, vol. I: *1917–1940* (Paris: Olivier Urban, 1987).

[2] Among the most valuable works on postwar working-class French radicalism, see Jean-Louis Robert, *Les ouvriers, la patrie et la Révolution: Paris 1914–1919* (Paris: Les Belles Lettres, 1995); John Horne, *Labour at War: France and Britain, 1914–1918* (Oxford University Press, 1991), 350–394; Chris Wrigley, *Challenges of Labour* (New York: Routledge, 1993), especially the article by Roger Magraw; Annie Kriegel, *Aux origines du communisme français: contribution à l'histoire du mouvement ouvrier français* (Paris: Flammarion, 1970).

marker for Parisians, as the lived experience of the war suggested, then what did it mean to be a worker in Paris in 1919? What, moreover, were the social and political ramifications of working-class identity, and how did it manifest itself at a series of levels, from the most local to the most global? In answering these questions, one must not only consider "objective" factors such as income, workplace experience, and family structure, but also investigate the more slippery questions of class identities and perspectives. Many cultural historians have questioned the value of class as a hermeneutical tool of historical exegesis. Joan Scott, Gareth Stedman Jones, and others have challenged the relevance of class analysis to certain periods in history by arguing, for example, that many working people in the past did not share a collective identity as workers, or that the working class itself was divided by more salient conflicts based on gender or ethnicity.[3] Such analyses have had the cumulative effect of raising an important and disturbing question: does the working class exist, and if so, how?[4]

I have tried to make this question the starting point of my analysis in this chapter and the one that follows. One can indeed speak of a Parisian working class in 1919, but in this chapter and the one that follows I emphasize and explore its heterogeneous, internally variegated character. Analyses of the material working and living conditions of Paris workers are crucial in pinpointing the basic parameters of their lives, revealing both the sharp distinctions among different types of workers as well as the distances separating them from other groups in society. Such analyses are fundamental, and no exploration of working-class identity is complete without them. Following Thompson, however, I shall argue that in 1919 the existence of the Parisian working class as a unified entity was primarily a subjective phenomenon, that is to say a matter of ideology and self-perception. However, I shall also assert that working-class consciousness was not the only factor of importance; rather, one must consider both middle-class and working-class representations of each other as forces that shaped this collective subjectivity.[5] Raymond

---

[3] Joan Scott, *Gender and the Politics of History* (New York: Columbia University Press, 1988); Gareth Stedman Jones, *Languages of Class* (Cambridge University Press, 1983); John R. Hall, ed., *Reworking Class* (Ithaca: Cornell University Press, 1997). For an excellent summary of these and other critiques of class analysis and labor history see Lenard Berlanstein, ed., *Rethinking Labor History* (Urbana: University of Illinois Press, 1993). For a critique of this approach, see William H. Sewell, *Logics of History: Social Theory and Social Transformation* (University of Chicago Press, 2005).

[4] For a stimulating cultural critique of the notion of social class, see Sarah Maza, *The Myth of the French Bourgeoisie: An Essay on the Social Imaginary, 1750–1850* (Cambridge MA: Harvard University Press, 2003).

[5] The classic study of bourgeois images of workers is Louis Chevalier, *Laboring Classes and Dangerous Classes in Paris during the First Half of the Nineteenth Century*, translated by Frank Jellinek (Princeton University Press, 1973); see also Donald Reid, *Paris Sewers and Sewermen: Realities and Representations* (Cambridge MA: Harvard University Press, 1991).

Williams once argued that both *bourgeois* and *working class* were not just groups of people but also conceptual frameworks and ultimately ideologies.[6] While such an approach can lead to essentialist stereotyping, it is very useful if placed in historical context and used to evaluate the perspectives of people living at the time. In 1919 both middle-class and working-class Parisians had their own views of what it meant to be working class, and these perceptions were the bedrock of working-class identity.

In particular, I argue in this section that during World War I working-class life in Paris assumed a character that would in many respects dominate the outlines of proletarian France during the twentieth century as a whole. In this chapter I underscore the tremendous diversity of Parisian workers, noting how it shaped the geography and politics of the capital and its suburbs. Following certain diasporic and postmodern theorists, I emphasize the idea that this heterogeneous quality was key to the nature of working-class community in Paris.[7] In the chapter that follows I consider the ways in which this diversity was both challenged and reaffirmed along race and gender lines, social divisions that would play a central role in the social and political life of the new century.

One useful way to proceed is by considering the Parisian working class in the context of certain dualities central to the life of Paris as a whole in 1919. In their fascinating study of the carnivalesque in modern Europe, Peter Stallybrass and Allon White emphasize the importance of symbolic oppositions in structuring European culture. Paul Fussell has noted that one impact of World War I on European thinking was to increase the importance of oppositional dualities, of "either/or" patterns of thought.[8] Paris was the site of numerous conflicts in the year after World War I, and this climate of contestation helped define the working class as an entity apart.[9] Not only war vs. peace, but also working class vs. bourgeois, male vs. female, white vs. nonwhite, and urban vs. suburban all contributed both to working-class identity and to the political turbulence of the era.

---

[6] Raymond Williams, *Culture and Society* (New York: Columbia University Press, 1960), 319–328.

[7] See Jean-Luc Nancy, *La communauté désoeuvrée* (Paris: Bourgois, 1986); Miami Theory Collective, ed., *Community at Loose Ends* (Minneapolis: University of Minnesota Press, 1991); Paul Gilroy, *The Black Atlantic: Modernity and Double Consciousness* (Cambridge MA: Harvard University Press, 1993).

[8] Peter Stallybrass and Allon White, *The Politics and Poetics of Transgression* (Ithaca: Cornell University Press, 1986); Paul Fussell, *The Great War and Modern Memory* (New York: Oxford University Press, 2000). This pattern was certainly not unique to World War I, but to an important extent arises frequently during wartime, past and present.

[9] On the rich potential of symbolic analysis for historians see Robert Darnton, *The Great Cat Massacre and Other Episodes in French Cultural History* (New York: Vintage Books, 1984); Darnton, *The Kiss of Lamourette: Reflections in Cultural History* (New York: Norton, 1990); see also the exchange on this subject between Robert Darnton and Roger Chartier: Chartier, "Texts, symbols and Frenchness," *Journal of Modern History*, 57 (1985); Darnton, "The symbolic element in history," *Journal of Modern History*, 58 (1986).

Yet if the strength of binary oppositions emphasized the importance of the working class as a social and political phenomenon in France at the end of the war, these oppositions were shifting and unstable. The year 1919 constitutes both a year of extreme dualities and a year in which these dualities existed in a state of transition and flux. Other dualities, such as those contrasting men and women, consumers and producers, and whites and nonwhites, also became manifest: at times they undercut working-class unity, at times they reinforced it. A central argument of this chapter, and of this study, is that the transitional nature of these oppositions helped open up new spaces in working-class life for alternative forms of popular struggle. The heightened climate of binary opposition increased the likelihood of clashes between bourgeoisie and proletariat, but the instability of this climate meant that these conflicts sometimes took unexpected forms.

This chapter will consider Parisian working-class identity from two perspectives. First, it will give a statistical analysis of workers in Paris and its suburbs, focusing in particular on occupational categories and neighborhood life. Second, I turn from this large general portrait of working-class Paris to study the lives of two individuals, Louise Deletang and René Michaud, looking at the ways in which they represented their own lives and the nature of class in general in wartime and postwar Paris. This chapter thus proceeds along both macro and micro levels, balancing the "objective" world of statistics with the subjective one of self-presentation. Ultimately it reveals a complex world of great diversity, one in which the binary thinking that was a legacy of World War I operated strategically to underscore new and unstable ideas of working-class identity and community.

Unfortunately, French statistical data, upon which much of this chapter is based, does not generally permit the historian to focus on a single year. I have therefore opted to use census data in particular from the 1921 and at times the 1926 censuses. I offer this information as a rough but nonetheless useful measurement of the statistical outlines of working-class Parisian life in 1919. Taken together with the writings of Deletang and Michaud, which do focus specifically on 1919, they provide a sense of class composition and class identity in that year, underscoring this chapter's emphasis on the turbulent nature of that year and its rootedness in the context of working-class life.

THE WORKING PEOPLE OF PARIS: AN OVERVIEW

Like many other labor historians, I choose to start my portrait of working-class Paris with an analysis of statistics gleaned from government sources. In using such material the historian must proceed with caution and an awareness of both the specific circumstances of their production and also the broader historical conjuncture out of which they arose.[10] Nonetheless, they represent a valuable source that, when used judiciously, can add enormously to our knowledge of working people, who did not usually leave written testimonies for posterity, those who did not count but were counted instead. In seeking to come to grips with the phenomenon of the Paris working class at the end of World War I they represent one place to start, not the Holy Grail of absolute knowledge.

The analysis presented in this section rests essentially on the data contained in French censuses of the 1920s, produced by the Statistique Générale de la France (SGF). A part of the Labor ministry, by the early twentieth century the SGF had refined the art of census taking almost to the level of an art, if not quite a science. National censuses were taken at a regular, rigidly fixed interval of five years, and census takers received specific instructions as to how to collect and present their data.[11] Of course, as anyone can attest who has ever looked at raw data from the French census, especially the more detailed *listes nominatives du recensement*, those hired to collect census information often ignored these directives, producing wide variations in the quality of census data. More generally, assumptions made by both individual census takers and the SGF as a whole often raise as many questions as they resolve. Census workers were normally poorly paid and poorly trained, so while the data they produced is useful in painting a broad statistical portrait, one must nonetheless take it with a grain of salt.

Defining a group as large and as heterogeneous as the working class of Paris and its suburbs with any accuracy is a daunting task in any case. The question of who should be included (and excluded) can be answered in many different ways. In his excellent, informative study of Parisian workers in the late nineteenth century, Lenard Berlanstein challenges the so-called *embourgeoisement* thesis, which argues that the population of the city of Paris had become predominantly middle class.[12] Based on his critical

---

[10] As Joan Scott has demonstrated, statistics are not neutral, objective facts, but rather embody value judgments and, ultimately, relations of power. See Scott, "A statistical representation of work," *Gender and the Politics of History* (New York: Columbia University Press, 1988). See also Bonnie G. Smith, *The Gender of History: Men, Women, and Historical Practice* (Cambridge MA: Harvard University Press, 2000).

[11] On the history of the French census during this period, see Michel Huber, "Quarante années de la Statistique générale de la France: 1896–1936," *Journal de la Société de statistique de Paris* (1937); Alfred Sauvy, "Statistique générale et Service national des statistiques de 1919 à 1944," *Journal de la Société de statistique de Paris* (1975); François Bédarida *et al.*, *Pour une histoire de la statistique* (Paris: Institut National de la Statistique et des Études Économiques, 1976).

[12] Lenard Berlanstein, *The Working People of Paris, 1871–1914* (Baltimore: Johns Hopkins University Press, 1984), 3–9. On the *embourgeoisement* theme, see Gerard Jacquemet, *Belleville au XIXe siècle*

reading of the 1911 census, Berlanstein asserts that a solid majority of the inhabitants of Paris, some 70 percent, were working people. Defining them as people who owned no property and lived off their paychecks, he divides the working people of Paris into several subcategories: craftsmen, factory workers, white-collar workers or employees, and service workers.[13]

Berlanstein's analysis of the Paris census data is skillful and well-informed, but does not conclusively resolve the question of who constituted the working class of that city. For an example, let us take the problem of the relationship between workers and employees. It is often extremely difficult to formulate any satisfactory definition of the latter, or to distinguish them from the former.[14] Often characterized as lower level white-collar workers, there was frequently little difference between their working and living conditions, and those of workers. By the 1920s most workers employed in the public sector were routinely defined as employees; this meant that workers for the Paris Metro, for example, were statistically divorced from the working class.[15] Some employees also had wages and living conditions not appreciably distinct from those of skilled workers. However, other factors distinguished the two groups more sharply. Conditions of employment were different, with employees usually enjoying much more job security than most workers. Employees also had higher levels of education, having often completed secondary school.[16] Most employees did seem to work in offices, not workshops or factories, making their work environments appreciably different from those of working-class Parisians. Finally, as far as can be determined many employees simply did not identify as workers, rarely forming unions and playing little or no role in labor and socialist movements.[17]

Additional problems arise when one tries to determine subcategories and gradations of skill among the working-class population. Scholars considering the French working class in the early twentieth century have usually divided it into three levels: skilled, semi-skilled, and unskilled (*ouvriers qualifiés, ouvriers*

(Paris: J. Touzot, 1984); Maurice Daumas and Jacques Payen, eds., *Évolution de la géographie industrielle de Paris et sa proche banlieue au XIXe siècle* (Paris: Centre de documentation d'histoire des techniques, 1976).

[13] Berlanstein, *Working People*, 15–38.

[14] Berlanstein provides an excellent discussion of this group in his study of the Paris Gas Company, *Big Business and Industrial Conflict in Nineteenth-Century France* (Berkeley: University of California Press, 1991), 191–257; see also Arno Mayer, "The lower middle class as a historical problem," *Journal of Modern History*, 47/3 (1975); Philip Nord, *Paris Shopkeepers and the Politics of Resentment* (Princeton University Press, 1986).

[15] Roger-Henri Guerrand, *L'aventure du métropolitain* (Paris: Éditions de la Découverte, 1986).

[16] Berlanstein, *Big Business*, 209–217.

[17] *Ibid.*, 228–257; see also Pierre Delon, *Les employés: un siècle de lutte* (Paris: Éditions Sociales, 1969); Judith Wishnia, *The Proletarianization of the Functionnaires: Civil Service Workers and the Labor Movement under the Third Republic* (Baton Rouge: Louisiana State University Press, 1990).

specialisés, manoeuvres). Yet these terms appear only sporadically in the French census during the 1920s.[18] The professional designations that are furnished, terms like *tourneur* or *manutentionnaire*, may indicate different levels of skill in different settings, such as small workshops versus large factories. In the case of craftsmen, it is virtually impossible to distinguish between the self-employed and those working for someone else, since the *listes nominatives* rarely list places of employment. Consequently, a poorly paid, low-skilled carpenter and the head of a construction firm can appear identical.[19]

The basic question of identity underlies these uncertainties. One cannot make a hard and fast distinction between objective facts gleaned from the pages of census records, and subjective considerations of self-representation; the two are completely intertwined. Since census takers primarily determined the occupations of their subjects simply by asking them, these classifications represent not abstract categories but the self-identities of the people of France.[20] Although census takers made their own observations and used their own judgments in deciding what to record, ultimately those being interviewed could choose to claim whatever professional status they either believed most represented them, or even desired for themselves. Consequently, as documents the French censuses hold keys to both subjective and objective parameters of class differentiation, in fact calling into question the real distinctions between the two.

The 1921 census of the City of Paris breaks down the population into several socioprofessional categories and lists their rough percentages as follows: heads of establishments, 9%; employees, 34%; workers, 44%; self-employed (*isolés*), 13%. Census figures for the Seine-*banlieue*, the mostly industrial suburbs of Paris within the Department of the Seine, tell a slightly different story: heads of establishments, 10%; employees, 18%; workers, 58%; and self-employed, 14%.[21] These figures emphasize the importance of the relationship between employees and workers in constructing an overall portrait of the class composition of the Paris area population in the early

---

[18] Semi-skilled workers in particular were both increasing in number and especially difficult to define during this period. In fact, there was often very little difference between unskilled and semi-skilled workers. On this group see Michel Collinet, *Essai sur la condition ouvrière* (Paris: Éditions ouvrières, 1951); and Alain Touraine, *L'évolution du travail ouvrier aux usines Renault* (Paris: Centre nationale de la récherche scientifique, 1955).

[19] At times the census would identify skilled craftsmen, especially masons, as "entrepreneurs," but this practice was both haphazard and rare in the census records I consulted.

[20] Since the term "absente" appears frequently in the *listes nominatives* under the occupational category, I have assumed that census takers determined people's jobs by asking them personally.

[21] Statistique Générale de France, *Résultats statistiques du recensement général de la population*, 2 (Paris: Imprimerie nationale, 1925), [hereafter *RS*], 1–3, 2–3.

twentieth century. If one combines the two groups into the broad category of working people, then Paris remains an overwhelmingly proletarian city, almost identical to the suburbs in this respect. If on the other hand one limits one's definition of working class to the census category "workers," then the idea of *embourgeoisement* makes somewhat more sense, and the distinction between urban and suburban populations appears much sharper.

For a number of reasons, some of which will become clearer below, I believe it is more useful to adopt the latter course. On balance, the differences in types of jobs, work experience, lifestyle, and *mentalité* seem to outweigh the similarities. By the 1920s the contrast between Paris and its suburbs had become marked by many contemporary observers, and a basic component of that contrast was the larger percentage of workers in the latter.[22] In addition, the fact that many people identified themselves as employees to the census takers reflects a choice not to identify with the working class. Therefore, for the purposes of this analysis, and this study, I will not include employees in my definition of the Paris working class.

The *Résultats statistiques* for 1921 does not subdivide the working class into specific skill levels, but it does analyze the "active industrial population" by different sectors. Since the industrial population seems to have been essentially working class,[23] a look at these subcategories should prove instructive in building a portrait of this class.

The statistics listed in Table 2.1 portray a working class that was highly diverse, concentrated in manufacturing, and significantly differentiated between urban and suburban sectors. In sharp contrast to many factory towns and provincial industrial regions in France, in the Paris area no one industry monopolized the working-class labor force.[24] Not surprisingly, given

---

[22] For contemporary accounts of the Paris suburbs, see Edouard Blanc, *La ceinture rouge* (Paris: Éditions Spes, 1927); M. Bonnefond, "Les colonies de bicoques de la région parisienne," *La vie urbaine*, 25, 26; Charles Collin, *Silhouettes de lotissements* (Paris: Bloud & Gay, 1931); Wladimir d'Ormesson, *Le problème des lotissements* (Paris: Éditions Spes, 1928); Jean de Vincennes, *Le Bon Dieu dans le bled* (Paris: G. Beauchesne, 1929); Alain Meyer and Christine Moissinac, *Representations sociales et littéraires: centre et périphérie, Paris 1908–1939* (Paris: IAURIF, 1979); Jacques Valdour, *Ateliers et taudis de la banlieue de Paris* (Paris: Éditions Spes, 1923).

[23] The *Résultats statistiques* for 1921 estimate the industrial population as 48 percent of the working population of the City of Paris as a whole; they also estimate that the category "workers" accounts for 44 out of 100 people employed. *RS* (1921), 1–3. According to the census, roughly 1.9 million Parisians were actively employed out of a city population of 2.9 million, or 67.7 percent, resulting in a very low dependency ratio. However, one must also note that the 1.9 million figure included roughly 250,000 suburbanites who commuted to work in Paris (minus 40,000 Parisians who commuted to work in the suburbs). *Ibid.*

[24] One can make an interesting comparison with Limoges and Saint-Etienne at roughly the same time, thanks to Kathryn Amdur's study, *Syndicalist Legacy* (Urbana: University of Illinois Press, 1986). Although both Limoges and Saint-Etienne were sizeable provincial cities with large industrial sectors, both were dominated by a few essential industries.

Table 2.1 *Parisian workers by industrial sector, 1921*

	City of Paris	Seine suburbs
Clothing	220,943 / 23.9%	67,931 / 13.3%
Basic metals	170,033 / 18.4%	156,377 / 30.7%
Chemicals	18,233 / 2.0%	39,016 / 7.7%
Construction	61,726 / 6.7%	27,308 / 5.4%
Wood	59,395 / 6.4%	31,673 / 6.2%
Leather	45,228 / 4.9%	12,201 / 2.4%
Printing	44,498 / 4.8%	9,127 / 1.8%
Food	39,534 / 4.3%	24,184 / 4.7%
Other	265,335 / 28.7%	141,413 / 27.8%
Totals	924,928 / 100.0%	509,230 / 100.0%

RS, 1921, 1–3, 2–3. In 1921 Paris had a population of roughly 2.9 million, the suburbs of the Department of the Seine roughly 1.5 million.

the position of the French capital as a world leader of the fashion industry, clothing is the largest single subcategory listed, but it accounted for less than one-quarter of the workers of the city.[25] Similarly, the largest sector of suburban labor, metals, reflecting the existence of industrial Behemoths like the Renault factory in Boulogne, employed less than one-third of the working people in that area. The category of "other" in the table, which included a whole range of smaller industries, such as rubber, paper, precious stones, and even agriculture, was the largest for Paris and the second largest for the suburbs of the Department of the Seine. Clearly, sheer occupational unity could not itself produce a broader spirit of class identity and consciousness for the Paris area.

This profile of the industrial economy in the Paris area also outlines a labor force very different from that of the nineteenth-century city. Perhaps most striking was the relatively small size of the construction industry. During the mid nineteenth century the various building trades accounted for a major proportion of the Paris working class, but by 1921 they were well under 10% in both the city and its suburbs.[26] This reflected not just the impact of the war, which had virtually halted residential construction, but more broadly the stagnation of the city's population in the early twentieth century. Significantly, while this sector had declined by 2% since 1906 in

[25] This category in the *Résultats statistiques* did not include textiles, which accounted for 24,481 people (2.6 percent) in Paris, and 10,692 (2.1 percent) in the suburbs.

[26] On the Parisian construction industry in the nineteenth century, see David Pinkney, *Napoleon III and the Rebuilding of Paris* (Princeton University Press, 1958); Jeanne Gaillard, *Paris, la ville, 1852–1870* (Paris: L'Harmattan, 1997).

the city, in the Paris suburbs it had grown by 25%, reflecting the population growth there. The basic metals industry, on the other hand, exemplified the opposite legacy of wartime production. Between 1906 and 1921 this industry increased its labor force by one-third in Paris, but more than tripled its numbers in the suburbs. If the carpenter, stonemason, and ditchdigger typified the world of Parisian labor in the nineteenth century, the metal-worker symbolized the working class of the twentieth.[27] Enshrined in Communist ideology and iconography during the interwar years, he[28] had already assumed a central role by 1919.[29]

The salient and growing differentiation between Parisian and suburban workers had also been spurred on by the war, and heralded the shape of the region's industrial economy in the twentieth century. Most of the industrial growth resulting from the war effort took place in the suburbs: whereas the industrial workforce of Paris grew by 3% from 1906 to 1921, that of the suburbs grew by 39%. The relative weight of specific industries differed in the two areas, with metals accounting for 18% of the Parisian industrial workforce, but 31% of that of the suburbs.[30] On the other hand, occupations requiring greater levels of craftsmanship, such as printing and leatherworking, had more prominence in the capital.[31] Moreover, suburban factories were larger than Parisian ones. The average Paris workshop had 9.2 workers, whereas the average for the suburbs was 14.5. This distinction between urban and suburban casts an important light on the question of the *embourgeoisement* of the Parisian population; ultimately, *embourgeoisement* was most significant as a relative concept. While many workers continued to live in the capital, in comparison to the suburbs the city's industry seemed small-scale and traditional. The suburbs, with their heavy industry, large factories, and more homogeneously working-class population, corresponded most closely to images of twentieth-century industry.[32]

[27] See Berlanstein, *Working People*, 8; Michel Coste, "Les métallos: une génération de pionniers de la proche banlieue parisienne," in Susanna Magri and Christian Topalov, eds., *Villes ouvrières, 1900–1950* (Paris: L'Harmattan, 1989). For an example of the "métallo" as working-class hero, see Lucien Monjauvis, *Jean-Pierre Timbaud* (Paris: Éditions sociales, 1971).

[28] As I shall explain below, the use of the masculine pronoun here is deliberate.

[29] Although sharply spurred on by World War I, the metals industry had already taken a leading role in the Parisian economy by the turn of the century. See on this point Daumas *et al.*, *Évolution de la géographie industrielle*.

[30] See Table 2.1.

[31] For example, the *Résultats statistiques* of 1921 listed over 32,000 printers working in Paris, but less than 6,000 in the suburbs.

[32] See on this point Jean Bastié, *La croissance de la banlieue parisienne* (Paris: Presses Universitaires de France, 1964); Louis Chevalier, "La formation de la population parisienne au 19e siècle," *Cahiers de l'Institut national des études démographiques*, 10 (1950); René Clozier, *La Gare du Nord* (Paris: J.-B. Bailliere et fils, 1940).

This overview of the working class of Paris and its suburbs serves to outline a few essential characteristics of that population. Its sheer size is most impressive, accounting for nearly half of the total population of the Department of the Seine, or over 2 million people.[33] Roughly one out of every twenty people in France was a Parisian worker in 1921.[34] The workers of Paris were also a diverse group, working in many different settings ranging from small laundries and sweatshops to giant metals and chemical factories. Given this size and diversity, such an overview is not adequate to provide any real insight into the structures of working-class life in Paris in the early twentieth century. Two reasons in particular make it imperative to take a closer look at this population by selecting certain neighborhoods for more in-depth analysis. The first is the nature of the sources: the *listes nominatives*, arranged by quarter in Paris or by suburban municipality, furnish a wealth of information on occupations, family structures, demography, ethnicity, and gender simply not available in the more general *Résultats statistiques*. The second has to do with the nature of working-class Parisian life at the time. Working people did not enjoy the kind of cosmopolitan perspectives on Paris so common of the bourgeois *flâneur*; for most, life was lived in the neighborhood, not in the city as a whole. Given this *esprit du clocher*, any analysis of working-class life in Paris that did not take into account neighborhood peculiarities would neglect a crucial part of that experience. Consequently, I have chosen to complete this numerical analysis of the Paris working class with a look at four communities within the metropolitan area with significant laboring populations: the quarters of Folie-Méricourt and Croulebarbe in the eleventh and thirteenth districts (*arrondissements*) respectively, and the suburban municipalities of Boulogne-Billancourt and Drancy.[35]

Stretching from the place de la République in the north to the places de la Bastille and de la Nation in the south, the eleventh district lay right in the heart of popular Paris in the early twentieth century. Along the southern edge of this district stretched the ancient Faubourg Saint-Antoine, fortress of the sans-culottes during the Revolution and still home to a dynamic furniture industry and artisanal culture.[36] Whereas the Faubourg Saint-Antoine

---

[33] The population of the Department of the Seine as a whole in 1921 was roughly 4.4 million people.
[34] I include suburbanites as Parisians in this sense; although residents of the suburbs may have distinguished themselves at times from those living within the city limits, they had much more in common with them than people in the provinces.
[35] Since unfortunately the *listes nominatives* done for the City of Paris in 1921 no longer exist, I was forced to use those from 1926 for Folie-Méricourt and Croulebarbe. I did, however, use the 1921 *listes nominatives* for Boulogne-Billancourt and Drancy.
[36] On Faubourg Saint-Antoine see Laurent Azzano, *Mes joyeuses années au faubourg* (Paris: France-Empire, 1985); Jacques Valdour (pseud.), *Le faubourg* (Paris: Spes, 1925).

represented in a sense the glorious past of popular Paris, the Folie-Méricourt quarter presented a more contemporary aspect. Lying at the northern end of the eleventh district, this area was bounded by the rue du Faubourg du Temple on the north, the boulevard de Belleville on the east, the rue Oberkampf on the south, and the boulevard du Temple on the west. Largely a product of the early nineteenth century, the neighborhood was dominated by the kind of five- to eight-story buildings that so typfied the poor neighborhoods of eastern Paris.[37] Over 55,000 people lived here in the early 1920s, in an area that had one of the highest population densities in the city.[38] Folie-Méricourt, and much of the eleventh district, abounded with small metallurgical shops, often located in the rear courtyards of otherwise residential buildings and employing a few skilled workers. In fact, small-scale industry and skilled labor character-ized much of the neighborhood's industry in general. So did the presence of a large foreign population, especially from eastern Europe.[39]

On the other side of the Seine lay the thirteenth district, one of the poorest in Paris. The Croulebarbe quarter constituted the northwest section of the district, bounded by the boulevard de Port Royal to the north, the Avenue des Gobelins to the east, the boulevard Auguste Blanqui to the south, and the rue de la Santé to the west. Although less impoverished than the Maison Blanche and Gare quarters to the south, Croulebarbe still harbored a large working-class population, nearly half of its total inhabitants and very close to the average for Paris as a whole. It had been an industrial neighborhood since the opening of the famous Gobelins tapestry works there in the fifteenth century, and still contained many metalworking ateliers and garment sweat-shops. Compared to the Folie-Méricourt quarter, Croulebarbe was much smaller and less densely populated, having only about 20,000 inhabitants in about the same amount of space. It also sheltered several military barracks and faced the Santé prison, all too well known to many working-class political leaders, across the rue de la Santé.[40]

---

[37] Fernand Bournon, *Paris-Atlas illustré* (Paris: Larousse, 1989), 93–95.
[38] On population densities see *Annuaire statistique de la ville de Paris, 1923–4* (Paris: Société anonyme de publications périodiques, 1927), 336.
[39] On the foreign population of Paris, see André Kaspi and Antoine Marès, *Le Paris des étrangers, 1919–1939* (Paris: Imprimerie nationale, 1992); Nancy Green, *The Pletzl of Paris: Jewish Immigrant Workers in the Belle Epoque* (New York: Holmes and Meier, 1986); Clifford Rosenberg, *Policing Paris: The Origins of Modern Immigration Control between the Wars* (Ithaca: Cornell University Press, 2006); Patrick Dewitte, *Les mouvements nègres en France, 1919–1939* (Paris: L'Harmattan, 1985); see also Azzano, *Mes joyeuses années*, and Valdour, *Le faubourg*.
[40] Bournon, *Paris-Atlas illustré*, 137–153; Jean-Jacques Leveque, *Vie et histoire du 13eme arrondissement* (Paris: Hervas, 1987).

Boulogne-Billancourt, to the southwest of Paris, represented in some ways the suburban equivalent of the Faubourg Saint-Antoine. Just as the latter symbolized the artisanal culture and politics of nineteenth-century Paris, so did the former symbolize the factory labor force of the twentieth century. In the early 1920s Boulogne had nearly 70,000 inhabitants, making it the largest single suburb of Paris. Dominated by the giant Renault auto plant, one of the largest in France, Boulogne represented French industrial might. On the face of it, there were few greater class contrasts in the metropolitan area than that between proletarian Boulogne-Billancourt and the neighboring affluent sixteenth *arrondissement* of Paris. Yet the reality of life in this factory town was more complex than its popular image suggested. It certainly contained a large working class, but not all of these worked at Renault or even in the metals industry in general. Moreover, the city was home to a sizeable group of property owners and middle-class liberal professionals, who lived primarily along the major boulevards near the Paris border.[41]

Boulogne-Billancourt may have symbolized proletarian life for the popular imagination in early twentieth-century France, but it was in actual fact a product of patterns of urbanization and industrialization set during the late 1800s. In contrast, the obscure little community of Drancy exemplified those processes that would shape the working-class suburbs of Paris between the wars. Situated at the northeast edge of the Department of the Seine, Drancy contained no industry to speak of, and transportation connections to Paris and more central industrial suburbs were adequate at best. Farmers still lived and worked in this town in the years after World War I. Yet it was Drancy and other similar communities that attracted the massive working-class migration to the Paris suburbs in the early twentieth century. With a population of barely 1,000 at the turn of the century, Drancy had 15,000 people in 1921, and over 50,000 ten years later. Peripheral both to the Paris area and to images of the working class in the early 1920s, Drancy nonetheless provided a prescient glimpse of future class relations in and around the capital.[42]

This brief survey of these four neighborhoods reveals the complex diversity of the worlds of working-class Paris. The crowded, lively streets and tenements of the Folie-Méricourt quarter might at first glance seem to have little

---

[41] Patrick Fridenson, *Histoire des usines Rénault* (Paris: Seuil, 1972).

[42] During the interwar years Drancy was known as "mushroom city" because of its extremely fast rate of growth. Jean-Jacques Peru, "Du village à la cité ouvrière, Drancy, 1896–1936" (Mémoire de maîtrise thesis, Université de Paris-1, 1977–1978). During the Occupation years Drancy became infamous for another reason: it was the site of the concentration camp that collected Parisian Jews for shipment to Auschwitz and other death camps in the East. See Maurice Rajsfus, *Drancy: un camp de concentration très ordinaire* (Paris: J'ai lu, 2004).

Table 2.2 *Social class in the Paris area during the 1920s*

	Workers	Employees	Middle class	Artisans / shopkprs	None
Folie-Mér.	225 / 48.6%	163 / 31.1%	32 / 6.1%	20 / 3.8%	55 / 10.5%
Croulebarbe	95 / 46.1%	64 / 31.1%	17 / 8.3%	21 / 10.2%	9 / 4.4%
Boulogne	362 / 53.8%	100 / 14.9%	89 / 13.2%	35 / 5.2%	77 / 11.4%
Drancy	114 / 74.0%	16 / 10.4%	0	18 / 11.7%	6 / 3.9%

Archives Départementales de Paris [ADP], *Listes nominatives*, Boulogne, 1921 (vol. II), D2M8, article 152; APP D2M8, 1926, article 250, eleventh *arrondissement* of Paris; APP D2M8, 1926, article 266, thirteenth *arrondissement* of Paris; APP D2M8; APP D2M8, 1921, article 167, Drancy. This and the other statistical tables about these four neighborhoods are based on 1/100th samples, not their entire populations.

Table 2.3 *Working-class occupations in Greater Paris in the 1920s*

	Clothing	Construction	Metals	Unskilled	Other
Folie-Mér.	33 / 22.2%	13 / 8.7%	38 / 25.5%	20 / 13.4%	45 / 30.2%
Croulebarbe	17 / 26.2%	4 / 6.2%	19 / 29.2%	15 / 23.1%	10 / 15.4%
Boulogne	31 / 17.6%	24 / 13.6%	51 / 29.0%	43 / 24.4%	27 / 15.3%
Drancy	11 / 18.6%	6 / 10.2%	13 / 22.0%	12 / 20.3%	7 / 11.9%

LN, Boulogne, 1921, 1931.

in common with the flat vistas and small allotment houses of Drancy. Working-class experience was not monolithic, but rested on many different material and social bases.

The categories presented in Table 2.2 give a very rough approximation of the actual class divisions in Paris after the war; they resemble static photographs that can sketch the main outlines of a living organism without rendering a true portrait of its soul.[43] As such, they need some clarification in order to provide the maximum amount of information possible. Each category comprises a myriad of professional designations. The group "working class" includes people of all skill levels, working in several industries; I have provided a more detailed breakdown of this class in Table 2.3. In general, workers were the most easy to identify from census records, reflecting perhaps a greater sense of definition of that class on the part of those who wrote the census.

---

[43] These categories include unemployed women and children in the class of the man usually listed as the employed person in the household.

Employees, on the other hand, were more difficult to categorize, and to differentiate from both workers and the middle class. One of the most diverse social groups, it included not just clerks and salespeople but also teachers, commercial representatives, insurance adjusters, postal employees, and many others. The percentages of employees are so much greater here for Paris than for the suburbs partly because I chose to include concierges in this category,[44] but they also reflect the relative *embourgeoisement* of Paris and the lesser importance of industry there in comparison to the suburbs.

Interestingly, the same was not true of the group labeled here "artisans and shopkeepers"; these people formed a greater part of the population of Drancy, the new working-class suburb, than they did of the Folie-Méricourt quarter, in spite of the latter's proximity to the Faubourg Saint-Antoine. These two groups had much in common as small entrepreneurs and property owners, but were not identical. Many of the artisans were concentrated in the construction trades, like carpenters and stonemasons, which partly explains their large numbers in a town growing as quickly as Drancy.[45] Shopkeepers, on the other hand, mostly ran food stores, the *boulangéries*, *crèmeries*, *charcuteries*, and others that still delight foreign visitors to Paris. I have also included in this category the costermongers, chandlers, and other pushcart vendors who still sold their wares in the streets of both Paris and its suburbs.[46]

The category "middle class" here similarly designates a wide range of occupations, including industrialists and factory owners, professors, doctors, and other members of the liberal professions, and *rentiers*.[47] In this survey Boulogne had the largest middle-class population, reflecting its proximity to the sixteenth *arrondissement* of Paris, and the Croulebarbe quarter could also claim many residents from this group. Both communities contained recognizably middle-class districts, such as the boulevard du Port-Royal in the Croulebarbe quarter, but many middle-class families also lived in the same buildings as working people. Also noteworthy is the complete absence of any middle-class population in Drancy. This could in part reflect the small size of

---

[44] For a fascinating insight into the world of Parisian concierges, see Bonnie Smith, *Confessions of a Concierge: Madame Lucie's History of Twentieth Century France* (New Haven: Yale University Press, 1985); also Sharon Marcus, *Apartment Stories: City and Home in Nineteenth Century Paris and London* (Berkeley: University of California Press, 1999).

[45] On Parisian artisans in the modern era see Berlanstein, *Working People*, 15–21; Nord, *Paris Shopkeepers*; Steven Zdatny, *The Politics of Survival: Artisans in Twentieth Century France* (New York: Oxford University Press, 1990).

[46] On these *métiers*, see especially Jacques Borge and Nicolas Viasnoff, *Archives de Paris* (Paris: Balland, 1981).

[47] Maza, *Myth*; Adeline Daumard, *La bourgeoisie parisienne de 1815 à 1848* (Paris: Albin Michel, 1996); Michael Miller, *The Bon Marché: Bourgeois Culture and the Department Store, 1896–1920* (Princeton University Press, 1981); Ezra Suleiman, *Elites in French Society* (Princeton University Press, 1973).

the sample taken, but also confirms the general image of the new residential working-class suburbs of the interwar years.[48]

One important consideration disclosed by Table 2.2 is the absence of any homogeneous working-class neighborhood or suburban community in the Paris area during the early twentieth century. While smaller concentrations of workers existed, they usually did not include more than a few streets or even a few buildings. Working people in most cases thus lived near to others from different social backgrounds. This was especially true of the Parisian neighborhoods. Because of the much greater density of the population in Folie-Méricourt and Croulebarbe, different people came into contact more frequently. Few streets, in fact few buildings, did not house a mixture of people from various social groupings.[49] The suburbs, on the other hand, combined lower population densities with larger numbers of workers to produce a greater level of class segregation. Drancy in particular, with a population that was nearly three-quarters working class in 1921, represented a trend toward more spatial separation of social classes in the Paris area. Working people in early twentieth-century Paris had contacts with others, but the patterns that would create huge working-class ghettos in the suburbs after 1945 were already apparent.[50]

The *listes nominatives* also make possible an analysis of different professions and levels of skill within the working-class population of Paris. In this case also workers varied significantly by neighborhood. One of the most striking things about Table 2.3 is the large number of people listed in the "other" category, especially in the Folie-Méricourt quarter. This group includes workers in the food industry, such as waiters, cooks, and butchers, and in transportation, such as taxi and truck drivers.[51] It was twice as large in Folie-Méricourt

---

[48] Peru, "Du village à la cité ouvrière," 14.

[49] David Pinkney's suggestion as to the gradual replacement of vertical by horizontal residential segregation in nineteenth-century Paris makes sense, but this was a gradual process that was by no means complete by the interwar years. Moreover, thanks to the resilience of the capital's urban fabric, it does not seem to have become as extreme as it did in the suburbs. Pinkney, *Napoleon III*; Gaillard, *Paris, la ville*; David Harvey, *Paris, Capital of Modernity* (New York: Routledge, 2003).

[50] On the Paris suburbs after 1945, see Bastié, *La croissance de la banlieue*; Pierre George, *Études sur la banlieue de Paris: essais methodologiques* (Paris: A. Colin, 1950); Colette Petonnet, *On est tous dans le brouillard: ethnologie des banlieues* (Paris: Galilée, 1980). In recent years the Paris suburbs have changed from a symbol of French Communism to one of the problems posed by immigration and race in French society. See Stovall, "From red belt to black belt: race, class, and urban marginality in Paris," in Sue Peabody and Tyler Stovall, eds., *The Color of Liberty: Histories of Race in France* (Durham NC: Duke University Press, 2003); Paul Silverstein, *Algeria in France: Transpolitics, Race, and Nation* (Bloomington: Indiana University Press, 2004); Jean-Paul Brunet, ed., *Immigration, vie politique et populisme en banlieue parisienne* (Paris: L'Harmattan, 1995).

[51] To a certain extent these groups overlapped with both employees (for example, railway workers) and shopkeepers (for example, butchers).

because of the large number of skilled craftspeople in that neighborhood; this included a sizeable group of furniture workers, thanks to the nearby Faubourg Saint-Antoine. In general, both Paris and its suburbs still played host to many different working-class occupations; one could still find *vitriers* walking the streets with panes of glass strapped to their backs crying out their professions, or cobblers making and repairing shoes in tiny little workshops in rear courtyards.

The census figures give little precise information about the relative levels of skill among Parisian workers in the 1920s. It is often virtually impossible to distinguish between skilled, semi-skilled, and unskilled laborers in a given industry. To the extent possible, I have tried to set up Table 2.3 to reflect skill levels; following the lead of the census takers, I have listed the unskilled (*manoeuvres* or *journalières*)[52] as a separate group, rather than including them in their own industries. People listed in both the metals and construction categories were almost all skilled workers, for example. The metals industry remained dominated by skilled labor in the early twentieth century; although by the late 1920s rationalization had created a large population of unskilled and semi-skilled workers in large factories like Renault and Citroen, in the small workshops that constituted the heart and soul of Parisian metallurgy turners, molders, mechanics, and other highly trained specialists predominated.[53] Similarly, in the construction industry skilled carpenters and stonemasons composed much of the workforce. In contrast, many of the clothing workers were laundresses with relatively small levels of skill. Those included in the category of unskilled workers labored in many different industries: large numbers worked as *terrassiers*, or ditchdiggers, while others were employed in steel factories or in the chemical plants that polluted many close-in Parisian suburbs.

In general, the data presented above confirm the widespread impression that Parisian workers were predominantly skilled in the early twentieth century, although it also reveals the existence of a large semi-skilled and unskilled population.[54] It is noteworthy that no overwhelming concentrations of single working-class occupations existed in the four areas studied. Even in Boulogne, famed as the home of Renault, metalworkers constituted less than one-third of

---

[52] Whereas male unskilled workers were usually called *manoeuvres*, women were almost always labeled *journalières*.

[53] On the Paris metals industry, see Touraine, *L'évolution du travail ouvrier*; Fridenson, *Histoire des usines*; Sylvie Schweitzer, *Des engrenages à la chaine: les usines Citroen 1915–1935* (Lyon: Presses Universitaires de Lyon, 1982); Laura Lee Downs, *Manufacturing Inequality: Gender Division in the French and British Metalworking Industries, 1914–1939* (Ithaca: Cornell University Press, 1995).

[54] This group has unfortunately been neglected not only by contemporaries but by historians as well. See for example Berlanstein, *Big Business*, 284–291.

all employed workers in the city.[55] By the 1920s, although some occupations retained a certain geographical concentration, housing pressures and transportation opportunities had produced a unified working-class job market in the Paris area.[56] The central characteristic of the working people of Paris remained occupational diversity. The concept "working class" encompassed a myriad of different work categories and experiences. The next section explores this internal class diversity from the standpoint of two very different individuals.

AUTOBIOGRAPHY, SELF-REPRESENTATION, AND IDENTITY

How did Parisian working people view their own lives, and to what extent did they consider themselves "workers"? What did this concept mean for them? While self-portrayals do not perforce constitute an objective or definitive guide to class as a social category or lived experience, no consideration of working-class history and identity can be complete without looking at how working people saw themselves.[57] Too often labor historians, both those using traditional perspectives and those operating within a postmodern paradigm, have tended to focus on bourgeois perceptions of the working class as the entire history of the representation of that group.[58] This not only ignores what workers had to say about their own lives, but also neglects their views of the bourgeoisie and of their world as a whole. Therefore, while the analysis of working-class self-perception does not in and of itself reveal the secrets of working-class identity, it is a fitting way to end this chapter.

I propose to approach this subject by analyzing two working-class memoirs from the time: René Michaud's *J'avais vingt ans: un jeune ouvrier au début du siècle*, and Louise Deletang's *Journal d'une ouvrière Parisienne pendant la guerre*. Self-perception and written self-representation are by no means the same

---

[55] *LN*, Boulogne, 1921. In 1921 Renault employed 10,400 workers; in 1926, 26,500. Fridenson, *Histoire des usines*, 328.

[56] Alain Faure, "A l'aube des transports de masse: les 'trains ouvriers' de la banlieue de Paris," *Revue d'histoire moderne et contemporaine*, 40/2 (April–June, 1993); also Faure, "'Nous travaillons 10 heures par jour, plus le chemin': les déplacements de travail chez les ouvriers parisiens, 1880–1914," in Magri and Topalov, *Villes ouvrières*.

[57] Here I would take issue somewhat with Joan Scott's celebrated article on this subject. Joan Scott, "The evidence of experience," *Critical Inquiry*, 17/4 (Summer, 1991); see also Martin Jay, *Songs of Experience: Modern American and European Variations on a Universal Theme* (Berkeley: University of California Press, 2005).

[58] For a classic example of this see Louis Chevalier, *Laboring Classes and Dangerous Classes in Paris during the First Half of the Nineteenth Century*, translated by Frank Jellinek (Princeton University Press, 1973); for an alternative approach see Donald Reid, *Paris Sewers and Sewermen: Realities and Representations* (Cambridge MA: Harvard University Press, 1991).

thing, as a substantial literature on the study of autobiography has established.[59] The autobiographer makes choices, both consciously and unconsciously, as to what aspects of his or her life to present to the public. In the case of published works, as the above two memoirs were, other considerations like the opinions of various editors also enter into play. In addition, even for those authors determined to tell "the truth, the whole truth, and nothing but the truth," memory is a subjective and mercurial phenomenon. In short, memoirs must be approached and studied not as organic historical evidence but as consciously constructed texts.

Over the last few decades several historians have written pioneering studies of working-class autobiographies.[60] Jacques Rancière's important and controversial book, *La nuit des prolétaires*, is perhaps the most significant example of new approaches to this subject. Traditionally, historians have used workers' memoirs to illustrate or buttress findings principally derived from more "objective" sources, believing that such autobiographical literature was itself too subjective and unreliable to be considered on its own. Rancière and others, however, reject this qualification, arguing that one should study workers' memoirs as texts whose inner workings and contradictions illuminate aspects of working-class perceptions and *mentalités*. What counts is not the representative nature of such works, or their correspondence with facts obtained from other sources, but rather the internal dynamic of each life story.[61]

In analyzing the memoirs of René Michaud and Louise Deletang I have borrowed from both approaches; this becomes evident in my reasons for choosing these two texts.[62] On the one hand, for my purposes both have the virtue of devoting considerable space to life in Paris during the war and 1919 in particular. Such detailed attention to the daily progression of events is often rare in autobiographical literature, and these two cases permit the historian to look at 1919 from an unusual angle. Yet Michaud's and Deletang's books

---

[59] On autobiography see Philippe Lejeune, *L'autobiographie en France* (Paris: A. Colin, 1998); Sidonie Smith and Julia Watson, *Reading Autobiography: A Guide for Interpreting Life Narratives* (Minneapolis: University of Minnesota Press, 2001); Jeremy D. Popkin, *History, Historians, and Autobiography* (University of Chicago Press, 2005).

[60] Mark Traugott, ed., *The French Worker: Autobiographies from the Early Industrial Era* (Berkeley: University of California Press, 1993); John Burnett, ed., *The Annals of Labour: Autobiographies of British Working-Class People, 1820–1920* (Bloomington: Indiana University Press, 1974); Victoria E. Bonnell, ed., *The Russian Worker: Life and Labor under the Tsarist Regime* (Berkeley: University of California Press, 1983).

[61] Jacques Rancière, *La nuit des prolétaires* (Paris: Fayard, 1981); Donald Reid, "Reflections on labor history and language," in Lenard Berlanstein, ed., *Rethinking Labor History: Essays on Discourse and Class Analysis* (Urbana: University of Illinois Press, 1993).

[62] For another example of a working-class autobiography that deals with wartime Paris, see Jeanne Bouvier, *Mes mémoires ou 59 années d'activité industrielle, sociale et intellectuelle d'une ouvrière 1876–1935* (Paris: La Découverte/Maspero, 1983).

are by no means simply one-person newsreels, but give uniquely personal interpretations of both their own lives and the larger issues of their day. On the other hand, Michaud and Deletang present narratives of their lives that are almost perfectly opposed to each other, both in style and in outlook. Rather than seeing them as ideal types, one may view Louise Deletang and René Michaud as extreme parameters of the working-class experience in Paris after World War I. The study of this opposition, and the internal contradictions upon which it is in part based, can reveal interesting insights about the nature of working-class identity in general. What ties bound Parisian workers together, made them into a social identity both concrete and yet broad enough to claim both René Michaud and Louise Deletang?

The basic outlines of the lives of René Michaud and Louise Deletang, as revealed in their life histories, are straightforward. Michaud was born with the twentieth century and grew up in a desperately poor neighborhood of Paris' thirteenth *arrondissement*. Michaud was raised by his mother, his father having committed suicide when he was five years old, and in his memoir he eloquently describes the poverty of his surroundings.

The Gare and Maison-Blanche were certainly not good neighborhoods. They sheltered a working class population formed in large part by small peasants and workers from the countryside who gained a poor living from the land . . . and who had come to the city, fascinated by the hope of more regular work, better pay, and an easier life.

These people, mostly without skills, little by little abandoned their taste for farm and fields to become a part of the uniform grayness of the great city, where they formed the most disadvantaged stratum, working as unskilled laborers, or as ditch-diggers building the Metro.[63]

He discusses how he started working as an apprentice in the shoemaker's trade at the age of thirteen, gradually relating the history of both his training and his growing appreciation of conflicts with the *patron* on the job. In 1919, a year which conveniently for the purposes of this study constitutes a turning point in the narrative, René Michaud proclaims his allegiance to anarchism as a political cause. The rest of the story, which ends in the mid 1920s, portrays the life of a young anarchist worker in Paris, providing lively and fascinating insights into both working-class politics and culture.[64]

---

[63] René Michaud, *J'avais vingt ans: un jeune ouvrier au début du siècle* (Paris: Éditions syndicalistes, 1967), 12–13.

[64] Among other things, Michaud's life reflects the attraction of many Parisian artisans to anarchism. See David Berry, *A History of the French Anarchist Movement, 1917 to 1945* (Westport CT: Greenwood Press, 2002).

We know much less about the life of Louise Deletang from her book. Unlike Michaud's memoir, Deletang's only covers the period of the war; she does not provide an introduction describing her early life, for example. We learn that Louise Deletang is a milliner working in the city's large dressmaking industry. She lived in the neighborhood around the rue Mouffetard, near the border of the fifth and thirteenth *arrondissements*. An ardent French patriot, Louise Deletang provides a precious account of how working people in Paris experienced the war years, discussing life on the job, material living conditions, and opinions on the course of the war and life in general.

It is done . . . Germany has declared war on us . . . A great wave of patriotism has lifted up the crowd. Both veterans and young people enlist. Greeks, Jews, Italians, Tunisians, Russians, who earn their daily bread in Paris, in France, enroll to defend her; an entire Jewish family has enlisted. The German junkmen of the rue Mouffetard have left. But at the train stations there are no cries, no wild enthusiasm . . . people reflect . . . but do not talk about it. One feels that all these men leave resolved on victory and they know they can die![65]

Sociologically, both Michaud and Deletang are working class, but they also represent important differences within that identity. In particular Deletang seems to be a settled woman, whereas Michaud is a young man just emerging from adolescence.[66] These contrasts of gender and age shape the two testimonies in important ways. For example, Deletang is far more concerned with food and questions of subsistence than Michaud, and in general themes of anxiety and worry about the future play a much greater role in her view of the world than in his.[67] At the same time, some similarities bind them. Both are single and self-supporting, and both have lots to say about life on the job. In addition, both René Michaud and Louise Deletang are deeply involved in the life of their particular Parisian neighborhoods, so that work and community constantly interact.

In reading these two memoirs, one is first struck by the contrasting styles used by each writer to tell his or her story. Michaud's *J'avais vingt ans* is a classic worker's autobiography. It closely fits the format of what has been called the heroic or political story of a worker's life, taking as its central theme the gradual dawning of class consciousness and its transformation into political activism, labor militancy, or some other type of participation in the class

---

[65] Louise Deletang, *Journal d'une ouvrière parisienne pendant la guerre* (Paris: Éditions Eugène Figuière, 1935), 12–13. This passage is dated August 4, 1914, 9 a.m.

[66] Deletang does not give her age in her diary, but she seems to occupy positions of responsibility, such as helping run charitable workhouses, that would suggest she was older than Michaud. At the same time, the fact that her mother was still working as a seamstress implies that she was not too advanced in years.

[67] Alex Hughes, *Heterographies: Sexual Difference in French Autobiography* (Oxford: Berg, 1999).

struggle.[68] As such, it is well known to historians, having been used by several to illustrate working-class life in Paris during the early twentieth century.[69] The book was published in 1967, and thus represents the author as a mature man looking back upon the days of his youth.[70] Drawing on the model of the *Bildungsroman*, Michaud thus presents his life as one example of the growth of a self-conscious and confident French proletariat.[71]

Deletang's *Journal d'une ouvrière parisienne pendant la guerre*, in contrast, is a detailed diary of her life in Paris during the war years. It consists of frequent entries, usually two or three per week, reflecting on different aspects of her wartime experiences. A much less streamlined product than Michaud's book, it does not present Deletang's life in a teleological mold, instead relating the history of various personal and political events in more haphazard fashion. Nonetheless, the story does emphasize a central theme, the war and the valiant struggle of the French people for justice and victory. The diary begins with an entry on August 1, 1914, and concludes on June 29, 1919, the day after the signing of the Treaty of Versailles. Whereas Michaud presents a relatively uncomplicated progression toward class consciousness that ends inconclusively, Deletang's narrative wanders randomly but ends on a happy and definitive note.

A key difference in the narrative styles of these two memoirs is the presentation of self, the role played by the author him/herself in the story. Whereas *J'avais vingt ans* is clearly the tale of René Michaud's life, *Journal d'une ouvrière parisienne pendant la guerre* portrays the history of the war as observed by an individual worker, Louise Deletang. Michaud is the center of his story, while Deletang plays a more retiring role. The difference is not one of personal modesty; even the most cursory reading of Deletang's diary reveals a woman of formidable character and opinions. Rather, it concerns the relation of each subject to his/her metaphorical reference point, the Working Class for Michaud, and the French Nation for Deletang. For Michaud a revolutionary working class is in its infancy, so that his growth from youth to adult parallels that of working-class consciousness. For Deletang, the point is not to create a national consciousness, but to defend the *patrie* from outside attack.

---

[68] Traugott, *The French Worker*, 28–37; Jacques Rancière, "The myth of the artisan: critical reflections on a category of social history," *International Labor and Working Class History*, 24 (Fall, 1983).

[69] For example, Berlanstein, *Working People*; Tyler Stovall, *The Rise of the Paris Red Belt* (Berkeley: University of California Press, 1990).

[70] Of course, memories of youth involve their own distortions, both willful and involuntary, since a large part of growing up lies precisely in forgetting how to view the world through the eyes of a child.

[71] The most extreme examples of this, of course, are the memoirs written by leading working-class politicians. See for example Jacques Duclos, *Mémoires* (Paris: Fayard, 1968); Maurice Thorez, *Fils du peuple* (Paris: Éditions Sociales, 1970).

This requires submerging one's own particularist desires and interests for the salvation of the nation as a whole. Since Deletang is especially concerned with working-class particularism and anti-patriotism, her narrative self-abnegation demonstrates in a formalistic sense the way workers should behave during the war, as undifferentiated members of the national community. In both cases the presentation of self thus structures and mirrors the main themes of each memoir.

The most striking difference between these two Parisian workers is, of course, their political perspectives. The heart and soul of Louise Deletang's outlook on life was a belief in the necessity of French victory: everything must be subordinated to achieving it. Consequently she was extremely antagonistic to French socialism and the unions, seeing them as factors of division in a nation whose only recourse was unity. Even the cooperation of organized labor with the war effort as part of the *Union Sacrée* did not mollify her. On August 22, 1914, Louise Deletang wrote in her diary:

They are thus guilty, all those who for years, with as much ardor as if they had been paid by the King of Prussia, have worked to disorganize the nation [Pays], to make the worker hate his labor, to destroy his pride in his profession, to completely discourage him by sowing in his soul feelings of envy and revolt. They are criminals, all those who have slandered and attacked the army, raising the people up against it, as if the army was not the people itself.[72]

The seemingly interminable nature of the war, and the growing hardships it imposed, only hardened Deletang's determination to see France victorious, as well as her disdain for her fellow workers who did not share her resolve. In particular, she observed the growing number of strikes after the beginning of 1917 with horror. Writing on May 20, 1917 (which was, she did not fail to note, the festival of Joan of Arc), Madame Deletang attacked working-class demands: "To profit from a state of war to demand the English work week is blackmail to a certain extent. Do those who are getting themselves killed to save these *midinettes* or *munitionnettes* enjoy the English work week …!"[73]

Such opinions could not have been farther removed from the beliefs of René Michaud. A young adolescent when the war broke out, Michaud first learned of it at work, right after one of his innumerable disputes with his boss. The first few years of the war did little to politicize the young shoemaker, who not only shared the patriotism of Louise Deletang but frequently sent portions of his meager salary to his two uncles fighting on the front lines.[74] The strikes and mutinies of the spring of 1917 shook his patriotic convictions,

---

[72] Deletang, *Journal*, 26–27.   [73] *Ibid.*, 337–338.   [74] Michaud, *J'avais vingt ans*, 78.

however, setting him on the road to his eventual anarchist conversion. René Michaud soon became a daily reader of *L'Humanité*, which he criticized for its political moderation, and eagerly followed the news of revolution in Russia. He also joined his first union, gradually taking a more active leadership role in its affairs. During the spring of 1917 Michaud took part in his first strike, moving from quarrels with his bosses to a more organized form of resistance. As he noted in his autobiography, "With the strike, I undertook a new apprenticeship, one of struggle, of solidarity, of tenacity at the test."[75] World War I coincided with the adolescence of René Michaud and constituted his coming of age. By the end of 1919 the boy had become a young man, not only professionally skilled but also a confirmed working-class militant.

The dramatic working-class struggles of 1919 further distinguished the outlooks of Louise Deletang and René Michaud. For Deletang, 1919 represented above all the conclusion of peace and victory for France; like H. Pearl Adam's book, her diary ends in the middle of the year, the last entry being dated June 29, the day after the signing of the peace treaty. Although she discusses strikes and demonstrations in some detail, she portrays them primarily as a disagreeable, shameful sideshow to the main drama of triumphant nationalism. For Michaud, in contrast, 1919 was the year he became a full-fledged revolutionary. The beginning of the year found him working in a cobbler's shop in Belleville which happened to be located next door to a printing cooperative, "La Fraternelle," run by the veteran anarchist Sebastien Faure. Attracted to their ideas, Michaud took part in both the Jaurès and May Day demonstrations. In July, while France was still rejoicing over its military triumph, René Michaud formally joined the *Jeunesses anarchistes*.

A comparison of Deletang's and Michaud's reactions to specific events during 1919 provides a more precise contrast of their attitudes. Direct comparisons are often not possible, because the two writers had different views as to what was important. For example, Louise Deletang only briefly mentions the acquittal of Raoul Vilain in her diary, and completely ignores Emile Cottin's attempt to assassinate Georges Clemenceau. In contrast, these events moved René Michaud to change his life:

The assassination attempt of Cottin . . . made a strong impression on me. His refusal to accept the war, the disinterested character of his gesture, assumed in my adolescent eyes a greater, more universal significance than all the recriminations and jeremiads of the working-class press. In the place of words one man, an ordinary, lone man like us, had substituted action. He identified with "his cause," and, devoid of all ambition,

<hr>

[75] *Ibid.,* 75–76.

hurled a challenge at the enslaved conscience of a humanity that had accepted this
war and glorified the man who had been one of those most responsible for it.

In fact, before having learned its principles, or even having opened the smallest
pamphlet, I had become an anarchist.[76]

Inspired by Cottin's example, Michaud joined the demonstration protest-
ing the acquittal of Vilain, where the clashes between the anarchists and
police further impressed him. His autobiography describes a young man
marching along, drunk with the emotion of the event: "I felt overwhelmed,
triumphant: our songs surrounded us with a halo of glory: *Arise, ye wretched
of the earth!*"[77]

In contrast, the problem of food shortages, caused by both lack of availability and high prices, occupies much of Louise Deletang's concern during
the first half of 1919. From 1916 on Deletang's diary contained numerous
complaints about shortages, vividly portraying the impact of wartime inflation on the working people of Paris. By the beginning of 1919 this has become
a source of constant worry. In her entry of January 8, 1919, Madame Deletang
describes the futile results of a day's attempted shopping:

No matter where one goes, one returns empty handed from one's errands.
  "Do you have any butter?"
  "It hasn't come in yet."
  "Any eggs?"
  "They are in short supply."
  "Any coffee?"
  "The delivery truck passed by empty; there won't be any all week."
  "Chocolate?"
  "None at all."
  "Macaroni?"
  "No more."
  "Cooking gas?"
  "We're waiting for some."[78]

In comparison, René Michaud makes little mention of food problems in
this period, aside from general allusions to the problem of inflation. Their
contrasting attitudes to problems of consumption underscore differences of
both gender and age between the two: food shopping remained overwhelmingly a woman's affair, and young men like Michaud generally devoted little

[76] *Ibid.*, 103.
[77] Note that whereas Michaud mistakes the date of Cottin's assassination attempt, he gets the date of the
Vilain demonstration exactly right.
[78] Deletang, *Journal*, 458.

attention to the problem of feeding their families.[79] Both Deletang and Michaud worried about questions central to working-class politics, but their engagement in these questions took radically different forms.

Both Michaud and Deletang, however, had lots to say about the events of May 1, 1919, and their perspectives could not have been further apart. For Louise Deletang, May Day represented another example of the impertinence and arrogance of organized labor. In contrast, René Michaud took part in the demonstrations and the riots, so that for him May Day 1919 constituted his first experience of violent class struggle and revolutionary militancy.[80] The comparison of René Michaud's and Louise Deletang's accounts of May 1, 1919 suggests that the events of the day exemplified a heightened level of intra-class as well as inter-class conflict. On May Day Deletang and Michaud found themselves literally on opposite sides of the barricades. At this level, therefore, the contrast posed by these two working-class memoirs calls into question the salience of a comprehensive sense of working-class identity for life in Paris immediately after World War I. How could a group with any concrete, functional sense of unity claim both Louise Deletang and René Michaud? Yet there are other parts of both these memoirs which tend to undermine the symbolic opposition between them, sections which indicate observations that are not so much identical as mutually recognizable. At points both Michaud and Deletang contradict or sidestep their own forthright ideological positions, and it is in these contradictions as much as in their more systematically presented views that one can discern a sense of Parisian working-class identity.

In spite of his newly found anarchism, for example, René Michaud retained an awareness, and even a certain level of empathy, for working-class patriotism and joy in victory. In his autobiography he describes his reaction and those of his workmates at a factory in the fourteenth *arrondissement* upon hearing the great news of the Armistice. While in the following description Michaud places his emphasis on peace rather than victory, on the end of suffering rather than national triumph, the heart of his portrayal remains spontaneous working-class action:

When on the morning of November 11 1918 the ringing of the bells announced the Armistice, the tools fell from our hands. Leaving our jobs and the factory behind, we threw ourselves into the street, happy and fraternal; we laughed, we lived again!

If the feelings of relief were general, not all hearts shared the same level of happiness. Numerous were those who suffered from sorrows, trials, and privations,

---

[79] Like many single young men, Michaud probably did little shopping for food, preferring to eat in cheap restaurants and cafés.

[80] See Chapter 4 for a more detailed treatment of Deletang's and Michaud's experiences on May 1, 1919.

and on this morning of peace found themselves broken and alone. How many had
lost their happiness, their hopes, their illusions? . . .
    I still see that old woman whose haggard sadness shattered my exaltation . . .
When, moved by her mute grief I stopped and took her hands, she murmured:
    "Ah! if only they were here . . ."
    She had lost two sons in the war.[81]

This passage presents an interesting interaction and tension between
Michaud's working-class militancy and the celebrations of the Armistice.
Michaud does not mention the word "victory" once in this description, and
clearly privileges themes of the cost of the war. Yet he never says that this cost
was in vain, and his depiction of the elderly woman's sorrow amid general
rejoicing could easily have been accepted by any French *jusqu'au-boutiste*. The
first section of the quotation cited above is also paradoxical. One can interpret
it either as an anarchist vision of liberation from the workplace, or as another
instance of the *Union Sacrée*, in which workers leave their specific concerns
and identity behind to join the national community celebrating in the streets.
Louise Deletang's description of the same event is much more straightforward: her diary entry of November 11 starts off with the sentence "Finally! the
hour of victory has sounded!"[82] Yet in general her account of Armistice
Day contains the same mixture of joy and sorrow as Michaud's, wild celebrations in the streets counterposed against mourning for those who did not
live to see the great day. The similarity between the descriptions of Michaud
and Deletang does not so much reflect an underlying objective reality as give
evidence of a view of war and peace common to many working-class Parisians.
In this case Michaud's leftist politics are firmly integrated into popular culture
in spite of the contradiction between his anarchist pacifism and the triumphant patriotism that reigned on November 11, 1918.
    Just as René Michaud's leftism did not necessarily entail a rejection of
working-class patriotism, Louise Deletang's patriotism and disdain for the
organized Left did not mean she had no sense of attachment to the working
class as a whole. She proclaims this forthrightly in her book's title, whereas
that of Michaud's autobiography alludes more vaguely to lost youth.
Madame Deletang's attitude to the working class and her place within it is
in many ways contradictory. To be sure, on many an occasion her contempt
for the socialists and union leaders extended to the behavior of ordinary
working people. When Paris came under enemy shelling in the summer of
1918 Louise Deletang attacked those of her neighbors who complained that
the bourgeois wanted to keep them out of the shelters, saying "Strange

[81] Michaud, *J'avais vingt ans*, 89–90.   [82] Deletang, *Journal*, 444.

bourgeois ... they are surely eating less well than the *regular guys* [pauvres bougres]."[83] She also argued at times that the lower middle classes were the ones who suffered most, both from the war and from working-class strikes: "What anguishing hours! The true laboring class, the artisans, the modest rentiers, the small shopkeepers suffer in silence and continue working, but no one notices them."[84]

Yet at other points in her diary Louise Deletang demonstrates both sympathy for other working people and a sense of class divisions and oppression. At one point, while discussing efforts to start workshops for women thrown out of work, she remarks, "Water always flows to the river ... and money always flows to the rich."[85] Unconsciously recalling the Jacobin patriotism of the French Revolution, she notes in October 1914 rumors that the national government is wallowing in luxury during its exile in Bordeaux.[86] More significantly, Madame Deletang participated actively in collective working-class undertakings. She and her sister belonged to a workers' mutual benefit association which helped members schedule rent payments, took part in organizing soup kitchens, and advanced small sums of money to those in need. Deletang describes movingly and in detail the sufferings of those thrown out of work as the Parisian economy adapted to the needs of war in 1914. In particular, she worked to help women in the clothing industry both to find jobs and to get decent treatment at the hands of their employers. This was not done out of disinterest, for she experienced personally the shortage of work and the lowering of piece rates early in the war. In discussing the piece rates imposed by a department store on seamstresses, Louise Deletang paints a portrait of working-class exploitation as clear as anything drawn by René Michaud:

"Why are you lowering your rates again? You know that the price of everything is going up, and that rents are expensive!"

"What do you want," they respond, "we've made major improvements, not because we are doing more business, but because our customers are looking for luxury; they demand carpets, plate glass, elevators, escalators, tea salons; we've got to catch up!"

Odious iniquity! ... It's not the customer who pays for this luxury! it's the miserable seamstress!

Moreover, is it really the customer who has insisted on such luxury? ... Isn't it rather the pride of the *big owners* [gros proprietaires] of the *great stores*? ...

---

[83] *Ibid.*, 402, entry of June 7, 1918.   [84] *Ibid.*, 340, entry of June 2, 1917.
[85] *Ibid.*, 76, entry of November 11, 1914.   [86] *Ibid.*, 61, entry of October 23, 1914.

Tick, tock, stitch, sew, apprentice . . . Madame will have her automobile . . .
Tick, tock, stitch, sew, apprentice . . . Monsieur will have his chateau.[87]

Writing in her diary on July 8, 1918, Louise Deletang began with the bitter
words "The proletariat disgusts me . . . and I am one of them!" This brief
sentence reveals much not only about Deletang's own relationship to working
people but more generally about the nature of working-class identity in Paris
at the end of World War I. Madame Deletang's diary clearly lives up to its
title, providing a wealth of information on popular Parisian working and
living conditions, as well as attitudes and concerns. It also reveals a central
contradiction in the views of its author: while identifying in many ways as a
worker, Madame Deletang was firmly hostile to the working-class Left, and
frequently contemptuous of her working-class neighbors as well.[88] While they
are less obvious, such contradictions also exist in the text of René Michaud.
In July 1919 Michaud took part as a man of honor in his uncle's wedding in
spite of his anarchist scorn of social conventions and religious ceremonies,
resolving the conflict between political principles and working-class family
culture in favor of the latter.[89] A clear concept of what it meant to be a worker
did not come easily for either writer.

The contrast between the memoirs of Louise Deletang and René Michaud
highlights the politicized nature of working-class identity in Paris at the end of
World War I. The symbolic opposition between bourgeois and proletarian
that informed so many aspects of Parisian life during 1919 in particular had its
counterpart here in the clash of two very different workers' political views. At
one level, this contrast suggests that the opposition between bourgeois and
proletarian was one of political discourses as well as sociology. Madame
Deletang could hardly have been more opposed to the views embraced by
René Michaud had she been a wealthy aristocrat. Yet at the same time the
comparison of the two memoirs reveals a number of experiences and perspectives that, while not identical, would be mutually comprehensible. It suggests
that Parisian workers not only faced many common problems, but also shared
ways of addressing and of conceptualizing their lives in general. Ultimately, if
both René Michaud and Louise Deletang could identify as workers, then in
spite of the vast size and diversity of the Parisian working class one can still

---

[87] *Ibid.*, 122–123, entry of January 16, 1915.

[88] For another example of a conservative working-class woman, see Carolyn Kay Steedman, *Landscape
for a Good Woman: A Story of Two Lives* (New Brunswick NJ: Rutgers University Press, 1986).

[89] Michaud, *J'avais vingt ans*, 112–114.

claim that a broad sense of identity played a significant role in the lives of its members.[90]

What strikes one most about this review of working-class life in the French capital is simply the tremendous diversity of experiences it embodied. Working people in Paris labored in large, anonymous factories and tiny, intimate workshops. They were employed in a variety of occupations ranging from domestic servants to metalworkers. They lived in crowded inner-city neighborhoods and barren suburban housing tracts. They were young and old, newcomers to the area and lifetime residents, men and women. They came from every corner of France, and from throughout Europe and beyond. They were people with life experiences and political views as different, even opposed, as René Michaud and Louise Deletang. All the contrasts of a major metropolitan area with several million inhabitants were reflected in the lives of those who washed the clothes, molded the steel, ran the trains, and provided the gas and electricity to light the lamps of the City of Light.

At first glance, such diversity would seem to fly in the face of a climate emphasizing hard-and-fast binary oppositions. It tends to support those who deconstruct social identities by focusing on their internal fissures, conflicts, and contradictions. Yet at the same time the many different characteristics of working-class life in Paris also revealed important points in common. More to the point, they suggest affinities with postmodern concepts of identity, those for which heterogeneity is integral to the nature of a community. A number of scholars, including Giorgio Agamben, Jean-Luc Nancy, and William Corlett, have wrestled with how to conceive of communities that champion difference while at the same time creating strong social bonds, in short communities that are inclusive without being exclusive. From such perspectives, communities that foreground rather than suppress difference enable a politics that is not just anti-essentialist but profoundly liberatory.[91] In other words, I suggest that the intense politicization of 1919 in particular both underscored and arose out of differences between Parisian workers, reaffirming the unstable nature of group identity in general.[92]

[90] One must also consider the other component of identity, how one is perceived by others. It is hard to imagine anyone regarding Louise Deletang as bourgeois, no matter how conservative her political opinions.

[91] Nancy, *La communauté désoeuvrée*; Miami Theory Collective, *Community at Loose Ends*; Giorgio Agamben, *The Coming Community*, translated by Michael Hardt (Minneapolis: University of Minnesota Press, 1993); William Corlett, *Community without Unity: A Politics of Derridian Extravagance* (Durham NC: Duke University Press, 1993).

[92] One approach to conceptualizing the idea of inclusive communities has come from scholars of diaspora, who have argued for an idea of communities based on heterogeneity rather than homogeneity, which draw their strength from diversity rather than sameness. Theoreticians of the African

This diversity is thus key to any attempts to comprehend the nature of working-class identity in early twentieth-century Paris. It raises the question, should one speak of identity, or identities? In seeking to answer this question, it is important to explore in greater depth the origins of this diversity. One naturally turns to what might be called the "melting pot" metaphor of modern urban life: romantic images of the metropolis as the crossroads of the world, or the play of the forces of international capital in breaking down all barriers to commerce, readily come to mind.[93] Yet the Parisian working class of the early twentieth century was not simply the product of gradual, organic evolution. The needs of the wartime economy had led to major shifts in its composition, producing such effects as the growth of the metallurgical sector, the influx of women into heavy industry, and the shortage of domestic servants. As was true of much of France's war effort, these changes were not planned but arose out of the exigencies of national war effort. The transition from war to peace in late 1918 and 1919, on the other hand, witnessed a much more concerted, organized effort to adapt Parisian working people to new realities. During the immediate postwar period, therefore, a conscious process of social construction reshaped the character of proletarian life in Paris, so much so that it is possible to speak of a remaking of the Parisian working class.

The next chapter will consider the ways working-class life was being reshaped by exclusions based on gender and race. Statistics, for all their utility, tend to give a static overview of a situation that was in fact constantly changing. A study of the forces promoting such changes can give us another picture of the working class of Paris after World War I. Such observations are always true of social classes and societies in general, but in 1919 the "artificial," socially constructed nature of working-class experience stood out in particularly sharp relief. The immediate postwar period thus provides a valuable opportunity to explore the process of the construction of social identity in modern France.[94]

---

diaspora in particular have explored this notion of diasporic communities. For a classic statement of this see Paul Gilroy, *The Black Atlantic: Modernity and Double Consciousness* (Cambridge MA: Harvard University Press, 1993).

[93] William Sharpe and Leonard Wallock, eds., *Visions of the Modern City* (New York: Proceedings of the Heyman Center for the Humanities, Columbia University, 1986); Mike Davis, *City of Quartz: Excavating the Future in Los Angeles* (London and New York: Verso, 2006).

[94] On the history of identity in France, see Fernand Braudel, *The Identity of France*, 2 vols., translated by Sian Reynolds (New York: HarperCollins, 1988–1990); Pierre Nora, *Realms of Memory: Rethinking the French Past*, 3 vols., translated by Arthur Goldhammer (New York: Columbia University Press, 1996); Emmanuel Todd, *The Making of Modern France: Ideology, Politics, and Culture* (Oxford: Basil Blackwell, 1991); Herman Lebovics, *True France: The Wars Over Cultural Identity, 1900–1945* (Ithaca NY: Cornell University Press, 1992).

CHAPTER 3

Remaking the French working class: race, gender, and exclusion[1]

At the beginning of January 1919, union activists held a mass meeting in Paris' Bourse du Travail to protest the firing of women workers from armaments factories at the end of the war. Attended by some 2,500 people, over 2,000 of them women, the meeting put in bold relief the sufferings of the *munitionnettes* thrown out of work in the months after the Armistice. Speaker after speaker rose to denounce the government and the bourgeoisie, often in revolutionary terms. Leclerc, of the automobile and aviation workers' union, saw in the plight of working women yet another example of the iniquity and bankruptcy of the capitalist system:

Already, a promising wind from the East is reaching us. Just as the Spanish flu came from the East, so will the Revolution. (Frenetic bravos). When the soldiers, your husbands, your brothers and your sons, learn that while they were defending the property of others you've been thrown in the street and that you can no longer send them a few cents from time to time, they will react with outrage and will make the appropriate response given the circumstances; that won't bother me at all, because they will bring to an end the war which, it must be said, is far from being over! (applause).[2]

This account of a protest meeting illustrates the complex interconnections between working-class identity, gender and difference, and radical politics in Paris during 1919. Organizers called the meeting to address the concerns of working women, yet it seems to have been mostly men who spoke, often only tangentially addressing the reasons why the audience was overwhelmingly feminine. While male union leaders devote relatively little attention to the demobilization of female war workers, some also viewed what they considered the victimization of women as further evidence of the need for

---

[1] Some material in this chapter appeared in the *Proceedings of the Annual Meeting of the Western Society for French History*, 14 (1987). My thanks to the editors for letting me reuse it here.

[2] AN F7 13356, report of January 10, 1919.

revolution. In 1919, the *munitionnettes* found themselves both hailed as a part of the working class and at the same time expelled from it. Here identity and politics intersected: in such a turbulent time, what and who was the working class?

Social identities are created by means of both inclusions and exclusions. One must define not only who belongs, but also who does not, in order to construct a sense of group cohesion and solidarity. The remaking of the Parisian working class in 1919 operated through the exclusion of two groups of working people: women in heavy industry and colonial subjects. The exigencies of the war effort brought new prominence to their position within the working class, but the end of the war raised questions about the continued desirability of their contributions. These exclusions functioned in very different ways, so that facile comparisons between the experiences of the two groups are misleading. Nonetheless, the relations of both to the Paris working class as a whole underwent rapid and dramatic shifts immediately after the war, in ways that suggested fundamental changes in the nature of working-class identity as part of the transition from war to peace. While government policymakers and industrial elites directed these changes, the desires of working people (including foreigners and women) played a central role in reshaping the working class. One must therefore consider this process not as something simply imposed by elites, but rather something that reflects different relations of power and contrasting conceptions of who was a worker.[3]

This chapter thus approaches the question of working-class identity from the perspective of difference, and in particular the interactions between class, gender, and race. The proliferation of identity studies on this theme in recent years has led one historian to refer to the "iron triangle" of race, class, and gender; certainly these three categories are not equivalent, nor are they the only important markers of social identities.[4] Yet Paris in 1919 provides a specific historical example of their interaction, in particular the ways in which ideas about race and gender redefined the nature of class identity. It

[3] Much of the historiography of French labor in this period has tended to treat the working class as a monolith. For a critique of this practice, see Laura Downs, "Women's strikes and the politics of popular egalitarianism in France, 1916–18," in Lenard Berlanstein, ed., *Rethinking Labor History* (Urbana: University of Illinois Press, 1993).

[4] Tom Holt, cited in Dwayne E. Williams, "Rethinking the African diaspora: a comparative look at race and identity in a transatlantic community," in Darlene Clark Hine and Jacqueline McLeod, eds., *Crossing Boundaries: Comparative History of Black People in Diaspora* (Bloomington: Indiana University Press, 1999), 106; see also Tom Holt, "Marking: race, race-making, and writing of history," *American Historical Review*, 106/1 (February, 1995), 1–20.

thus contributes to our broader understanding of the polyvalent and historically shifting character of social identities in general.[5]

Whereas in the last chapter I considered the nature of working-class community from the standpoint of heterogeneity rather than unity, in this chapter I focus more closely on the ways in which social identity, in this case working-class Parisian identity, arose out of processes of differentiation. Scholars from a variety of different disciplines, including anthropology, philosophy, linguistics, feminist theory, and postcolonial studies, have considered the ways in which perceptions and conceptualizations of the Other have helped define group identities. Hegel's parable of the master/slave dialectic constituted one of the first modern manifestations of this approach to identity, and the psychoanalyst Jacques Lacan and the philosophers Jacques Derrida and Emmanuel Levinas have made significant use of this concept. Simone de Beauvoir deployed the idea of the Other in her pioneering work in feminist theory, *The Second Sex*, as did Frantz Fanon in *Black Skin, White Masks* and Edward Said in *Orientalism*.[6]

In this chapter I consider how some segments of Parisian labor conceptualized others as the Other and tried to exclude them, in the process attempting to redefine what it meant to be a worker. The chapter will analyze the history of these exclusions as a key aspect of the transformation of working-class identity in 1919. I argue that while the nature of this process was transitional, it nonetheless set forth themes crucial to the lives of French working people during the twentieth century as a whole. Moreover, I argue that this exclusionary process played a role in the political turbulence of 1919; far from dividing and depoliticizing the working class, divisions of race and gender paralleled if not directly contributed to the broader sense of uncertainty and instability central to the revolutionary climate of the year after the Armistice. An increased focus on the Other within the working

---

[5] Historians and other scholars studying difference have begun to move beyond a simple additive approach to race, class, and gender, instead analyzing the intersections between various types of difference in concrete situations. Much of this work has been done by feminists, especially black feminists, considering the relationship between race and gender; in the 1990s some began to employ the concept of intersectionality to analyze this phenomenon. See Kimberle Crenshaw, "Mapping the margins: intersectionality, identity politics, and violence against women of color," *Stanford Law Review*, 43/6 (1991); Patricia Hill Collins, "It's all in the family: intersections of gender, race, and nation," *Hypatia*, 13/3 (Summer, 1998).

[6] Lorenzo Chiesa, *Subjectivity and Otherness: A Philosophical Reading of Lacan* (Cambridge MA: MIT Press, 2007); Jacques Derrida, *Of Grammatology* (Baltimore MD: Johns Hopkins University Press, 1976); Emmanuel Levinas, *Humanism of the Other* (Urbana: University of Illinois Press, 2003); David Fryer, *The Intervention of the Other: Ethical Subjectivity in Levinas and Lacan* (New York: Other Press, 2004); Simone de Beauvoir, *The Second Sex* (New York: Vintage, 1952); Frantz Fanon, *Black Skin, White Masks* (New York: Grove Press, 1967); Edward Said, *Orientalism* (New York: Vintage, 1979).

class went hand in hand with heightened notions of working-class solidarity. In other words, the nature of both working-class identity and working-class politics were very much up for grabs at the end of World War I, so that the possibilities for a fundamental change in the latter were hinted at by the transformations of the former. At the same time, I contend that ultimately the attempt to redefine Parisian labor failed, on a number of levels, and thus reaffirmed the diversity of that class as outlined in the previous chapter.

Before looking at this process of exclusion, I wish to continue the work done in Chapter 2 by giving a portrait of gender, ethnicity, and race in working-class Paris during the era of World War I. Such an overview is vital to understanding how the exclusions of female and colonial labor in 1919 shaped working-class identity in general. This description reinforces the importance of diversity as a key to working-class life in Paris, as noted in Chapter 2, illustrating why challenges to aspects of this diversity should have political consequences in 1919.[7]

GENDER, RACE, AND ETHNICITY IN WORKING-CLASS PARIS

In considering the nature of working-class life in early twentieth-century Paris, one must also look at key differences in the working-class population, differences that not only affected its statistical profile but also fundamentally shaped working-class identities. Of these gender is perhaps the most important.[8] Men and women worked in different spaces in Paris during the 1920s; the central division between workplace and home was reinforced by the gendered nature of many occupations. Both metalworking and construction were heavily masculine, although one can find indications of women mechanics in the census data. Domestic service, clothing, and increasingly clerical and shop employment, in contrast, primarily employed women. A more specific analysis of women's

---

[7] For an exploration of these issues see Laura Levine Frader, *Breadwinners and Citizens: Gender in the Making of the French Social Model* (Durham NC: Duke University Press, 2008).

[8] There now exists a very large and dynamic literature on both the history of working-class women, and also the theoretical relationship between class and gender, in both modern Europe and America. Useful overviews of the various questions and debates involved in this subject include Scott, *Gender*; Louise Tilly and Joan Scott, *Women, Work, and Family* (New York: Holt, Rinehart, and Winston, 1978); Judith Newton, Mary Ryan, and Judith Walkowitz, eds., *Sex and Class in Women's History* (Boston MA: Routledge and Kegan Paul, 1983); Laura L. Frader and Sonya O. Rose, eds., *Gender and Class in Modern Europe* (Ithaca NY: Cornell University Press, 1996).

Table 3.1 *Occupations of working-class women*

	Service	Clothing	Clerks	Metals	Furni.	Unskil.	Housewv.
Boul., '21	11 / 7.6%	17 / 11.7%	5 / 3.4%	2 / 1.4%	1 / 0.7%	18 / 12.4%	91 / 62.8%
Dran., '21	1 / 2.8%	9 / 25.0%	1 / 2.8%	0	1 / 2.8%	2 / 5.6%	22 / 61.1%
F-M., '26	7 / 7.0%	23 / 23.0%	7 / 7.0%	6 / 6.0%	10 / 10.0%	7 / 7.0%	40 / 40.0%
Crlb., '26	3 / 6.4%	20 / 42.6%	3 / 6.4%	4 / 8.5%	0	5 / 10.6%	12 / 25.5%

LN, 1921, 1926. Again, these are based on 1/100th population samples.

employment patterns will give a very different view of Parisian working-class life.[9]

Two things stand out in Table 3.1: the heavy predominance of house-wives and the different occupations women found when they did work outside the home. In both Boulogne and Drancy housewives formed a solid majority of the adult working-class female population, while in Folie-Méricourt they constituted the largest occupational group. Only in Croulebarbe did this group come in second place, behind workers in the clothing sector. In general, therefore, Parisian working-class women were more likely to work inside the house than to engage in any single occupation. However, this did not mean that a woman's place was simply in the home, as far as this community was concerned. Whether or not a woman held paid employment varied according to her age and family status. Young women and women living alone were more likely to have jobs than were married women with children. Thanks in part to the war[10] many women were widows living alone or with their children, and they generally supported themselves until their children were old enough to lend a hand. Many women, especially the young, who were married without offspring also worked outside the home. On the other hand, working-class married mothers overwhelmingly stayed home, at least while their children were

---

[9] On the history of working-class women in France, see Sylvie Schweitzer, *Les femmes ont toujours travaillé: une histoire de leurs métiers, XIXe–XXe siècles* (Paris: O. Jacob, 2002); James McMillan, *Housewife or Harlot: The Place of Women in French Society* (New York: St. Martin's Press, 1981); Charles Sowerine, *Sisters or Citizens? Women and Socialism in France since 1876* (Cambridge University Press, 1982); Rachel Fuchs, *Poor and Pregnant in Paris: Strategies for Survival in the Nineteenth Century* (New Brunswick NJ: Rutgers University Press, 1992); Marie-Hélène Zylberberg-Hocquard, *Femmes et féminisme dans le mouvement ouvrier français* (Paris: Éditions ouvrières, 1981).

[10] On the demographic impact of World War I on French women see Michel Huber, *La population de la France, son évolution et ses perspectives* (Paris: Hachette, 1937); Colin Dyer, *Population and Society in Twentieth Century France* (London: Hodder & Stoughton, 1978).

young.[11] In addition, Table 3.1 reveals a significant neighborhood contrast in the occupational patterns of working-class women. Suburban women were much more likely to work as housewives than their urban counterparts. The underdeveloped commercial sector, the concentration of industry and relative lack of small workplaces, transportation difficulties, and the culture of domesticity in the allotment communities all tended to render working outside the home less of an option for women in communities like Boulogne and Drancy.[12]

The choices available to those *Parisiennes* who did work for wages remained limited in the 1920s, but also reflected shifts in the metropolitan economy since the beginning of the century. The most important occupational category for women in the late nineteenth century, domestic service, had clearly diminished in importance. Since most maids and other servants lived in the homes of their bourgeois employers, Table 3.1 with its focus on working-class neighborhoods cannot accurately estimate their numbers in the Paris area. However, it does confirm the general portrait of a "servants crisis" in the period after World War I.[13] More women worked in the clothing industry than in any other sector, primarily as laundresses and dressmakers. Conditions in this industry varied enormously; much of the garment trade in particular used sweated labor, so women obtained thread, cloth, and other raw materials from their suppliers, who then paid them by the piece for finished articles of clothing. Laundresses also frequently worked out of their homes. Yet many women worked in garment factories, dressmakers' shops, or laundries scattered throughout the Paris area.[14] Much of women's work was classified as unskilled, and generally included jobs like packing and cleaning in factories. Finally, in spite of the undeniable growth of women's clerical work after World War I, such jobs still employed a relatively small percentage of working-class women in 1920s Paris.[15]

---

[11] Tilly and Scott, *Women, Work, and Family*; McMillan, *Housewife or Harlot*, 37–41.

[12] On the life of women in suburban areas, see Martine Segalen, "L'esprit de famille à Nanterre," *Vingtième siècle*, 14 (April–June, 1987); Peter Willmott and Michael Young, *Family and Class in a London Suburb* (London: Routledge and Kegan Paul, 1960).

[13] McBride, "A woman's world"; Mary Louise Roberts, *Civilization without Sexes: Reconstructing Gender in Postwar France, 1917–1927* (University of Chicago Press, 1994). Jean-Louis Robert has argued that one main cause of the postwar servants crisis was the departure of German maids from Paris at the beginning of the war. Jean-Louis Robert, "Ouvriers et mouvement ouvrier parisiens pendant la grande guerre et l'immédiat après-guerre" (Doctorat d'Etat thesis, Université de Paris-1, 1989), 391.

[14] Henriette Vanier, *La mode et ses métiers: frivolités et luttes des classes, 1830–1870* (Paris: A. Colin, 1960); Tilly and Scott, *Women, Work, and Family*; Jeanne Bouvier, *Mes mémoires* (Paris: Découverte, 1983).

[15] Roberts, *Civilization without Sexes*.

In general, therefore, the working-class labor market in Paris continued to be segmented along gender lines. This is all the more striking given the experience of working-class Parisian women during the war. Hundreds of thousands of them had gone to work in heavy industry, especially in munitions plants, for the first time.[16] Even more significant is the heavy preponderance of housewives, especially in the suburbs. Places like Boulogne and especially Drancy represented the future of urban France in the early twentieth century, and thus of urban working-class women as well. As I shall discuss in greater detail below, these changes did not simply result from the evolution of the labor market, but were constructed by powerful social and political discourses. Such forces ensured that the world of working-class Parisian women remained in more than one sense separate and unequal during the interwar years.[17]

Ethnicity and foreign nationality also served to differentiate working people in Paris from each other during the 1920s. For several reasons, most notably the loss of 1.6 million young Frenchmen on the battlefields of World War I and the adoption of new, highly restrictive limits on immigration by the government of the United States, France became one of the world's leading recipients of immigrants during the interwar years.[18] Paris in particular became host to a large foreign population; the 1926 census counted nearly 300,000 foreign nationals living in the city, or 10.3 percent of the population, while the suburbs of the Department of the Seine were home to another 140,000, or 8.1 percent.[19] This foreign population was nothing if not cosmopolitan during the 1920s, including people as diverse as Ernest Hemingway and Ho Chi Minh, but most were certainly working

---

[16] Margaret H. Darrow, *French Women and the First World War: War Stories of the Home Front* (Oxford and New York: Berg, 2000); McMillan, *Housewife or Harlot*, 101–162; Françoise Thébaud, *La femme au temps de la guerre de 14* (Paris: Stock, 1986); Yvonne Delatour, "Le travail des femmes pendant la première guerre mondiale et ses conséquences sur l'evolution de leur role dans la société," *Francia*, 2 (1974); M. Dubusset, F. Thébaud, and C. Vincent, "Les munitionnettes de la Seine," in Patrick Fridenson, ed., *1914–1918: l'autre front* (Paris: Éditions Ouvrières, 1977).

[17] There is a broad consensus among historians that the use of women workers in the munitions industries of World War I did not produce lasting results. See Laura Lee Downs, *Manufacturing Inequality: Gender Division in the French and British Metalworking Industries, 1914–1939* (Ithaca NY: Cornell University Press, 1995); Susan Grayzel, *Women's Identities at War: Gender, Motherhood, and Politics in Britain and France during the First World War* (Chapel Hill: University of North Carolina Press, 1999).

[18] On immigration into France during the interwar years see Mary Dewhurst Lewis, *The Boundaries of the Republic: Migrant Rights and the Limits of Universalism in France, 1918–1940* (Stanford University Press, 2007); Clifford Rosenberg, *Policing Paris: The Origins of Modern Immigration Control Between the Wars* (Ithaca NY: Cornell University Press, 2006); Gary Cross, *Immigrant Workers in Industrial France* (Philadelphia PA: Temple University Press, 1983); Gérard Noiriel, *Gens d'ici venus d'ailleurs: la France de l'immigration, 1900 à nos jours* (Paris: Chêne, 2004).

[19] *Annuaire statistique de la ville de Paris, 1923–4*, 296–297.

Table 3.2 *Foreigners in the Paris area, 1926*

Boulogne	9,916 / 13.4%
Drancy	2,346 / 7.5%
Folie-Méricourt	6,770 / 12.7%
Croulebarbe	1,624 / 8.1%

Annuaire statistique de la ville de Paris, 1923–4, 296–297.

people. Observers of Parisian working-class life in this period commented frequently on the striking presence of a colorful, polyglot population in the faubourgs. Jacques Valdour, an assiduous commentator on the worlds of French workers in the early twentieth century, described in his book *Le faubourg* the newly international character of the Faubourg Saint-Antoine:

> For the last fifteen or twenty years genuine foreigners have joined the population, so characteristic and homogeneous, of the Parisian cabinet makers of the Faubourg: Belgians and Italians who relatively quickly become naturalized and integrated into the French masses, and, since the war, Spaniards, also easily assimilable, Czechs, Poles, and Jews ... The Italians, settled especially in Charonne, are spilling over into the eastern edges of the Faubourg ... a large number of signs labeled "Franco-Italian restaurant" are displayed on the rue de Dahomey, Boulevard Diderot, Avenue Daumesnill; in the upper part of the rue du Faubourg there is a "Piedmontese restaurant" and a stationer's shop that sells several Yiddish newspapers, several Spanish newspapers, and two dozen Italian newspapers, both dailies and weeklies, including an anarchist one.[20]

The foreign population of the four neighborhoods studied in the previous chapter corresponded closely to the general shape of immigrant life in Paris, as well as to the above description (see Table 3.2). The largest groups of immigrant workers in the Paris area, as elsewhere in France, were Belgians, Italians, Poles, and Spaniards. The city also contained a sizeable population of Jews from eastern Europe, especially in the Marais and eastern districts, and a small Arab colony, principally Algerian.[21]

Gérard Noiriel has distinguished between two models of immigrant worker settlement in early twentieth-century France: that of factory towns and that of city-center neighborhoods.[22] Both models existed in Paris in the

---

[20] Jacques Valdour (pseud.), *Le faubourg*, 133. Valdour's real name was Louis Martin.

[21] Nancy Green, "Quartier et travail: les immigrés juifs dans le Marais et derrière les machines à coudre, 1900–1939," in Magri and Topalov, *Villes ouvrières*; Norbert Gomar, *L'Émigration algérienne en France* (Paris: Presses Universitaires de France, 1931); G. Meynier, "Les Algériens en France, 1914–1918," *Revue d'Histoire Maghrébine*, 5 (1976); Neil MacMaster, *Colonial Migrants and Racism: Algerians in France, 1900–1962* (New York: St. Martin's Press, 1997).

[22] Gérard Noiriel, "Les espaces de l'immigration ouvrière," in Magri and Topalov, *Villes ouvrières*.

1920s. Boulogne exemplified the first, with its large population of unskilled and semi-skilled workers employed at Renault and other local factories. Folie-Méricourt, in contrast, represented the second, a neighborhood with many carpenters, furniture makers, and other artisans of foreign origin. While certain nationalities tended to specialize in certain occupations, such as Italian stonemasons or Jewish tailors, the occupational distribution of the foreign population as a whole does not seem that different from that of French workers. Family structure, on the other hand, differed between native and immigrant workers. Whereas among French workers the nuclear family dominated, most French families consisting of couples without or with a small number of children, among foreign workers there were both more single-person households (usually male) and more large, extended families.

Workers who shared the same foreign nationality were much more likely to live grouped together in the same *quartier* or street than those who shared the same occupation. Scattered throughout the census records one can find small colonies of different immigrant populations, such as the Italians of the rue Larochefoucauld in Boulogne, or the eastern Europeans of the rue d'Angouleme in Folie-Méricourt. Although many foreigners lived in working-class suburban areas, they had a greater visual and cultural impact in urban neighborhoods like the Marais or the Faubourg Saint-Antoine, where their concentrated presence lent an air of exoticism to the decrepit streets of old Paris. During the 1920s the overwhelming majority of Parisians were born in France,[23] and the French capital could not compete with the mosaic of diversity offered by a city like New York at the turn of the century.[24] Nonetheless, ethnicity both contributed to and helped differentiate conceptions of working-class identity in early twentieth-century Paris. As Laurent Azzano noted in his memoir, *Mes joyeuses années au faubourg*:

I was thirteen years old, and I belonged to a family of Italian furniture makers who had emigrated to France. At that time the Faubourg received many émigrés from all over the world, Czechs, eastern Jews, Hungarians, people who possessed a solid level of skill in their profession but who were often ignorant of French techniques

[23] There were of course many Parisians who were French citizens and born in France, but whose parents were foreigners. Although French nationals, these people usually belonged to immigrant communities and claimed an ethnically distinct identity.

[24] Similarly, the historiography of ethnicity is far more sophisticated and extensive in the United States than in France. For purposes of comparison, see Nancy L. Green, *Ready-to-Wear and Ready-to-Work: A Century of Industry and Immigrants in Paris and New York* (Durham NC: Duke University Press, 1997).

more advanced than those of their homelands. In the workshops which produced inexpensive goods they preferred foreigners to the French, since they received lower wages and worked faster, without stopping. The Italians were particularly numerous, settling into the Faubourg where they rapidly began to produce furniture more cheaply than the French houses.[25]

The diversity of Parisian labor in the early twentieth century revolved not just around occupation and neighborhood, but also around gender and ethnicity.[26] Yet along with this diversity went a significant amount of segregation, primarily occupational in the case of women and men, both occupational and spatial in the case of French and foreign workers. Ultimately the exclusion of female and colonial labor in 1919, to which we now turn, promoted new levels of segregation in the postwar period rather than eliminating these groups from the working class as a whole. Although many parties to this process hoped to restore prewar stereotypes of French workers (stereotypes which were themselves never quite accurate in any case), instead they succeeded in producing a newly segmented labor force whose diversity would anticipate that of the Parisian working class as a whole in the twentieth century.

REDEFINING THE PARIS WORKING CLASS

Even before 1914 France had played host to a large working-class population of foreign origin, but wartime needs for both industrial and agricultural labor sharply increased the size and significance of this group.[27] Over half a million foreigners worked in French factories and fields between 1914 and 1918. The majority of these, like most immigrant workers before the war, came from different European countries, principally Spain, Greece,

---

[25] Azzano, *Mes joyeuses années*, 17. In *Peasants into Frenchmen* (Stanford University Press, 1976) Eugene Weber compares the dissemination of French urban values into the countryside to French imperial expansion overseas in the late nineteenth century. I would suggest one could make a similar comparison between immigrants to Paris from the French provinces and from other nations.

[26] To give one example of the interaction of gender and ethnicity in France, many officials favored the immigration of women from southern Europe (or "the Latin race"), seeing them as relatively assimilable into French culture yet more fecund than French women. See Elisa Camiscioli, "Producing citizens, reproducing the 'French race': immigration, demography, pronatalism in early twentieth century France," *Gender and History*, 13 (November, 2001), 593–621.

[27] On foreign workers in France before 1914, see Paul Frezouls, *Les ouvriers étrangers en France* (Montpellier: G. Fermin, 1909); J. Didion, *Les salariés étrangers en France* (Paris: M. Giard, 1911); Michelle Perrot, "Les rapports entre ouvriers français et étrangers (1871–1893)," *Bulletin de la Société d'Histoire moderne*, 12/15–16 (1960).

3.1 Vietnamese working in the Trianon gardens, Versailles, World War I

Portugal, and Italy. Although their greater numbers during and after the war made an impact on observers of working-class life like Jacques Valdour, still white-skinned foreigners were not so unusual in French workshops and working-class neighborhoods. However, the war also brought a large population of nonwhite workers, over 300,000, to France from China, North Africa, and Indochina. The introduction of a group of laborers who differed so strikingly in language, customs, and skin color from French workers raised the possibility, at least temporarily, of a fundamental shift in what it meant to be working class in France (Illustration 3.1).[28]

---

[28] There is now a large and growing literature on the history of colonial labor in France during World War I. See Rosenberg, *Policing Paris*; Mary Lewis, "Une théorie raciale des valeurs? Démobilisation des travailleurs immigrés et mobilisation des stereotypes à la fin de la Grande Guerre," translated by Sandrine Bertaux, in Hervé Le Bras, ed., *L'invention des populations: biologie, idéologie et politique* (Paris: Odile Jacob, 2000); John Horne, "Immigrant workers in France during World War I," *French Historical Studies*, 14/1 (Spring, 1985); Jean Vidalenc, "La main-d'oeuvre étrangère en france et la première guerre mondiale (1901–1926)," *Francia*, 2 (1974); Bertrand Nogaro and Lucien Weil, *La main-d'oeuvre étrangère et colonial pendant la guerre* (Paris: Presses Universitaires de France, 1926). My own contributions include T. Stovall, "Colour-blind France? Colonial workers during the First World War," *Race and Class*, 35/2 (October–December, 1993).

3.2 Colonial soldiers at a café in the Gare de Lyon, September 1914

Establishing the number of foreign workers who came to Paris during the war, and gauging their impact on working-class identity in the metropolitan area, remains a difficult task. Before the war Paris not only had one of the largest concentrations of immigrant workers in France, but also more foreigners (not all working class) than any other European capital. Moreover, its foreign population was one of the most cosmopolitan in France, containing not just Belgians and Italians but people of many other nationalities as well.[29] World War I temporarily changed this situation (Illustration 3.2). As both Gary Cross and John Horne have noted, wartime immigration differed from its prewar predecessor in being much more organized and controlled by both the state and private industry. Both groups shared an interest in directing foreign labor to where it was needed most, generally to French farms and provincial armaments factories. In contrast Paris, with its high wages and large numbers of French refugees from the occupied north of France, was not targeted as a place where foreign workers were needed. In fact, the French government set up an elaborate (if less than completely effective) set of controls designed to prevent immigrant

[29] Robert, *Les ouvriers, la patrie et la révolution*, 364–365.

workers from leaving their assigned workplaces and moving to Paris in search of better salaries.[30]

Colonial workers in particular occupied a relatively small place in the life of the Parisian working class. Non-Europeans were brought in under the auspices of the French military, and consequently were subject to a much stricter series of controls than their European compatriots. Whereas many Spaniards, for example, succeeded in eluding governmental controls and migrating to Paris and other cities, immigrants from the colonies and China had fewer opportunities to do so.[31] Most of the colonial workers who ended up in industrial labor worked in State-owned factories, such as the powder works in Saint Medard, near Bordeaux; since most of the war plants in the Paris area were privately owned and did not use this source of labor very much, relatively few nonwhite workers came to the Paris area.[32] On the other hand, some colonial subjects did find work with other public agencies, particularly the City of Paris. The figure of the man of color sweeping the streets of the French capital, one of the most common and visible images of Parisian working-class life from the 1960s on, first became a reality during World War I.[33]

To an important extent, therefore, foreign workers were already excluded from the Parisian working class before 1919, as a result of the mechanics set up to provide France with vital workers for its fields and factories. The official preference for keeping foreign labor out of Paris also reflected a desire to segregate foreign workers from French society in general. This attitude applied particularly to colonial workers, and reflected deep-seated racial anxieties. Colonial workers were much more strictly controlled than European foreigners; subject to military discipline, they were housed and fed in isolated barracks, and generally not allowed to live in private residential accommodation.[34] Government authorities justified this practice by arguing that the workers' unfamiliarity with the French language and customs necessitated this policy of concentration. Furthermore, some asserted that isolating colonial workers from the French civilian population was necessary to keep the latter from corrupting the former with the maladies of "civilization":

---

[30] Cross, *Immigrant Workers*, 38–41; Horne, "Immigrant workers in France."

[31] On the regimentation system see Stovall, "Colour-blind France?"; Horne, "Immigrant workers in France."

[32] These war plants were in Vincennes and Puteaux. Robert, *Les ouvriers, la patrie et la révolution*, 392.

[33] *Ibid.*

[34] Given the cost and shortage of wartime housing, this was not a realistic possibility in Paris in any case.

3.3 Women and Chinese workers in a French factory, World War I

From the point of view of morality, the Annamite is a big child, little prepared for our civilization and susceptible to contract its vices. It is necessary to watch over him in order to stop him from falling into bad habits or listening to bad advice . . . one must, in particular, make sure that he doesn't start drinking alcohol. Intelligent, good natured, a little lazy, the Annamite has a tendency toward lying, gambling, and petty larceny. One must be just with him, command him calmly without either anger or weakness.[35]

In actuality, however, French officials worried less about the moral fiber of colonial workers and more about their relations with French civilians, especially French women. Fear of conflict between colonial and French workers was a major preoccupation, and authorities concerned with managing the former frequently referred to such worrisome precedents as the clashes between Chinese and white workers in the United States. However, concerns about relations between nonwhite workers and French women gradually became a key justification for separating colonial laborers from the French working-class population (Illustration 3.3). Judging from the

---

[35] "Instruction relative à l'emploi de la main-d'oeuvre annamite," Société historique de l'armée de terre (hereafter SHAT), 7 N 144, 20/2/1916.

numerous letters written by colonial workers to friends and relatives back home, such relations were fairly frequent.[36] In the summer of 1917 a Madagascan named Rabetanety wrote that he had applied to remain in France: "I invoked . . . my great desire to continue to serve the Patrie, but in reality I find French women very sweet and beautiful, and I would be heartbroken if I had to leave them already."[37]

Government and industrial leaders were not the only people who worried about the presence of foreign workers in France. In general, French workers remained suspicious of the colonial subjects in their midst. Many workers and union leaders continued to believe, with ample justification, that immigrant labor was used by government and industrial leaders to lower wages in general and, after 1916, to break strikes.[38] In particular, some feared that French workers replaced by foreigners would then be drafted and sent to fight on the front lines. There was also the concern that unskilled colonial workers would be used to introduce labor-saving machinery and Taylorist methods, thus weakening the workplace autonomy of skilled workers. The reasons advanced by union representatives to oppose the use of immigrant labor therefore emphasized not hatred of foreigners per se but fears that they would be used as tools of the employers to worsen the working conditions of the French proletariat.[39]

Some of the opposition manifested by French workers toward foreigners had little to do with economic advantage, however. Sexual competition frequently hardened attitudes toward outsiders, at times bringing French and foreign male workers to blows with each other. Some men feared that immigrant workers would take not only their jobs but their women as well:

It is frequently said (in the munitions factories), . . . "If this continues, there will not be any men left in France; so why are we fighting? So that Chinese, Arabs, or

---

[36] One Tunisian worker claimed to have four girlfriends, and noted that where he worked "fornication was as abundant as grains of sand." Letter from Mahmoud ben Arrar, 4/17, SHAT 7 N 1001. See Tyler Stovall, "Love, labor, and race: colonial men and white women in France during the Great War," in Tyler Stovall and Georges Van Den Abbeele, eds., *French Civilization and its Discontents: Nationalism, Colonialism, Race* (Lanham MD: Lexington Books, 2003).

[37] SHAT 7 N 997.

[38] For example, Chinese workers were used as strikebreakers during the general strike of May 1920. Judith Van Der Stegen, "Les chinois en France, 1915–1925" (Mémoire de maîtrise thesis, Université de Paris X, 1974), 24–25. The regimentation system also worked to keep their wages lower than those of French workers.

[39] American historians in particular have done pioneering work on the role of race in the lives of both white workers and workers of color. See Roediger, *The Wages of Whiteness*; Roediger, *Working Toward Whiteness*; Noel Ignatiev, *How the Irish Became White* (New York: Routledge, 1995).

Spaniards can marry our wives and daughters and share out the France for which we'll all, sooner or later, get ourselves [killed] at the front."[40]

In July 1917, for example the Pas-de-Calais miners' union complained about local North African workers, claiming that they posed problems of morality, given the proximity of families whose men were absent, and of sanitation.[41] In November of the same year the Paris City Council approved a resolution from the street cleaners' union insulting Kabyles working for the municipality and requesting their exclusion from jobs as street sweepers.[42]

With the end of the war France faced a dilemma as far as its continued use of foreign labor was concerned. On the one hand, many government, industry, and union officials decided that the use of foreign labor had been a failure, justified only by extreme wartime shortages of French workers. This attitude was especially pronounced where colonial workers were concerned. Many employers refused to hire colonial workers, claiming that they lacked necessary skills and aptitudes, that language problems were insurmountable, that they were weak and lazy.[43] Now that the war was over, French authorities often felt they were no longer needed. Some also feared the problem of competition with demobilized French soldiers returning home to look for work, predicting riots if foreign workers were allowed to stay.[44] On the other hand, it was clear to many French policymakers in 1919 that labor shortages would not end with the war. France had lost roughly 1.6 million young men during the conflict, and many more returned wounded and unfit for many kinds of work. Moreover, the devastation of much of northern France in particular by occupying German armies meant that more workers would be needed to rebuild the country. One writer estimated that as many as 400,000 additional laborers would be required.[45] If the French economy was to recover and prosper in the 1920s, someone would have to replace these lost Frenchmen in the nation's workplaces. The question was, who?

---

[40] AN F7 13619, police report from Le Havre of May 21, 1917, cited in Horne, "Immigrant workers in France," 85.

[41] AN F14 11334, CIMO report of July 7, 1917. It is worth considering the idea that such racist complaints constituted a kind of rhetorical strategy to win sympathy for workers from elites less disposed to acknowledge complaints about wages.

[42] Conseil Municipal de Paris procès-verbal, November 30, 1917, 55. The report uses the derogatory term "sidi."

[43] On this point see especially the numerous complaints about Chinese workers contained in AN F14 11331.

[44] As Léon Jouhaux put it in August 1917, "If the workers return from the front to find themselves faced with foreign workers, who, because there are no guarantees against their exploitation, may cause wage decreases, the discontent will be widespread and violent." Cited in Cross, *Immigrant Workers*, 49.

[45] Cross, *Immigrant Workers*, 54.

Immediately after the Armistice the national government closed France's borders to further immigration, but within a matter of months it became clear that this was only a temporary expediency to allow time for the reorganization of immigration, not a permanent policy. By the spring of 1919 State authorities had reopened several French industries, including dock work, construction, and mining to foreigners. In March of that year the government established a new organization, the Conférence permanente de la main-d'oeuvre étrangère, to oversee the process of recruiting workers from abroad. Within a year this group had negotiated treaties with the governments of Italy, Poland, and Czechoslovakia to facilitate bringing laborers from those countries to France. By the end of 1924 over one million new foreign workers entered France as a result of these and other agreements.[46]

This new cosmopolitanism had its limits, however. Although French labor, industry, and government representatives were willing, if sometimes reluctantly, to countenance large-scale importation of foreign labor from other parts of Europe, they drew the line at colonial workers. During the war these two groups of immigrant workers had been treated very differently, and these differences reached their logical conclusion at the end of the war. Since most officials concerned with foreign labor concurred in a negative view of the potential and achievements of colonial workers, they agreed to repatriate those remaining in France at the Armistice, and not to renew this experiment with "exotic" labor. Once decided upon, the expulsion of colonial labor was accomplished with breathtaking rapidity. Thanks to the regimentation system, rounding up these workers and sending them home was a relatively simple matter. By the middle of 1919 less than 30,000 remained of the nearly quarter of a million North Africans, Indochinese, and Chinese who had come to work in France during the war. The 1921 census gives an indication of numbers by national group, listing 13,000 Chinese, 6,500 Algerians, 4,000 Moroccans, 1,500 Tunisians, 175 Indochinese, and only 37 Madagascans resident in France during that year.[47]

In part, French authorities justified this massive repatriation of colonial workers by arguing that their experience in France had been an unhappy one and that most were only too happy to return home. Given the harsh and bewildering conditions experienced by laborers from the French empire and

[46] *Ibid.*, chap. 3; Louis Pasquet, *Immigration et la main-d'oeuvre étrangère en France* (Paris: Rieder, 1927).
[47] Huber, *La population de la France*, 506–511.

China during the war, there is probably a good deal of validity to this point of view; certainly many of the letters they wrote home indicate a desire to leave France as soon as possible.[48] The point is, however, that the French were unwilling to permit colonial workers to decide for themselves, taking steps to expel them whether they wanted to go or not. This was especially true of North Africans. More than the Asians or Madagascans, they had created a certain, tiny presence in prewar France and had established small communities in some French cities by the end of the war, notably Paris and Marseilles.[49] They were therefore more likely to want to stay in France, and more able to do so, once the war ended.

Paris occupied a central position in the expulsion of colonial labor in 1918 and 1919. While most of these workers found themselves stationed else-where during the war, French officials feared that once the conflict ended, in the confusion surrounding repatriation many would gravitate to the French capital and disappear into its large, polyglot, and anonymous population.[50] Some also worried that because of the high wages offered by the city's industries and the fact that many soldiers were demobilized there, a large population of foreign workers in Paris would be particularly likely to provoke clashes with French laborers returning from the war in search of jobs. Consequently during 1919 and 1920 Parisian police systematically raided the city's Arab neighborhoods in search of illegal immigrants, summarily deporting all those who fell into their nets. While a certain North African population remained in Paris, much of it existed on a clandestine basis in isolation from French working people in the city.

The expulsions of the immediate postwar period created an enduring legacy for the working-class experience, in Paris and in France as a whole, during the 1920s and 1930s. Although during the interwar years France became one of the world's leading recipients of foreigners, almost all of these came from other parts of Europe, notably Poland and Italy. Over 1 million European aliens lived in France according to the census of 1931. On the other hand, few nonwhite laborers found much of a reception there during these years. This was especially noteworthy in Paris. The *Annuaire statistique de la ville de Paris* counted 120,000 Italians, 98,000 Belgians, 39,000 Spaniards, and 33,000 Poles residing in the Department of the Seine at the

---

[48] Thanks to the diligence of wartime censors in France, historians have at their disposal thousands of letters written by foreign workers during the war. See in particular SHAT 7 N 1001, 6 N 149, 7 N 435, 5 N 134, 7 N 144, 7 N 997.

[49] Meynier, "Les Algériens en France"; Gomar, *L'émigration algérienne*; Benjamin Stora, "Les Algériens dans le Paris de l'entre-deux-guerres," in Kaspi and Marès, *Le Paris des étrangers*.

[50] See the official reports contained in AN F 22 2565, report of March 8, 1919.

end of 1924. In contrast, only 9,000 Moroccans, 2,400 Chinese, 600 Tunisians, and 11 Indochinese (*Annamites*) found their way into its statistics.[51]

The French government did not in fact terminate all importation of labor from outside Europe during the interwar years. Algerians in particular were allowed to come to France to work. They came in under the auspices of the French Labor Ministry, which in 1919 established a center in Marseilles to organize their recruitment and distribution throughout the country. In effect the Algerians constituted the exception that proved the rule about the exclusion of nonwhite labor from France after World War I. During the war, Algerians were generally regarded by French employers and government officials as the least desirable workers, only to be hired when no French or European laborers could be found. They were also, as during the war, kept segregated from other workers. Moreover, most Algerians came to France on a very temporary basis; although close to half a million entered the country during the twenties, during several years more returned home than arrived. Their presence was a transitory phenomenon that did little to alter the character of French working-class life.[52]

This exclusion of nonwhite workers took place with the full accord and participation of the major French unions. Indeed, many organized workers wished to go further and bar virtually all foreign workers from French soil. Fear of postwar unemployment was especially sharp in early 1919, and prompted many union attacks on the use of immigrant labor.[53] The issue of foreign labor also played a small role in the burgeoning struggle between the centrist majority and the antiwar radical minority in the *Confédération Générale du Travail* (CGT), with the latter claiming that one of the evils of war (and by extension, of the majority's support of the national war effort) had been the increased use of foreign workers.[54] The important point here is simply that both sides wanted to limit the number of foreign workers in France. By the end of the year, however, national CGT leaders had largely conceded that, in the face of the need for economic reconstruction, France would have to continue to bring in foreigners for the foreseeable future.[55]

---

[51] *Annuaire statistique de la ville de Paris, 1923–4*, 300–301.
[52] Cross, *Immigrant Workers*, 123–126; Stora, "Les Algériens dans le Paris"; MacMaster, *Colonial Migrants*; Rosenberg, *Policing Paris*.
[53] Robert, *Les ouvriers, la patrie et la révolution*, 419; AN F 7 13356.
[54] On this point see Mireille Favre, "Un milieu porteur de modernisation: travailleurs et tirailleurs Vietnamiens en France pendant la première guerre mondiale" (thesis for the diplome d'archiviste-paléographe, École nationale des Chartes, 1986), 370–382.
[55] The factional struggles within the CGT and the French Left at this time also prevented labor from exercising much influence over the question of immigrant workers. Cross, *Immigrant Workers*, 46–55.

Yet all sides – labor, capital, and government – were able to agree that this should not include non-Europeans. Therefore, the fact that during the 1920s France imported large numbers of Europeans but few from outside the continent to work in its fields and factories reflected both a compromise between organized French labor, industry, and the government, as well as a strikingly rare unanimity of opinion among all three parties after the war.

The expulsion of wartime colonial labor underlined the new importance of race in the constitution of the French working class during the early twentieth century. World War I provided the first example of the introduction of a large population of people of color into metropolitan France, and the reaction to this experiment was overwhelmingly negative from most parts of French society. Consequently France chose to restructure its working class after the war, attempting to restore its prewar shape and reverse the errors of wartime. Since the abundant hostility to all foreign workers was tempered by the looming postwar labor shortage, this hostility focused not on all immigrants but on those whose presence had encountered the most resistance during the war. Not only the nation's government and industrial leaders, but also the leaders of the working class itself, participated in this process of reconstitution. The exclusion of colonial workers thus becomes not just an aspect of the social history of demobilization, but also an important example of the way in which French workers defined their own collective identity. This process created a rather artificial demographic phenomenon in interwar France, especially Paris: a working class that seemed more cosmopolitan than ever, but whose heterogeneity remained firmly circumscribed by the color line. Although in the 1920s and 1930s European foreigners continued to be marginal to this class as a whole, I would argue that in this period the relative absence of nonwhite workers meant that race must be considered a key component of working-class identity.[56]

---

[56] In *Policing Paris* Clifford Rosenberg challenges this conclusion, arguing that (at least as far as North Africans were concerned) "Hostility toward colonial workers during World War I was not discernibly more racially charged than that toward any earlier wave of newcomers, and the idea that colonial workers were 'racially distinct' is difficult to sustain" (118). I would respond by noting that race certainly did play a part in views of white foreigners (and for that matter French provincials) before 1914, but that the presence of peoples of color during the war tended to confer white status upon those groups during the war. The fact that the Chinese, who should have been treated the same as Spaniards and other European foreigners, were instead universally lumped in with colonial laborers underscores this. Given the manifold differences between the treatment of European and colonial workers in World War I France, Rosenberg's objections fall into a longstanding refusal of many scholars of France to recognize race as a factor in the nation's history. See Herrick Chapman and Laura Frader, eds., *Race in France: Interdisciplinary Perspectives on the Politics of Difference* (New York: Berghahn Books, 2004).

This process of redefinition also radically altered the position of women workers in France during the immediate postwar period. One cannot, of course, draw the parallels too far: working women were much more widely used than their nonwhite colleagues, and they were not simply kicked out of the country once the war ended. In another sense, however, they also found themselves excluded, if not from working-class life altogether, at least from their wartime status as workers in heavy industry. Moreover, this process took place at the same time as the expulsion of colonial workers, from the Armistice through the early months of 1919. In spite of the differences between the two groups, both government and industrial leaders, as well as male workers and their representatives to a certain extent, looked upon them as temporarily functioning in roles that really belonged to others, and sought to remove them from these roles at the end of the war. The experience of both groups, and the attitudes of government, industry, and labor to them, raise interesting questions about the impact of both race and gender in structuring French working-class identity in the early twentieth century.

Like foreigners, women were no strangers to the paid labor force in France before 1914. As the nation industrialized during the nineteenth century millions of working-class Frenchwomen toiled in the various workplaces of the non-agricultural economy.[57] World War I not only increased the number of women engaged in the paid labor force but, more significantly, dramatically shifted the nature of women's work in France. Initially many women lost their jobs as non-essential industries like fashion were effectively shut down at the start of the war.[58] Large numbers of domestic servants also lost their jobs.[59] This period soon came to an end, however, as French authorities began to realize the important contribution women's work could make to the war effort. As with foreign workers, initially scattered and haphazard efforts gave way to more systematic steps to mobilize women on the economic front.

In July 1916 the national government officially began to promote the hiring of women to work in war industry. Women consequently began to appear in many previously all-male workplaces, making their most

---

[57] On women's work in nineteenth-century France see McMillan, *Housewife or Harlot*, 46–75; Fuchs, *Poor and Pregnant*; Tilly and Scott, *Women, Work, and Family*; Elinor Accampo, *Industrialization, Family Life, and Class Relations in Saint-Chamond, 1815–1914* (Berkeley: University of California Press, 1989); Gay Gullickson, *Spinners and Weavers of Auffray: Rural Industry and the Sexual Division of Labor in a French Village, 1750–1850* (Cambridge University Press, 1986).

[58] On this point see Louise Deletang, *Journal d'une ouvrière parisienne pendant la guerre* (Paris: Eugène Figuière, 1935).

[59] Robert, *Les ouvriers, la patrie et la révolution*, 391.

important, and most dramatic, contribution to the wartime economy by working in the munitions plants. Close to 700,000 women worked as "*munitionnettes*" during the course of the war. At the same time the numbers of women engaged in more traditional occupations like clothing and textiles dropped somewhat, so that war also brought a fundamental reshaping of the nature of women's work in general. Many of the women who took up munitions work had either never worked for wages at all, or had no previous experience in heavy industry. The war brought about, therefore, the emergence of a new female labor force in France.

As with foreign labor, France viewed this new reliance on women's work with decidedly mixed feelings. Many, perhaps most, Frenchmen believed that the woman's place was in the home, and the necessity of bowing to the exigencies of the war did not change this belief. Industrialists had some hesitations about introducing large numbers of women into their factories; not only were they seen as weaker physically, but also as less skilled and adapted to the rhythms of shopfloor life. However, given their extreme need for labor by 1915, most employers in the metals industry were more than willing to take advantage (in more than one sense) of this new resource.[60] Public authorities had more serious reservations. At the beginning of August 1914 René Viviani had called upon Frenchwomen to "replace on the field of labor those who are on the field of battle," and it soon became clear that using female labor could in fact be a matter of national survival.[61] Yet government leaders also worried about the moral and demographic effects of permitting large numbers of women to work in heavy industry. In particular, many agonized about the impact of war work on young mothers or mothers-to-be. While the war created a new need for women's industrial labor, it also underscored the demographic consequences of France's low birthrate, especially vis-à-vis Germany. Public authorities feared heavy labor in war plants would harm the health of French mothers, who would thus produce weak sons unfit to serve as the soldiers of tomorrow. Should Frenchwomen engage in the battle of production at the cost of losing the battle of reproduction?[62]

---

[60] On this point see in particular Laura Lee Downs, *Manufacturing Inequality: Gender Division in the French and British Metalworking Industries, 1914–1939* (Ithaca NY: Cornell University Press, 1995).

[61] Cited in Delatour, "Le travail des femmes," 482.

[62] Martin Fine, "Albert Thomas: a reformer's vision of modernization, 1914–1932," *Journal of Contemporary History*, 12 (1977); Annie Fourcaut, *Femmes à l'usine en France dans l'entre deux guerres* (Paris: Maspero, 1982). On the problems of natality see Roberts, *Civilization without Sexes*; William Schneider, *Quality and Quantity: The Quest for Biological Regeneration in Twentieth Century France* (New York: Cambridge University Press, 1990). See also Joshua Cole, *The Power of Large Numbers:*

Male workers and union leaders shared this concern, but they also had their own, more specific anxieties about the expansion of women's paid labor during World War I. The French union movement before 1914 had a long history of opposing the use of women in industrial labor. During the war unions and most male workers accepted the national need for women to work in the war plants, but still expressed many misgivings. One was the fear that working women would be used to free men to be drafted and sent to the front lines. They also feared that employers would use women to lower wages for all workers, and to promote Taylorist means of workplace organization that would devalue the talents of skilled workers and weaken workplace control. Some union leaders believed that since women had lower rates of union membership than men, employers would use women workers to weaken the union movement.[63]

These concerns about the use of women in wartime industry parallel to a large extent those expressed about foreign workers. Public authorities did take concrete steps to address some of them. In 1916 they founded a Comité du Travail Féminin to watch over the conditions of women factory workers, and the following year introduced women superintendents into the war plants to protect their moral and physical well-being.[64] French unions also devoted efforts to organizing women workers, especially after they began to go on strike in large numbers in both the clothing industry and war plants after 1917. Motivating both sets of action was the belief that women would continue to work in large numbers in heavy industry after the end of the war, so that France would have to adapt to this new social reality. However, misgivings about this kind of women's work did not simply go away, but reappeared with greater force after the Armistice.

As noted above, fear of a postwar recession and the need to find jobs for demobilized soldiers dominated considerations of French economic planning and labor recruitment immediately after the war. However, the move to dismiss women workers from postwar industry had cultural as well as economic roots. As Laura Downs has demonstrated in her work on British

---

Population, Politics, and Gender in Nineteenth Century France (Ithaca NY: Cornell University Press, 2000). As Elisa Camiscioli has noted, the issue of reproduction also had a racial dimension. During and especially after the war French policymakers and pro-natalists worried not just about the quantity but also the quality of the national population, and in trying to increase the number of French people distinguished between "good" and "bad" immigrants, a distinction that was often racialized. Elisa Camiscioli, *Reproducing the French Race: Immigration, Intimacy, and Embodiment in the Early Twentieth Century* (Durham NC: Duke University Press, 2009).

[63] Jean-Louis Robert, "La CGT et la famille ouvrière, 1914–1918," *Mouvement Social*, 116 (July–Sept., 1981); Downs, "Women's strikes." As with concerns about the use of colonial labor, these fears certainly had legitimacy, as the lower wages paid to women in war plants made clear.

[64] Delatour, "Le travail des femmes," 491.

and French women in the metals industry, pro-natalist and Taylorist ideas
battled to define the role of working women once the war ended. For those
concerned above all with increasing France's lackluster birthrate the issue
was simple: "what is woman's highest duty . . . the sacred task which the
Nation expects from her? To bear children, bear them again, to always bear
children!"[65] While not disagreeing with this position, many employers felt
that a modernized, mechanized factory plus the new social services provided
for female workers during the war could both protect motherhood and
assure the postwar labor supply so crucial to reconstruction.

The combination of the economic stresses of the transition from war to
peace and these cultural concerns about the role of women in industry and
in the nation shaped the process of women's demobilization after the war.
In 1918 and 1919 the war plants got rid of most of their female labor force.
Two days after the Armistice Louis Loucheur, Minister of Industrial
Reconstruction (formerly Armaments), appealed to women workers to
leave their jobs in state-owned war plants voluntarily and return home; he
also announced that those who did so before December 5 would receive a
severance bonus of thirty days' pay. Since few women initially took
advantage of this offer, in late November Loucheur issued a new policy
reassigning women employed in state munitions plants to part-time labor at
reduced wages, 6–9 francs per day. By the end of December over two-thirds
of the female labor force in this sector had quit.[66]

Demobilization took place much more suddenly and brutally in privately
owned war plants. In contrast to the government, which anticipated economic problems after the Armistice and took preventative steps to deal with
them, most private employers waited until December, when postwar
uncertainties, the cancellation of wartime contracts, transportation difficulties, and shortages of raw materials had disrupted the economy, to lay off
masses of women workers. By February 1919, for example, the Citroen
factory in Paris had discharged all its female workforce of close to 6,000,
firing some and persuading others to take severance bonuses and leave. In
spite of urgings by public authorities, most industrialists did not provide
severance pay for these women, in many cases simply dumping them on the
street in the weeks before Christmas. By the spring of 1919 over half the
women who worked in the war plants of the Paris area had lost their jobs; an

---

[65] Cited in Downs, "Women's strikes," 207.
[66] *Ibid.*, 271–275; Loucheur, "Circulaire aux ouvrières des usines et établissements de l'État travaillant
pour la défense nationale," AN F7 13356, November 13, 1918; Léon Abensour, "Le problème de la
démobilisation féminine," *La Grande Revue* (January, 1919).

April survey by the Metalworkers' Federation estimated that half a million women had left the industry in France.[67]

Like colonial workers, some *munitionnettes* probably welcomed the chance to leave dirty, difficult, and dangerous jobs to return to more traditional employment or to life at home; those who argued that such work, even at high wages, was hardly liberating certainly had a point.[68] The emphasis on getting rid of women rested on the belief that they could always return to the *foyer* and let themselves be taken care of by their husbands or fathers. Unfortunately, this rosy image of working women returning to a warm family haven simply did not correspond to the realities of life after the Armistice for many. Thanks to the war, many husbands and fathers would not be coming home at all, so their widows and daughters would have to fend for themselves. Moreover, the demobilization of women war workers took place much more rapidly than the demobilization of male soldiers. Therefore, even those women who could count on an eventual return to the role of housewife found themselves out of work, during the coldest months of the year, well before they could count on their husbands' wages. In addition, some women undoubtedly enjoyed earning a decent salary and wished to continue doing so. Also like colonial workers, women could not vote and thus had little influence on the formation of state policy. One must therefore regard the demobilization of women factory workers in 1918 and 1919 as patronizing at best, punitive at worst.

The protests made by the *munitionnettes* underscore their widespread opposition and resistance to demobilization. The files of the Paris police from December 1918 through March 1919 are full of reports on mass meetings held by women to protest the government's lack of action on their behalf. A large rally held in the capital's Bourse du Travail on January 9, 1919 attracted some 2,000 participants (mostly women), according to police, while another that took place two weeks later, on the 25th, rallied 6,000.[69] At the Bourse du Travail meeting, which was presided over by Madame Geoffroy of the Military Clothing Workers' Union, several speakers described the plight of women workers thrown out of work and denounced the failure of public authorities to address their concerns. The feminist and antiwar activist Hélène Brion took the podium to attack the double oppression of women workers by both their employers and their husbands:

---

[67] McMillan, *Housewife or Harlot*, 159.
[68] J. Servière, "La peine des femmes," *L'Information ouvrière et sociale* (May 5, 1918).
[69] AN F7 13367, police reports of January 9 and January 25, 1919.

The woman who is obliged to work in the factory . . . is in addition forced to do housework; she has to wash and iron the linen. We are now in an impasse from which we can only escape with difficulty. It could happen that very soon women, tortured by hunger, will become revolutionaries.

A woman in the audience at another meeting condemned the government for sending troops to intervene in the Russian civil war: "They are going to spend billions . . . but for those of us here who are asking for work they don't want to give us a piece of bread to eat."[70]

The attitude of the unions and of male workers in general toward the demobilization of women at the end of the war is complex. In general, the unions sympathized with the plight of the dismissed women workers and attempted to mobilize their members to support their demands for higher indemnities. They helped organize and sponsor many of the mass meetings held to protest the situation, for example. The Metal Workers' Union of the Department of the Seine was particularly active on this issue; Loze, Gabriel Pericat, and other leaders often played a prominent role in such meetings.[71] The labor press also dealt with the problems of laid-off women; on January 16, 1919 *France Libre* ran an article noting that "In Paris, in the suburbs, all over France an intense period of unemployment has broken out. Thousands of women have been deprived of their wages. They are thrown into the street without even being given a reasonable indemnity."[72] This concern with women's issues even altered the language of protest; most of the protest rallies were advertised with titles like "Meeting des Chomeurs et Chomeuses des Usines de Guerre." This explicit attention to the gendered nature of class oppression, extremely rare at the time in the language of working-class activism, symbolized the attention of the unions to women's concerns.[73]

Yet the unions' opposition to the demobilization of the *munitionnettes* did not go as far as it might have done. Most importantly, labor leaders did not actually call for the reinstatement of women who had lost their jobs, in either public or private industry. While condemning government policy in general on this issue and in particular demanding a higher level of severance pay for dismissed women, they generally stopped well short of insisting on

---

[70] AN F7 13367, police report of January 16, 1919.

[71] In fact, most of the speakers at these meetings were male union representatives, even though most of the audience was female. This conformity to the stereotypical dichotomy between activist men and passive women underscored both the weakness of union attempts to organize women workers and their complex views of the role of gender in working-class life.

[72] *France Libre*, "Le chomage à Paris," January 16, 1919, in AN F7 13367.

[73] Note it also represents the limits of this concern – men were still listed first in the titles of these articles, even though this was a woman's issue and most of the people who came to these meetings were women.

their right to work, or commenting on the inequality of treatment of men and women. An extensive police report on women's unemployment in the Department of the Seine at the beginning of January 1919 commented on this reluctance:

As far as the layoffs of women in particular are concerned, the majority of them [union leaders] only devote relative and perfunctory attention to the problem. The elimination of the feminine element, largely resistant to union organizing, even offers an advantage from their point of view, that of limiting the competition faced by male workers. However, they can't appear to accept the dismissal without compensation of their old comrades and they would wish to see them given, at least provisionally, an unemployment indemnity of three francs per day. The women would thus have the minimum of resources necessary to await the return of their mobilized husbands, or to devote themselves to other professions.[74]

The conclusions of this particular report are confirmed by the statements of most union representatives. While they expressed deep sympathy with the plight of women workers and anger at their employers, ultimately their speeches and their actions did not contradict a belief that Frenchwomen did not belong in heavy industry.[75]

This attitude seems characteristic of working-class Frenchmen as a group at the end of the war. In his study of Parisian workers Jean-Louis Robert has concluded that most union leaders expressed more progressive, pro-female opinions on this issue than did their rank and file constituents.[76] Many male workers had disapproved of the new role war had given to women in the labor force, and felt that since the war was over it was time for women to return to their homes. The fear of unemployment resulting from the transition from war to peace, especially the return to civilian life of French soldiers, was of course a prime concern. Yet, as with French working-class views of colonial labor, one also finds traces of moral and sexual reprobation. Some male workers complained about the supposed tendency of *munitionnettes* to flaunt their charms in the street, thus besmirching the moral standing of the working class as a whole.[77] At one meeting in Paris called to protest the layoffs of women factory workers, a soldier rose to attack the behavior of these women, citing wartime rumors in

---

[74] "Au sujet de chomage dans la region parisienne," AN F7 13367, report of January 4, 1919.
[75] Many of the speeches at these meetings focused on the inadequate nature of the unemployment indemnities. For example, those assembled at the meeting of January 9 voted a resolution demanding payments of 250 francs to all fired workers, plus 3 francs per day (with 1.50 francs additional for every child).
[76] Robert, *Les ouvriers, la patrie et la révolution*, 489.   [77] APP BA 1386, police report of June 8, 1919.

the trenches to the effect that "women working in the factories cheated on their husbands with the male workers of these factories."[78]

While organized labor and male workers did not actively applaud the demobilization of women war workers as they had the expulsion of non-European labor, neither did they effectively oppose this process. Given this absence of effective opposition, women quickly lost much of the position in heavy industry they had gained from 1914 to 1918. By the end of December 1918, half of the *munitionnettes* in the Department of the Seine had lost their jobs (in contrast to 12 percent of male munitions workers). State munitions factories actually banned the hiring of women, whereas private concerns gave priority to demobilized soldiers.[79] The postwar exclusion of women from heavy industry took place in a larger context of shifting views about women as a whole. One of the fruits of peace, indeed of victory, was to be the ability of the soldier who had fought so hard for France to be able to return to a nurturing, loving household created by the woman of his dreams. Consequently, the demobilization of *munitionnettes* was the concrete representation of a much larger symbolic return of all women to the *foyer*.[80] Two music hall artists, Joullot and Lemarchand, portrayed this climate with hilarious accuracy in a skit entitled "The Demobilization of the Typists":

My young women, I have something very important to tell you ... My young women ... we have now been working together for four years ... what we did ... was not that important, but we did it well ... I have just received an order from the Personnel Office to demobilize you ... you will return to your families. You will found your own households, and when later in life you are snuggling up to your husband, remember your Secretary's motto: don't work too hard on his instrument [*ne tapez pas trop fort sur sa machine*].[81]

During the period from December 1918 to the end of 1919 different sectors of French society, including working people themselves, redefined the French working class. This process of redefinition operated principally by the exclusion of two groups of workers, nonwhites from the French colonies and China, and women in heavy industry. The situation of the two groups

---

[78] AN F7 13367, police report of January 16, 1919. Such anxieties about the wartime fidelity of French women were common. See Louis Barthas, *Les Cahiers de guerre de Louis Barthas, tonnelier, 1914–1919* (Paris: Maspero, 1978); Stéphane Audoin-Rouzeau, *Men at War, 1914–1918: National Sentiment and Trench Journalism in France during the First World War* (Providence RI: Berg, 1992, translated by Helen McPhail).

[79] Robert, *Les ouvriers, la patrie et la révolution*, 459.   [80] McMillan, *Housewife or Harlot*, 157–162.

[81] "Revue d'Excelsior," by Joullot and Lemarchand, June 18, 1919, APP, BA 861.

was by no means parallel.[82] Women workers were excluded from certain sectors of heavy industry, but not from France as a whole. While their role within the French working class shifted, in some cases dramatically, they still remained a vital part of that class. Moreover, the exclusion of women from heavy industry was largely temporary. By the end of 1919 factory owners were beginning to rehire women, as the economy recovered from the uncertainties of the transition to peace and generated a need for more labor. In 1921 the census indicated that women constituted over 10 percent of the workforce in the metals industry (14 percent in the Department of the Seine).[83] This was twice the percentage of women in that industry in 1914, and indicated that while French women had not completely regained their wartime position, still they retained a significant presence in the factory.[84]

In contrast, colonial workers left metropolitan France altogether. Algerians constituted the one significant exception to this situation, and their extremely high turnover rates plus their position at the very bottom of the nation's occupational hierarchy confirmed the racialized character of French labor during the interwar years. Yet even here one can see certain parallels. If one rejects, as do many students of French colonialism, the division between France and her empire as artificial in favor of a unitary conceptualization of imperial France, then as with women workers the expulsions of 1919 represented a reassignment of colonial labor, not its permanent exclusion.[85] In particular, the repatriations from the metropole occurred at the same time as a new emphasis on the use of native labor in the colonies. In 1922 colonial minister Albert Sarraut published *La mise en valeur des colonies françaises*, and the projects inspired by this new policy, such as the construction of the Brazzaville–Atlantic railway in French Equatorial Africa, depended heavily upon the exploitation of native

---

[82] At times, for example, advocates of working women attacked the use of foreign labor. In January 1919 a group of women workers in the Loiret requested the expulsion of Chinese labor from national war plants to prevent the firing of French nationals. AN F7 13356, report of January 16, 1919. By way of contrast, during the war the journalist Pierre Hamp recommended the hiring of Chinese workers as a way of forestalling the use of French women in heavy industry. Pierre Hamp, *La France, pays ouvrier* (Paris: Nouvelle revue française, 1916).

[83] Downs, *Manufacturing Inequality*, 205.

[84] To place these figures in context, women in the Department of the Seine composed 7 percent of the labor force of the metals industry in 1906, and 30 percent in 1918. While the demobilization of 1918–1919 did serve to "correct" the unusual wartime levels of women's participation in this industry, it did not alter the more long-term trend toward the increased presence of Parisian women workers in heavy industry. Robert, *Les ouvriers, la patrie et la révolution*, 459–460.

[85] See on this point Gary Wilder, *The French Imperial Nation-State: Negritude and Colonial Humanism between the Wars* (University of Chicago Press, 2005).

workers. The repatriation of colonial workers from the metropole thus went hand in hand with a new emphasis on labor in the empire itself.[86]

This parallel underscores the observation that the creation of working-class identity in the year after the Armistice involved reformulating the relationship of both groups to that class as a whole. The war had brought these groups into greater prominence within the French working class, and during late 1918 and 1919 there was a concerted attempt by industry and government, with the participation and approval of much of organized labor, to restore the prewar situation. However, one cannot stuff the genie back into the bottle once it has escaped, and this attempt was only partially successful. The goal was to create (or recreate) a working class whose prototype was a white male employed in a factory, married to a housewife and producing many (preferably male) offspring. Yet women's participation in heavy industry and other sectors of the paid labor force remained much higher than prewar levels, and French natality continued to decline. While the 1920s did not represent the triumph of the working woman, neither did they make her disappear.[87] Similarly, the attempt to reassign native labor back to the colonies not only produced new levels of working-class formation there, but also helped create a new consciousness about race and racial difference in the metropole as well.

The fact that the attempt to exclude women and colonial workers as paid labor from the French working class ultimately failed does not lessen the importance of the effort to do so. Whatever the end result, the process itself is central to any discussion of working-class identity and the working-class experience in France at the end of World War I. It underlines the unstable, transitional character of that identity, demonstrating that the working class was no fixed entity but one whose character and very existence resulted from processes of social construction and definition. In particular, this process provides a glimpse into the ways elite images of the working class interacted with workers' self-perceptions to bring about new realities. 1919 established the margins, and thus the center, of working-class identity through a dynamic process of exclusion, whose very dynamism made it all the more transparent. The next chapter will consider the ways in which working-class

---

[86] Tyler Stovall, "National identity and shifting imperial frontiers: whiteness and the exclusion of colonial labor after World War I," *Representations*, 84/1 (2003).

[87] On the new woman of the 1920s see Roberts, *Civilization without Sexes*; Whitney Chadwick and Tirza True Latimer, eds., *The Modern Woman Revisited: Paris between the Wars* (New Brunswick NJ: Rutgers University Press, 2003); Shari Benstock, *Women of the Left Bank, 1900–1940* (Austin: University of Texas Press, 1986).

politics and workers' own conceptions of class identities imprinted themselves on public space in the French capital. It will show how working-class discontent in Paris interacted with international negotiations and conflicts to produce a radical political upsurge in which local and global concerns reinforced each other.

CHAPTER 4

Spectacular politics

I was attracted, drawn in by the power that flowed from this indignant crowd, from this grumbling tempest. Mixed in with this mass of
people I felt as if seized by a state of grace, as if my body, my legs
moved to the slow rhythm of this vast chain, beyond my own
control.

And I believed that my humble strength, added to that of the others
constituted a power such that Power (by which we meant the cops, the
judges, all officials) would have to reckon with ... I took my place
behind the red flags of the leather workers federation and those of the
shoe workers union. Shoulder to shoulder, we went down the street,
men and women, my brothers, my sisters, singing at the top of our
lungs, in a state of wonder, my heart overflowing with love. Masters of
the streets, we marched along peacefully.[1]

So did René Michaud describe his experience of the protest march held by
Parisian labor against the acquittal of Raoul Vilain, assassin of the great
Socialist leader Jean Jaurès, in April 1919. In his narrative the personal and
the political, the individual and the collective, intertwine, the young activist
feeling himself swept away by the passion he shared with his comrades.
From this perspective, not only power but one's own very sense of identity
lay in the streets.

One of the most popular motifs for describing modern Paris has been
that of spectacle. A number of commentators, most notably Walter
Benjamin, have pointed out the various ways in which the capital's urban
culture appealed to, seduced, or assaulted the senses. Whether it be the
opulent display of the city's department stores, the careful placing of monu-
ments and boulevards, or the ornate public displays and demonstrations
that celebrated and shaped the exercise of power, Parisian life in the modern
era has seemed to center around the spectacular. In particular, the rise of

[1] Michaud, *J'avais vingt ans*, 104–105.

mass consumer culture in the modern period seemed to highlight this sense of urbanity, so that the city as a whole became a commodity to be consumed. The idea of the *flâneur*, for example, exemplified the power of elite males (for the most part) to enjoy Paris and make it their own.[2]

In recent years a number of historians have turned to an analysis of the politics of spectacle. For Roger Shattuck, the modern era in Paris began with the mass public funeral of Victor Hugo in 1885, when 2 million Parisians accompanied the great writer on his last journey across Paris to the Pantheon. In her study of Parisian mass culture in the fin-de-siècle, Vanessa Schwartz argues that the specter of the revolutionary crowd in the nineteenth century gave way to a crowd conceived of as the consumers of the spectacles of mass culture. More recently, James R. Lehning has suggested that the literary trope of melodrama is key to modern political culture in France.[3]

This chapter addresses the nature of political spectacle and its relationship to working-class radicalism and identity in Paris after the Armistice. In it I argue that politics and political life were transformed rather than sidelined by the rise of spectacle, and that in 1919 working-class politics assumed a spectacular quality, emphasizing public contests over urban space. In this study I use the term spectacle to convey a sense of public presentation geared to a mass audience. In particular, I am interested in those spectacles that used urban space to appeal to the emotions as well as the intellect. In this reading, spectacular politics combines ideology and drama in pursuit of its goals. Both bourgeois representations of working-class life and workers' own sense of identity reflected and responded to the descent of politics into the streets of the capital.

[2] The classic statement of Paris as spectacle is Walter Benjamin, "Paris, capital of the nineteenth century" (1935), in Uwe Steiner, ed., *Walter Benjamin: An Introduction to His Work and Thought* (University of Chicago Press, 2010); see also Charles Rearick, *Pleasures of the Belle Epoque* (New Haven: Yale University Press, 1985). On the *flâneur* see Aruna D'Souza and Tom McDonough, eds., *The Invisible Flâneuse? Gender, Public Space and Visual Culture in Nineteenth Century Paris* (Manchester University Press, 2006); Deborah Parsons, *Streetwalking the Metropolis: Women, the City and Modernity* (New York: Oxford University Press, 2000); Keith Tester, ed., *The Flaneur* (London and New York: Routledge, 1994).

[3] Perhaps the most influential theoretical discussion of the politics of spectacle is Guy Debord, *The Society of the Spectacle* (Detroit: Black and Red Press, 1983). See also Mona Ozouf, *Festivals and the French Revolution*, translated by Alan Sheridan (Cambridge MA: Harvard University Press, 1988); Roger Shattuck, *The Banquet Years: The Origins of the Avant-Garde in France, 1885 to World War I* (New York: Vintage, 1968); Vanessa R. Schwartz, *Spectacular Realities: Early Mass Culture in Fin-de-siècle Paris* (Berkeley: University of California Press, 1999); James R. Lehning, *The Melodramatic Thread: Spectacle and Political Culture in Modern France* (Bloomington: Indiana University Press, 2007).

Spectacular politics was very much shaped by the city's global role in 1919. As the site of the peace negotiations for the treaty to end the war, Paris seemed literally a stage upon which all the passions of the world were enacted. Never before or since in the city's history has it been so central to global affairs. The title of Margaret MacMillan's history of the peace negotiations, *Paris 1919: Six Months that Changed the World*, sums up the city's importance nicely.[4] The experience of Parisian workers lay at a vast remove from that of the diplomats gathered in their city to remake the world. Yet these different spheres of high and low politics, local concerns and global visions, intersected in a variety of ways, underscoring the dualities that had so characterized Parisian life during the war itself. Paris in 1919 was a city whose inhabitants by and large were both witness to and excluded from the councils of the powerful. The spectacular nature of working-class politics thus paralleled and complemented the dramas surrounding the peace negotiations. Ideas of class war and world peace coexisted uneasily in a city struggling to define the postwar era.

PARIS, CAPITAL OF THE WORLD

Of all the dualities that shaped life in 1919, certainly the most important was that of war and peace. The transition from one to the other was the central fact of life in Paris during 1919, just as war had been for the four and a half previous years.[5] But exactly when did the war end? Both for the historian looking back and for people at the time the question was not as simple as it might first appear. The Armistice ended the fighting on November 11, 1918, but as soon became clear during the course of the tortuous negotiations that finally produced the Treaty of Versailles, this did not equal a definitive peace. As far as the popular press of the capital was concerned, the Allies were willing, ready, and able to resume hostilities immediately if Germany's peace delegation did not stop its obstreperous delaying tactics and sign the treaty.[6] The treaty was signed on June 28, 1919, but even that did not make peace an established fact, since national legislatures still had to ratify it. In

---

[4] Margaret MacMillan, *Paris 1919: Six Months that Changed the World* (New York: Random House, 2002).

[5] Charles Maier, *Recasting Bourgeois Europe: Stabilization in France, Germany and Italy in the Decade of World War I* (Princeton University Press, 1975); Joshua Cole, "The transition to peace, 1918–1919," in Jay Winter and Jean-Louis Robert, eds., *Capital Cities at War: Paris, London, Berlin, 1914–1919* (Cambridge University Press, 1997).

[6] *Le Figaro*, April 22, 1919, 1; June 6, 1919, 2.

fact, in one sense World War I did not finally end until Turkey signed the Treaty of Sèvres in August 1920.[7]

The year 1919 thus represented neither wartime nor peacetime, but a confusing, unstable mixture of both. Certainly the killing had stopped, masses of young men no longer traveled through Paris on their way to the front, and Parisians no longer fearfully watched the skies in anticipation of bombardment as they had a year earlier. Yet many young Parisians remained at the front lines, and for much of the year foreign soldiers still crowded the streets of the French capital.[8] Moreover, World War I had not been just an affair for generals and soldiers, but had entailed the radical restructuring of much of French life. Therefore, the transition from war to peace involved much more than simply signing a treaty. Whole areas of Parisian existence, including industrial production, food pricing, housing, entertainment, political life, and cultural policies, had to be carefully rethought.[9] Remembering her wartime childhood in Montmartre, Mrs. Robert Henrey commented on the concrete impact of the end of hostilities in November 1918:

The armistice did not make any immediate difference to our lives. Women waited anxiously for the return of their husbands. Jules Alexis, who had burnt himself so cruelly so as not to be sent back to the front, was drafted to Russia. Little Louis was packed off to occupy the Rhineland. Both were safe, but they were being deprived of liberty.[10]

The transitional character of 1919 opened spaces for conflict and contestation in many areas of daily life, so that the unstable duality of war and peace became fertile ground for struggles that pitted one class against another.

Another key duality was one that has shaped Paris throughout the modern period. For centuries Paris has enjoyed a rich and very localized culture. Yet at the same time Paris is the capital of France, a city where the most important people are often those who have only the most abstract ties to most local residents, a city where the business of the nation is, precisely, local life, and as such takes precedence over the concerns of the *quartier*.

---

[7] The historical literature on the peace settlements that ended World War I is voluminous. Some useful general references include MacMillan, *Paris 1919*; William Keylor, ed., *The Legacy of the Great War: Peacemaking, 1919* (Boston MA: Houghton Mifflin, 1998); Arno Mayer, *Politics and Diplomacy of Peacemaking* (New York: Knopf, 1967).

[8] William Klingaman, *1919* (New York: St. Martin's Press, 1987), 71–73, 184; Charles Seymour, *Letters from the Paris Peace Conference* (New Haven CT: Yale University Press, 1965).

[9] Henri Sellier, A. Bruggeman, and Marcel Poëte, *Paris pendant la guerre* (Paris: Presses Universitaires de France, 1926); Richard Kuisel, *Capitalism and the State in Modern France* (Cambridge University Press, 1981); Tom Kemp, *The French Economy, 1913–1939* (London: Longman, 1972).

[10] Mrs. Robert Henrey, *The Little Madeleine* (New York: E. P. Dutton, 1953), 205.

This contradiction was never more intense than in 1919, when the various peace negotiations made Paris the capital not just of France but in effect of the entire world. From shortly after the Armistice until the end of the summer of 1919 the city was packed with presidents, kings, diplomats, reporters, and various other official and unofficial onlookers from every corner of the globe.[11]

Like the contrast between war and peace, that dividing Paris as world city from Paris as local community was unstable, giving rise to conflicts and affinities at both concrete and symbolic levels. For the world leaders who came to Paris in 1919, especially those from France's allies, did not fail to take the average Parisian into account. The reopening of music halls, cabarets, and nightlife in general after the Armistice represented the rebirth of *la gaieté parisienne*, thanks to the valiant efforts of the Allied soldiers. In 1919, therefore, the entertainments of Paris represented one of the fruits of victory; as a character noted repeatedly in John Dos Passos' novel *1919*, "Fellers, this ain't a war, it's a goddam whorehouse!"[12]

Ordinary Parisians also played an important role in forming the cheering crowds that welcomed the Allied leaders come to the French capital to negotiate the peace treaties. The model for this was set in December 1918, on the occasion of Woodrow Wilson's arrival in Paris. Symbolizing both victory and peace, the American president enjoyed immense popular appeal in France and throughout Europe, but Georges Clemenceau and many other conservative French leaders viewed his idealism with skepticism.[13] Accordingly his arrival in the French capital was a carefully planned and orchestrated performance, in which the masses of Parisian spectators played the role of a laudatory Greek chorus. The Socialists and the *Confédération Générale du Travail* (CGT) organized a large demonstration on December 14, both to welcome Wilson to Paris and to criticize by extension France's own leadership.

I could look all the way up toward the Arc de Triomphe, the broad avenue all clear, but the spaces on each side, the benches, the trees, the roofs all black with

---

[11] The memoirs of foreign leaders, diplomats, and journalists attending the peace conference provide important observations of Parisian life in 1919. See for example David Lloyd George, *Memoirs of the Peace Conference* (New Haven: Yale University Press, 1939); Edward House, *What Really Happened at Paris: The Story of the Peace Conference, 1918–1919* (New York: C. Scribner's Sons, 1921); Charles Seymour, *Letters from the Paris Peace Conference* (New Haven: Yale University Press, 1965).

[12] John Dos Passos, *1919* (New York: Harcourt, Brace, and Co., 1932); on the experiences of John Dos Passos in Paris during 1919, see Dos Passos, *Mr. Wilson's War* (Garden City NY: Doubleday, 1962).

[13] Mayer, *Politics and Diplomacy*, 167–193; A. Walworth, *Wilson and His Peacemakers: American Diplomacy at the Paris Peace Conference* (New York: Norton, 1986); Arthur Link, *Woodrow Wilson: War, Revolution, and Peace* (Arlington Heights IL: Harlan Davidson, 1979).

people ... From the talk all about me I felt that the People were genuinely and honestly sympathetic ... There were many working men and women in the crowd all about and many children ... Wilson with President Poincaré was in the first carriage ... He was loudly cheered. Mrs. Wilson's carriage was ... smothered in flowers ... I am told that the reception was in every way larger and more enthusiastic than that accorded to any of the kings or generals who have been here ... However, there was not just an abandon of joy. Certainly the labor leaders must have put their millions on the streets ... There has been no organized demonstration, but an enormous number of workmen and socialists were on the streets.[14]

Wilson's entry into Paris assumed symbolic importance not just for the "high" world of international politics, but also for the "low" world of Parisian popular culture. At a time when American films (often including newsreels) were beginning to enjoy major popularity among the working-class population of the city, Wilson's reception bore all the trappings of the frenzied greeting accorded a Hollywood movie star. In Paris and throughout Europe, the titled nobility of the Old World would soon bow down their heads before the celluloid kings and queens of the New.[15]

Foreign views of popular Paris after the Armistice were not always so encouraging, or so controlled. Most diplomats and other officials had few contacts with ordinary Parisians during their work on the peace negotiations, and the images they formed of this aspect of the life of the capital usually emphasized its distance and strange character. John Dos Passos' novel, *Three Soldiers*, gives a vivid portrayal of this sense of otherness, representing working-class Paris as another world. John Andrews, one of the major characters in the novel, deserts from the American Army at the end of the war. After escaping the military police by taking a highly symbolic swim in the Seine, Andrews finds refuge with a Parisian family. As a deserter, Andrews is a transitional figure, caught between the official American presence in Paris he has rejected, and the world of average Parisians to which he can never belong. Even his socialist sympathies will not suffice to bridge the gap.

---

[14] Ray Stannard Baker, December 14, 1918, quoted in Mayer, *Politics and Diplomacy*, 176–177. The organized demonstration originally planned by Parisian labor for Wilson was cancelled in response to the hostility of the French government.

[15] On the history of film in France see Marc Ferro, *Cinema et histoire* (Paris: Denoel, 1977); Richard Abel, *French Cinema: The First Wave, 1915–1929* (Princeton University Press, 1984); on the cinema and working-class Parisians, see the various works of Jacques Valdour, especially *Ouvriers parisiens d'après-guerre* (Paris: Arthur Rousseau, 1921), and *Ateliers et taudis de la banlieue de Paris* (Paris: Éditions Spes, 1923); W. Scott Haine, "The development of leisure and the transformation of working-class adolescence, Paris 1830–1940," *Journal of Family History*, 17/4 (1992).

When Andrews walked by the M.P. at the Gare St. Lazare, his hands were cold with fear. The M.P. did not look at him. He stopped on the crowded pavement a little way from the station and stared into a mirror in a shop window. Unshaven, with a check cap on the side of his head and his corduroy trousers, he looked like a young workman who had been out of work for a month.

"Gee, clothes do make a difference," he said to himself . . . On a side street the fumes of coffee roasting attracted him into a small bar. Several men were arguing boisterously at the end of the bar. One of them turned a ruddy, tow-whiskered face to Andrews, and said:

"Et toi, tu vas chomer le premier mai?" ["And you, will you strike on May Day?"]

"I'm on strike already," answered Andrews laughing.

The man noticed his accent, looked at him sharply a second, and turned back to the conversation, lowering his voice as he did so. Andrews drank down his coffee and left the bar, his heart pounding.[16]

This passage neatly sums up the ultimately hopeless position of John Andrews, deserter. He has succeeded in escaping from his former world, but the new one he embraces will not accept him. Every aspect of his brief interchange with the French worker bespeaks the difference between them, not just the fact that they literally speak different languages, but also their contrasting views of politics and even the different tones of their voices, the Frenchman serious, Andrews mocking. Clothes do not make such a difference after all. *Three Soldiers* ends with Andrews giving himself up to the American military police, despairing of the possibility of creating a more just, humane world.[17]

If a rebel soldier like John Andrews could not bridge the gap between the international elite and the Paris working class, most representatives of the former had no interest in doing so. For most of the foreign officials, Paris in 1919 was a whirl of limousines and fancy hotels, long meetings in sumptuous surroundings, celebratory dinners and dress balls.[18] Strikes did attract some attention, especially the brief work stoppage staged by the city's waiters in mid-July.[19] But such events merely confirmed the alien, incomprehensible nature of popular Paris for the diplomats, reporters, and politicians.[20] The

---

[16] John Dos Passos *Three Soldiers* (Boston: Houghton Mifflin, 1921), 388–389.

[17] American deserters in fact seem to have been plentiful in Paris after the war. Louis Chevalier, *Montmartre du plaisir et du crime* (Paris: R. Laffont, 1980), 377.

[18] As William Klingaman notes, "Food prices were high, of course, which wrought a severe hardship on the working population of Paris, but the Americans always seemed to have enough cash to get by handsomely," *1919*, 72.

[19] *Le Petit Parisien*, July 12, 1919, 1; *ibid.*, July 13, 1919, 2.

[20] *Le Figaro* noted the bemusement of Americans watching the May Day demonstrators in the rue Royale from their balconies in the Hotel Crillon. *Le Figaro*, May 2, 1919, 1.

description of the May Day riots recorded by Yale University historian (and future president) Charles Seymour summed up this opposition nicely:

I shall never forget the sight of that black crowd coming down the street waving its red flags at the moment it ran into the troops. It might have been Petrograd, or the Revolution of 1848, which started close to here and in very much the same manner. They say there are various fights in other parts of Paris. Gladys came over to see the later part of the fuss, the passageway from the Crillon to the office running behind bars and the gates being closed.

Tonight we are having dinner with the two Polish delegates – Paderewski and Dmowski – with flowers, cigars, and wines, inasmuch as it is a "state dinner."[21]

They considered the distance between these two worlds enormous, when they noticed it at all; their concerns were Belgium and the Polish corridor, not Belleville and Popincourt.

If, on the other hand, one looks at this duality through the eyes of Parisian workers, one at first glance finds a parallel situation. The working people of Paris had their own problems, ones that may have seemed mundane to international diplomats but were deeply felt nonetheless. The application of the eight-hour day, or the price of vegetables in neighborhood markets bore little immediate relevance to questions of German reparations or the status of Trieste. This distance has been replicated by much of the historiography of French labor in the era of World War I. Yet Parisian working people were aware of the peace negotiations going on in their midst, and did form opinions as to their significance. For example, at the beginning of the year some CGT activists called for a labor demonstration in Paris to coincide with the opening of the peace conference, to ensure that the concerns of the working class were addressed.[22] During the June metalworkers' strike a striker at the Citroen auto factory claimed that French industrialists would agree to labor's demands once the Germans signed the peace treaty, since they were so eager to take advantage of the new markets peace would open up.[23] And in January a member of the metalworkers' union linked the high cost of living to the conference:

They tell us . . . that everything is expensive because of the transportation crisis. This is false, there are trains and railway cars sitting idle in the large railway stations. They find plenty of railroad cars to organize trains to bring deputies to Alsace, or bring sovereigns to France.[24]

[21] Seymour, *Letters*, 220–221.
[22] Police report, "Au sujet de chomage dans la région parisienne," AN F7 13367, January 4, 1919.
[23] APP BA 1386, police report of June 23, 1919.
[24] AN F7 13367, "Réunion des chomeurs et chomeuses de la métallurgie," police report of January 5, 1919.

The programs of the Paris music halls, a key institution in Parisian cultural life, provide an interesting perspective on popular views of the peace negotiations and the international elite in 1919. Located primarily near the *grands boulevards* and Montmartre, they were by no means a purely proletarian voice. Much of their audience was middle class or bourgeois, and working people often appeared as figures of fun in their skits and songs.[25] However, in the period after the war they did address working-class concerns at times, especially those like the housing shortage and the high price of food that were also shared by the middle class.[26] Music hall lyricists and scriptwriters frequently poked fun at the numerous foreign officials to be found in Paris during 1919, often comparing them with ordinary Parisians. For example, in January a musical review called "Paris Awakens" contained a song lampooning the impact of the imminent peace negotiations on the housing crisis:

> There are nice diplomats, very small, small
> The over-full hotels will become very small, small
> And for our great friends, the willing government [gouvernement soumis]
> Will have to find other furnished rooms in Paris
> So that, in order to find housing all those who come to Paris
> Will have to, if it's okay, find shelter under the bridges
>
> And the bridges of Paris will become exquisite places
> Under each we'll be able to admire dukes, princes, and even factory owners
> There will be receptions, five o'clocks and bostons,
> And even all-night restaurants.[27]

In another skit, a song parodying Parisian concerns about *la vie chère* claimed that "since the arrival of the Americans chickens [i.e. prostitutes] are outrageously expensive."[28]

The Parisian workers whose opinions addressed most clearly the peace conference and the foreign elite were those on the political Left. The

---

[25] For example, see the script for the musical revue, "C'est tout syndiqué," APP BA 860, June 17, 1919.

[26] On the history of the Paris music hall during this period see Edouard Beaudu *et al.*, *Histoire du music-hall* (Paris: Éditions de Paris, 1954); Jacques Charles, *Cent ans de music-hall* (Paris: Jeheber, 1956); André Sallée and Philippe Chauveau, *Music-Hall et café-concert* (Paris: Bordas, 1985); Andre Warnod, *Les bals de Paris* (Paris: Les Éditions G. Crès, 1922). In particular, see Regina Marie Sweeney, *Singing Our Way to Victory: French Cultural Politics and Music During the Great War* (Middletown CT: Wesleyan University Press, 2001).

[27] "Paris s'éveille," APP BA 860, January 14, 1919.

[28] Song "La vie chère," in the musical revue "La Révue Ce . . . leste," by Paul Cartoux, Jean de Merry, at the Gaité Rochechouart theater, APP BA 860, February 8, 1919.

widespread popularity enjoyed by President Wilson among the popular masses in Paris and throughout Europe in the early part of the year provides one important example of this. Wilson was no Socialist, as labor leaders were well aware in France. Yet his calls for self-determination of all peoples and a peace without annexations or indemnities struck a deep chord in the hearts of many Parisian workers exhausted after over four years of warfare.[29] Wilson's appeal was so strong that even much of the revolutionary French Left supported him, if not all his specific ideas or programs, during the first few months of 1919. What Arno Mayer has called the Wilson cult[30] did not last long, victim of both the radicalization of many Parisian workers and a general disenchantment with the peace process; by March H. Pearl Adam could write that "President Wilson's waning popularity with the mob should not, in his own interests, be submitted to any rude shock just now. The word 'idealist' is rapidly acquiring a half-humorous, half-acid flavour in the general vocabulary."[31] The popular acclaim of Wilson provided a significant glimpse into the ways in which Parisian workers perceived the doings of the international high and mighty in their midst, and how a growing spirit of class conflict among them gradually shifted their attitudes from warm adulation to indifference and hostility.

But the question of Allied intervention in the Russian civil war sparked the most intense working-class attention to the peace conference. Lenin and the Bolsheviks were of course the great outsiders at the Paris peace negotiations, yet the unfolding revolutionary civil war in Russia, not to mention the prospect that it might spread to other parts of Europe, haunted the conferees.[32] Although the impact of the Revolution was greatest in eastern and central Europe, many French workers, especially in Paris, also eagerly supported and followed the struggle of the Bolsheviks to establish full control in Russia and build the world's first socialist state.[33] At a

---

[29] For example, the song "La Wilsonienne" was popular in Paris at the beginning of 1919. AN F7 13367, police report of January 19, 1919.

[30] Mayer, *Politics and Diplomacy*, 167–177.

[31] H. Pearl Adam, *Paris Sees It Through* (London: Hodder and Stoughton, 1919), 297.

[32] Mayer, *Politics and Diplomacy*, 284–343; A. Zaîontchkovsky, *Les Alliés contre la Russie avant, pendant et après la guerre mondiale (faits et documents)* (Paris: A. Delpuech, 1926); J. M. Thompson, *Russia, Bolshevism, and the Versailles Peace* (Princeton University Press, 1966).

[33] On French labor and the Russian Revolution, see Annie Kriegel, *Aux origins du communisme français, 1914–1920; contributions à l'histoire du mouvement ouvrier français* (Paris: Flammarion, 1970); Christian Gras, *Alfred Rosmer et le mouvement révolutionnaire international* (Paris: Maspero, 1971); I. Sinanoglou, "Frenchmen, their Revolutionary heritage and the Russian Revolution," *International History Review*, 2/4 (October, 1980); Claude Willard, "La connaissance de la révolution russe et l'expérience soviétique par le mouvement ouvrier français en 1918–1919," *Cahiers de l'institut Maurice Thorez*, 12–13 (1975).

metalworkers' meeting in January, Gabriel Pericat declared that "they want to overthrow the Soviet Republic in Russia because everyone there lives equally and the bourgeois has to work if he wants to eat."[34] Solidarity with the Russian Revolution became a key theme of workers' meetings in Paris during 1919, especially in reaction to the material and military aid furnished by France and other Allied powers to the counterrevolutionary White armies.[35] Speakers frequently, almost ritualistically, condemned the policies of Clemenceau's government toward the Russian and Hungarian revolutions. At times, however, they broadened their critique to include the leaders of all the Allied governments. Speaking at the beginning of the June metalworkers' strike, Weber of the ditchdiggers' union declared that:

The moment has come to show our solidarity with the proletariat of all nations. Everywhere the working masses protest the domination of capitalism. In Italy, in England, in France these masses must act to hinder by all possible means the Entente governments from continuing their intervention against the workers' revolutions in Russia and Hungary.[36]

The case of Allied intervention in the Russian civil war reinforced the idea among many workers in Paris that the foreign diplomats and officials in the French capital represented an international capitalist plutocracy, and that therefore Parisian labor had the obligation to stand up for the international proletariat. A symbolic coincidence reinforced this linkage of the local and international class struggles: by June 28, the day the peace treaty was signed, the massive Paris metalworkers' strike had clearly run out of steam, its final defeat just a matter of days.[37] Capitalism had triumphed, both in the streets of Paris and in the halls of Versailles, or, to use an analogy from the days of the Commune, once again Versailles had defeated Paris.[38] At a strike meeting held that day in Saint-Denis, one speaker condemned the newly signed peace treaty as a victory of the international capitalist class over the international proletariat, claiming that "as soon as we return to work we will engage in both union and political action to obtain the revision of this wicked peace."[39]

[34] AN F7 13367, "Réunion des chomeurs et chomeuses de la métallurgie," police report of January 5, 1919.
[35] In his study Jean-Louis Robert provides a statistical analysis of references made to the Russian Revolution during working-class meetings in Paris, noting that opposition to Allied intervention in the Russian civil war played a central role in such assemblies. Robert, "Ouvriers et mouvement ouvrier parisiens," 1826–1830, 1871.
[36] APP BA 1386, "Réunion des grevistes de la métallurgie," Paris, police report of June 4, 1919.
[37] The history of this strike, and others during 1919, will be the subject of Chapter 6.
[38] As I shall discuss in greater detail throughout this study, points of comparison between the Paris Commune and working-class life and politics in 1919 are legion.
[39] APP BA 1386, police report of June 28, 1919.

The representatives of Russia's new revolutionary government were not the only people effectively excluded from the peace negotiations in Paris: by whom it chose not to invite, the conference forecast not only the divisions between East and West that would dominate world politics in the twentieth century, but also those between North and South. Many colonial subjects followed the events in Paris closely, in the hope that Woodrow Wilson's pronouncements about bringing democracy and self-determination to the world would include those outside Europe. A variety of individuals and delegations came from European colonies to plead their nations' cases for liberty. Nguyen-Ai-Quoc, the future Ho Chi Minh, who in 1920 took part in the Congress of Tours that created the French Communist Party, was merely the most famous of those.[40] In February blacks from Africa and the Americas assembled in Paris to hold the world's second Pan-African Congress to plead for better treatment for those of African descent in world affairs.[41]

As is well known, the diplomats assembled for the Paris peace conference turned a deaf ear to the demands of the colonized.[42] None bothered to attend the Pan-African Congress, and colonial delegations in general were shut out of the deliberations. Moreover, the delegates rejected Japan's request to include a clause supporting racial equality in the treaty. The British and French colonial empires remained intact, and the conferees gave the colonies of the defeated Axis powers to the Allies as "mandates," colonies in all but name. Just as colonial workers were excluded from French labor in 1919, so were colonial delegations excluded from having a say in the constitution of the new world order. Yet in both cases these exclusions set the tone for developments throughout the twentieth century. If the expulsion of colonial labor foreshadowed the rise of a new postcolonial France, the silence about the colonies at the Paris peace conference anticipated the traumas of decolonization. The flagrant contrast between the victorious powers' destruction of empire within Europe and their reinforcement of it

---

[40] Raymond Betts, *Tricouleur: The French Overseas Empire* (London: Gordon & Cremonesi, 1978), 121–122; Jean Lacouture, *Ho Chi Minh, A Political Biography* (New York: Random House, 1968); Gaspard Thu Trang, *Ho Chi Minh à Paris, 1917–1923* (Paris: L'Harmattan, 1992); Genevieve Barman and Nicole Dulioust, "Les années françaises de Deng Xiaoping (1920–1925)," *Vingtième Siècle*, 20 (1988).

[41] Clarence G. Contee, "DuBois, the NAACP, and the Pan-African Congress of 1919," *Journal of Negro History*, 57/1 (January, 1972), 13–28.

[42] Unfortunately, this deafness has been replicated by the historiography of the Paris peace conference, which has largely ignored colonial questions. For an important recent account, see Erez Manela, *The Wilsonian Moment: Self-Determination and the International Origins of Anticolonial Nationalism* (Oxford University Press, 2007).

overseas did not of course go unnoticed in the colonies: in Egypt, the refusal of the British to allow a delegation to travel to Paris prompted a major uprising, the Wafd rebellion, in March. The same month news of Wilson's 14 points prompted students in Korea to demonstrate against Japanese rule, launching the March 1st rebellion. A month later British attempts to repress nationalist agitation in India exploded in the Amritsar massacre. In China, the calls for a new world order, and the interest of Chinese students in Wilsonianism, helped inspire the May 4th movement. Both in Paris and worldwide, 1919 witnessed attempts to defuse the colonial question that a new world war would bring back to haunt the imperial powers.[43]

The symbolic contrast between the international diplomatic elite and the working people of Paris played a significant role in shaping the subjective identity of the latter during 1919. Hostility and conflict did not always enter into this construction of difference; for many diplomats in Paris the workers of that city represented The People, the anonymous ordinary citizens throughout the world for whom they were working to build a lasting peace. The adulation given by many Parisian workers to Woodrow Wilson was the most important example of popular praise for the peace negotiations. The essential point, however, was that the presence of so many foreign officials in Paris created a new version of the city light years removed from the world of workshop, cheap café, and *hotel garni*. Fictional attempts to bridge this gap, whether by John Andrews in *Three Soldiers* or the songs and skits of the Paris music halls, most clearly demonstrated the futility of trying to do so. This sense of distance and difference, therefore, reinforced for both Parisians and foreigners the conviction that a working-class presence did indeed exist in Paris. The radical Left was able to extrapolate from this a belief that the international class struggle had come to Paris. The year 1919 was a year of sharp class and political conflicts throughout the world, and most of these were represented, at least symbolically, in the French capital thanks to the peace negotiations.[44] The Parisian working class thus drew a sense of its own identity from its position as a symbol for the global contrast between Capital and Labor.

[43] Michael D. Callahan, *A Sacred Trust: The League of Nations and Africa, 1929–1946* (Brighton: Sussex Academic Press, 2004); An Sang-gyo, *The Nature and Spirit of Korea: The March First Independence Movement versus Japanese Colonization* (Seoul: Korean Publishing Co., n.d.); Maurice Deeb, *Party Politics in Egypt: The Wafd and Its Rivals, 1919–1939* (London: Ithaca Press, 1979); Alfred Draper, *Amritsar: The Massacre That Ended the Raj* (London: Cassell, 1981).

[44] For a general overview of the revolutionary nature of world politics in that year, see Klingaman, *1919*; David Mitchell, *1919: Red Mirage* (London: Cape, 1970).

CLASS IDENTITY AND URBAN PUBLIC SPACE

In his classic study *Napoleon III and the Rebuilding of Paris*, David Pinkney argued that one effect of the creation of broad new boulevards in nineteenth-century Paris was to render barricades obsolete, opening up the crowded central neighborhoods of the city not just to light and air but also to cavalry charges and artillery fire. Historians have debated this question ever since, noting for example that Baron Haussmann's urban renovations did not prevent the outbreak of the Paris Commune.[45] What has often gone unnoticed is the fact that, while Haussmann's boulevards may have challenged the efficacy of barricades in Paris, they made the city an excellent site for demonstrations. Haussmann created broad avenues perfect for massing large numbers of people, and surrounded them with buildings tall enough to ensure a critical mass of spectators but not so tall as to dwarf the action in the streets. Moreover, his emphasis on monumentality had the effect of channeling crowds toward major sites of symbolic and political power. As a result, *la manifestation* became a central popular political ritual in twentieth-century Paris. Even the dominance of the automobile in Parisian streets after World War II has not changed this: from the drivers parading in mass during the 1950s sounding their horns to the beat of "*Algérie française*" to the tractors of José Bové and his followers, wheels as well as feet have taken part in this tradition. Whereas barricade fighters sought above all to defend their own turf, demonstrators laid symbolic claim to the city as a whole.

Parades and demonstrations played a key role in shaping Parisian public life during the year after the Armistice. Politics lay in the streets of Paris in 1919, and historians of postwar France and French labor have underscored the significance of workers' demonstrations to the class struggles of the era.[46] However, the workers were not the only Parisians to take to the streets during this period. The year 1919 was also a year of victory marches, when

---

[45] David Pinkney, *Napoleon III and the Rebuilding of Paris* (Princeton University Press, 1958); David Harvey, *Paris, Capital of Modernity* (New York: Routledge, 2003); Alain Corbin, ed., *La barricade* (Paris: Presses Universitaires de la Sorbonne, 1997); Mark Traugott, "Barricades as repertoire: continuities and discontinuities in the history of French contention," *Social Science History*, 17/2 (Summer, 1993).

[46] Robert Wohl, *French Communism in the Making* (Stanford University Press, 1966), 128–138; Mayer, *Politics and Diplomacy*, 662–672; Alfred Rosmer, *Le mouvement ouvrier pendant la guerre*, 2 vols. (Paris: Librairie du Travail, 1936–1956); John Horne, *Labour at War: France and Britain, 1914–1918* (Oxford University Press, 1991), 370–375; Roger Magraw, "Paris 1917–1920: labour protest and popular politics," in Chris Wrigley, ed., *Challenges of Labour: Central and Western Europe, 1917–1920* (London and New York: Routledge, 1993), 136–140.

soldiers representing not only France but all the Allied nations marched down the boulevards of the capital in a living demonstration of military prowess and triumph. Paris in that year thus presented the spectacle of a dialog of public parades, working-class demonstrations versus military celebrations. Not until the early years of the Popular Front would the French capital witness comparable levels of public political mobilization and opposition.[47] In particular, the May Day demonstration contrasted sharply with the great victory march of July 14, 1919. May Day and Bastille Day have been regarded as bookends of the politics of the French Left throughout the twentieth century.[48] In 1919, however, both demonstrations assumed a spectacular and unusual character; Bastille Day because of its role as the official World War I victory march, May Day because of the rioting that marked the occasion. These two public events symbolized the over-heated nature of political and class conflict during a very unusual year.

I shall argue, however, that the study of these two events is useful not just for illuminating the shape of postwar French politics, but is also crucial for coming to an understanding of the nature of Parisian working-class identity. Many anthropologists and anthropologically inspired historians have pointed to the importance of parades, festivals, and other public gatherings in revealing general cultural norms, both arising from and reinforcing broadly accepted goals and patterns of behavior.[49] Mary Ryan has effectively used a study of parades in New York, New Orleans, and San Francisco to analyze the creation of urban ethnic cultures in nineteenth-century America. In considering social movements and culture in Barcelona, Temma Kaplan describes how various kinds of public spectacles ranging from celebrations of the Virgin Mary to mass funerals of bombing victims functioned as rituals to promote both social cohesion and conflict.[50] Such

---

[47] On the demonstrations of February 6, 9, and 12, 1934, see Julian Jackson, *The Popular Front in France* (Cambridge University Press, 1988), 17–29.

[48] Maurice Dommanget, *Histoire du premier mai* (Paris: Éditions de la Tête des Feuilles, 1972); Andre Rossel: *Premier Mai: 90 ans de lutte populaire dans le monde* (Paris: Éditions de la Courtille, 1977); Rosemonde Sanson, *Les 14 juillet, fête et conscience nationale, 1789–1975* (Paris: Flammarion, 1976); Michelle Perrot, "The first of May 1890 in France: the birth of a working class ritual," in Pat Thane, Geoffrey Crossick, and Roderick Floud, eds., *The Power of the Past* (Cambridge University Press, 1977).

[49] John Berger, "The nature of mass demonstrations," *New Society*, May 23, 1968; Clifford Geertz, *Negara: The Theatre State in 19th Century Bali* (Princeton University Press, 1980); Susan Davis, *Parades and Power: Street Theatre in 19th Century Philadelphia* (Philadelphia: Temple University Press, 1986).

[50] Temma Kaplan, *Red City, Blue Period: Social Movements in Picasso's Barcelona* (Berkeley: University of California Press, 1992); Mary Ryan, "The American parade: representations of the nineteenth-century social order," in Lynn Hunt, ed., *The New Cultural History* (Berkeley: University of California Press, 1989).

approaches are also very useful in illustrating Parisian working-class life in 1919. Since the study of such events allows the historian to consider the interesting tensions between the goals of the planners and leaders of the marches, on the one hand, and the behavior of individual participants in them, on the other, they are particularly appropriate for trying to understand how class identity could work in a large urban area. The symbolic opposition of May Day and Bastille Day offers insights into the ways both Parisian elites and Parisian workers perceived the working class. Whereas May Day provides an example of the ways in which workers tried to create a sense of both community and opposition to the bourgeoisie, the contrast between it and the victory parade of July 14 set up an oppositional duality of order and disorder which symbolically relegated the working class to the margins of society.

The observation that urban parades and demonstrations can represent a symbolic conquest of urban space is not a new one, but it is particularly relevant to Paris in 1919.[51] After over four years of war military tropes played a dominant theme in the life of the city. Paris was full of soldiers from all over the world, so that to a certain extent even the daily life of the street came to resemble a military parade.[52] In this climate the parade became a key way of symbolizing victory, as the ceremonies of July 14 so magnificently demonstrated. However, a parade could also symbolize defeat, and some Parisians still held bitter memories of the German army's arrogant march through the city at the end of the Franco-Prussian war.[53] The themes of victory and defeat haunted the French capital in 1919, and worked to underline the symbolic importance of the demonstration in the expression of postwar French politics and class identities.

These demonstrations often had the effect of symbolizing working-class unity, indeed uniformity. The organizers of events like the May Day march certainly desired this, and much of the public commentary on them also underscored the idea of the workers as an undifferentiated mass. Yet as this study has taken pains to point out, distinctions of gender and race shaped working-class identity in 1919. Even though these distinctions rarely appeared overtly in discussions of working-class spectacular politics, they did nonetheless manifest themselves from time to time, as we shall see. While one encounters few mentions of women or colonial subjects in

[51] Kaplan, *Red City*, 43; Vernon Lidtke, *The Alternative Culture: Socialist Labor in Imperial Germany* (Oxford University Press, 1985).
[52] Sellier, Bruggeman, and Poëte, *Paris pendant la guerre*, 84–87.
[53] On the German victory march through Paris at the beginning of 1871 see Stewart Edwards, *The Paris Commune, 1871* (London: Eyre and Spottiswoode, 1971).

discussions of these demonstrations, distinctions of race and gender at times played a role in their overall profiles. As the relationship between the peace conference and Parisian public space showed, questions of difference had a political dimension in 1919, including the politics of the street.

The symbolic opposition between the May Day and Bastille Day marches in 1919 was prefigured earlier in the year by the contrast between two events, which one British journalist termed collectively "the Affair of the Two Verdicts." On the morning of February 19, a young anarchist named Émile Cottin attempted to assassinate President Clemençeau by emptying his revolver into the great man's car as he rode from his home in the city's elegant Passy neighborhood to the Ministry of War. Cottin succeeded only in wounding Clemençeau lightly in the shoulder, and was himself immediately apprehended. He showed no remorse for his actions, declaring "I am a friend of humanity . . . both Germans and French, both Chinese and Negroes. I only have one hatred: Clemençeau, because he is war and an obstacle to the renovation of society."[54] The act outraged most Parisians, and few expressed much surprise or regret when on March 14 a military tribunal condemned Cottin to death.[55]

Two weeks later the Cottin verdict appeared in a very different light for many. On March 24 Raoul Vilain went on trial for his assassination of Jean Jaurès on the eve of World War I. Whereas Cottin's trial had been all but open and shut, Vilain's trial lasted five days. Since there was no question that Vilain had committed the deed in question, much of the testimony turned on the questions of the motivations that prompted it. In effect the proceedings placed Jaurès on trial: the defense emphasized Vilain's extreme devotion to France, portraying the assassination as an act of misguided but understandable super-patriotism,[56] while the prosecution struggled to defend Jaurès' record as a lover of France who would have backed the national war effort had he lived. In the postwar climate of both patriotic triumphalism and fears of rising working-class militancy, the Vilain trial, by targeting the one great French Socialist who never embraced the *Union Sacrée*, allowed the French Right to play upon fears of revolutionary subversion. Consequently, after five days of testimony but only twenty minutes of deliberation, the jury voted to acquit

---

[54] Cited in Elisabeth Hausser, *Paris au jour le jour: les événements vu par la presse, 1900–1919* (Paris: Les Éditions de Minuit, 1968), 715.
[55] *L'Humanité*, March 15, 1919, 1.
[56] It argued, for example, that he had also wanted to assassinate the Kaiser. *Le Petit Parisien*, March 25, 1919, 1.

Vilain, requiring only that he pay a symbolic indemnity to the widow of the martyred Socialist leader.[57]

Now came the turn of the French Left to react with shock and outrage. It was ironic and fitting, at a time when factional struggles in both the Socialist Party and the CGT were daily becoming more intense and acerbic, that Jean Jaurès, the great unifier of French socialism, should one more time provide a cause that all could rally around. As one, all the major figures of the Left rushed to condemn the verdict as not only a gross miscarriage of justice but also an insult to the working people of France.[58] But the contrast between the Cottin and Vilain verdicts prompted the most bitter commentaries. Both were admitted assassins; the primary difference between their acts was that Vilain succeeded where Cottin failed. Yet the young worker Cottin[59] was sentenced to death whereas Vilain barely received a slap on the wrist from the French judicial system. At a meeting of Parisian metal-workers on March 30, one union leader denounced this contrast in ringing terms:

Yesterday, a verdict of acquittal was rendered in favor of the assassin of our great JAURES, a man who did not want war; with this verdict the ruling capitalist class has once more made its intentions known, once again throwing down the gauntlet before us, since it has just condemned to death a son of the proletariat who did not kill anyone. Ah! if only Jaurès was here now![60]

Not only the Socialists labeled this dichotomy unfair: as H. Pearl Adam noted, "Everybody felt that there was here a serious injustice; the Socialists gained in a moment the support of every fair-minded observer in their dismay and fury at the acquittal."[61]

In spite of such sympathies, however, the contrasting nature of the two verdicts underlined the separate character of the French Left and the working class as a whole. The Socialists and CGT were not content to issue verbal protests, but soon organized a mass demonstration to give working-class discontent a visible presence in the streets of Paris. The demonstration was set for Sunday, April 6, and succeeded as an impressive display of working-class power in the French capital. That day, 300,000 people

---

[57] *Le Petit Parisien*, March 30, 1919, 1. On Jean Jaurès see Harvey Goldberg, *The Life of Jean Jaurès: A Biography of the Great French Socialist and Intellectual* (Madison: University of Wisconsin Press, 1962).

[58] Mayer, *Politics and Diplomacy*, 663; see especially *L'Humanité* and *La Vie Ouvrière*, March 31–April 1.

[59] Cottin claimed to have acted partly out of desperation at finding himself on the verge of unemployment, something that was not alien to many Parisian workers at the time.

[60] Couergou, cited in AN F7 13367, police report of March 31, 1919. There were 800 people present at the meeting.

[61] Adam, *Paris Sees It Through*, 301.

marched behind the banners of the SFIO and the CGT, leading *Le Petit Parisien* to call it "an imposing homage to the memory of Jaurès."[62] The demonstration certainly was that, but it also provided an interesting display of the symbolic opposition between bourgeoisie and proletariat. Especially significant in this regard was the route taken by the marches. Departing from the usual pattern of working-class demonstrations in Paris, which generally took place on major boulevards in the eastern part of the city, the organizers of the Jaurès march placed it in the heart of the wealthy and residential sixteenth district.[63] The parade started at the place du Trocadero, right across the river from the ultimate symbol of bourgeois Paris, the Eiffel Tower,[64] and proceeded down the avenue Henri-Martin toward the Bois de Boulogne. It thus neatly counterposed two kinds of visual order: the elegant, symmetrical facades of the late nineteenth-century *immeubles bourgeois* that lined the avenue Henri-Martin contrasted with the stately procession of the disciplined working-class corteges moving through the street (Illustration 4.1). At the same time, however, the presence of large numbers of working people in a place where they so clearly did not belong, the plush residential streets of Passy, underlined the difference between the two worlds.

The demonstration did not proceed completely without incident. Anarchists established their own presence in the march, at one point shouting "Clemenceau assassin! Vive Cottin!"[65] Fighting broke out between some demonstrators and the police at the margins of the march; several agents were wounded including the director of the Paris police, Paul Guichard, who was struck in the left eye. Although images of working-class dignity, strength, and discipline dominated coverage of the march, countervailing representations of working-class rioting and anarchy also attracted attention, especially in the bourgeois press.[66] Yet for the most part the Paris press commented favorably on the peaceful, orderly tone of the march, and the restraint shown by its participants. *Le Figaro* described it

---

[62] *Le Petit Parisien*, April 7, 1919, 1, 2. As is often the case, estimates of the size of the crowd varied widely; *Le Figaro* estimated 15,000 to 25,000.

[63] The organizers decided on, and won state approval for, this highly unusual itinerary in order to march by Jaurès' house in the Villa de la Tour, off the rue de la Pompe. A personal and commemorative itinerary, the route of the march also underscored working-class claims to the city as a whole. *L'Humanité*, April 6, 1919, 1; *ibid.*, April 7, 1919, 1.

[64] The Eiffel Tower symbolized not only the confidence of nineteenth-century liberal republicanism, but also the strength and artistic quality of French artisanal traditions. See Debora Silverman, *Art Nouveau in Fin-de-Siècle France* (Berkeley: University of California Press, 1989), 2–5; Miriam R. Levin, *When the Eiffel Tower Was New: French Visions of Progress at the Centennial of the Revolution* (Amherst: University of Massachusetts Press, 1989).

[65] *Le Petit Parisien*, April 8, 1919, 2.   [66] *Ibid.*

4.1 Demonstration against the acquittal of Raoul Vilain, place du Trocadero, April 1919

as "Calm, a little confused, silent in general and silently received ... all in all, a three hours' demonstration. A calm day, with few incidents."[67]

This unanimity of press opinion disappeared a few weeks later. If certain aspects of the Jaurès demonstration suggested working-class violence and marginality, the violence that accompanied May Day in Paris strongly confirmed this view. During the three weeks that separated the two working-class *journées* two events of note occurred. First, two days after the Jaurès march Clemençeau personally commuted Émile Cottin's sentence from execution to ten years in prison. While not of course changing the lenient verdict in the Vilain case, this act did nonetheless somewhat redress the balance between the two and vindicate the tactic of militant working-class street demonstrations.[68] More importantly, on April 17 the Chamber of Deputies officially and unanimously granted French workers the eight-hour workday; the bill was officially signed into law on April 25 after a unanimous yes vote by the Senate.[69] This had long been a goal of

---

[67] *Le Figaro*, April 7, 1919, 1, 2.   [68] *Le Petit Parisien*, April 9, 1919, 1.

[69] As Roger Magraw has suggested, the Jaurès demonstration played no small role in convincing parliamentary representatives that it was better to grant a key working-class demand than risk revolution. Magraw, "Paris 1917–1920," 136–137.

French labor activists, as well as a centerpiece of the CGT's economic Minimum Program for the postwar period, and workers throughout the country greeted it as a signal victory.[70] However, the mechanics of the eight-hour day remained to be worked out industry by industry, to ensure both the implementation of the new workday and that workers did not suffer a pay cut as a result of it. Consequently, the CGT and the SFIO decided to use the upcoming May Day festival both to celebrate the achievement of the eight-hour day, and to make manifest the determination of the French working class to ensure its implementation.[71]

However, the importance of May Day 1919 transcended the issue of the eight-hour day. For four years the traditional workers' holiday had been essentially ignored in France, as the needs of the war effort took precedence over labor struggles. This had begun to change in 1917 and 1918, but here the *Union Sacrée* held until the end.[72] May Day 1919 thus represented a celebration of the end of both the war and the *Union Sacrée*, and a return to the custom of militant, public class struggle. Moreover, for those on the Left of the SFIO and the CGT, the day came at a time when hopes for world revolution were at a fever pitch. A new Communist International had been founded, Trotsky's armies were mobilizing in the east, and Germany, Austria, and Hungary were in political turmoil. All in all, Europe trembled on the brink of a springtime of peoples such as it had not known since 1848. May Day 1919 thus came as an opportunity to show the bourgeois of France and the peoples of the world that Paris had not lost its traditional revolutionary *élan*.[73] As the railway workers' leader Sirolle thundered at a mass meeting of 6,000 on April 29, "We will go to the demonstration; if they touch one single hair on a worker's head, blood will flow, the massacre will begin and not stop until we are the masters, when the rulers and the bourgeois will be under our boots."[74]

This larger significance helps explain why the French government decided at the last minute to ban all public demonstrations in Paris (but not

---

[70] See my discussion of the eight-hour day in Chapter 6.   [71] Mayer, *Politics and Diplomacy*, 667.

[72] Dommanget, *Histoire du premier mai*, 258–277.

[73] Helmut Gruber, ed., *International Communism in the Era of Lenin* (Ithaca NY: Cornell University Press, 1967); Albert Lindemann, *The "Red Years": European Socialism versus Bolshevism, 1919–1921* (Berkeley: University of California Press, 1974); James Cronin and Carmen Sirianni, *Work, Community, and Power* (Philadelphia: Temple University Press, 1983); Charles Bertrand, *Revolutionary Situations in Europe, 1917–1922* (Montreal: Interuniversity Centre for European Studies, 1977); Chris Wrigley, *Challenges of Labour* (London and New York: Routledge, 1993).

[74] AN F7 13273, police report of April 30, 1919, "La manifestation du 1er Mai et les cheminots."

elsewhere in France) for May Day.[75] At the same time it began quietly concentrating large numbers of troops in the Paris area, in readiness to cope with any disturbances. The government justified these moves by pointing to the riots that had accompanied the Jaurès demonstration, but many workers, especially in the minoritaire factions of the SFIO and CGT, considered its actions a provocation. This was further grist to the mill of those who saw May Day as the first step toward revolution, but it left the majoritaires, especially the leadership of the CGT, in a difficult position. Rather than simply accept the ban and cancel already planned demonstrations, thus risking the wrath of the minoritaires, the CGT leaders left the decision to departmental union organizations.[76] On April 29 the Departmental Union of the Seine, influenced by anarchist elements in the ditchdiggers' union, voted by a narrow margin to defy the government ban and proceed with a Paris demonstration.[77] The stage was thus set for a dramatic confrontation with public authorities in the French capital.

Thursday, May 1, 1919 dawned with the kind of grey, persistent drizzle that makes a mockery of songs like "April in Paris." During much of the morning Paris seemed like a ghost town; most shops and businesses closed for the day, and neither busses, taxis, nor the Metro operated. Few ventured out into the rain-slicked streets except for the soldiers stationed at strategic points throughout the capital.[78] Not until the afternoon did groups of workers start marching into the streets of the city, and as they did, violent clashes broke out between them and the forces of order, both soldiers and police, at several points. The original plan had been for the march to proceed from the place de la Concorde up the rue Royale and along the *grands boulevards* to the place de la République. Obeying the government's orders, soldiers and police moved to prevent groups of workers from concentrating at any of the main staging points of the demonstration. As a result, during the afternoon and evening of May Day pitched battles developed between contingents of demonstrators trying to enter the city center from the suburbs, and troops and police struggling to force them back.[79]

[75] AN F7 13273, police report of May 2, 1919. The CGT was informed of this ban on April 29, at a point when large demonstrations had already been planned.

[76] AN F7 13273, police report of May 2, 1919, "Quelles étaient les dispositions prises par la CGT pour le premier mai?"

[77] AN F7 13273, police report of May 1, 1919, "Dans quelles conditions a été organisé le cortège du 1er mai à Paris?"

[78] Adam, *Paris Sees It Through*, 302–303; Deletang, *Journal*, 468.

[79] See the various detailed police reports contained in AN F7 13273. On May Day police agents sent in their dispatches on an hourly basis.

In spite of the general confusion surrounding the events of the day, one can discern two main waves of rioting, one centering around the area between the place de la Concorde and the place de l'Opéra, the other located between the place de la République and the Gare de l'Est. At 2 p.m. a large crowd of railway workers, estimated at from 800 to 3,000 people, left a mass meeting in Clichy to march into Paris. Sweeping aside initial resistance from police, this group made its way to the Gare du Nord area where fighting broke out with the forces of order stationed there. Meanwhile, another contingent of demonstrators, shouting "Vivent les Poilus" and occasionally singing the "Internationale," overwhelmed police barricades in the rue Royale after marching down from the place de l'Opéra to end up near the Pont des Invalides. At one point a group of railway workers attempted to cross the pont Alexandre III, only to be thrown back by soldiers defending the bridge. For roughly an hour marchers battled an odd array of police, mounted cavalry, and firemen throughout the Faubourg Saint-Honoré, finally giving way at around 4.30.

The most serious fighting occurred in the area around the place de la République, the destination of the original march. By 3 p.m. roughly 4,000 demonstrators had gathered near the square, their numbers reinforced by those who succeeded in marching from the Opéra down the rues du Quatre Septembre and Réaumur (the *grands boulevards* being blocked by police). The arrival of this latter group, at around 4 p.m., precipitated fighting between the crowd and the police that continued for several hours. The melée reached its climax after 5.30 p.m., when between 15,000 and 20,000 more demonstrators, shouting "A Bas Clemençeau" and "Vive les Soviets," marched down from CGT offices in the rue Grange-aux-Belles toward République (Illustration 4.2). Although the forces of order succeeded in preventing them from joining forces with those already battling in the square, this new contingent was able to reach the boulevard Magenta, four blocks away. There they tore up the iron grilles protecting the boulevard's trees to use as weapons against the soldiers and police, as well as throwing stones and attacking the barricades of their opponents. The demonstrators were gradually forced up the boulevard Magenta away from the place de la République, the crowd dwindling in size as many escaped into the surrounding streets. By 8 p.m. the police were masters of the situation, with the final fighting taking place in the halls and corridors of the Gare de l'Est.[80]

The events of May Day loomed large in the commentaries of both Louise Deletang and René Michaud. In her diary entries at the time Deletang refers

[80] *Le Petit Parisien*, May 2, 1919, 1.

Place de l'Opéra, à 3 h. ½ : les gardes municipaux à cheval dispersent les manifestants venant de la Madeleine

Une bagarre sur le boulevard des Italiens

Après les manifestations : un barrage de municipaux
devant le café de la Paix.

A 5 heures du soir : fantassins occupant la place de l'Opéra
« secteur tranquille ».

LE 1ᵉʳ MAI A PARIS

4.2 Images of May Day in Paris, 1919

to strikes as blackmail and labels the union leadership "His Majesty the CGT." Deletang notes that she, a friend, and their apprentice worked on May 1 in defiance of union orders, and then goes on to criticize the government for being too soft on the demonstrators:

Everywhere there is rage and indignity, and people ask themselves if the eagerness of all the unions (even the newspapers!) to obey the orders of the CGT, if this governmental tolerance is a tactic to deprive the Bolsheviks of any excuse for rioting while the German delegation is at Versailles! . . . Has the *Tiger* [Clemençeau] used up all his teeth?[81]

Like many other French men and women, Louise Deletang was horrified by the prospect of strife between French soldiers and workers while representatives of the enemy sat a few miles away. However, unlike H. Pearl Adam for example, she placed the blame for the violence firmly on the heads of the "revolutionaries." As she noted in her diary on May 2, "This *journée* was certainly the last *boche* offensive, as can be seen by the increase of German demands." In the view of Louise Deletang, if this was class war, then it was a war waged against the French nation and a continuation of the conflict that had begun in August 1914.

René Michaud was one of those demonstrators, so hotly condemned by Louise Deletang and many others, who took to the streets of Paris on May 1, 1919.[82] As he noted in his memoirs, "The first of May 1919 was to mark an important stage in my revolutionary orientation, giving me the occasion to measure my dynamism, to test my character and my convictions."[83] Michaud and a few friends from Belleville were among those who gathered at the Bourse du Travail in order to discover the plan of action for the day. He soon found himself near the boulevard Magenta, in the thick of the worst fighting that day.

Suddenly, bursting out from everywhere, the cops attacked, striking out with might and main at everyone in their way. They cleared the square.

The counterattack from our ranks was immediate and no less brutal. In an instant the iron grilles surrounding the trees were torn up – it's strange how in such moments of exaltation one's strength seems multiplied tenfold – and broken into pieces of iron to be thrown at the adversary, striking when and where they could. This hindered the charge of the police, compelling them to exercise some prudence.

---

[81] Deletang, *Journal*, 468, entry of May 1, 1919.
[82] Although, as we have seen, Michaud and Deletang had their own individual ideas and personalities, their difference here to a certain extent reflects the gendered nature of May 1, and of most Parisian demonstrations. With some notable exceptions, such as the dressmakers' strike two years earlier, men usually dominated public demonstrations in Paris.
[83] Michaud, *J'avais vingt ans*, 109.

Scattered for a moment, the mass of demonstrators dispersed in the neighboring streets reformed a little farther up, this time armed with improvised defensive weapons. Did they want a riot! Well then, they would certainly get one!
This May Day was a cruel and bloody *journée*.[84]

René Michaud spent the entire afternoon fighting the police along the boulevard Magenta, ending up in the Gare de l'Est with the rest of the demonstrators. He fled the demonstration after witnessing mounted dragoons firing their weapons at the crowd. For Michaud, May Day confirmed his belief in collective action and in anarchism. A baptism of fire, it symbolized his revolutionary commitment and his self-image as merely one of millions who soon would bring about the Great Day.

The events of May Day 1919 provide a rich symbolic repertoire for the shifting nature of working-class politics and identity in Paris at the end of World War I. Certain aspects of the rioting recalled the Paris Commune. The fact that May Day demonstrations in all other French cities proceeded in a peaceful and disciplined manner recreated the distinction between revolutionary capital and quiescent provinces so prevalent in 1871, and the struggle of soldiers to force insurgent workers out of the city center back to the periphery was highly reminiscent of events during another Parisian May forty-eight years before.[85] More significantly, like 1919 itself, the May Day events that year were a confusing and unstable mixture of war and peace. Was this a peaceful, civil demonstration, or was it class war? No one seemed sure. The demonstrators proclaimed their desire for the former, and strove primarily to reach points along the parade route fixed earlier; one group did succeed in staging a peaceful march before becoming embroiled in the fighting in the place de la République. Yet troops patrolled the city streets and fierce fighting raged all over the Right Bank. The very language used by commentators seemed borrowed from the war that had just ended: journalists and police reporters wrote of charges, battles, encirclement, advances and retreats, maneuvers, columns, and reinforcements.[86]

---

[84] *Ibid.*, 109–110.

[85] As historians have since noted, this dichotomy between rebellious Paris and the peaceful provinces in 1871 was more symbolic than real. Louis Greenberg, *Sisters of Liberty* (Cambridge MA: Harvard University Press, 1971); Jeanne Gaillard, *Communes de province, Commune de Paris* (Paris: Flammarion, 1971); Jacques Girault, *La Commune et Bordeaux* (Paris: Éditions Sociales, 1971).

[86] For example, *Le Figaro* reported that "The plan was to advance, at the same time, from different parts of Paris, troups of demonstrators supposed to converge on the place de la Concorde, singing and deploying red flags." *Le Figaro*, May 2, 1919, 1. For press reports on May Day 1919, see *Le Figaro*, "The Day of the Agitators," May 2, 1919, 1; *L'Humanité*, May 2, 1919, 1; *ibid.*, May 3, 1919, 1; *La Vie Ouvrière*, May 7, 1919, 1.

And of wounded. The casualties of the May Day rioting were numerous, evenly distributed on both sides, and in a few cases notable. Roughly 300 demonstrators and 400 police received injuries during the fighting, the former from police batons and, in a few cases, gunshots, the latter from rocks, bottles, and other projectiles. Two demonstrators were killed: Charles Lorne, an eighteen-year-old garage mechanic, shot to death near the place de l'Opéra, and Alexander Auger, a 48-year-old bill collector, killed by gunfire in the Gare de l'Est.[87] But it was not only the labor rank and file who suffered. Léon Jouhaux himself was struck in the left eye by a policeman's billy club in the fighting around the place de la République, Socialist leader and deputy Marcel Cachin was seriously wounded in the Gare de l'Est, and another SFIO parliamentarian, Paul Poncet, was likewise beaten by the police. Several witnesses emphasized the brutality displayed by soldiers and police alike in suppressing the May Day demonstration.[88] H. Pearl Adam, no fan of French Socialism, expressed shock at the spectacle she witnessed that day:

the May-Day demonstration of Labour was treated with the utmost brutality by the Paris police, who declared they were acting under orders. They kicked and trampled men and women, they were far too ready with their revolvers, and those who saw their behaviour were absolutely sickened ... The police at this time are heavily censoring reports of what happened, and, one can only remark, just like them! They have deliberately joined battle with an enemy who was lacking in every arm save this, which the police have vouchsafed them, of a legitimate grievance ... When you see a policeman running about with a naked sword seeking whom he may slash, simply because he feels he would like to do some slashing and here's an opportunity, nobody can help feeling that there is something wrong with that policeman or with the man who gave him his orders.[89]

The May Day riots provided a dramatic representation of the Parisian working class as a symbol of disorder, chaos, and danger. This danger lay not so much in the Socialist ideals of the SFIO and CGT leadership, but rather in the indiscipline and arrogance of the working people as a whole. The beatings of Jouhaux, Cachin, and Poncet symbolized this demarcation between labor and its leaders. Most of the latter had opposed or at least remained neutral on the issue of whether labor should march in Paris on

---

[87] Mayer, *Politics and Diplomacy*, 670. See the interview with Charles Lorne's mother in *Le Petit Parisien*, May 3, 1919, 1.

[88] AN F7 13273, police report of June 14, 1919. See in particular the testimonies by M. Sohier, a music teacher who was passing by and got shot in the foot, and M. Lepicard, a mechanic from Courbevoie who took part in the demonstration and ended up with two bullets in his back.

[89] Adam, *Paris Sees It Through*, 301, 305.

May Day in defiance of the government's ban. During the chaos that erupted on that day, they tried unsuccessfully to keep the peace between demonstrators and police, thus winning the image of ineffective moderates pathetically and vainly trying to hold back the unruly forces of revolution. Although in actuality Jouhaux, Poncet, and Cachin received their blows at the hands of the police, symbolically they were beaten by the Leftist minoritaires and the mob in general. Their inability to control their followers undermined the image of working-class power and discipline they had tried so hard to create during the Jaurès demonstration, instead reinforcing preconceived notions of the dangerous rabble on the march.[90]

To the images of disorder the Jaurès and May Day demonstrations also contributed another powerful and even more timely metaphor: invasion. The unusual physical location of both events in the urban space of Paris provides striking confirmation of this. Most working-class Parisian demonstrations during the late nineteenth and twentieth centuries have taken place on the boulevards of the eastern half of the capital; the march from the place de la Bastille east to the place de la Nation is a favorite of May Day marches to this day.[91] The Parisian demonstrators of April and May 1919, in contrast, took their message into the heart of bourgeois Paris. During the Jaurès demonstration an imposing, and intimidating, number of Parisian workers marched peacefully through an elegant, quiet neighborhood on a Sunday (which underlined the residential character of this *quartier*) to erect a bust to the Socialist martyr in the square Lamartine.

The May Day riots suggested the invasion metaphor much more forcefully. The basic pattern of the demonstration was fighting between workers from the outer districts and the suburbs trying to reach the city center, and soldiers and police struggling to force them back. Since the late nineteenth century the working population of Paris had been gradually moving from the center to the periphery of the urban area. The suburbs of the Department of the Seine in particular had grown rapidly, and in 1919 were poised on the edge of their most spectacular period of growth ever.[92] Whereas the fighting that destroyed the Paris Commune in May 1871 represented working-class expulsion from the city center, May Day 1919

---

[90] For example, in his article "The Day of the Agitators" Alfred Capus wrote, "A somber, wretched day, without any other meaning than a desire for riot and disorder, a day of social hatred deprived of any grandeur or dignity. The police were visibly disgusted at having to maintain order against a few groups of rabid activists in this Paris just emerging from its hour of trial." *Le Figaro*, May 2, 1919, 1.

[91] Dommanget, *Histoire du premier mai*, 246–346.

[92] T. Stovall, *The Rise of the Paris Red Belt* (Berkeley: University of California Press, 1990); Annie Fourcaut, *Bobigny, banlieue rouge* (Paris: Éditions Ouvrières, 1986); Annie Fourcaut, *Banlieue rouge, 1920–1960* (Paris: Éditions Autrement, 1992).

symbolized a brief and unsuccessful return from exile. Henceforth in the twentieth century suburban working-class organizations and municipalities would reenact this ritual in a symbolic and non-threatening manner, packing demonstrators into chartered busses to come into the city and march along carefully delineated routes.[93] But May Day 1919 was the real thing. Marchers forced their way into the Faubourg Saint-Honoré and at one point surrounded the offices of the respectable bourgeois daily *Le Matin*.[94] It was a day that seemed to justify all those fears of working-class suburbia as a horde of barbarians held at bay by urban civilization.[95] Finally, it was more than fitting that the final battles of the day should take place in the Gare de l'Est. Both the site of countless embarkations for the front lines during the war, and a key transportation link between the city and the burgeoning working-class suburbs to the east, the great railway station constituted a near-perfect symbol of the perils of working-class invasion in 1919.

Finally, if the May Day demonstration in particular recalled the street fighting that accompanied the suppression of the Paris Commune, it also foreshadowed another bloody event that would take place in Paris forty-two years later. On October 17, 1961, representatives of the Algerian FLN in Paris organized a demonstration in the city to protest the curfew imposed on Algerians in the city. As on May Day 1919, the marchers invaded the city from the surrounding suburban slums, targeting areas like the Opéra, and to an even greater extent were met with ferocious police repression.[96] The parallels between May 1, 1919 and October 17, 1961 underscore the perils of transgressing class and racial boundaries in Paris, and the ways in which French workers in 1919 were both determined to expel the colonial Other from their ranks, and at the same time found themselves subjected to treatment similar to that meted out to the colonized. The expulsion of the rioters from the center of Paris foreshadowed the increasing

[93] This is further emphasized by the contemporary Fête de l'*Humanité*, the annual festival of the French Communist Party. It takes place every Fall in the Paris suburbs, safely removed from the seats of governmental and industrial power.

[94] AN F7 13273, police report of May 1, 1919, 5 p.m.

[95] As John Merriman has demonstrated, such fears went back to the early nineteenth century. Merriman, *The Margins of City Life: Explorations on the French Urban Frontier, 1815–1851* (Oxford University Press, 1991).

[96] There has been a recent explosion of literature on the events of October 17, 1961. See Jim House and Neil MacMaster, *Paris 1961: Algerians, State Terror, and Memory* (New York: Oxford University Press, 2006); Jean-Luc Einaudi, *La Bataille de Paris: 17 Octobre 1961* (Paris: Seuil, 1991). For a contrary view of the events see Jean-Paul Brunet, *Police contre FLN: le drame d'octobre 1961* (Paris: Flammarion, 1999). The article by Joshua Cole, "Remembering the Battle of Paris, 17 October 1961, in French and Algerian memory," in *French Politics, Culture, and Society*, 21/3 (Fall, 2003), provides a useful summary and critique of the debate.

suburbanization of the city's labor force, grouped in peripheral settlements whose marginality replicated the relationship of the colonies to the metropole.[97]

The comparison between May 1 and October 17 thus illustrates the racialized dimension of spectacular politics in 1919. As the peace conference made clear, intersections of class and race shaped both global and local politics in the year after the Armistice. Some commentators on May Day noted the presence of foreign workers, suggesting both Bolshevik agitators and the colonial Other.[98] More generally, the sheer visuality of the great marches and parades of 1919, coupled with the intense dualism of politics in Paris and in the world, underscored the salience of racial distinctions. The repeated references to the "blackness" of the massive crowds in the streets indicate this point. As noted elsewhere in this study, even though the French were actively trying to get colonial subjects out of the capital and the metropole in general, their presence could not be so easily erased.

The Jaurès and May Day demonstrations were not the largest examples of working-class mobilization during 1919; pride of place must go to the massive metalworkers' strike that followed closely in June. However, they were the most impressive in terms of their impact on Parisian public space. While the striking metalworkers limited their militant actions to working-class neighborhoods and factory entrances, the events of April and May occurred in the middle of the city, representing a symbolic attempt to place working-class life at the center of urban and national life. The successful repression of the May Day demonstration by the forces of order entailed the defeat of this attempt. This was not the last public activity staged by Parisian workers in May 1919: 100,000 attended the funeral of Charles Lorne in Père Lachaise cemetery on May 8, and 60,000 returned there to honor the memory of the Communards on May 25.[99] Yet the threat to the center of Paris, and to public order, had clearly passed. The final symbolic act in this drama took place the day after May Day, while city streets still bore traces of the riots. Public authorities had long desired to dismantle the fortifications

[97] The idea of a parallel between French suburbs and French colonies is not new, but gathered force in the late twentieth century as the suburbs became increasingly identified with postcolonial populations. See Stovall, "From red belt to black belt," in Peabody and Stovall, *The Color of Liberty*. One of the most prominent to make this point was Jean-Paul Sartre: see his "Le Tiers Monde commence en banlieue," *Situations VIII* (Paris: Gallimard, 1972). I owe this reference to Susan P. Arthur; see her "Unfinished projects: decolonization and the philosophy of Jean-Paul Sartre" (Ph.D. dissertation, University of California, Berkeley, 2004).

[98] *Le Figaro*, May 2, 1919, 1.

[99] *L'Humanité*, May 9, 1919, 1; *ibid.*, May 26, 1919, 1; *Le Figaro*, May 26, 1919, 2; Mayer, *Politics and Diplomacy*, 672; Hausser, *Paris au jour le jour*, 730.

around Paris, seen as a medieval relic and a barrier to traffic.[100] The onset of
war had postponed efforts to do so, but by the beginning of 1919 the city was
ready to proceed. On May 2 workers began the task of demolishing the
walls. France was now at peace, and Paris was no longer threatened by
invasion. The Armistice may have been declared in November 1918, but the
outcome of May Day 1919 made this a reality.

The great victory celebration held in Paris on Bastille Day, 1919, thus
marked a triumph in two senses: over the Germans and their allies, and over
the forces of anarchy and revolution. Like May Day, it was preceded by a
similar event that functioned as an introductory act, the spontaneous
celebrations that took place on both June 24 and June 29 as Germany
announced it would sign the Versailles Treaty, then did so. Like the
demolition of the Parisian fortifications, it followed closely upon a working-
class setback, the end of the metalworkers' strike.

And yet it is the differences between the two that loom largest in the
present discussion. Most obviously, they had different outcomes: whereas
the May Day marchers were bloodily expelled from the French capital,
those of Bastille Day paraded through it in unchallenged triumph. July 14
was thus not just a celebration of victory, but a victory in its own right. The
two demonstrations also differed radically in their style and public presentation, emphasizing the contrast between bourgeois order and proletarian
disorder that has been a central theme of this analysis. The choreographed
display that took center stage on July 14 could not have been more unlike
the screaming chaos of May 1. Yet the class oppositions represented by the
two events were more ideological and symbolic than sociological. Working
people played a major role in the victory celebrations of both late June and
Bastille Day. Thus the contrast between May 1 and July 14 also symbolized
conflicting conceptions of working-class identity in Paris after the war. Who
were the "real" workers, those who fought the police in the place de la
République on May Day, or those who climbed lampposts along the
Champs-Elysées to wave the national flag and sing the Marseillaise on
Bastille Day? Or were they one and the same? (Illustration 4.3).[101]

---

[100] On the trend toward removing walls around French cities in the nineteenth century, see Merriman,
The Margins of City Life, 31–35. On the demolition of the Parisian fortifications in 1919, see Adrian
Rifkin, *Street Noises: Parisian Pleasure, 1900–1940* (Manchester University Press, 1993), 27; Marie
Charvet, *Les fortifications de Paris: de l'hygiène à l'urbanisme, 1880–1919* (Rennes: Presses
Universitaires de Rennes, 2005).

[101] In her commentary on the May Day riots H. Pearl Adam describes watching cavalry parade along the
boulevard near the place de la République, contrasting the silence of the onlooking crowd with the
enthusiastic cheering that greeted soldiers throughout Paris on the day after the Armistice. Adam,
Paris Sees It Through, 302–303.

4.3 Crowds at the 1919 Victory Parade

The public demonstrations in Paris that greeted the news of the final signing of the peace treaty in Versailles at the end of June provide an important example of working-class patriotism. They began on June 23, 1919, when Parisians learned that after many difficult negotiations the German delegation to the peace talks had at last agreed to sign the peace treaty. Shortly before 7 p.m. cannons fired and sirens wailed for twenty minutes to announce the glad tidings.[102] As happened on November 11, 1918, spontaneous celebrations erupted throughout the city, Parisians greeting the news of the final end of the war with joy and abandon. People staged their own quickly organized victory marches, parading along streets carrying flags and shouting "Long live France! Long live peace! Long live the Allies!" Students marched in mass up the boulevard Saint-Michel, followed by a cortege of war wounded wearing their decorations. All over the city soldiers, both French and Allied, celebrated with Parisians, singing and dancing until dawn.[103]

Similar scenes took place on Friday, June 27, as Parisians breathlessly awaited the ceremonial signing of the treaty the next day. Tens of thousands

[102] Elisabeth Hausser, *Paris au jour le jour*, 733–734. [103] *Le Petit Parisien*, June 23, 1919.

came out into the streets, marching along the *grands boulevards* to converge
in the place de l'Opéra. The neighborhood which less than two months
before had witnessed violence and barricades now affirmed the unity of all
the people of France. The dressmaker Louise Deletang, firmly patriotic
throughout the conflict, joined the crowd surging up the rue de la Paix. In
her diary she emphasized the good spirits and sense of decorum that
animated those present: "A procession of young women marched singing
toward the Carousel; their voices were pure, their procession disciplined and
rhythmic."[104] The crowd eventually came together in the place de l'Opéra
between the Café de la Paix and the Opera itself. A young American soldier
present described the occasion:

The Opera was draped in tricolor as were the buildings on either side. One of the
great sopranos of the Opera company appeared just as the day was beginning to
fade and the immense crowd began to quiet down . . . Then came the pure tones of
this great artist singing, without accompaniment, La Marseillaise. The location of
the Opera looking out into the Place made it a perfect outdoor theater and as that
beautiful voice washed over the stilled crowd, it held them enthralled. Then a male
member of the Opera company stepped to the front and led the vast crowd in its
singing of the Marseillaise. Suddenly people were in each other's arms, tears were
openly shed, and I confess to having a lump in my throat. There was almost a
religious fervor to it.[105]

The descriptions of these Parisian demonstrations celebrating peace and
victory at the end of June 1919 give interesting views of working-class
identity. While many of these accounts mention the presence of working
people, it is as one element in the vast array of Parisians of all kinds cheering
the triumph of French arms. Often articles about these celebrations that
appeared in middle-class newspapers like *Le Matin* and *Le Temps* failed to
note workers' contributions to the festivities at all. Urban social geography
also contributed to this interpretation of the celebrations: most newspapers
focused on events in central Paris, while briefly indicating that revelry also
took place in the working-class faubourgs. The socialist and labor press, on
the other hand, paid little attention to the working-class' role in the peace
celebrations. By mid 1919 neither majoritaire nor minoritaire factions
wished to call attention to working-class contributions to the French war
effort. The Parisian press thus effectively portrayed the victory celebrations
at the end of June as the *Union Sacrée* reborn, as an event that abolished the
existence of the working class as a social identity. By either praising it in

[104] Deletang, *Journal,* 477.
[105] John Maginnis, "The big parade: Paris-1919," *Laurels,* 55/2 (Fall, 1984), 80–82.

these terms or ignoring it altogether, both the Left and the Right concurred in this representation of events.

I would suggest, however, that this view is at least somewhat mistaken, and that the popular festivities in Paris at the end of June should be considered a part of Parisian working-class culture and identity.[106] It is impossible to estimate what percentage of the crowds in the place de l'Opéra and the *grands boulevards* were working class, but if the diary of Louise Deletang is at all representative many must have been. Moreover, Montmartre, Belleville, and the Faubourg Saint-Antoine all hosted their own lively celebrations. Demonstrators shouted "Vive les Poilus!" on both May 1 and June 27, emphasizing once again the centrality of workers to the nation as a whole. Even more than May Day, and certainly more than the carefully orchestrated pageantry of Bastille Day to come, the June festivities arose spontaneously as a direct expression of the Parisian mood. Working people could play a central role in the celebrations, as they had in the war itself. The June celebrations thus both affirmed and denied Parisian working-class identity. The dominant discourses of both Left and Right presented them as something opposed to the collective consciousness of working people. At the same time, a more subaltern conception of the festivities could be glimpsed, one in which the distinctive cultures of popular Paris conceptualized victory as something that working people had achieved and deserved to celebrate.[107]

Whereas the June victory celebrations mixed both the rejection and the affirmation of working-class identity, the formal parade that took place on Bastille Day 1919 was much more straightforward. Its championing of patriotic ideas, its celebration of elites and hierarchy generally, and its precise, stately form all constituted a powerful statement of what France should be, and by extension of what working-class Paris assuredly was not. First and foremost, it was a formal military parade, composed of units from both the French and Allied armed forces. Spontaneity was not even conceivable, let alone permitted, and all civilians were firmly relegated to the sidelines.[108]

Like the May Day march, on Bastille Day the parade moved from the outskirts into the center of the city, but the resemblance stopped there.

[106] On the history of popular festivals in Paris, see Rifkin, *Street Noises*; François Gasnault, *Guinguettes et lorettes: bals publics à Paris au XIXe siècle* (Paris: Aubier, 1986); Alain Faure, *Paris Careme prenant: du carnaval à Paris au XIXe siècle* (Paris: Hachette, 1978).

[107] As historians of British labor have pointed out, working-class culture and popular culture are not necessarily the same thing. See Gareth Stedman Jones, *Languages of Class* (Cambridge University Press, 1983); Patrick Joyce, *Visions of the People* (Cambridge University Press, 1991).

[108] *Le Petit Parisien*, July 15, 1919, 1, 2.

Starting from their encampments in the Bois de Boulogne at dawn, the
participating soldiers entered Paris through the Porte Maillot, where they
were welcomed by the President of the Paris City Council and the Prefect of
the Seine. They then marched up the soon-to-be-named avenue Foch
through the Arc de Triomphe and down the Champs-Elysées. From the
place de la Concorde, the march continued along the *grands boulevards* to
the place de la République, where the great parade ended shortly after noon.
It was a magnificent spectacle, a dramatic theatrical climax to five years of
human struggle and suffering. As such, it furnished a perfect Happy Ending
for H. Pearl Adam's *Paris Sees It Through*.

Behind the acolytes came marshals and generals, and after them many armies with
banners. The blue shadow fell upon them all as they passed, the sunshine received
them, and the Arch, clean once more after forty-eight years, its stain washed out
beneath the dust of their steps, reared its grey brow into the sky as they left it and
passed on to salute the Dead, and thence into the waiting city. But the shadow and the
sunshine seemed to keep, as the Arch did, a star and a flag especially for those first
three figures, who, steady and unswerving, carried with them that oblation of suffering
and loss and the splendour of sacrifice which France and her Allies laid, day and night,
through five long years, upon the altar of national honour and universal right.[109]

With its chiaroscuro imagery and its references to the exorcized specter of
l'année terrible, this passage reflects both the undeniable majesty of the
Bastille Day march, and the symbolic oppositions upon which that majesty,
at least in part, rested (Illustration 4.4).

   The contrast between the routes of May Day and Bastille Day underlines
that symbolic opposition. The march into the city, welcomed by Parisian
officials and the population as a whole, constituted a ritualistic inversion of
invasions by both the Germans and the revolutionary Left. Where the latter
had failed, the French and Allied armies succeeded brilliantly. The parade
through the Arc de Triomphe and down the Champs-Elysées obviously
recalled the military glories of Napoleon I, and served to endow the military
march with the glamour of the city's most majestic thoroughfare. Yet it also
emphasized the elite nature of the occasion. The rest of the march covered
much of the same urban space that the May Day demonstrators had
attempted to use. By concluding at the place de la République, the
Bastille Day parade reaffirmed the conquest of that square by soldiers and
police on May 1. It also reinforced the division between western and central
Paris, through which it wound its way in triumph, and the mostly working-
class districts east of the place de la République, into which it did not

---

[109] Adam, *Paris Sees It Through*, 314–315. Adam's memoir in fact ends with this passage.

4.4 July 14, 1919 Victory Parade, Arc de Triomphe

venture. The Bastille Day parade not only functioned to reclaim Paris for the bourgeoisie, it also constituted a symbolic purification of urban space, cleansing it of the memories of class strife left by the May Day riots.

By both its size and its form Bastille Day also served to refute the demonstrations of May. Whereas the participants in the May Day riots probably totaled less than 50,000, the officers and soldiers who marched on July 14, 1919 numbered in the hundreds of thousands. When one adds the number of spectators who lined the entire parade route and cheered the marchers as they passed, one can say that millions of people took part in the victory parade, in one form or another. This size difference graphically illustrated the contrast between the massive unity of a victorious France and a small, marginal population of discontented Parisian workers. The beautifully choreographed character of the military march also contrasted sharply with the chaotic disorder of May Day, to the credit of the former. The Bastille Day marchers proceeded along the parade route in perfect, unchanging order. The march was led by two of the great architects of the French victory, Marshalls Foch and Joffre, riding on horseback. The generals were preceded by a contingent of wounded veterans, making the point that the march did not just celebrate victory but also commemorated sacrifice.[110] Units from the various Allied nations followed them. The Americans came first, then the Belgians, British, Italians, and other nationalities. Finally, and most impressively of all, the regiments of the French armed forces marched, with Marshall Pétain at their head. Unlike the May Day march, a festival of desperate anarchy where working-class leaders were often beaten, Bastille Day emphasized the beauty of hierarchy and tight organization. It presented a universe where everyone knew his place, and everyone received symbolic recompense (through applause) in due measure.[111]

The presence of the Allied contingents also posed an interesting contrast with May Day, illuminating the images of foreigners held in France during 1919. Formally, the ceremony of July 14, 1919 was the Allied victory parade to mark the official end of World War I. However, this ostensibly international festival took place on the French national holiday, not only in the French capital but along a route laden with the historical presence of France's great warrior, Napoleon. Moreover, the foreign contingents were in effect bracketed by the French: two French generals led the march, and units of the French military, by far the largest in the parade, brought up the rear. The Bastille Day parade thus presented an image of foreigners not only serving the French cause, but also in effect integrated into France as a whole, a dynamic vision of the "nation of one hundred million Frenchmen" on the march. The presence of sizeable contingents of colonial soldiers in the French armies on July 14 further bolstered this image.[112] On Bastille Day the presence of these groups was admired and loudly praised, whereas during the May Day riots many newspapers had condemned the violence as the work of foreign agitators, not true French workers.[113] Moreover, the ostentatious display of colonial soldiers at a time when French authorities were actively deporting colonial workers further underscored the difference between nationalistic and working-class identity. The contrast between May Day and Bastille Day, 1919, thus also served to highlight intersections between discourses of patriotism and xenophobia. As a (carefully controlled) part of the national community foreigners symbolized the strength and universality of French values and culture; as part of the working class, they represented the denial of French values and the greatest danger to that culture.

---

[110] *Ibid.*, 314.   [111] Ryan, "The American parade," 132–134.

[112] By way of contrast, the US military banned African American soldiers from taking part in the victory parade. Arthur E. Barbeau and Florette Henri, *The Unknown Soldiers: Black American Troops in World War I* (Philadelphia PA: Temple University Press, 1974). See also Jennifer D. Keene, *Doughboys, World War I, and the Remaking of American Culture* (Baltimore MD: Johns Hopkins University Press, 2001).

[113] Mayer, *Politics and Diplomacy*, 671.

The June celebrations of the signing of the peace treaty had made it clear that while workers were welcome to take part in festivals of the national community, they must strip themselves of any conceptions of working-class consciousness based on conflict in order to gain admission to that community. Bastille Day reinforced this in a much more extreme manner. Many of the French *poilus* who marched that day were of working-class origin, of course, but their public presence was that of soldiers, not workers. Many working people were part of the huge crowds that lined the parade route, so that in a strictly numerical sense Bastille Day was much more of a working-class event than May Day, because more workers took part in it. Yet they took part as spectators, in dramatic contrast to the battling workers who took to the streets of Paris on May 1. In general, the sharp division between active participants and cheering but non-participatory crowds was one of the most vivid aspects of Bastille Day 1919.[114] It replicated a key theme of the mass culture that already loomed large in Parisian life and whose importance would only increase during the interwar years.[115] Bastille Day thus contrasted not only with May Day in this regard, but also with the December 1918 celebration of President Wilson's arrival in Paris. Whereas French labor turned that event into a demonstration of its own strength and presence in the capital, July 14 demonstrated to the contrary the integration of working people into an undifferentiated mass culture. It represented in effect the triumph of that mass culture over the more oppositional conception of working-class life symbolized by the burning barricades of May.

Any great public demonstration offers a rich treasure of symbolic practices, and the two great public events of 1919 in Paris, May Day and Bastille Day, certainly conformed to this rule. However, I would argue it is the contrast between the two that is especially revealing, particularly as far as conceptions of working-class identity are concerned. Not that the two events did not have a lot in common. Both took traditional French public celebrations and reshaped them to reflect the unstable, transitional character of 1919. Both in their own ways reflected the dominant theme of that year's public life, the contrast between war and peace. Both used Parisian public

---

[114] Scholars of spectatorship have called into question the idea that the observer is always passive. See Michele Aaron, *Spectatorship: The Power of Looking On* (London and New York: Wallflower, 2007); Jonathan Crary, *Techniques of the Observer: On Vision and Modernity in the Nineteenth Century* (Cambridge MA: MIT Press, 1990); Linda Williams, ed., *Viewing Positions* (New Brunswick: Rutgers University Press, 1994).

[115] This underscores a central point made by Vanessa Schwartz in *Spectacular Realities*, 4–5. However, I would argue that the revolutionary crowd of Paris did not disappear by the twentieth century, absorbed into commercial spectacle. Rather, people could play multiple roles, including devotees of both mass culture and oppositional politics.

space to address themes of national and universal significance. Yet in doing so May Day and Bastille Day 1919 symbolically represented not just contrasts but also conflicts that went to the heart of life in Paris after the war. Central was the opposition between order and disorder highlighted by the two demonstrations. Whereas May Day was not only poorly planned but erupted onto the streets of Paris in chaos and violence, Bastille Day was tightly controlled and displayed all the beauty and precision of a classical ballet. The contrast between the two events symbolized the conflict between bourgeois order and working-class disorder in 1919. Not just in politics and ideology, but also in form and style, the demonstrations represented two different worlds.

Yet May Day and Bastille Day also symbolized contrasts within working-class Parisian life. If May Day stood for working-class militancy and isolation, Bastille Day resembled working-class reception of the products of capitalist mass culture like the cinema. Much of the history of twentieth-century labor, in France and throughout Europe and the industrialized world, would revolve around this contrast between class-conscious working-class culture and integrative capitalist consumer culture.[116] The symbolic opposition of May Day and Bastille Day, 1919, represented this dichotomy powerfully, yet it was not absolute. Behind this symbolic opposition lurked instances of interaction between the two visions. After the impressive military march, for example, the traditional *bals populaires* took place on the night of July 14 in working-class neighborhoods throughout Paris.[117] Such instances, while not necessarily undermining bourgeois perceptions of the working class as symbols of disorder and the Other in 1919, did posit the existence of alternative conceptions of working-class identity. These alternative conceptions involved both conflict and interaction between the poles constituted by May Day and Bastille Day. Ultimately, the two great public events served to demonstrate the complexity of Parisian working-class life; while the opposition between them tended to promote ideal types of the worker and the bourgeois, it also subverted these types, shedding new light on what it meant to be a worker in Paris at the end of World War I.

[116] Michael Seidman, *Workers against Work: Labor in Paris and Barcelona during the Popular Fronts* (Berkeley: University of California Press, 1991); Gary Cross, "Consumer history and dilemmas of working-class history," *Labor History Review*, 62/3 (1997); Ellen Furlough and Carl Strikwerda, eds., *Consumers against Capitalism? Consumer Cooperation in Europe, North America, and Japan, 1840–1990* (Lanham MD: Rowman and Littlefield, 1999).

[117] ". . . et la fête commence!," *L'Humanité*, July 14, 1919, 1.

Social identities are never fixed, but change incessantly over time, and working-class identity is no exception to this rule. 1919 was unusual, however, in that the process of identity formation was particularly transparent and therefore open to challenge. Workers in Paris were workers because they were not bourgeois, and rarely before had the bourgeoisie represented such power and self-assurance. For a brief time in 1919 all the movers and shakers of the world gathered in the French capital, by their presence vividly underlining the contrast between the powerful and the powerless. To be a worker meant not to be one of them. At the same time, however, the nature of the working class itself lay open to question. The process of exclusion of nonwhite and female laborers from those industrial spaces symbolizing working class graphically shows the constructed nature of this social group. Street politics both contrasted the gap between labor and capital in Paris, and at the same time subtly undermined it. In back of all this instability lay the metaphoric experience of the war itself, which had created an either/or world that the international peacemakers meeting in Paris both nourished and hoped to bring to an end.

In 1919 Paris and the world had yet to settle into a comfortable postwar routine. Consequently, the popular struggles that took place in that year strongly reflected both the wartime climate of binary opposition and the instability of a working class that had changed during the war and now confronted different possibilities for the years of peace ahead. This instability opened up new options for popular struggle. In particular, it highlighted the spectacular nature of working-class politics and working-class identity. Acts that demonstrated what it meant to be a worker, ranging from marching in a demonstration to writing in a diary, became especially important in an era that both insisted upon and yet challenged normative patterns of class identification.

The next chapter will consider one specific example of working-class identity and politics, consumer movements. For various reasons, struggles over consumer goods emerged to the fore as a prime example of these alternative strategies. Concretely, even people as different as René Michaud and Louise Deletang could agree that the price of vegetables was too high. More broadly, the struggle over the deregulation of consumer goods crystallized the opposition between war and peace in terms of working-class living standards. Finally, the politicization of everyday commodities like food, clothing, and shelter both reflected and reinforced a Manichean vision of the world, in which everything revolved around class conflict. Alsace-Lorraine might be won and the Kaiser humbled, but the struggle for one's daily bread still expressed itself in the language of war.

CHAPTER 5

Consumer movements

In September 1919 a comedy troupe performed a skit entitled "Everything's Rising!" at the Lune Rousse theater in Paris. A clever mixture of commentary on local events and a satire of the relationship between politics and war, the skit underscored the importance of consumer movements for Parisians after the Armistice.

[ALL]: Long live the League! Long live the President!

BALTHA: Thank you my children, all is going well and your President is happy to tell you that the campaign led by the Montmartre League has begun to bear fruit – and fruit these days is something rare ... Let us listen to the latest communiqué of the League! ...
Rue des Abbesses front.
We have advanced from the Lepic sector to the Marché Saint-Pierre after a violent barrage of tomatoes and cauliflowers and an emission of poison gas using ripe Livarot and Camembert cheeses. Between Clignancourt and Grande Carrières potatoes have retreated from 40 to 35 centimes. Rotten eggs selling at 75 centimes tried an attack but were repulsed by a counterattack from the Vilgrain barracks. Wine, which had moved up to 1 franc 80 centimes, was forced back to its initial position of 1 franc 65 ... milk, after having advanced under violent fire to 1 franc 25 has been forced back to 90 centimes.

ALL: Victory![1]

At the heart of the revolutionary upsurge in the year after the Armistice lay struggles over the basic commodities of food and shelter. In Paris and its suburbs 1919 brought an unprecedented level of consumer activism, as thousands sought to ensure that the protections for consumers enacted by public authorities during the war were not abandoned with the peace. In an era when political insurgency was very much at the forefront of public concerns, they raised the prospect that the consumers' war could turn into the consumers' revolution. If working-class activism assumed a spectacular

[1] Archives de la Préfecture de Police de Paris, BA 861, "He! La Hausse!," September 1, 1919.

public dimension, as noted in the previous chapter, it also surfaced in more mundane and everyday spheres of life. In 1919 politics lay not just in the streets, but in the apartments and food markets of the city as well.

The consumer activism of 1919 grew naturally out of the wartime tensions and movements discussed in Chapter 1. The movements around both housing and food reflected wartime struggles, in particular emphasizing the preservation of the benefits of wartime cost regulations into the postwar era. In contrast, 1919 did not see the kind of activism around clothing that had marked the war years. This was certainly not because fashion had lost its political significance, far from it; as Mary Louise Roberts and others have noted, the war years gave rise to the triumph of the New Woman in fashion and style during the 1920s in Paris.[2] Yet even though the less ostentatious, more understated character of this new style might betray a certain popular influence, during 1919 at least it did not share the overt politicization so central to food and housing consumerism. Instead, in her sartorial rejection of prewar tradition the New Woman anticipated the blue-jeaned, long-haired rebels of the mid twentieth century. Consumer activism in 1919 remained rooted in working-class organizational structures even while challenging them, and the time had not yet come for the kind of middle-class postmodern militancy that the aftermath of a new world war would bring.[3]

The importance of consumer struggles in 1919 played a key role in reformulations of working-class identity. On the one hand, as noted in the discussion of Louise Deletang and René Michaud, discontent over consumer issues had the power to bring together Parisian workers of very disparate views and circumstances. On the other hand, movements around food and housing at times underscored the role of difference in working-class identity. This was particularly true of gender differences. Paradoxically, during a period in which women were losing their jobs in heavy industry, Parisian labor was also engaged in movements, especially those around the cost of food, that gave pride of place to female activists and consumers. If on

---

[2] Mary Louise Roberts, *Civilization Without Sexes: Reconstructing Gender in Postwar France, 1917–1927* (University of Chicago Press, 1994); Valerie Steele, *Paris Fashion: A Cultural History* (New York: Oxford University Press, 1988). Steele has noted that in many ways the New Woman as fashion idea antedated the war. *Ibid.*, 237.

[3] One exception to this lack of attention to the politics of clothing in 1919 concerned the clothing of demobilized soldiers. Those leaving uniform were given small allowances to purchase civilian clothes, and there were numerous complaints about the inadequacy of these allowances. Interestingly, this issue showed up most in popular entertainment, as music hall artists satirized the dilemma of the poor unfashionable veteran. See Archives de la Préfecture de Police, BA 860, "Scene du demobilisé," April 1919.

one level, as shown in Chapter 3, women were excluded from working-class identity, on another they received increased prominence in it. One can make sense of this paradox by seeing it as advocating a more traditional view of female militancy and gender segregation in the face of the challenge to the latter posed by the *munitionnettes* during the war. At the same time, the emphasis on women's consumer activism (which, as we shall see, had its limits in 1919) and the close proximity of two such disparate views of working women highlights the instability of class identity so prominent in the year after the Armistice. Here again, the collision of different streams produced a frothy explosion of white water.

The Paris consumer movements of 1919 shared a few central themes. While most of their participants belonged to or identified with the organized working-class Left, their focus on issues of food and shelter departed from and at times challenged the productivist workplace orientation of workers' parties and unions at the time, as did their emphasis on relatively spontaneous forms of organization. In addressing consumer issues they organized around what were traditionally seen as women's concerns, and in consequence they at times tried to give prominent roles to women, while at the same time remaining largely dominated by male activists. Finally, these movements addressed issues that resonated with many middle-class consumers as well, and at times they tried to take advantage of that broader appeal. At the same time, however, many if not most of their adherents espoused revolutionary sentiments, seeing their struggles as part of the broader struggle for a new day. In both their anti-capitalist fervor and in their heterodox styles of organization and militancy, the Parisian consumer movements perfectly summed up the revolutionary nature of 1919.

Any historical analysis of consumer movements in 1919 must contend with two major bodies of scholarship. The first concerns popular movements of moral economy. Students of Europe in the eighteenth and nineteenth centuries have devoted a great deal of attention to food riots in particular, presenting them as examples of popular protest and revealing illustrations of popular *mentalités*. In a celebrated article E. P. Thompson argued that men and women in pre-industrial England held certain basic ideas as to what constituted fair treatment by food producers and merchants. Transgressions of this "moral economy of the crowd" could and did provoke food riots.[4] Although such food riots varied considerably in character, they often shared several essential traits: attempts to punish food

---

[4] E. P. Thompson, "The moral economy of the English crowd in the eighteenth century," *Past and Present*, 50 (February, 1971). For responses to this article, see A. W. Coats, "Contrary moralities: plebs,

merchants and regulate food prices by means of *taxation populaire*, or popular price fixing; an insistence on the obligation of public authorities to regulate food prices; and the active participation of women.[5] Some historians of this phenomenon have argued food riots were a pre-industrial form of protest that largely disappeared after the mid nineteenth century, with the rise of national food markets that increasingly prevented local food shortages, and centralized price levels.[6] Others have challenged this view, pointing to the existence of food riots in the years before World War I. In an article on the 1911 food riots in northern France, Paul Hanson argues that these movements demonstrate the continued survival of traditional *mentalités* and forms of protest well into the contemporary era.[7]

The second scholarly approach to popular mobilization concerns the study of new social movements in the late twentieth century. The New Left social and political struggles that arose throughout Europe and America during the 1960s and 1970s, and the decline of the postwar *modus vivendi* between capital and organized labor, led many social scientists during the 1980s and 1990s to re-theorize the nature of collective movements in advanced capitalist countries. They heralded the rise of "new social movements," creations of post-industrial society characterized by a non-working-class social base, a concern with quality of life rather than bread and butter issues, a concern with race and gender identities rather than (or in addition to) class, and an emphasis on participatory and spontaneous forms of organization in contrast to traditional Marxist political parties and working-class trade unions.[8] New social movement theory has also attracted criticism from historians, some of whom have

---

paternalists and political economists," *Past and Present*, 54 (February, 1972); Elizabeth Fox Genovese, "The many faces of moral economy: a contribution to a debate," *Past and Present*, 58 (February, 1973). See also E. P. Thompson, *Customs in Common* (New York: New Press, 1993).

[5] Among the most important works on food riots in early modern Europe are Steven L. Kaplan, *Provisioning Paris: Merchants and Millers in the Grain and Flour Trade during the Eighteenth Century* (Ithaca NY: Cornell University Press, 1984); Georges Rudé, "La taxation populaire de mai 1775 à Paris et dans la région parisienne," *Annales historiques de la Révolution Française*, 143 (April–June, 1956); Eric Richards, "The last Scottish food riots," *Past and Present*, Supplement, 6 (1982).

[6] Roger Price, *The Modernization of Rural France* (New York: St. Martin's Press, 1983); Charles Tilly, "Food supply and public order in modern Europe," in Charles Tilly, ed., *The Formation of National States in Western Europe* (Princeton University Press, 1975); Louise Tilly, "The food riot as a form of political conflict in France," *Journal of Interdisciplinary History*, 2/1 (Summer, 1971).

[7] Paul Hanson, "The 'vie chère' riots of 1911: traditional protests in modern garb," *Journal of Social History*, 21/3 (Spring, 1988).

[8] On new social movement theory, see in particular Alain Touraine, *The Voice and the Eye: An Analysis of Social Movements* (Cambridge University Press, 2003); Jean Cohen, "Rethinking social movements," *Berkeley Journal of Sociology*, 28 (1983); Klaus Eder, *The New Politics of Class: Social Movements and Cultural Dynamics in Advanced Societies* (London: Sage Publications, 1993); Jan Willem Duyvendak, *The Power of Politics: New Social Movements in France* (Boulder CO: Westview Press, 1995). For a useful summary of the literature see Nelson A. Pichado, "New social movements: a critical review," *Annual Review of Sociology*, 23 (1997).

contended that there is very little new about such movements, and that the rupture with the industrial era is less sharp than is often assumed. Some have argued, for example, that many of the characteristics of new social movements also typified popular struggles in the early nineteenth century, such as Chartism. In an important article, Craig Calhoun suggests that one can usefully distinguish both the early industrial and postindustrial eras from the late nineteenth to mid twentieth centuries, noting that even in that latter period Marxist-inspired forms of social struggle were always contested.[9]

The consumer movements that struck Paris in 1919 exhibit similarities with both moral economy riots and new social movements. Their focus on consumption rather than production, their relatively spontaneous nature, and the prominent involvement of women (and their concern with what were frequently considered women's issues) all recall an earlier period of popular struggles in France and elsewhere in Europe.[10] The connection to the late twentieth century is less clear, since Parisian consumer activists did not adopt the frontal challenge to working-class parties and unions that typified the militants of 1968 and other New Left struggles. However, their spontaneity and their ability to appeal to middle-class concerns did foreshadow some aspects of the new social movements of the post-1945 period. Rather than view 1919 as an intermediate stage along a teleologically defined history of social movements, one should consider food and housing struggles as tactics in a repertoire of popular practices, to be used when conditions were appropriate.[11] The Paris consumer movements of 1919 showed that traditional attitudes remained strong among French workers in the early twentieth century, but that in confronting threats to their living conditions working people consciously and creatively adapted these traditions to produce new strategies of resistance. Such movements played a major role in Parisian life during 1919, and surfaced in other parts of Europe and America as well.[12]

[9] Craig Calhoun, "'New social movements' of the early nineteenth century," *Social Science History*, 17/3 (Fall, 1993); Paul D'Anieri *et al.*, "New social movements in historical perspective," *Comparative Politics*, 22 (July, 1990); Alberto A. Melucci, "A strange kind of newness: what's new in new social movements?" in E. Larana *et al.*, *New Social Movements: From Ideology to Identity* (Philadelphia PA: Temple University Press, 1994).

[10] Historians of Britain during World War I have also noted this. See Matthew Hilton, *Consumerism in Twentieth-Century Britain: The Search for a Historical Movement* (Cambridge University Press, 2003); Bernard Waites, "The government of the Home Front and the 'moral economy' of the working class," in Peter H. Liddle, ed., *Home Fires and Foreign Fields: British Social and Military Experience in the First World War* (London: Brassey's Defence Publishers, 1985).

[11] On the concept of repertoires of popular practices, see Charles Tilly, *The Contentious French* (Cambridge MA: Belknap Press, 1986).

[12] See Temma Kaplan, "Female consciousness and collective action: the case of Barcelona, 1910–1918," *Signs*, 7/2 (Winter, 1981); Jean-Marie Flonneau, "Crise de vie chère et mouvement syndical 1910–1914," *Mouvement Social* (July–September, 1970); Anthony James Coles, "The moral economy of the crowd: some twentieth-century food riots," *Journal of British Studies*, 18/1 (Fall, 1978).

In particular, struggles over housing and food highlighted transformations of working-class activism and life in general wrought by World War I. They showed how, while neighborhood and local concerns retained their importance, they were increasingly interpreted in national and even international contexts. Here again the phenomenon of glocalization, made so evident by the presence of the world peace negotiations in the city, helped structure working-class strategies in defense of their living standards. These movements also illustrated new attitudes toward politics and the state. The conflicts around state regulation of consumption and the economy in general caused by the war had effectively destroyed the old anarcho-syndicalist rejection of politics. State action became a key focus of these new consumer movements, constituting a powerful legacy for the twentieth century as a whole. At the same time, these movements fostered a recognition of the micro-politics of power that went well beyond that offered by the unions and parties of the Left. In adapting traditions of working-class activism to meet the challenges created by the war and postwar era, the consumer movements of 1919 ultimately created new forms of activism for the twentieth century. Ultimately, the vision of revolution arose out of and underscored this politicization of everyday life.

Finally, as in many other parts of this study, it is useful to consider this history in the context of colonial consumerism and consumer movements.[13] One can look at this from two different perspectives. First, if the Parisian consumer movements represent a departure from normative patterns of French industrial unrest that both recall moral economy and forecast new social movements, they also demonstrate notable affinities with consumer politics in Europe's overseas empires. As examples as disparate as the Boston Tea Party and Gandhi's 1930 Salt March to the sea make clear, food and other consumer goods have played a central role both in the attempts of colonial states to enforce their power over colonized populations, and in the anti-colonial struggles of the latter.[14] A major theme of imperial rule in the

---

[13] In pointing to the relationship between colonialism and consumerism in modern France I take inspiration from the work of Kristin Ross. See her *Fast Cars, Clean Bodies: Decolonization and the Reordering of French Culture* (Cambridge MA: MIT Press, 1996).

[14] A leading scholar of anti-colonial peasant resistance and its roots in ideas of moral economy is James Scott. See his *The Moral Economy of the Peasant: Rebellion and Subsistence in Southeast Asia* (New Haven: Yale University Press, 1976); and *Weapons of the Weak: Everyday Forms of Peasant Resistance* (New Haven: Yale University Press, 1985). See also Timothy Burke, *Lifebuoy Men, Lux Women: Commodification, Consumption, and Cleanliness in Modern Zimbabwe* (Durham NC: Duke University Press, 1996).

modern era has been the attempt of European rulers to impose standards of consumption on the colonized as a means of transforming them into wage laborers and tax payers, as well as creating markets for their own products. Britain's opium wars with China are perhaps the most prominent example of this.[15] In his dissertation Gerard Sasges demonstrates that the French alcohol monopoly was the single most prominent European institution in colonial Indochina.[16] At the same time, scholars have argued that colonizers did not simply impose European styles of consumption upon the colonized, but that the latter at times embraced, rejected, and transformed consumer goods from the west. Jeremy Rich has shown how French food became a contested symbol of colonial rule, a site of both administrative power and native resistance, in central Africa.[17] With the growth of urban centers in colonial areas struggles over housing, especially concerning racial segregation, also became social and political flashpoints.[18] As anti-colonialism began to achieve a mass base between the world wars, in many cases consumer as well as workplace issues loomed large in activist strategies.[19] In both Asia and Africa anti-colonial militants used consumer boycotts to challenge imperial rule.[20]

Second, the consumer movements of 1919 took place in a culture that was embracing colonialism and the exotic as consumer products to an unprecedented degree. The year 1919 represented not only the end of World War I but also the beginnings of the *années folles*, an era that celebrated African and

---

[15] Peter Ward Fay, *The Opium War, 1840–1842* (Chapel Hill: University of North Carolina Press, 1998).

[16] Gerard Sasges, "The alcohol regime in Indochina 1897–1933" (Ph.D. dissertation, University of California, Berkeley, 2006). See also Jonathan Crush and Charles Ambler, eds., *Liquor and Labor in Southern Africa* (Athens: Ohio University Press, 1992).

[17] Jeremy Rich, *A Workman Is Worthy of His Meat: Food and Colonialism in the Gabon Estuary* (Lincoln: University of Nebraska Press, 2007); Louis A. Pérez, *On Becoming Cuban: Identity, Nationality, and Culture* (Chapel Hill: University of North Carolina Press, 1999). A classic study in this regard is Sidney W. Mintz, *Sweetness and Power: The Place of Sugar in Modern History* (New York: Penguin, 1985).

[18] Zeynep Celik, *Urban Forms and Colonial Confrontations: Algiers under French Rule* (Berkeley: University of California Press, 1997); see also the essays in W. Brian Newsome and Tyler Stovall, eds., "French colonial urbanism," special issue of *Historical Reflections / Réflexions Historiques*, 33/2 (Summer, 2007).

[19] Janaki Nair, "Contending ideologies? The Mass Awakener's Union and the Congress in Mysore, 1936–1942," *Social Scientist*, 22/7–8 (July, 1994); Charles Ambler, "Alcohol, racial segregation, and popular politics in Northern Rhodesia," *Journal of African History*, 31/2 (1990); Frederick Cooper, "Conflict and connection: rethinking colonial African history," *American Historical Review*, 99/5 (December, 1994).

[20] Peter Stearns, *Consumerism in World History: The Global Transformation of Desire* (New York: Routledge, 2001), 119.

African American culture in particular.[21] The famous *Banania* ads depicting a genial African soldier first appeared during the war, and by 1919 the popularity of jazz in France had become a major item of discussion for cultural commentators in Paris.[22] Such exoticism represented the new prominence of the French empire in the metropole, the colonies as consumer product. There is of course a huge, seemingly unbridgeable gap between demands for cheap rents and the triumphs of a Josephine Baker on the Paris stage. Yet both drew a link between consumerism and identity, both represented affinities between daily life and questions of national, indeed global politics. In short, Parisian workers emphasized the right to consume as central to working-class politics and identity in a national context in which consumption of the colonial Other increasingly defined French identity.

This parallel does not of course work perfectly. Whereas many anti-colonial struggles around consumer products emphasized resistance to the imposition of European commodities, Parisian consumer movements fought for the right to consume. Certainly the city's housing and food activists did not see themselves as colonized by unscrupulous landlords and merchants. Nonetheless, the relationship between consumerism and identity was a key facet of the modern colonial encounter, and by moving consumer consciousness to the center of Parisian working-class life the consumer movements of 1919 reflected that centrality in a metropolitan context. This parallel reflects that between the exclusion of colonial workers from Paris and the silencing of colonial protest at the peace conference, and underscores the latter's conception of a unified world based upon hierarchies of class and race. The fact that Parisian workers and colonial subjects should adopt, completely independently of each other, similar modes of protest illustrated the interpenetration of those two forms of difference. Ironically, in an era when Parisian workers were emphasizing their difference from colonial labor, they chose activist patterns that highlighted their similarities. Here as in other respects, the Parisian

---

[21] Petrine Archer-Shaw, *Negrophilia: Avant-Garde Paris and Black Culture in the 1920s* (New York: Thames and Hudson, 2000); Elizabeth Ezra, *The Colonial Unconscious: Race and Culture in Interwar France* (Ithaca NY: Cornell University Press, 2000); Brett Berliner, *Ambivalent Desire: The Exotic Black Other in France* (Amherst: University of Massachusetts Press, 2002); Jody Blake, *La Tumulte Noir: Modernist Art and Popular Entertainment in Jazz-Age Paris* (University Park PA: Pennsylvania State University Press, 1999).

[22] Anne Donadey, "'Y'a bon Banania': ethics and cultural criticism in the colonial context," *French Cultural Studies*, 11/31 (2000); Jeffrey Jackson, *Making Jazz French: Music and Modern Life in Interwar Paris* (Durham NC: Duke University Press, 2003).

consumer struggles of 1919 had certain postcolonial as well as postindustrial affinities.

The urban consumer movements that erupted in Paris after the war contributed significantly to the revolutionary spirit of the times. Not only did many of their leaders and activists invoke revolutionary slogans, but their spontaneous, unstable character underscored the idea of a world in flux, where old patterns no longer held and alternative visions of society were possible. Conversely, the unprecedented politicization of mundane concerns like rents and the price of potatoes testified to the extraordinary character of 1919. Above all, they showed that the uncertain transition from war to peace provided space for new types of popular movements, ones that seemed, at least at the time, to have the potential to bring about a new day in France.

DEMOBILIZING THE CONSUMER ECONOMY

For France, World War I marked a quantum increase in the state's direction of the national economy. The French had never embraced economic liberalism to the extent of their neighbors across the Channel; not only did the nineteenth-century Bonapartist state emphasize economic protectionism and government-funded economic projects, but, as Janet Horne has argued, the period before the war saw the development of solidarism and other ideologies advocating a more interventionist state in matters of social reform.[23] Nonetheless, on the eve of World War I state authorities only intervened fitfully and reluctantly to improve the lot of ordinary French men and women. World War I created a crisis profound enough to force national authorities to modify, at least temporarily, this hands-off approach to protecting popular living standards.

The increased powers of the French state during the war, especially its increased levels of consumer regulation, also changed working-class attitudes toward government. France had a long tradition of public oversight of the consumer economy; for example, the regulation of bread prices went back to the French Revolution and indeed earlier centuries. During the war,

---

[23] Jean-Marie Mayeur and Madeleine Rebérioux, *The Third Republic from Its Origins to the Great War, 1871–1914* (Cambridge University Press, 1984), 90–94; Janet R. Horne, *A Social Laboratory for Modern France: The Musée Social and the Rise of the Welfare State* (Durham NC: Duke University Press, 2002); Judith F. Stone, *The Search for Social Peace: Reform Legislation in France, 1890–1914* (Albany: State University of New York Press, 1985).

however, French state organizations acted to an unprecedented degree in protecting the living standards of working people by controlling the prices and supply of both housing and food, as well as encouraging the growth of the cooperative movement. The state thus prompted French workers to view it as, at least in part, responsible for the maintenance of those living standards. Therefore, when protesters in 1919 looked toward public authorities to do something about housing shortages or the high cost of food, they not only drew on historical traditions but also based their beliefs on lessons learned during the war itself.[24]

Many historians have argued that the end of the war brought about a rapid return to normal attitudes toward state involvement in the French economy. Pierre Rosanvallon, for example, states that "Less than a year after the end of the war, the state edifice that had grown up between 1915 and 1918 was in effect almost totally dismantled."[25] Others, however, have noted certain continuities between wartime and postwar economic policies. In considering the wartime history of French labor, John Horne shows how in 1919 reformist labor leaders concentrated on state policies, notably the eight-hour day, which built upon principles of state intervention established during World War I.[26] The corporatist principles pioneered by wartime minister of production Albert Thomas also seemed to leave a legacy for postwar France.[27] Just as some cultural historians have contended that the impact of World War I was not entirely reversed with the peace, so it may be that the process of economic demobilization after 1918 did not in fact involve a complete return to prewar policies. More recently some historians have gone further, calling into question the idea that the creation of the welfare state in France represented a major rupture after 1945 and suggesting instead that World War I constituted the essential beginnings of the modern interventionist state. For example, Timothy B. Smith argues that major currents of urban and municipal social reform began during World War I, providing an important template for national efforts after Vichy.[28]

[24] Patrick Fridenson, "The impact of the war on French workers," in Richard Wall and Jay Winter, eds., *The Upheaval of War* (Cambridge University Press, 1988), 241–244.
[25] Pierre Rosanvallon, *L'État en France de 1789 à nos jours* (Paris: Seuil, 1990), 228.
[26] John Horne, *Labour at War: France and Britain, 1914–1918* (Oxford University Press, 1991).
[27] Alain Hennebique, "Albert Thomas and the war industries," in Patrick Fridenson, ed., *The French Home Front, 1914–1918*, translated by Bruce Little (Providence RI and Oxford: Berg, 1992).
[28] Timothy B. Smith, *Creating the Welfare State in France, 1880–1940* (Montreal: McGill-Queen's University Press, 2003). On the idea that the beginnings of the French welfare state go back to the Third Republic, see John Weiss, "Origins of the French welfare state: Poor Relief in the Third Republic, 1871–1914," *French Historical Studies*, 13 (Spring, 1983); Philip Nord, "The welfare state in France, 1870–1914," *French Historical Studies*, 13/1 (Spring, 1994).

From this perspective as well, economic demobilization after 1918 did not bring about a return to prewar normality.

The demobilization of the consumer economy tends to support the idea that the liberal state did not reassert itself completely after 1918, at least not without a struggle. Unfortunately few historians have written about the regulation of civilian consumption during the war, and fewer still have considered debates about the termination of those controls at the war's end.[29] Yet as we have seen in this study, the war introduced a level of government intervention in French consumer life unprecedented during the Third Republic. Moreover, precisely because the consumer economy seemed less central to the war effort than did the armed forces or the munitions industrial sector, the transition from war to peace was less clear-cut; whereas it obviously made no sense to keep a large army or numerous munitions factories after the Armistice, it was easier to make an argument for the maintenance of consumer regulations. In addition, the idea that the sacrifices of the *poilus* had entitled them and their families to a better standard of living, to be guaranteed by the state if necessary, directly targeted the availability and prices of consumer goods. Much more so than military and industrial mobilization, wartime consumer regulation had become identified with improvements in the quality of working-class life in particular.

For these reasons, the demobilization of the consumer sector in France was less straightforward than demobilization in general, and led to major popular struggles in 1919. These struggles underscored the unstable character of that year, divided between war and peace and unsure as to whether or not wartime experiments would become peacetime norms. Although not necessarily revolutionary in and of themselves, they highlighted the revolutionary atmosphere and potential of 1919. As we shall see, the impact of such struggles varied according to their goals, strategies, and concerns. Whereas housing activists generally succeeded in maintaining wartime restrictions on rents, those advocating continued controls of food prices largely failed. The ideology of the liberal, non-interventionist state may have prevailed in general during the postwar era, but it was not universally triumphant. Even when authorities succeeded in deregulating consumer life after the Armistice, they had to contend with forces that, much more than before

[29] On the transition from war to peace in general, see Joshua Cole, "The transition to peace, 1918–1919," in Jay Winter and Jean-Louis Robert, *Capital Cities at War: Paris, London, Berlin 1914–1919* (Cambridge University Press, 1997); Bruno Cabanes, *La victoire endeuillée: la sortie de guerre des soldats français (1918–1920)* (Paris: Seuil, 2004); John Horne, "Démobilisations culturelles après la Grande Guerre," special issue of *14–18 Aujourd'hui* (May, 2002).

1914, challenged their right and shaped their abilities to do so. In 1919 the consumers' war continued, emphasizing the continuation of the struggle for consumer rights after the termination of hostilities with Germany. It suggested not so much that the war should continue, but rather that peace should perpetuate and build upon the wartime achievements of the interventionist state. The question of consumer demobilization after World War I bears more than a passing resemblance to the much more extensive development of *l'état providence* in France and throughout Europe after 1945. As in the case of postcolonial society in the late twentieth century, one can trace the beginnings of the modern welfare state to the conflicts over consumerism and consumer regulation at the end of World War I.

THE STRUGGLE FOR A PLACE TO LIVE

As noted in Chapter 1, the rental policies enacted by the national government during the war had sharpened the opposition between landlords and tenants in Paris. The successive moratoria on eviction for non-payment of rent, finally codified in the law of March 9, 1918, had embittered most Parisian landlords, who often viewed their tenants as taking unfair advantage of the war to profit at their expense. Many tenants, accusing the city's landlords of wanting to exploit soldiers fighting and dying for the nation and hoping to kick their widows into the street if they couldn't pay, joined the new renters' union, the *Union confédérale des locataires* (Federal Union of Tenants). The passage of the March, 1918 law, and the approaching end of hostilities, did nothing to ease the harsh feelings surrounding the housing question in Paris. On the contrary, the end of the war seemed to intensify the conflict as both landlords and tenants jockeyed for advantage amidst the uncertainties of the transition to peace.[30]

The powerful social struggles around housing that took place in Paris during the year after the Armistice arose in the context of one of the worst housing crises in the city's history (Illustration 5.1). The French capital had a long history of inadequate and substandard housing. The years immediately before the war had witnessed a certain increase in the availability of affordable housing, but virtually all of that was in the suburbs; in 1914 the vacancy rate for apartments renting for under 300 francs per year was 1 percent, as opposed to 8 percent ten years earlier.[31] The socioeconomic

---

[30] Susanna Magri, "Housing," in Winter and Robert, *Capital Cities at War.*

[31] Tyler Stovall, "*Sous les toits de Paris:* the working class and the Paris housing crisis, 1914–1924," *Proceedings of the Annual Meeting of the Western Society for French History,* 14 (1987), 265.

5.1 "Struggle for Home!"

processes that would gradually transform Paris into an affluent, bourgeois city surrounded by working-class suburbia during the twentieth century were already well under way before 1914.[32]

The war of course made things much worse, for a variety of reasons. The population of the Department of the Seine grew substantially during the war, thanks not only to the needs of wartime industry, but also because of the expansion of the national government, which created a need for more clerks and other low-level white-collar workers to staff its offices. At the same time, the reorientation of the French economy to meet the needs of war brought housing construction to a virtual halt after August 1914: some Parisian buildings that had been partially completed when hostilities broke out remained in that condition for the duration of the war. From 1915 to 1919 there was a net increase of 1,480 apartments in Paris, compared with 4,745 from 1910 to 1914; residential construction in the suburbs fell off to an

---

[32] Jean Bastié, *La croissance de la banlieue parisienne* (Paris: Presses Universitaires de France, 1964); Jean-Paul Brunet, *Saint-Denis la ville rouge* (Paris: Hachette, 1980); Tyler Stovall, *The Rise of the Paris Red Belt* (Berkeley: University of California Press, 1990).

even greater extent. Moreover, both higher construction costs and a trend toward commercial building in Paris fueled the shortage of affordable housing during World War I.[33]

This combination of factors by itself would have ensured a crisis of affordable rental housing during the war. Yet state policies, notably residential rent control and the wartime moratoria on the Paris housing market, reinforced their impact and made the issue a political one. The national government's decisions to curtail the ability of landlords to raise rents or to expel tenants for non-payment of rent were a major cause of disinvestment in residential housing construction, thus contributing to the severity of the housing crisis as a whole. In effect, the housing crisis was the downside of rent control, a policy that had a considerable upside for most Parisians. Thanks to wartime controls, housing costs constituted a shrinking share of the average Parisian's budget. Whereas the costs of food, clothing, and heating fuel all roughly tripled from 1914 to 1922, the cost of housing only rose about 10 percent. Accounting for 16 percent of the Parisian working-class budget in 1914, by 1924 housing took up only 4 percent.[34]

It was this situation that underlay the near collapse of residential construction in Paris during and after the war, the major cause of the housing crisis. However, owners of apartments also took steps in response to rent control that made it more difficult for Parisians to find a place to live. Many owners of vacant apartments, especially inexpensive ones, simply refused to rent them out. In what amounted to a landlords' strike, owners often preferred to let apartments sit empty rather than take a chance on bringing in tenants who would have the legal right to pay low rents for the indefinite future, and who could not be evicted if they refused to pay. When they did rent their apartments, many owners did so to friends or relatives without any public announcement; one police officer noted that, although there were no vacancy notices in his district, one could often observe moving vehicles at work.[35]

Far from bringing relief to those desperately searching for shelter, the end of the war brought a worsening of the Paris housing crisis. One problem was housing demobilized soldiers. Those originally from the area presumably

[33] Henri Sellier, *La crise du logement et l'intervention publique en matière d'habitation populaire dans l'agglomération parisienne* (Paris: Éditions de l'office public d'habitations à bon marché du département de la Seine, 1921), 131.

[34] *Revue Internationale du Travail*, 7 (June, 1923), 6; Susanna Magri, *La politique du logement et besoins en main d'oeuvre* (Paris: Centre de sociologie urbaine, 1972), 94–97.

[35] Archives de la Préfecture de Police de Paris [hereafter APP], series BA 1614, police report of October 16, 1919.

had homes to return to, but many provincial soldiers who left the army in Paris decided to stay there. Similarly, many wartime refugees chose not to return to their homes in the formerly invaded regions of France, or if they did, they sometimes hung onto their Parisian lodgings just in case. Moreover, precisely because housing was so tight, people who already had apartments either chose not to move, or if they did, opted to keep their old apartments until they were firmly established in their new homes, further decreasing the housing supply at any given time. Consequently, vacancy rates plunged in the two years after the Armistice. For example, after rising slightly during the war, the vacancy rate for Paris apartments renting for 500–1,000 francs per year dropped sharply at the end of 1918. By 1920 the rate for them was less than 0.2 percent; fewer than 300 such apartments were available in the entire city.[36] The war might be over, but the battle for affordable housing remained to be won.

Reports by police and other public officials from throughout the city and the suburbs of the Department of the Seine testified to the near-impossibility of finding housing after the war. They noted that landlords were demanding much higher rents as well as substantial security deposits, and that even those prospective tenants able to accept such terms often searched in vain. Concierges, the powerful gatekeepers of Parisian housing, also often took advantage of the situation by demanding and getting the "*denier à dieu*," a substantial tip often worth several hundred francs, in exchange for reserving lodgings for people (Illustration 5.2). As one report from eastern Paris in February 1919 noted:

The renters in search of rooms or small apartments are tired of looking.

The landlords, fearful of not being paid, don't advertise their vacant lodgings.

Moreover, those tenants fortunate enough finally to have found the housing that they want have to confront the exaggerated importance of the *denier à dieu* demanded by the concierges who, in spite of what they promise, end up giving the apartment to the highest bidder.

This is currently a deplorable abuse but one that is impossible to stop.[37]

A report from April commented that "The situation remains the same; a few refugees have returned home, but the influx of a fairly large number of new

---

[36] Departement de la Seine, commission des Habitations ouvrières et du plan d'extension, *Rapport relatif à la crise du logement*, 129, 145. Unfortunately this report did not provide statistics for apartments renting at less than 500 francs per year. One should also take into account the fact that these statistics were drawn up by the Tax Commission of the City of Paris. A landlord who declared an apartment to have a taxable value of 500 francs a year was not always actually willing to rent it out at such a price.

[37] APP BA 1614, report of February 24, 1919.

Toto. — *C'est lui..., Dieu ?*

5.2 "Le denier à dieu"

railway workers has largely filled the gap they could have left in the twelfth *arrondissement* and the number of available apartments remains null."[38] One February report noted that not only were the hotels around the Gare du Nord and the Gare de l'Est packed with families looking for more permanent housing, but many of their proprietors had evicted their traditional clientele, prostitutes, to make room for them.[39]

For many would-be tenants in Paris and its suburbs in 1919, the problem was not just the shortage of housing in general but the arrogance of landlords and their agents in particular. And Parisian landlords were certainly in no mood, after four years of wartime rent moratoria, to accept anything less than the maximum rents they could get. In 1919 many landlords continued their wartime practices of withholding rental units from the market, demanding substantially higher rents, and insisting on payment of several months' rent in advance. However, they also sought to take advantage of the end of hostilities by ending what they saw as a free ride for those who already had apartments. The successive moratoria on rent payments, renewed every three months since August 1914, were scheduled to expire with the end of

[38] APP BA 1614, report of April 7, 1919.   [39] APP BA 1614, report of February 10, 1919.

the war. The housing law of March 9, 1918 had reaffirmed the wartime exemption from paying rent for the poorest tenants. However, at the same time the law permitted landlords to petition for rents from others. In 1919 many landlords used this provision of the 1918 law to try to recoup their wartime losses.

At the heart of this conflict lay the arbitration commissions established by the 1918 housing law. The law established these commissions in all the districts of Paris and the suburbs of the Department of the Seine. Each consisted of five members: a magistrate (who had the tie-breaking vote) and two representatives each of landlords and tenants. They began working with the promulgation of the law, hearing rental disputes, and until September 1918 seem to have worked regularly and quietly. As the end of the war approached, however, the number of cases brought before the commissions by landlords increased sharply. By the end of December plaintiffs had brought over 100,000 cases before the arbitration commissions of the Department of the Seine. These increases continued in 1919. By June 30, 1919 the number of complaints formally registered in Paris alone stood at over 160,000, as opposed to less than 60,000 at the beginning of the year. For Parisian landlords, accustomed during the war years to government intervention in favor of their tenants, the end of the war meant that they could finally use the 1918 housing law to their own advantage.[40]

The arbitration commissions could benefit the landlords in two ways. First, they could rule in their favor and order tenants to accept rent increases, or even to pay back rent. Just as those with housing to offer did so at much higher prices in 1919, so did they demand similar rent increases of already established tenants. As a report to the Paris City Council in June 1919 noted, "Certain landlords, too often without taking into account the situation or good will of their tenants, and desiring to recuperate the rental 'losses' they suffered (or even the rent increases they have not been able to implement) . . . raise their rents by 300, 400, and up to 500%."[41]

More significantly, in cases where tenants would not or could not pay the mandated rent increases, the arbitration commissions had the power to order evictions. Once the war ended landlords rushed to evict those who had been allowed to postpone rent payments during the conflict. Thus the specter of eviction from one's home for non-payment of rent, essentially

[40] Magri, "Housing," 409–410.
[41] Conseil Municipal de Paris, "Proposition tendant à remédier à la crise du logement," *Rapports et documents*, 3 (1921). As noted earlier, landlords simply believed that rent increases were their only way to recoup wartime losses, especially given the possibility that rent controls might be imposed again.

nonexistent during the war, reappeared with a vengeance in Paris and its suburbs during 1919. As with rent increases, the period from the Armistice to October 1919 represents the high point of such expulsion attempts. In June alone the authorities sent 50,000 eviction notices to Parisian tenants.[42] Landlords had clearly had enough of tenants who refused to pay rent, and in 1919 it seemed they would finally succeed in resolving the problem on their terms. As a report in the *Gazette des Tribunaux* noted:

The process of evicting renters, which had been suspended during the war, has begun.

In virtue of article 34 of the law of March 9, 1918, the arbitration commissions have been called to rule upon special cases. Decisions for eviction have been rendered ... the affected tenants not having left their homes, the bailiffs have proceeded to evict them with the aid of the police commissioner.[43]

As noted in Chapter 1, the war had created a climate of sharp opposition between landlords and tenants in Paris. The specter of mass evictions, however, brought this hostility to a whole new level, and lay at the base of the upsurge in tenant activism in 1919. Public authorities were very well aware of the problems for public order that widespread evictions could create, and frequently tried to intervene by finding new housing for those expelled or at risk of being expelled from their apartments. In February 1919, the Paris Prefect of Police wrote to the Minister of Justice about the problem:

The housing question deserves close examination, since the difficulties [of finding housing] get worse each day both because of the return of demobilized soldiers to Paris and because of the evictions pronounced by the arbitration commissions; the decisions of the latter cannot be executed without endangering public order, except when it is possible to assure shelter for those evicted.

My services are frequently asked to come to the aid of the homeless; but, in spite of all their good will, the officials of the Prefecture of Police can only rarely satisfy these requests. Currently, in effect, the few vacant apartments and rooms are not made available for rent by the landlords, who fear they won't be able to collect their rents.[44]

Another police report a month later expressed "a strong concern about what will happen when the Police commissioners have to undertake the first evictions ... where will we house those evicted?"[45]

Ironically, the arbitration commissions, which had been established to mediate the discord between landlords and tenants by searching for

---

[42] Conseil Municipal de Paris, *Rapports et documents*, 3 (1921), 8.
[43] "Chronique," *Gazette des Tribunaux*, May 30–31, 1919, 2. The report goes on to note that two evictions took place in Ivry, but that fortunately the police were able to find alternative housing for the evicted tenants.
[44] AN F7 13755, letter of February 10, 1919.   [45] APP BA 1614, police report of March 7, 1919.

compromises that would satisfy both, instead came to symbolize the opposition between the two groups, and class conflict in general. As Susanna Magri has pointed out, while one option for resolving landlord/tenant disputes submitted to the commissions was conciliation, in less than a third of the cases registered was such conciliation even attempted.[46] The tenants' union had opposed the 1918 housing law largely because of the role given to the arbitration commissions in adjudicating landlord/tenant disputes, and it felt that the evictions of 1919 fully justified its position. The members of the commissions themselves seemed to recognize that they were stepping into a hornets' nest; as one police report noted in April:

M. Michel, president of an arbitration commission in the 20th *arrondissement,* having submitted to me the fears expressed by certain judges, prompted me to undertake an investigation, from which it seems that such fears are not entirely well founded. Nonetheless, we will exercise surveillance to the extent possible.

In any case, the tenants who are called before the arbitration commission have shown that they plan to be even less open to compromise in the future.[47]

"LONG LIVE THE RENTERS! LONG LIVE THE WORKERS' INTERNATIONALE!"

The landlords' use of the arbitration commissions to expel Parisian tenants for non-payment of rent gave renters' unionism a new lease on life after the war. As noted in Chapter 1, activists had founded the Federal Union of Tenants (*Union Confédérale des Locataires*) in 1915. A national organization, it was largely dominated by the Renters' Federation of the Seine (*Fédération des Locataires de la Seine*), or FLS. During the war the FLS competed with other renters' unions in Paris and its suburbs, but the housing and evictions crises of 1919 propelled it to a size and prominence unprecedented in the history of French tenant unionism. Affiliated with the Socialist Party, it was led by veteran activists like Lucien Dieulle, its general secretary in 1919, and Louis Muller, both of whom had been active in tenant unionism before the war. However, this affiliation was fairly loose; although the FLS generally espoused Left-wing ideas and prioritized a working-class base, it did not for the most part work in concert with other socialist or working-class organizations. It was a tenants' union pure and simple, and all those concerned with promoting the well-being of renters in Paris were welcome to join.[48]

---

[46] Magri, "Housing," 409–410.   [47] APP BA 1614, police report of April 28, 1919.
[48] Susanna Magri, "Le mouvement des locataires à Paris et dans sa banlieue, 1919–1925," *Mouvement social,* 137 (October–December, 1986).

Although the FLS was active from 1915 well into the 1920s, by far its most important year was 1919, the year of evictions in Paris. Its structure was a loose confederation of affiliates in each Parisian *arrondissement* and suburban municipality. It was in these local assemblies that most of the business of the FLS took place: there was not much central administration and general meetings were only held a few times a year. The scale of tenant unionism in Paris during 1919 dwarfed prewar movements, giving organized consumer politics unprecedented significance in the French capital. At the height of its strength in 1919, the FLS had perhaps 40,000 to 50,000 members and active sympathizers in the Department of the Seine (it claimed as many as 200,000). Local meetings generally attracted from 100 to 400 participants. FLS affiliates met frequently; there were 110 meetings during 1919 alone. Far more than during the war, therefore, in the year after the Armistice tenant unionism became a powerful social movement.[49]

In terms of popular involvement and frequency, the most important activities of the FLS were the local meetings. First and foremost, they allowed tenants to give voice to their grievances and difficulties in a sympathetic setting. At the same time, they constituted a space for sharing information about the housing crisis, and for debating possible ways of defending tenants' interests against the landlords. Horror stories, especially concerning evictions, often featured prominently. At a meeting held in Clichy in early January, a refugee from the Nord got up to tell the 300 people assembled at a local FLS meeting how he, his wife, and two children had been kicked out of their apartment by their landlord. He noted that he and his wife were staying in the apartment regardless of the landlord's orders, while the children slept in the workshops where they were employed. Several of the outraged listeners wanted to leave immediately to go demonstrate in front of the landlord's house, but were persuaded by the meeting's leaders to pursue official channels instead. The meeting then ended after passing the following motion:

The tenants of Clichy, meeting on January 3 . . . send their greetings to President WILSON, to those comrades detained in the jails of the Republic for political offenses, and to those in the armies, commit themselves to struggle ever more strongly to obtain satisfaction from the landlords . . . "Long live the renters! Long live the workers' Internationale!"[50]

In another instance, a speaker related the case of a tenant in St.-Maur, a father with a five-month-old baby. Because this individual had refused to

---

[49] *Ibid.*   [50] AN F7 13755, police report of January 3, 1919.

accept a rent increase of 30 percent the landlord had seized the baby's effects, on the pretext that he owed 7 francs back rent.[51] Sometimes such stories strained the bounds of credibility, as in the case of an FLS meeting in the second *arrondissement*. On this occasion one speaker told of a war amputee who, upon returning from Germany after forty-eight months in a prisoner of war camp, was ordered by the local arbitration commission to pay back rent or face eviction.[52]

These and other tenants' horror stories served rhetorically to underscore the iniquity of landlords and the vulnerability of tenants. The frequent references to children losing their homes and being thrown into the street painted a picture of martyred innocence prey to capitalist cupidity. They also underlined the need for collective action, emphasizing that anyone could lose his or her home unless backed up by a strong tenants' movement. One detects in the reports of FLS meetings a certain tension around how to react to such stories. On the one hand, they were clearly intended to promote tenant organizing and hatred of landlords. On the other hand, as happened in Clichy, it was only natural that some people, on hearing such stories, wanted to take immediate action, and had to be shown the advantages of more systematic strategies. The rhetoric of tenant victimization was not intended just to underscore tenant solidarity and the gap between renters and property owners, but also to help build an effective union movement to safeguard tenants' rights.

As during the war itself, tenants' union activists emphasized the theme of wartime sacrifice as justification for their demands. The hostilities may have ended in November 1918, but wartime analogies and references remained alive and well in 1919. As the embattled soldiers were demobilized into victorious veterans searching for a place to rest their laurels, the idea that affordable housing was something the nation as a whole owed them, and should force landlords to provide them, became a centerpiece of tenant activist rhetoric. As far as many FLS members were concerned, tenants had won the war, and landlords should be appropriately grateful. A speaker at an FLS meeting in the fourth *arrondissement* expressed this viewpoint succinctly:

BLOCH criticized the landlords "who ... dare to pursue those soldiers who defended their houses. We won the victory, it is true, but we must not forget that we came close to defeat. It's true that the Germans didn't capture Paris, but they were at the gates. If they weren't able to enter, it is because of the soldiers who made a rampart of their bodies to protect the buildings of the property owners

---

[51] AN F7 13755, police report of February 16, 1919.   [52] AN F7 13755, police report of January 4, 1919.

(applause). If their houses are still standing, it is because we were there, we the tenants, while they fled to Bordeaux or to Nice (applause). And they pay us back with scandalous rent increases, and by dragging us before the arbitration commissions and threatening us with eviction."[53]

In a similar vein, a Socialist deputy argued at an FLS meeting in Pré-St.-Gervais that "The *boches* often forced women and children to march in front of them in order to shield themselves from French gunfire. The big landlords are doing the same thing. They have placed in the foreground the small landlords in order to win the sympathy of the Government and the Assembly."[54] For tenant activists, the view of landlords as enemies of the nation continued to serve as an effective rallying cry in 1919.

The numerous, often well-attended, meetings held by the FLS throughout Paris and its suburbs in 1919 served to create a sense of identity and cohesion among many low-income tenants as well as dramatizing the difficulties they faced in trying to find a place to live. However, the FLS was not just a debating society, but also sought ways to satisfy the grievances of renters and demonstrate their power as an organized group in the capital. During 1919 the FLS formulated a series of demands that it argued were necessary to ensure equitable treatment of renters. These included the suppression of the *denier à dieu*, of requirements to pay rent in advance, and of the seizure of tenants' property for non-payment of rent. Such demands were not original, having been raised frequently by prewar tenants' unions. In contrast, the demand for government regulation of rent levels (*la taxation des loyers*) was new, reflecting the unprecedented level of state intervention in consumer pricing during the war. Also new, and a reflection of the severity of the housing crisis, was the demand that the government force landlords to advertise publicly vacant apartments available for rent, rather than withholding them from the market. Finally, the postwar FLS made improving the quality of affordable housing a major demand, calling upon public authorities to clear the worst slums and build new apartments to provide working people with a better standard of living. This demand not only for state regulation of housing but ultimately public housing echoed the arguments of many specialists in urbanism, notably the Socialist leader Henri Sellier, and would become a major legacy of the movement for the twentieth century as a whole.[55]

Elaborating its own positive vision of social housing was important, of course, but the activists of the FLS were most concerned with preventing

[53] AN F7 13755, police report of July 30, 1919.   [54] AN F7 13755, police report of January 6, 1919.
[55] Magri, "Le mouvement des locataires."

the abuses of the present and protecting Parisian renters. They devoted much of their meetings to debating strategies to resist the landlords and protect fellow tenants. In 1919 the FLS focused on the arbitration commissions as key to their struggle to defend renters' interests. In spite of their mixed composition, the FLS generally viewed the arbitration commissions as "entirely in the hands of the landlords."[56] At a meeting in the second *arrondissement* Périvier of the national leadership spoke bitterly about the arbitrary rulings of the commissions:

everyone is found guilty. If you show up without worn-out shoes or a filthy hat they assume that you are rich and therefore able to pay. If a young widow appears before them, she is told, "but you are still young you can remarry and make a new life, so you can pay" (murmurs). If you have gray hair they say: "What! At your age, you are rebelling against the law even though you seem to be such a decent sort!", and they find you guilty; they condemn en masse.[57]

Above all, since the arbitration commissions had the authority to order evictions, the key issue in 1919, any struggle for renters' rights had to begin with them. Although some members of the FLS proposed boycotting the commission hearings, in general tenant activists preferred the strategy of trying to intimidate them into ruling in favor of the renters and against the landlords. Sometimes this took the form of FLS members packing the hall where the hearing was held, making so much noise that they forced the abandonment of the session, at times leading the landlord to drop his complaint. At times the FLS would negotiate with arbitration commissions to convince them to treat renters more sympathetically. At a meeting in Clichy in June, Périvier explained how they had dealt with the commission of the second *arrondissement*:

in the second *arrondissement* we made a small pact with the President of the arbitration commission. We have already noted how all those brought before him were condemned without mercy. We therefore concluded, "Since this [commission] is an execution machine, let's set up our own 'fighting machine', and we began consciously to sabotage all the meetings of the commission.

When we had shown what we were capable of, we met with the President of the commission and told him: "If you are nice to us, if you don't condemn our members, we will leave you in peace. Otherwise we will sabotage all your meetings." As you can well imagine, the President told us to take a hike, saying that he wasn't going to make any agreement with us; the day after he continued condemning everybody.

---

[56] AN F7 13755, police report of January 11, 1919.   [57] AN F7 13755, police report of January 4, 1919.

Without missing a beat, the day after we all came to the commission meeting and I can tell you that our presence was noticed. When he saw that, the President changed his mind. Since then, when we learn that one of our members will appear before the arbitration commission, we write a letter to the President three days in advance giving him the details of the case he will rule upon. We are then pleased to see our member come out of the hearing completely exonerated, or at least with a very small penalty (applause).[58]

The decision to focus on the arbitration commissions made sense, given that they had the power to order evictions, but it also reflected a shift in tenant activism compared with the prewar period. In 1919 the FLS emphasized state action as key to resolving tenant disputes, in contrast to prewar traditions like the *demenagement à la cloche des bois.* The role assumed by the government in regulating the rental housing market had left its mark, so that the renters' union saw the maintenance and extension of wartime controls as ultimately more significant than attacking landlords directly. At times, as noted during the Clichy meeting, this meant trying to persuade irate tenants to follow a more nuanced course of action. In speaking to an FLS group in the third *arrondissement*, Périvier argued for calm and orderly procedures:

But in asking you to take action, I don't want to tell you to take to the streets; I don't want to lead you to the kind of extremities that will only result in earning you punches and saber blows from the agents of M. the Prefect of Police.

In telling you to take action, I mean actions that are well thought-out.[59]

Yet in fact the activists of the FLS did often pursue direct actions against the landlords, both because they felt the need and because their followers pushed them to do so. At times renters' activists would demonstrate against landlords to show the power of the tenants' union. In April, for example, FLS leaders announced, before a meeting in the eleventh *arrondissement* attended by 800 people, plans for a demonstration against a landlord in Ménilmontant who had threatened his tenants with expulsion if they didn't pay up.[60] On another occasion union members demonstrated against landlords in the rues Sedaine and Vaucouleurs, also in the eleventh *arrondissement*, for failing to maintain elementary standards of hygiene in their buildings. At an FLS meeting reporting this event, speakers claimed that the demonstration had led a majority of the buildings' tenants to join the FLS.[61]

[58] AN F7 13755, police report of June 27, 1919.
[59] AN F7 13755, police report of September 11, 1919.   [60] AN F7 13755, police report of April 5, 1919.
[61] AN F7 13755, police report of February 27, 1919.

The most important, and widespread, type of direct action was resistance to evictions. On several occasions FLS members took steps to stop tenants from losing their homes, either by trying to hinder the work of bailiffs or by literally moving renters' belongings back into their apartments. On June 25, 1919, for example, 1,500 people gathered in Paris to prevent an eviction. An FLS meeting in May described a similar action, noting how: "in the twelfth *arrondissement* a police commissioner and a bailiff, having tried to evict a renter, were met by 2,000 people who stopped them from accomplishing their mission."[62] The secretary of the FLS committee of the eleventh *arrondissement* described his group's actions to prevent evictions in October:

Recently, two elderly ladies having been evicted, we carried their furniture back into their apartment and, in the presence of the 150 comrades who took part in the operation, the landlord didn't dare to do anything.

Another time, having been warned that a tenant was about to be evicted, we sent a letter to the Minister of Justice asking him to stop this eviction. We also noted that, in case of an unfavorable response, we would set up a permanent watch near the home of this tenant and we would use all necessary means to stop his eviction.

The next day, the bailiff approached the police commissioner, but this latter having received his orders did not budge.[63]

FLS activists tried to organize such direct actions systematically by forming action committees charged with defending renters' interests. These committees were based in the local FLS sections, and took the lead in mounting demonstrations, attempts to halt evictions, pressure on arbitration committees, and other activities in defense of tenants. By the end of 1919 many of the FLS local sections in Paris and its suburbs had created action committees: the FLS of the eleventh *arrondissement* alone boasted forty such committees by March 1920.[64] At a city-wide FLS conference in June, one speaker noted that "action committees have been constituted in all sections to defend members who are visited by the cops, replace furniture thrown into the street, and correct those who tried to evict the tenants."[65] At an Asnières meeting in January the FLS section created an action committee of thirty members, chosen from among those present at the meeting, and voted to pay them by asking all FLS section members to donate one franc every three months.[66] There are also suggestions of action committees creating a kind of "early warning system" enabling members of a given area to alert other FLS members as quickly as possible of a pending eviction in order to take

[62] AN F7 13755, police report of May 19, 1919.   [63] AN F7 13755, police report of October 10, 1919.
[64] Magri, "Le mouvement des locataires," 74, fn. 88.
[65] AN F7 13755, police report of June 13, 1919.   [66] AN F7 13755, police report of January 20, 1919.

action.[67] Such trained cadres of housing activists, often working clandestinely to avoid police repression, spoke both to the FLS' recognition that direct action was needed to prevent evictions, and also to its determination to channel popular resentment of landlords into organized and effective means of expression.

In contrast to the attention devoted to challenging the arbitration committees and to resisting evictions, the prospect of organizing rent strikes of Parisian tenants received much less attention from the FLS. One does find at times mention of this tactic by speakers at FLS meetings. At a meeting in the eleventh *arrondissement*, one speaker argued: "Since direct action is our only defense, we will make sure to use it (applause) to the maximum extent necessary, even a rent strike."[68] In counseling moderation to the FLS members of the third *arrondissement*, Périvier noted:

There is a very simple way to solve the housing crisis. If you can't find housing, stay where you are, stay and don't pay!

There are 800,000 renters in Paris; they will never find 800,000 bailiffs to evict them all.[69]

Yet there is no indication that the FLS ever organized any systematic rent strikes. Of course, given that many low-income Parisian tenants had used the wartime moratoria to stage what were in effect rent strikes (at least from the point of view of the landlords) since 1914, adopting this as a tactic did not address the central concerns of tenants in 1919. They worried most about evictions in 1919, not rent increases, and when the FLS thought of direct action, it generally considered means of resisting those, something that rent strikes could not really do.

As we have seen with consumer issues during the war, differences of gender played a key role in shaping tenants' unionism in postwar Paris. The social movement around renters' rights brought two contrasting views of popular activism into relation with each other, and gender was central to this contrast. On the one hand, they recalled traditional movements around moral economy, movements typically dominated by women. The progressive separation between home and work in the nineteenth century had gradually transformed the former into a female space, placing the wife and mother in charge of the *foyer*. On the other hand, the organization of the FLS as a tenants' union, traditionally a male-dominated if not exclusively masculine form of social movement, placed men at the center of the struggle

---

[67] AN F7 13755, police report of August 9, 1919.   [68] AN F7 13755, police report of April 5, 1919.
[69] AN F7 13755, police report of September 12, 1919.

over housing. An emphasis on paternalism, on the duty of men to protect their wives, children, and homes, to a certain extent resolved this contrast. Nevertheless, as we shall see even more sharply in the case of the food riots the same year, a tension existed between the movement's emphasis on home and hearth and its organizational structure.[70]

The classic example of this was the fact that only men spoke at FLS meetings. Moreover, they generally spoke in gender-neutral terms, addressing all renters or all workers regardless of sex. While women certainly attended at least some of the meetings, they did not assume leadership roles. When the speakers did talk about gender, they often exhorted women to take a more active role in the union. Speaking before an FLS meeting in Clichy, Maury of the national organization addressed the impact of the housing crisis on women in particular:

it is especially on you women that we rely, because you are the ones who really suffer from the housing crisis. We men, we leave in the morning and often don't come home until late in the evening, and when we have put our daily wages on the table we believe we have fulfilled our duty and don't worry about anything else.

But you women, the home is your responsibility; it is your job to make it pleasant, something that's not always easy when you only have a little room and inadequate fresh air and sunlight.

You have another responsibility, care of the child ... Your child will die, in effect, because he lives in a foul atmosphere, deprived of light and air.[71]

This image of women as the aesthetic angels of hearth and home, and as nurturers and defenders of innocent children, underscored classically patriarchal ideas of gender so prevalent in French labor while at the same time emphasizing the duty of women to take an active role in defending their homes. In essence, male tenant activists found themselves in the position of asking women to take action in the public sector in order to protect their isolation in the private sector. Given the deeply contradictory nature of such an appeal, it is not surprising that the men generally occupied the leading positions in the FLS.[72] It does not necessarily follow, however, that women played a passive role in the movement. Women often joined direct action campaigns in defense of renters' rights. The most popular seems to have

---

[70] See on this point Laura L. Frader and Sonya O. Rose, eds., *Gender and Labor in Modern France* (Ithaca NY: Cornell University Press, 1996); Tessie Liu, *The Weaver's Knot: The Contradictions of Class Struggle and Family Solidarity in Western France, 1750–1914* (Ithaca NY: Cornell University Press, 1994); Louise A. Tilly and Joan W. Scott, *Women, Work, and Family* (New York: Holt, Rinehart, and Winston, 1978).

[71] AN F7 13755, police report of March 13, 1919.

[72] One should also note in this context, however, the history of women's activism in Right-wing movements, including those that advocated traditional roles for women. See Paola Bacchetta and

been taking part in disrupting arbitration commission meetings; phalanxes of FLS women would attend, booing, hissing, and in general interrupting the work of the commissioners. The prospect of female activists as a kind of militant Greek chorus, angrily reacting to male attempts to deprive them of their homes, neatly illustrates both the gendered nature of tenant unionism and the very real dynamism exhibited by women as part of this consumer social movement.[73]

Finally, the politics of the housing crisis, and political approaches to resolving it, generated a lot of debate among FLS members. In sharp contrast to prewar tenant unionism, political action emerged as a central focus of Parisian renter activists in 1919. Given the role of the wartime state in ordering the wartime housing moratoria then attempting to regulate the housing sector systematically with the law of 1918, not to mention the actions of the arbitration committees, this was perhaps unavoidable. As we shall see with the movement around food prices, maintaining wartime controls and in general appealing to state intervention to guarantee social justice was a key theme in postwar consumer activism. Although it had opposed the 1918 housing law, in general the FLS viewed legislation as a very effective way to improve conditions for renters. Many members of the Paris City Council appeared at FLS meetings, and the organization actively supported political candidates. Moreover, members seemed aware that political campaigns and elections could be used to tenants' advantage. In recommending a rent strike, Périvier argued: "you have nothing to fear, they won't evict anyone before the election campaign."[74]

Not all members agreed with this emphasis on political struggle. Prewar French unionism, dominated by anarcho-syndicalism, had generally rejected alliances with political parties or movements, and many FLS activists still believed in this tradition.[75] At a May meeting of the FLS in the eighteenth *arrondissement*, the secretary of the section, Crepet, rejected a

---

Margaret Power, eds., *Right-wing Women: From Conservatives to Extremists around the World* (New York: Routledge, 2002); Donald T. Critchlow, *Phyllis Schlafly and Grassroots Conservativism: A Woman's Crusade* (Princeton University Press, 2005).

[73] On women in new social movements, see Sara M. Evans, *Personal Politics: The Roots of Women's Liberation in the Civil Rights Movement and the New Left* (New York: Random House, 1979).

[74] AN F7 13755, police report of September 12, 1919.

[75] While French labor before the war encompassed a variety of doctrines, this aversion to politics was shared by most, so that a peculiarity of the French Left was the strained relations between union movements and socialist parties. On French anarcho-syndicalism, see Peter Stearns, *Revolutionary Syndicalism and French Labor: A Cause Without Rebels* (New Brunswick NJ: Rutgers University Press, 1971); Barbara Mitchell, *The Practical Revolutionaries: A New Interpretation of the French Anarchosyndicalists* (New York: Greenwood Press, 1987); Jacques Julliard, *Autonomie ouvrière: études sur le syndicalisme d'action directe* (Paris: Gallimard/Le Seuil, 1988).

request to discuss the mutiny of France's Black Sea fleet, in spite of his own sympathies with the mutineers, stating that "as secretary of the organization, I cannot let you speak about such questions, because our group has formally banned the discussion of all political questions."[76] In September Laroche, the general secretary of the FLS, discussed this question with members at a meeting in the fourth *arrondissement*:

"The elections approach, you have a formidable weapon in your hands. We will designate those outgoing parliamentary deputies who supported your interests during the vote on the law of March 9 [1918], and those who still support you. But we will also designate those others, those who voted for this iniquitous law; you will know what to do about them."

This last phrase prompted a member of the audience to say "We are here to engage in unionism, not politics; you would do better to tell us what we should do when the landlord tells us to pay up. Otherwise we will leave tonight, like other nights, without knowing what we need to do. It's not politics that interests us, but the housing question."

LAROCHE responds that one can't build a union without engaging in politics.

"Politics is everywhere, it is in everything, the evil laws we protest against were made by politicians. The right that you have to meet here tonight was given you by politicians. Therefore you need to take them into account . . . We are not dealing with electoral questions but we have the duty to designate our enemies in Parliament and to tell you: Watch out, be on your guard!" (applause).[77]

Clearly the position of the FLS on political activism was more than a little ambiguous, as Laroche's final sentence above demonstrates. This tension not only illustrates changing conceptions of unionism and of the state in France as a result of World War I, but also corresponds to a major theme in the history of twentieth-century social movements: can they retain their own autonomy and mass activist base while at the same time negotiating with political actors, or do they risk being marginalized by the latter? [78]

Whatever their views on political activism, it seems clear that ideologically FLS members leaned overwhelmingly to the Left, even the revolutionary Left, in 1919. Repeatedly during meetings speakers referred to revolutionary events both at home and abroad, often portraying them as models for how to deal with the plight of tenants in Paris. At a January meeting in the twentieth *arrondissement*, a speaker concluded his critique of the government by saying "Let us be strong and be ready, because perhaps

---

[76] AN F7 13755, police report of May 29, 1919.
[77] AN F7 13755, police report of September 13, 1919.
[78] See on this point Frances Fox Piven and Richard Cloward, *Poor People's Movements: Why They Succeed, How They Fail* (New York: Vintage, 1979).

we will soon be obliged to make the revolution like in Germany and Russia."[79] Other speakers called for the abolition of the propertied class and the triumph of Communism as the only sure remedy for the housing crisis.[80] As one speaker proclaimed in Malakoff, "A strong wind is blowing from the East; I hope it will reach us soon, and then we will be able to rise to an assault of the citadel."[81]

Such revolutionary rhetoric, however heartfelt, only went so far, and did not extend to revolutionary direct action. In general, FLS activists were willing to take to the streets to prevent evictions, but not for other reasons. One speaker at a meeting in the fourth *arrondissement* appealed for the constitution of an action committee "not for the sake of a revolutionary action, but with the firm intention of preventing the victims of the arbitration commissions from being thrown in the street."[82] Nor were they necessarily willing to take part in other working-class struggles at the time. At a meeting in late June, during the metalworkers' strike, FLS activists decided not to hold a demonstration for fear that strikers would join and thereby expose renters and their families to the possibility of police repression.[83] A report on a large FLS festival, attended by 5,000 people, held in Paris in March 1920 succinctly characterized the organization's ideological ambivalence:

Although the Renters Federation is not in general composed of people with profound revolutionary sentiments, but rather those guided only by immediate interests, even shopkeepers and small industrialists, one should nonetheless underline, as a sign of the times, the presentations by artists of definitely internationalist songs and poetry, and the enthusiastic reception given them by the crowd.[84]

During 1919 thousands of tenants in Paris and its suburbs organized to defend their rights, and more specifically to fight the evictions resulting from the suspension of wartime rent controls. They used the fundamental issue of access to affordable housing to bring together not just workers but also many middle-class renters, challenging the idea that the end of the war meant a return to non-interventionist state policies. While their focus on a consumer issue recalled notions of moral economy, their insistence upon state regulation both forecast and contributed to the rise of *l'état providence* later in the twentieth century. As we shall see with the movement to regulate

[79] AN F7 13755, police report of January 6, 1919.
[80] AN F7 13755, police reports of January 26, 1919; September 12, 1919; June 30, 1919.
[81] AN F7 13755, police report of August 29, 1919.   [82] AN F7 13755, police report of January 11, 1919.
[83] AN F7 13755, police report of June 30, 1919.   [84] AN F7 13755, police report of March 8, 1920.

food in Paris, the consumer movements of 1919 looked both to the past and
to the future at the same time.

RIOTS IN THE MARKETPLACE

The Paris food riots of 1919 took place in both Les Halles and different
neighborhood marketplaces during late July and August, forming part of a
summer of widespread and dramatic working-class discontent in the
capital. In taking direct action against the high prices of food, working
people in Paris demonstrated both their determination to master the
conditions of their own lives, and the limits of their abilities to do so.
Like the tenants' movement, the food riots and the subsequent attempts
to control food prices reflected very concrete concerns yet also contributed
to a sense of revolutionary crisis in the year after the Armistice. In the right
circumstances aggrieved housewives could bring down a government, and
some Parisians saw the potential for just such a development in 1919
(Illustration 5.3).

5.3 "La vie chère"

In their actions to cope with the food crisis during and immediately after World War I, both local and national public authorities in France were guided by two main goals. Assuring that the population had adequate supplies of food received top priority. Thus the national government took steps to purchase grain, meat, and other foods from a growing number of sources abroad and overseas, and as the war dragged on both central and local governments implemented ever-stricter rationing plans. Second, public authorities tried to retard the rise in food prices as much as possible. The national government attempted to do so by expanding the food supply, which according to the laws of supply and demand would counteract rising prices. The City of Paris, on the other hand, chose to create a sector of stores selling food at prices fixed below market levels, in the hope that such competition would lower prices in general.[85] On the whole, the government designed its policies to facilitate the workings of the free market, not to override it. Although national authorities did set some maximum price ceilings for certain foods, for the most part they did so hesitantly and briefly.[86]

By the beginning of 1919, some argued that even this measure went too far in hindering the efficient workings of the free market. They asserted that price ceilings, far from lowering food prices, actually helped keep them high by restricting the food supply. Abolishing them, on the other hand, would encourage shopkeepers to sell more food and thus naturally lower prices for everyone. One writer, R. Lavollée, claimed that state intervention increased the price of potatoes by 66 percent.[87] Not everyone advocated this position: in February a commission appointed by the Chamber of Deputies to study the question recommended retaining price controls, arguing that municipal food stores and cooperatives could keep food costs down more effectively.[88] Yet the forces demanding a return to freedom of commerce carried the day.

---

[85] *Ibid.*, 12–39; Pierre Pinot, *Food Supply in France during the War* (New Haven: Yale University Press, 1927), 245–286.

[86] "First of all, the government always believes that its intervention in the provisioning of the nation should not have the effect of substituting an administrative system of state food supply for the normal play of market forces and, even for those foodstuffs for which a veritable monopoly of purchase and distribution had to be instituted – grains and sugar – the Provisioning services constantly looked to free market competition." Pinot, *Food Supply in France*, 5. See also Michel Auge-Laribé, *Agriculture in France during the War* (New Haven: Yale University Press, 1927), 69–99.

[87] In November 1920 Senator Chauveau attacked government controls over bread: "They perpetuate, during peacetime, a large part of the evils created by the war. They lie at the source of the imbalance of production, of the depreciation of our currency, and of the increase in public expenses." Cited in Alfred Sauvy, *Histoire économique de la France entre les deux guerres*, 4 vols. (Paris: Fayard, 1965–1975), vol. I, 316–317.

[88] AN F12 8019(2): Chambre des Deputés, *Procès-verbal*, February 16, 1919.

By spring the government had terminated price ceilings on most foods, except grain.[89]

This did not bring all efforts to control food prices to an end. In fact, the Provisioning Office and the Paris City Council stepped up their efforts to sell food at subsidized prices. Led by M. Vilgrain, Undersecretary of State in the Provisioning Ministry, the Provisioning Office decided to create its own food stores to sell directly to the public at fixed prices. In mid-February the Paris municipality agreed to cooperate with the program, and on March 6, 1919 the first nine stores, nicknamed Vilgrain barracks by Parisians, opened at locations scattered throughout the city. At first the barracks' stocks were limited to rice, beans, and salted meats, and they sold a maximum of 2 kilograms of food to a customer. Even so, they were extremely popular with Parisians, who waited in long lines to get in. Taking note of this, many merchants doing business near Vilgrain barracks lowered their prices in order to remain competitive. Consequently, the Provisioning Office expanded the program rapidly, so that by the end of the year 162 Vilgrain barracks were operating in Paris, and 60 in the suburbs. In late 1919 the Provisioning Ministry followed up this success with a new program of popular restaurants, serving three-course meals for the price of 2 francs.[90]

The Vilgrain barracks and popular restaurants may not have lowered overall food prices in the Paris area significantly, but they did nonetheless make an important difference to local consumers, who took full advantage of them. The full impact of these programs was not felt until the fall and winter of 1919–1920, however; in the summer months that preceded the outbreak of food rioting, by way of contrast, the government's major activity concerning food seemed to be directed toward weakening price controls. Given that food costs continued to rise as fast as they had before the Armistice, the crisis which had necessitated government intervention had not come to an end. Many Parisians therefore felt that the government still needed to do more to restrain speculation and inflation.[91] By mid-summer, some began to translate this anger at food prices into direct action.

---

[89] Pinot, *Food Supply in France*, 287–294.

[90] *Ibid.*, 295–301; Sellier, Bruggeman, and Poëte, *Paris pendant la guerre*, 24–31, 63–67; APP BA 1614, reports of March 4, 1919; March 11, 1919; March 17, 1919; March 24, 1919; March 31, 1919; June 2, 1919; October 16, 1919; *Humanité*, March 7, 1919, 2; March 12, 1919, 2; March 21, 1919, 2; September 25, 1919, 2.

[91] "The high cost of living remains the essential cause of the general unrest; the population is disturbed by the scandalous actions of the merchants who profit from workers' wage increases to raise the prices of their merchandise to incomprehensible levels. People feel that this kind of behavior will never lead to an accord between employers and employees, and many blame the public authorities for this situation, accusing them of not intervening in a more energetic fashion against the profiteers." APP BA 1614, report of June 16, 191.

The first riots broke out at the end of July in Montmartre's rue des Abbesses marketplace. On Sunday, July 27, women from the neighborhood crowded into the street to do their shopping, as usual on Sundays. A dispute soon arose between a shopkeeper, M. Guay, and a woman who claimed to have been overcharged for a piece of rabbit. When the customer pointed out that the posted price for rabbit was 3.50 francs apiece, instead of the 4 francs she had been charged, the shopkeeper claimed that the price had just gone up. Not surprisingly, this failed to satisfy the aggrieved customer, who continued to protest. Other women joined in, attacking the arrogance of shopkeepers and the high prices they charged for food,[92] so that soon the street in front of the *épicerie* was full of angry, shouting people. This situation escalated into violence when suddenly about twenty individuals attacked the store, throwing food into the street accompanied by cries of "Hang the thieves!" (Illustration 5.4).[93]

5.4 Guay's grocery store in Montmartre

[92] This view of shopkeepers did not suddenly arise in 1919, but was a constant of Parisian life during the war. In the eyes of many, shopkeepers who charged high prices were, like arms manufacturers, war profiteers. See on this question Françoise Thébaud, *La femme au temps de la guerre de 14* (Paris: Éditions Stock, 1986), 210–214.

[93] *L'Information ouvrière et sociale*, July 31, 1919, 1, 2; AN F23 199; *L'Echo de Paris*, July 28, 1919; *Le Petit Parisien*, July 28, 1919; *Le Matin*, July 31, 1919.

The police intervened to restore order and closed the shop. It reopened the next day, but, as observers were quick to note, M. Guay not only displayed a more courteous attitude but also showed himself willing to compromise on price levels. A journalist recorded the following conversation between the shopkeeper and one of his customers:

"How much are these tomatoes?"
    "Seven cents, my dear . . ."
    "Seven cents! No, really . . . Over there they cost five cents . . ."
    "Yes, but look, these are beautiful tomatoes . . . Oh well, I'll let you have them for six cents!"
    "No, five cents!"
    "Don't get angry, my little one. OK, go ahead . . . and with that? Will that be all? Wouldn't you like some of this lovely melon?"[94]

The incident in the rue des Abbesses was soon followed by a similar protest in the nineteenth *arrondissement*. When a shopkeeper in the marketplace of the place de Bitche refused to sell mutton at 4.75 francs, the crowd immediately demolished his stall. Violent conflicts also took place in the working-class suburbs of the capital. In Boulogne-Billancourt, shopkeepers attacked a local cooperative that had agreed to sell food at prices well below the ones they offered. This led to a battle with neighborhood housewives who rushed to defend the cooperative. Another fight between consumers and merchants took place in Clichy over two days, August 18 and 19.[95]

Most frequently, these riots involved indignant women attacking male shopkeepers. While contemporary sources do not give an accurate account of the gender composition of the rioters, most reports tend to mention crowds of housewives as the main instigators of the disturbances. The initial riot in Montmartre was certainly a women's riot: men ran most of the food stores attacked by the crowds in the summer of 1919. The quotation cited above, in which an angry housewife confronts a defensive male merchant, typifies the central conflict in this drama. The 1919 food riots did not simply turn on struggles between men and women, however. Men also took part in the rioting crowds, and several women shopkeepers became the objects of their wrath. A week after the first riot in Montmartre, for example, housewives overturned the cart of a woman selling tomatoes in the rue des

---

[94] *L'Information ouvrière et sociale*, July 31, 1919, 2.
[95] *Ibid.*; *L'Humanité*, August 20, 1919, 1; *L'Humanité*, August 21, 1919, 1; AN F 23 199: *Le Journal*, August 6, 1919; *L'Avenir*, July 31, 1919; *Le Journal*, August 7, 1919.

Abbesses, claiming that her price of 70 centimes per kilogram was too high.[96]

Rioting broke out not only between consumers and shopkeepers, but also between shopkeepers and wholesale food merchants. The Parisian food protests of the summer of 1919 found small shopkeepers caught in the middle, facing both the anger of working-class consumers and steadily rising wholesale prices. During August Les Halles in particular became the scene of several violent confrontations. On the morning of Thursday, July 31 several hundred fish sellers rioted against wholesale merchants at the Seafood Pavilion of Les Halles. Claiming that the wholesalers charged them too much for their fish, the *petits commercants* attacked their booths, hurling the fish to the ground and jumping up and down on them.[97]

In mid-August small butter and egg sellers staged similarly violent protests for two days running in Les Halles, protests in which many consumers enraged at the high price of food also participated. By Wednesday, August 13, produce merchants had joined in, attempting to prevent the delivery of fruits and vegetables out of Les Halles to the city's produce stores. The boycott forced many neighborhood stores to close, prompting the government to requisition vegetables. In response, Parisian food merchants sent hundreds of telegrams to provincial wholesalers telling them not to send any more food to Paris, a move that proved embarrassing when workers in the central post office intercepted the telegrams and made them public. This disclosure outraged many Parisian consumers, leading *L'Humanité* to run the headline "Shopkeepers and Les Halles brokers want to starve Paris" in its August 14 issue.[98]

The August 13 episode provides a revealing example of the contradictory position of small shopkeepers in the Paris food crisis. It is not at all clear whether their attempt to prevent food deliveries from Les Halles was aimed at consumers, at wholesale food merchants, or at both groups. There were some indications of accords between consumers and shopkeepers, especially

---

[96] AN F 23 199: *Le Journal*, August 6, 1919. It is impossible to say whether or not any men were involved as food rioters at this point; the available sources do not mention any. Male involvement in the movement to control food prices seems to have been tied to the vigilance committees to a much greater extent. This reflected the prevalent division of labor in French working-class families at the time, according to which women did the shopping and cooking whereas (some) men joined unions and other working-class organizations.

[97] *L'Information ouvrière et sociale*, August 3, 1919, 2.

[98] *L'Humanité*, August 14, 1919, 1. In contrast to its stance at other times, here the newspaper did not exempt small shopkeepers from blame for high food prices. See also *L'Humanité*, August 13, 1919, 1; *L'Information ouvrière et sociale*, August 14, 1919, 2; AN F 23 199: *L'Intransigeant*, August 12, 1919; *Le Matin*, August 13, 1919; *L'Echo de Paris*, August 13, 1919; *Le Petit Journal*, August 13, 1919.

the small "merchants of four seasons," or food peddlers. During the latter half of August these peddlers staged strikes against high wholesale prices, and at times appealed to consumers to join them in seeking to lower food costs by eliminating the middlemen. This kind of unity between consumers and small shopkeepers certainly did not typify the food protests as a whole, however. At the same time as a strike by the peddlers, for example, shopkeepers in the rue des Abbesses closed their stores for a day in protest against the attempts of consumer organizations to enforce lower prices.[99]

The shopkeepers' protests differed significantly from those by consumers. The first group was predominantly male, the second overwhelmingly female. The relationship between shopkeeper and wholesaler was much more impersonal than that between housewife and shopkeeper, and the consumer protests seem to have been much more widespread and spontaneous. The actions by shopkeepers recall less eighteenth-century food riots than those by late twentieth-century French farmers geared to keeping food prices high.[100] Yet there were similarities as well: each group felt it had to pay too much for food, and each used violence to make that point manifest. These similarities did inspire some working-class activists to call for common attacks on wholesalers, yet the fact that such ideas had little impact in the summer of 1919 underscored the fact that shopkeepers and housewives saw themselves as adversaries, not allies.[101]

The marketplace riots of 1919 recalled certain aspects of eighteenth-century protest movements. Customers reacted spontaneously and violently when shopkeepers refused to compromise on food prices, and consciously used these attacks to force such compromises. Women's participation also reveals a connection with eighteenth-century popular practices. Both in practice and in the popular imagination, shopping for food remained very much a woman's job.[102]

These similarities raise questions about the motivations that lay behind the Paris riots during the summer of 1919. What do they reveal about the beliefs of Parisian workers at the end of World War I? Were they spurred by

---

[99] *L'Humanité*, August 13, 1919, 1, 2; August 19, 1919, 1; August 30, 1919, 1.

[100] I have not found any indications in the literature on food riots in the eighteenth century or in 1910–1911 of the existence of similar shopkeeper protests.

[101] For example, a member of a food cooperative wrote a letter to *L'Humanité* arguing that shopkeepers were not the real enemy, and that the crisis could only be resolved by requisitioning food in the countryside. *L'Humanité*, August 17, 1919, 2.

[102] On the role of women in food riots, see Kaplan, "Female consciousness"; John Bohstedt, "Gender, household and community politics: women in English riots," *Past and Present*, 120 (August, 1988); Cynthia Bouton, "Gendered behavior in subsistence riots: the French flour war of 1775," *Journal of Social History*, 23/4 (Summer, 1990).

a vision of a "moral economy" similar to that emphasized by historians of Europe in the eighteenth century? While the 1919 riots illustrate a certain affinity between eighteenth- and twentieth-century beliefs, their history suggests that this affinity may have arisen more from contemporary conflicts than from the persistence of popular memory. Small marketplace riots had broken out during the latter years of the war, as the high cost of living grew more oppressive. In particular, the bitter winter of 1916–1917 created coal shortages to which a few women responded violently. During April 1917 police had to guard the Bois de Boulogne to prevent desperate housewives from chopping down its trees for fuel, and the seamstress Louise Deletang noted in her wartime diary a demonstration of women in Paris demanding "Coal or our men."[103] Many Parisians resented what they saw as the termination of government controls on food prices and a return to economic liberalism in 1919, at a time when the price of food continued to climb. The widespread (and largely accurate) belief that prices had outstripped wages reinforced this desire to retain the restrictions on food prices enacted during the latter half of the war. In July, just before the outbreak of food rioting, the newspaper *L'Oeuvre* published the results of an enquiry into the changes in working-class budgets in Paris since 1914:

Employed for more than twenty years in one of the leading commercial establishments of Paris, married, father of two children, responsible for the care of his elderly 75-year-old mother, the writer informs us that before the war his monthly salary of 475 francs allowed him and his family to live in a modest but sufficient manner. After his return from the Army his salary was increased to 600 francs . . . his budget of expenses is now 775 francs per month.

And he adds, "I anticipate with terror the moment when my pitiful savings, already diminished by four and a half years of military service, will be completely exhausted. What shall I do then?"[104]

Most importantly, the presence of something resembling an *ancien régime* popular moral economy is indicated by the widespread occurrence of *taxation populaire* practiced in Paris during the summer of 1919, as well as by the determination of protesters to force government action to deal with the crisis. Such traits reinforce the conclusion that the 1919 Paris food riots were motivated by a hostility to unrestricted food prices that in significant ways resembled the classic moral economy of the pre-industrial crowd.[105] However, these practices reveal that ultimately the 1919 food protests were

---

[103] Thébaud, *La Femme au temps de la guerre*, 216; Louise Deletang, *Journal d'une ouvrière parisienne pendant la guerre* (Paris: Eugène Figuière, 1935), 333, entry of April 25, 1917.

[104] Reprinted in *L'Information ouvrière et sociale*, July 20, 1919, 6.

[105] Tilly, "The food riot"; Hanson, "The 'vie chère' riots."

something new under the sun. *Taxation populaire* in 1919 assumed new organizational forms radically different from those of the eighteenth century, whereas the protesters' view of governmental accountability was founded not just on traditional attitudes but also on specific policies adopted by the state during World War I.[106] An illumination of these differences calls for an in-depth exploration of popular price fixing and government action during 1919.[107]

RISE AND FALL OF THE VIGILANCE COMMITTEES

All of the marketplace riots that occurred in Paris broke out spontaneously, usually as violent conflicts between housewives and shopkeepers. However, many consumers soon decided that smashing the stalls of local merchants would not in and of itself bring lower prices, and that more systematic means of persuasion were called for. Therefore groups of shoppers began policing local marketplaces throughout Paris and its suburbs, forcing neighborhood merchants to adopt lower prices if they wanted to avoid the wrath of the crowd. Adopting many different names, they became generally known as "vigilance committees," and by the second week of August had established a central presence in the protests over food prices. At the end of July the founders of a vigilance committee in the nineteenth *arrondissement* issued the following manifesto:

The comrades of the Pont-de-Flandre invite all those who are discontented to stop their complaining about government inertia and instead take action!

Last Sunday, armed with the official price lists from Les Halles, we gave a fruitful lesson on the spot to the profiteers of the market of the rue de Joinville.[108]

Like the market riots, the vigilance committees originated and spread rapidly in August. Although consumer violence probably spurred their activities, the vigilance committees were not simply created as a response to the riots; chronologically, they seem to have occurred at roughly the same time. Instead, the committees represented a different type of attempt to deal

---

[106] My analysis thus underscores the limits of the moral economy model in explaining these movements. See Cynthia Bouton's similar argument in the conclusion to her *The Flour War: Gender, Class, and Community in Late Ancien Régime French Society* (University Park PA: Pennsylvania State University Press, 1993), 257–258.

[107] On eighteenth-century popular price fixing, see Thompson, "The moral economy of the English crowd," 108–120; Tilly, "The food riot"; Georges Rudé, "La taxation populaire de mai 1775 en picardie en normandie et dans le beauvaisis," *Annales historiques de la révolution française*, 165 (July–September, 1961).

[108] *L'Information ouvrière et sociale*, July 31, 1919, 2.

with the problem of high food prices, one that represented a more systematic view of the situation.

The relations between the vigilance committees and other working-class organizations are by no means clear. The committees seem to have attracted militants from the unions and the Socialist Party, yet no prominent working-class activists took part in their work. Their leaders were for the most part obscure: perhaps the most important, President Mugnier of the eighteenth *arrondissement* vigilance committee, had lived in Montmartre for fifty years but had no significant presence in previous organizations.[109] Moreover, to all appearances the vigilance committees guarded their autonomy and their focus on consumer issues jealously.[110] In Paris the committees were organized in individual *arrondissements*, but for the most part limited their scope to particular *quartiers*, or even market areas; the suburban committees usually covered a particular *commune*. They grew up throughout the Paris area, spreading rapidly in August. Working-class areas, such as the eighteenth and nineteenth *arrondissements* of Paris and suburbs like Clichy, Pantin, and Puteaux, took the lead in creating vigilance committees. Yet by the end of the month such organizations had been founded in a majority of Parisian *arrondissements* and over twenty suburbs, including wealthy locales like the sixteenth *arrondissement* and Saint-Germain-en-Laye.[111] There are no clear figures on the numbers of people who joined vigilance committees or participated in their activities. In their initial, price-fixing phase actual committee membership generally consisted of a few activists, who coordinated marketplace demonstrations and played a broad leadership role. The twelfth *arrondissement* committee had sixteen members. At the same time, they attracted many participants who did join formally. Around 2,000 people came to a meeting held by the vigilance committee of Choisy-le-Roi in late August. As the committees began emphasizing common purchases they gained many more formal members, while losing the supporters attracted by market demonstrations and mass

---

[109] *L'Information ouvrière et sociale*, August 7, 1919, 3.

[110] The statutes of the Consumer's League of the Eighteenth *arrondissement* specified that "political or religious discussions are not permitted in the league." AN F 23 199: *Le Petit Journal*, August 7, 1919. A vigilance committee in Courbevoie publicly disassociated itself from a group in Beçon-les-Bruyères which it accused of caring more about politics than about consumer concerns. *L'Humanité*, August 16, 1919, 2.

[111] For August and September I have uncovered indications of the existence of vigilance committees in *arrondissements* 3–6, 10–13, and 15–20 of Paris, and the suburbs of Asnières, Becon-les-Bruyères, Bois-Colombes, Choisy-le-Roi, Clichy, Corbeil, Courbevoie, Fontenay-sous-Bois, Gennevilliers, Kremlin-Bicêtre, Levallois, Les Lilas-Bagnolet, Maisons-Alfort, Montreuil, Nanterre, Palaiseau, Pantin, Pré-Saint-Gervais, Puteaux, Rosny, Saint-Germain-en-Laye, Suresnes, Villeneuve, and Vitry.

meetings. The Latin Quarter vigilance committee signed up about 500 people at the height of its collective purchases program.[112]

One of the more interesting characteristics of the vigilance committees was their ability to reach out to a middle-class audience. Even though they were predominantly, if not overwhelmingly, composed of workers and *employés*, and their leaders were usually working-class activists, the committees did attract some middle-class participants, and many more sympathizers.[113] One of the most important vigilance committees, the *Ligue contre la vie chère* of the fifth and sixth *arrondissements*, was in large part directed by university students.[114] This ability to appeal to middle-class consumers was noteworthy at a time of sharp class tensions and bourgeois fears of the bloody Red Revolution.[115] Much of the bourgeois press, for example, which had shown itself firmly opposed to working-class strikes and demonstrations during 1919, commented on the vigilance committees and the general movement against high food prices in neutral, even approving tones.

Since unionism is in vogue, why not use this weapon to combat the high cost of living? Cooperative societies are nothing other than unions of consumers; they defend, in the most concrete and practical manner, the interests of those whom one can call "professionals," because isn't it one of the most tiring and least fruitful professions today to shop for food provisions for consumption? It takes up several hours a day.[116]

Vigilance committee activists did try to avoid overt political stances, and for the most part downplayed themes of class struggle, insisting that malevolent, avaricious merchants were the enemy. This explains some of the

---

[112] *L'Humanité*, August 13, 1919, 3; August 26, 1919, 1; August 27 1919, 2; September 6, 1919, 2; Archives de la prefecture de police de Paris [hereafter APP], BA 1614, reports of September 11, 1919; September 25, 1919. One of the traditional sources on the identities of participants in food riots, arrest records, is not available for 1919 simply because the police did not arrest any of the rioters. This has significance for the relationship between the Paris police and food riots in 1919, and will be discussed below.

[113] In spite of this, it seems clear that they were heavily working class. Most of the vigilance committees arose in working-class neighborhoods; there were none in bourgeois areas like the seventh and eighth *arrondissements*, Neuilly, or Saint-Mandé. Moreover, there is some evidence that even those committees established in affluent neighborhoods had a working-class membership. For example, the Saint-Germain-en-Laye vigilance committee was composed of "workers' organizations." *L'Humanité*, September 17, 1919, 2.

[114] AN F 23 199: *Le Matin*, September 9, 1919; September 15, 1919; *L'Avenir*, October 10, 1919; APP BA 1614, police reports of September 11, 1919, September 25, 1919, October 16, 1919, December 11, 1919, January 1, 1920. The Latin Quarter committee took the name "La Plume et l'Outil" (The Pen and the Tool) to symbolize the unity of workers and students in its ranks.

[115] Charles Maier, *Recasting Bourgeois Europe* (Princeton University Press, 1975), 22–53; Charles Bertrand, ed., *Revolutionary Situations in Europe, 1917–1922: Germany, Italy, Austria-Hungary* (Montreal: Interuniversity Centre for European Studies, 1977).

[116] AN F 23 199: *Le Figaro*, October 6, 1919.

5.5 Members of the vigilance committee of the sixth *arrondissement*

breadth of their appeal, yet the issue itself was perhaps more crucial. The severe inflation of the period also affected middle-class consumers, not only worsening their own living standards but also threatening them with a sobering loss of status (Illustration 5.5).[117]

The activities of the vigilance committees in the Paris area took different forms, but all of them had as their primary goal lowering the prices of food and other consumer goods. They were responsible for organizing instances of popular price fixing, which in most cases provided the committees' first major action and reason for being. After the initial community meeting that constituted the vigilance committee, members would agree to rally at the local marketplace on Sunday or another important shopping day. Before then, they would usually check wholesale prices at Les Halles, in order to

---

[117] Unfortunately, from the standpoint of bourgeois commentators, consumer activists did not always avoid politics. After reporting favorably on the actions of a vigilance committee in Corbeil, *L'Echo de Paris* noted that "Unfortunately, the majority of the speakers talked about politics, attacking the government and the bourgeoisie!," AN F 23 199: *L'Echo de Paris*, August 16, 1919.

determine fair retail prices for food. Upon arrival at the marketplace, the committee would usually hold a brief rally against price-gouging merchants to attract shoppers' attention. Having done so, they would then go from merchant to merchant, demanding that they lower their prices to acceptable levels. The vigilance committees explicitly rejected violence as a tactic, but the threat of it was always present in the crowds of housewives that followed them on their rounds.[118] The actions of the vigilance committee in Villeneuve-Saint-Georges provide a good example of such procedures:

Wednesday morning, as soon as the market opened, several hundred railwaymen and workers of all kinds were present, divided up into groups, and armed with price lists drawn up by the vigilance committee.

Without any violence, but very firmly, the delegates of each group invited the shopkeepers to adopt the prices fixed by the vigilance committee, warning them that no higher prices would be tolerated. To say that they welcomed our decision with a smile would be an exaggeration, but in general the majority of shopkeepers submitted with good grace to a measure whose inevitability they recognized.

It goes without saying that if the merchants were not all happy, in contrast the housewives beamed.[119]

The vigilance committees generally sought to win the cooperation of shop-keepers, and in some cases succeeded in doing so without the threat of demonstrations. For example, a committee active in the western suburbs of Paris met with local merchants and together drafted a common resolution.[120]

One grocery store in Montreuil even carried a sign reading "all food sold at wholesale prices under the regulation of the action committee" (Illustration 5.6).[121]

Such direct action, according to those active in the vigilance committees, produced quick results. However, these short-term price cuts did little to ameliorate the general problem: food and other basic necessities remained expensive in August and September 1919. Moreover, some feared that *taxation populaire* would simply lead to wholesalers withholding supplies from local markets and thus aggravate the problem of food shortages. Therefore, by late August vigilance committees began to apply a new tactic to lower food prices. Downplaying demonstrations and confrontations with local merchants, some decided to bypass the problem by organizing collective purchases of food and clothing at wholesale rates for their members.

---

[118] *L'Information ouvrière et sociale*, July 31, 1919, 1; *L'Humanité*, August 9, 1919, 1; August 11, 1919, 2; August 12, 1919, 1, 2; August 13, 1919, 3; August 26, 1919, 1; AN F 23 199: *Le Journal*, August 6, 1919; *L'Echo de Paris*, August 8, 1919; *Le Figaro*, August 10, 1919.
[119] *L'Humanité*, August 8, 1919, 2.   [120] *Ibid.*, August 13, 1919, 2.   [121] *Ibid.*, August 14, 1919, 2.

5.6 Vigilance committee members monitoring food prices at Les Halles

The Federation of Vigilance Committees, the umbrella organization of the groups in the Paris area, took the lead in this new endeavor.

Founded at the beginning of August with the slogan "consumers unite!" the Federation represented an attempt by some vigilance committee activists to give some centralized direction to an extremely localized phenomenon. The Federation actually did very little, but it does deserve credit for starting the practice of collective purchases among vigilance committees. On August 7, Federation members went to Les Halles where they bought food at wholesale prices and sold it to members of vigilance committees.[122]

---

[122] *L'Humanité*, August 8, 1919, 2. See also *L'Humanité*, August 1, 1919, 1; August 14, 1919, 2; August 18, 1919, 1; October 4, 1919, 2.

By the first week of September local committees in Bois-Colombes, Gennevilliers, Montreuil, and the fifth, sixth, and nineteenth *arrondissements* had taken up this practice. In contrast, there were no marketplace riots and few examples of price-fixing demonstrations after the end of August.[123]

Initiatives follow each other ... and take different forms. Under the force of circumstance and following the natural law of adaptation, leagues against the high cost of living adopt in turn the most varied tactics of struggle. We have seen regulation by "vigilants" which perhaps has not produced satisfactory results; we have seen consumers' leagues conclude accords with shopkeepers. Now some of them have transformed themselves into buyers' leagues. Through a gradual process of trial and error, one will eventually discover the most effective strategies.[124]

This switch involved more than mere strategy; it marked an important change in orientation as well. With the decline of food riots organized attempts at *taxation populaire* lost their persuasiveness, and the decision of the vigilance committees to abandon them constituted an implicit recognition of this fact. In replacing them with collective purchases they moved from an orientation toward confrontation to one that sought to avoid, not change, the free market in consumer goods. Many members of the vigilance committees did not view the issue this way; during a general meeting of committees at the end of August, members listed as a top priority, "To desire to achieve, by the establishment of purchases and distribution in common, by deliveries directly from the producer to the consumer, the extension of their action to the national level for the total suppression of all middlemen."[125] Yet the vigilance committees never attempted to expand their purchase programs beyond the neighborhood level, let alone pose an economic challenge to small shopkeepers. Therefore, their claim that common purchase programs would eliminate middlemen was based on fond hopes, not harsh realities.

In adopting the common purchase program the vigilance committees moved farther away from traditional food riots, turning instead to the model of consumer organization pioneered by French cooperatives. French consumer coops had a history dating back to the 1830s, creating a national organization in 1885. Like the food riots, consumer cooperation had roots in early nineteenth-century ideas of moral economy, and

---

[123] *L'Humanité*, September 3, 1919, 2; September 6, 1919, 2; September 17, 1919, 2; September 30, 1919, 2; October 17, 1919, 2; Archives de la Préfecture de Police, BA 1614, reports of September 11, 1919; September 25, 1919; October 16, 1919; AN F 23 199: *Le Matin*, September 9, 1919; September 15, 1919; *L'Avenir*, October 10, 1919.

[124] AN F 23 199: *La Lanterne*, August 27, 1919.   [125] *L'Humanité*, August 27, 1919, 2.

particularly in Britain flourished under the leadership of utopian socialists like Robert Owen. In England Owenites, ex-Chartists, and others came together in 1844 to create the Rochdale Pioneers, probably the most influential consumer cooperative in modern history. As Ellen Furlough and Carl Strikwerda have shown, consumer cooperatives played a key role in labor movements in modern Europe and America. Although cooperation initially strove to challenge capitalist enterprise on all fronts, by the late nineteenth century consumer cooperatives had taken the lead of the movement.[126]

The food riots of 1919 came at an important juncture for French cooperation. Many *coopés* saw their work as integral to working-class struggles, and themselves as the "third pillar" of labor movements alongside the unions and socialist parties. The onset of World War I would reinforce their importance yet also alter their political significance, especially in Paris. Parisian consumer cooperatives had grown and prospered during the war; in the Department of the Seine, the value of their sales rose from 20 million francs in 1914 to 90 million in 1919. At the same time they began working more closely with government authorities, while softening their revolutionary ideology.[127] In particular, French coops portrayed themselves as a movement for all consumers, not just workers, and as a regulator of capitalist commerce rather than an alternative to it. Nonetheless, in 1919 the consumer cooperatives remained the most important working-class organizations in Paris concerned with consumer politics. Coop members actively supported the vigilance committee movement, believing it demonstrated the validity of their own analysis of the position of the consumer under capitalism. They also saw the movement as a way of recruiting new coop members; while difficult to prove, it is possible that this occurred.[128]

---

[126] Ellen Furlough and Carl Strikwerda, *Consumers against Capitalism? Consumer Cooperation in Europe, North America, and Japan, 1840–1990* (Lanham MD: Rowman and Littlefield, 1999); Peter Gurney, *Co-operative Culture and the Politics of Consumption in England, 1870–1930* (Manchester University Press, 1996).

[127] See on this point Jean-Louis Robert, "Cooperatives and the labor movement in Paris during the Great War," in Patrick Fridenson, ed., *The French Home Front, 1914–1918* (Providence RI and Oxford: Berg, 1992); Robert, "La Bellevilloise dans la tourmente de la Grande Guerre," in Jean-Jacques Meusy, *La Bellevilloise (1877–1939): une page de l'histoire de la cooperation et du mouvement ouvrier français* (Paris: Créaphis, 2001); Ellen Furlough, *Consumer Cooperation in France: The Politics of Consumption 1834–1930* (Ithaca: Cornell University Press, 1991), 227–258. The increasing reformism of the Parisian coop movement as a result of the war provides an interesting contrast with the food riots of 1919, demonstrating that consumer activism could take different directions.

[128] *L'Humanité*, July 2, 1919, 4; August 17, 1919, 2; August 26, 1919, 2; August 31, 1919, 2; September 4, 1919, 2; September 30, 1919, 2; *L'Information ouvrière et sociale*, April 20, 1919, 4; July 24, 1919, 1; September 18, 1919, 2; October 26, 1919, 1–5; AN F 7 13936(2); Sellier, Bruggeman, and Poëte, *Paris pendant la guerre*, 40–43. See also Furlough, *Consumer Cooperation in France*.

This change in tactics did keep the vigilance committees alive for a few more months, but by the end of September the movement had clearly lost most of its momentum. There are no records of any new committees starting up after early September. The common purchase programs continued on a very small scale, bringing lower food prices to committee members but posing no real threat to shopkeepers.[129] Lacking the drama and public presence of the price-fixing demonstrations, these programs failed to bring the vigilance committees the attention and followers they needed to survive. As the winter took hold in Paris, the shortage of coal brought about a brief outburst of consumer discontent and violence in November, but the vigilance committees took no part in trying to organize it.[130] By the beginning of 1920 the committee movement had effectively ceased to exist. In January the police reported that the President of the Latin Quarter's *Ligue contre la Vie Chère*, one of the most successful in Paris, had absconded with the group's funds. Most groups did not self-destruct so dramatically, but rather quietly faded away in late 1919 and early 1920.[131] While inflation rates remained high into the early months of 1920, the success of government programs to lower food prices by late 1919 prevented new food riots and thus undercut the ability of the vigilance committees to mobilize Parisian consumers. Without the dynamic popular mobilization produced by the food riots ultimately the committees lacked the organizational stability to survive.

The vigilance committees occupied a central position in the food protests of 1919, mobilizing thousands of Parisians and suburbanites in the struggle for lower prices. Their existence and their efforts to organize food rioters in a systematic consumers' movement provide a clear contrast with eighteenth-century food riots. These committees did not represent a complete break with the past. In fact, vigilance committees were by no means new in 1919. Neighborhood organizations with the same name played an active role in Parisian working-class life during the siege of Paris and the Commune.[132]

---

[129] "The league against the high cost of living of the fifth *arrondissement* is no longer selling food on Sundays like it used to do. This group, directed by students, no longer exists. Their small-scale actions did not succeed in lowering the price of food." APP BA 1614, report of December 11, 1919.

[130] In Ménilmontant a crowd of roughly 100 invaded a coal store, broke its windows, and forced the proprietor to sell them coal; in Montmartre another storeowner, fighting off a similar assault by a group of women, wounded several of them with a knife. In general, Parisians demanded primarily more coal, rather than lower coal prices. APP BA 1614, reports of November 5, 1919; November 6, 1919.

[131] APP BA 1614, report of January 1, 1920.

[132] See Stewart Edwards, *The Paris Commune 1871* (London: Eyre and Spottiswoode, 1971). As noted before in this study, in many ways Parisian working-class life and activism in 1919 suggests parallels with the events of 1870–1871. The atmosphere of transition from war to peace, the strong concern

During the food riots of 1911 women had created their own housewives' leagues to organize boycotts of certain shopkeepers. Some aspects of vigilance committee actions in 1919 were reminiscent of earlier practices. For example, their emphasis on attacking middlemen as the root cause of high food prices closely resembles themes common in the eighteenth century.[133] The strong localism of the movement, in spite of the creation of the Federation and of calls for extending the struggle nationwide, also recalled earlier food riots. Moreover, the short lives of the committees, lasting only a few months, mark them as something different from more permanent trade unions.

Yet in many other ways the vigilance committees betrayed their roots in the early twentieth century. The role they assigned to women provides an important indication of this. Although the food riots were for the most part women's riots, the vigilance committees followed the example of many contemporary French workers' organizations in relegating women to subordinate roles. Most of the leaders in the vigilance committees seem to have been men, whereas women generally played the role of rank and file supporters. The demonstration of the Villeneuve-Saint-Georges committee, described above, exemplifies this dichotomy. In this incident men acted as delegates and confronted the shopkeepers, while women stood passively in the background thankfully praising their efforts. A typical committee meeting involved several male activists speaking to an audience made up predominantly of housewives.[134] This situation differed significantly from the food riots of both the eighteenth century and 1911, in which women often acted as leaders. Whereas the leagues of 1911 were created and led by women, men founded and controlled 1919's vigilance committees, relegating women to a supporting role.[135]

The vigilance committees represented an attempt to apply some of the approaches involved in organizing unions and political parties to consumer issues. As the food riots erupted in Paris during the summer of 1919, working-class activists recognized the importance of the issue and moved to channel the anger of the crowd toward their own ends. However, the

with housing issues, the shortages of food, and the general radicalization of the population, not to mention the central role played by Montmartre, all link the two eras together. There were certainly Parisians in 1919 with personal memories of the Commune (Georges Clemençeau being the most outstanding example), and it is possible that the food riots were directly linked by popular memory to this earlier working-class upheaval.

[133] "War against the middlemen! That is the new slogan of this crusade against those who profit from inflation, who are frequently at the same time responsible for it." *L'Humanité*, August 19, 1919, 1.

[134] See for example the description of a Pré-Saint-Gervais vigilance committee meeting given in *L'Humanité*, August 27, 1919, 2.

[135] Flonneau, "Crise de vie chère," 62–63.

vigilance committees owed their existence to more than tactical opportunism. By 1919, after several years of war-induced inflation, many militants had come to recognize that wage increases could not fully compensate for runaway price levels, that one must deal with the consumer sphere on its own terms in order to address the problem effectively.[136] Therefore, like the renters' committees springing up around the city in 1919, the vigilance committees tried to organize workers as consumers, in order ultimately to transform consumer life from a series of individual sacrifices to a process of collective struggle.

However, this did not mean that traditional working-class organizations led or even wholeheartedly adopted the protest movement around food. In 1911 the Confédération Générale du Travail had actively supported the food rioters in the Nord, converting several protest organizations into housewives' unions. CGT leaders like Benoit Broutchoux and Georges Dumoulin spoke at housewives' rallies and were consequently arrested in September on the charge of inciting to riot. In April 1912, Léon Jouhaux, the head of the CGT, spoke out in favor of continued organizing against high prices.[137] In 1919, on the other hand, no working-class leaders of any stature involved themselves with the vigilance committees or tried to convert them into unions.[138] While the CGT and the Socialist Party supported in general terms the attempt of these groups to control prices, they made sure to condemn violent attacks against shopkeepers. Moreover, in terms that recall classic descriptions of "primitive" rebellion, some activists criticized the vigilance committees for their lack of systematic organization, and for failing to address the fundamental causes of inflation.

The increasing cost of living has mobilized the public into a movement of revolt, presaging a new era. Leagues have arisen. But their action, dispersed, intermittent, was often brutal and disorganized. Born of popular irritation, organs of impassioned minorities, without staff or doctrine, without discipline or method, they have been up to now factors of anarchy, not of reform; instruments of repression, not of collaboration. Rioting is not a system, punches are not a means of regulation.[139]

---

[136] "[T]he constant wage increases condemn our comrades to turn in a vicious circle, not allowing them to resolve the problem. The high cost of living: it transcends the bounds of union activity. It forces the unions to go beyond the narrow limits of this action and, inspired by the general interest, to force the public authorities to take serious measures." Letter from the Postal Workers' Federation to the Minister of Post, Telephone, and Telegraph, *L'Information ouvrière et sociale*, July 20, 1919, 6.

[137] Flonneau, "Crise de vie chère," 62–79.

[138] However, rank and file members of both the CGT and the Socialist Party certainly played a major role in the vigilance committees. In a few cases it seems likely that local union and party organizations even took part.

[139] *L'Information ouvrière et sociale*, December 25, 1919, 3.

Why did the CGT in particular react so differently to the food riots of 1911 and of 1919? One answer is simply that the war had taught the CGT the value of "collaboration and reform," that in particular the leadership's involvement with the government during the war had made it more skeptical of the need for such popular movements. However, to comprehend the CGT's position one must consider the relationship between popular unrest in Paris and the burgeoning conflict between the majority and minority factions within the organization during the summer of 1919. The violent demonstrations on May Day and the numerous strikes in Paris during May and June, most notably the metalworkers' strike, convinced many on the Left of the CGT that France was headed toward revolution, and that only the timidity and conservatism of the CGT leaders stood in the way. Members of the majority faction, on the other hand, felt it was more important to concentrate on achieving concrete reforms in cooperation with the state, doubting the imminence of revolution.[140]

Preoccupied with this increasingly bitter dispute, neither CGT faction paid much attention to the Paris food riots, or the issue of high prices in general. The authors of the CGT's key Minimum Program of December 1918 only mentioned this question very briefly on the seventh and last page of that document. For the majoritaires, both the riots and the vigilance committees represented one more example of the lack of discipline and rationality that threatened the labor movement in the summer of 1919. For the minoritaire leaders, the riots were too scattered and too apolitical to merit much concern. Neither the majority nor the minority resolutions presented at the CGT's Orléans national congress in September–October 1920 referred to *la vie chère* at all. This general lack of interest was demonstrated by the fate of the CGT's proposed one-day general strike scheduled for July 21, 1919. Stung by minoritaire criticism of its ambivalent attitude toward the June metalworkers' strike, in July the CGT leaders agreed to stage a general strike against Allied intervention in the Russian civil war. However, the majoritaires insisted that the strike also address economic issues, so that it called for demobilization and condemned the high cost of living into the bargain. The strike thus turned into an unwieldy compromise between majority and minority factions; as one of a number of wildly

[140] On the postwar disputes within the CGT see Robert Wohl, *French Communism in the Making* (Stanford University Press, 1966); Annie Kriegel, *Aux origines du communisme français: contribution à l'histoire du mouvement ouvrier français* (Paris: Flammarion, 1970); Maurice Labi, *La grande division des travailleurs* (Paris: Éditions Ouvrières, 1964); Jean-Louis Robert, *La scission syndicale de 1921* (Paris: Publications de la Sorbonne, 1980); Kathryn Amdur, *Syndicalist Legacy: Trade Unions and Politics in Two French Cities in the Era of World War I* (Urbana: University of Illinois Press, 1986).

divergent issues *la vie chère* received little attention from the CGT in preparations for the strike, which in any case never got off the ground.[141] Even after the outbreak of food rioting in August proved the importance of this issue, a sharply divided CGT could spare little effort for it.[142]

The vigilance committees constituted one response by Parisians to the high cost of living, particularly as it affected food, during the summer of 1919. The committees only survived a short time, never achieving the kind of long-term institutional presence enjoyed by the unions that composed the CGT, for example. They demonstrated that the organization of consumer life had a long way to go when compared to that of the workplace. Yet they also demonstrated that, as far as consumer protests were concerned, the early twentieth century was not the eighteenth century. The vigilance committees certainly drew some inspiration from union and political models, but were not just a simple application of such models to the consumer sphere. Instead, they arose out of a combination of neighborhood activism on an issue of concern to all, and the attempt to develop an institutional framework related to other organizations of the labor movement. They gave the Parisian protests of 1919 a variegated character and underlined their differences from earlier food riots in French history.

Finally, the actions of national and local governments were key in shaping the evolution of the 1919 crisis. The national government undertook two new actions during the summer of 1919 to control the rise of the cost of living. On July 31 a presidential decree established what came to be known as the normal price commissions. These commissions, the brainchild of the new Minister of Agriculture and Food, J. Noulens, were set up in each Department with a membership composed of city councilors, food merchants, and shopkeepers, as well as representatives of trade unions and cooperatives. They met on a weekly basis to draw up lists of normative retail prices for major foodstuffs, in order to keep consumers informed of market price levels. A second presidential decree, on August 14, required shopkeepers to display prominently the prices of all foods and beverages. Those

---

[141] After a meeting with Premier Clemençeau on July 18, the CGT leaders called off the strike one day before it should have occurred, prompting further recriminations from the minority faction. Wohl, *French Communism*, 138–139; see also the police reports in AN dossier F7 13310.

[142] The CGT did not completely ignore the issue of wartime inflation. During the early years of the conflict the CGT, together with various Socialist Party organizations and the Fédération Nationale des Coopératives de Consommation, had participated in a joint Comité d'Action, which devoted considerable attention to the war's impact on working-class consumers. The Comité strongly advocated price controls on food and also promoted the use of frozen meat as a way of keeping costs down. See John Horne, "The Comité d'Action (CGT-Parti Socialiste) and the origins of wartime labor reformism (1914–1916)," in Fridenson, ed., *The French Home Front*, esp. 246–248.

who sold goods at prices higher than those marked could be liable to prosecution.[143]

These two government actions revealed the ambiguities of its approach to price control. While echoing the popular hatred of food speculation, the government refused to abandon, in theory at least, its support of free-market principles.

The cost of food has reached excessive levels. Economic and social considerations demand that all possible efforts be made to lower as much as possible the cost of living . . .

Today, one must think of immediate palliative measures. Not only has the price of food been increased by the disturbances caused by the war, but also an excessive spirit of lucre has developed among certain middlemen. Wholesale traders in food have let themselves be persuaded to demand benefits out of proportion to those that their trade should reasonably and morally provide . . .

Our proposals . . . in no way damage the principle of the free market, hallowed by the constituent assembly as the fundamental law of the land.

The proposed decree only hopes to exercise a moral constraint on merchants and to permit consumers to discuss intelligently their exaggerated demands.[144]

This text illustrates the difficulties faced by government authorities in trying to satisfy both those clamoring for government intervention to lower food prices and those demanding the abolition of all government economic controls. During 1919 the French business community led a massive and furious assault against wartime regulations;[145] passages in this text supporting free enterprise were certainly designed to mollify such sentiment. Yet at the same time government authorities believed they had to do something about high food prices, and they justified their actions in terms that had some affinities with Parisian popular attitudes.

Although the document cited above rejects any definite policy of price fixing, it implies the existence of certain moral norms that should govern the

---

[143] Pinot, *Food Supply in France*, 301–303; *Journal Officiel de la République Française*, 51/206, August 1, 1919, 8006; *ibid.*, 51/219, August 14, 1919, 8748–8750; *L'Humanité*, August 15, 1919, 1; *ibid.*, August 26, 1919, 2; *L'Information ouvrière et sociale*, August 24, 1919, 2.

[144] *Journal Officiel*, 51/206, August 1, 1919, 8006, J. Noulens, "Ministère de l'Agriculture et du ravitaillement – rapport au président de la république Française." This report accompanied the presidential decree establishing the normal price commissions.

[145] "There is no longer any reason to make commerce and the populace bear the heavy constraints of prohibitions, restrictions, taxes, monopolies, and the economic dictatorship of public authorities and the consortiums . . . The bureaucrats who have become accustomed to running everything must not continue to impede the country's commercial activity under the pretext that they have been doing this for four years. Restoring freedom to commerce is urgent." Petition from the Béziers Chamber of Commerce to the government, February 11, 1919, cited in Richard Kuisel, *Capitalism and the State in Modern France* (Cambridge University Press, 1981), 51.

cost of food. In general, the national government's position on food prices contained some traces of beliefs germane to the traditional moral economy of the crowd. Attacks on middlemen, suggestions that food prices should reflect the ability of the consumer to pay, and references to morality all bear witness to this. Although the government argued that the decrees mandating the normal prices commissions and the posting of prices merely constituted a policy of consumer awareness, working-class consumer activists could read into them governmental intentions actively to limit food costs.

The actions of public authorities in Paris demonstrated that this interpretation had some basis in fact. The normal prices commission of the Department of the Seine, which met every Sunday from August to October 1919, worked closely with members of Parisian consumer cooperatives and vigilance committees. At times it sought to transcend its narrow mandate by attempting to set prices in the metropolitan area. The police of Paris not only sometimes turned a blind eye to violent attacks upon shopkeepers, but often seemed to be working in concert with the vigilance committees. During the attack on the store of M. Guay in Montmartre several gendarmes stood idly by and watched, finally intervening to save the shop from total destruction. In Corbeil, the police led a crowd of demonstrators in inspecting food prices in the local marketplace, doing nothing to prevent two members of the crowd from lowering the price of vegetables at one stall and selling them over the objections of the proprietress. The popular belief in governmental approval of vigilance committee actions was strong enough to force the Provisioning Ministry to deny it specifically:

Contrary to certain tendentious rumors that are barely worth mentioning, the Minister of Supply can only deplore violent attacks committed against some shopkeepers, under the pretext of exaggerated pricing. No one person has the right to take the law into his own hands. The organs of repression that the public authorities create and reinforce every day are sufficient to bring an end to such abuses.[146]

In general, the history of government policy on food prices in Paris at this time underlines the strength and resilience of liberal ideology. Politicians and administrators ultimately rejected both paternalist and corporatist approaches to food regulation. However, this history also reveals that, given popular demands for public intervention, in practice certain government sectors were willing to bend this policy. In spite of the rhetoric of

---

[146] AN F 23 199: *La Victoire*, August 9, 1919; *L'Echo de Paris*, July 28, 1919; *ibid.*, August 16, 1919; *Le Petit Parisien*, August 12, 1919; *L'Humanité*, August 13, 1919, 3; *ibid.*, August 18, 1919, 1; *ibid.*, August 21, 1919, 1.

neutral consumer education surrounding them, the normal prices commissions constituted both a response to and a collaboration with the Parisian food riots of the summer of 1919. The fact that the Paris commission disappeared at roughly the same time as the riots underscores this. The interaction of an activist popular moral economy and government commitment to liberal principles produced new forms of price controls whose brief existence illustrated both sharp conflicts and certain affinities between two very different views of the world.

CONCLUSION

An assessment of the achievements of the consumer movements of 1919, and their legacies for the future, reveals both strengths and weaknesses. Both the housing and food movements mobilized large numbers of Parisians from a variety of backgrounds in a very short time, and both developed original and often effective techniques for achieving their goals. At the same time, neither was able to sustain a solid organizational framework over the long haul. The FLS largely ceased operation by 1925, and the vigilance committees created by food activists disappeared even faster. In 1919, therefore, consumer struggles remained at the level of a dramatic but evanescent social movement rather than a consumers' union or political party.

Nevertheless, the two movements had very different records of success. The struggle to retain the kinds of public controls over rental housing introduced by the war was vindicated by a series of laws and decrees in the immediate postwar period. A decree of August 13, 1919 required landlords to post notices of vacant apartments, complete with the amount of rent. The national government followed this two months later with the law of October 23, 1919, which essentially extended wartime controls on rent levels. Further legislation in 1922 and 1923 permitted very small rent increases, but in general functioned to maintain the cost of apartments in the Paris area at levels well below market rates. Not until the years after World War II would Parisian landlords be able to raise rents substantially.[147] Although rent control not only survived but prospered after 1919, plans for public housing did not progress very far. To be sure, not only most experts and politicians concerned with affordable housing, but also most FLS militants, recognized that rent control on its own could not provide suitable lodging for the poor, but had to be supplemented by state

---

[147] Anthony Sutcliffe, *The Autumn of Central Paris: The Defeat of Town Planning 1850–1970* (London: Edward Arnold, 1970), 256–257.

intervention in housing supplies as well as prices. In 1913 the Paris City Council had established an *Office publique des habitations à bon marché* and funded it with a loan of 200 million francs. After the war the housing crisis plus the danger to public health constituted by fetid slum areas led the municipality to undertake some residential construction. An outbreak of bubonic plague in the eighteenth *arrondissement* in 1921 prompted the city of Paris to demolish forty-seven buildings and put up new housing for 4,000 inhabitants. But in general public authorities abstained from developing housing during the interwar years, building only 85,000 units of public housing in the Department of the Seine before 1939. Local and national governments in France after World War I thus pursued contradictory strategies that in the end only worsened the housing crisis: while they hindered private residential construction by discouraging capitalist investment, they failed to substitute alternative means of housing the people of Paris.[148]

Unlike rent control, government attempts to control food prices in Paris only survived the end of the war by a few years. The normal price commissions, the most controversial of attempts to regulate price levels, proved strikingly ephemeral. Soon after it came into existence, conservatives attacked the Paris commission for going beyond consumer education to restricting food prices. At the same time, many working-class activists condemned it for not going far enough: members of Parisian consumer cooperatives, in particular, often argued that the commission was ineffective. Moreover, several individuals, including members of the Paris City Council, charged that by recommending certain price levels the commission actually increased food costs; merchants selling at a discount would raise their prices to those suggested by the commission. As a result of these various criticisms, the Paris normal price commission ceased effective operations after October 1919. The Vilgrain barracks and popular restaurants operated successfully during 1920 and 1921, but were phased out in 1922. In October 1920, the national government decreed the establishment of Consumer Councils throughout France, but these remained a dead letter. By the early 1920s the ideology of the free market dominated government actions concerning Parisian food prices.[149]

All in all, the 1919 Paris consumer movements provide a significant glimpse into the interaction of Parisians' attitudes and the forms of struggle

---

[148] *Ibid.*, 258.
[149] Pinot, *Food Supply in France*, 303; *L'Humanité*, August 22, 1919, 2; *ibid.*, August 26, 1919, 2; *L'Information ouvrière et sociale*, September 18, 1919, 2; AN F 23 199: *Le Petit Parisien*, August 31, 1919; *ibid.*, October 5, 1919; *Le Journal*, August 24, 1919; *ibid.*, October 4, 1919.

they adopted in a notably turbulent era. Many aspects of the food riots and renters' actions, especially the belief system they reflected, the language in which those beliefs were expressed, and the role of women in them, recall Thompson's pre-industrial crowds. At the same time, their forms of organization and relationship to state organizations indicate the rise of new ideas and practices.[150] The participants in these riots faced a situation in which workplace and political actions did not seem capable of dealing with the ravages of inflation, so they responded with a complex synthesis of old and new forms of protest, one that in many ways foreshadowed the new social movements of the late twentieth century. Their ability to appeal to many middle-class Parisians, their concern with direct action and popular mobilization beyond the limits of established working-class organizations, and even their tentative approaches to dealing with questions of gender and difference, resonate with the popular and political struggles of the New Left. In this respect as in others, 1919 both looked back to popular tradition and heralded the advent of postmodernity.

As this chapter has tried to demonstrate, the consumer movements of 1919 constituted an important aspect of the revolutionary temper of the immediate postwar era. While their relationship to ideas of political revolution was ambivalent, to say the least, their instability and impact in politicizing mundane aspects of daily life in the capital and its suburbs underscored the feeling that revolution might very well lie on the horizon.[151] Moreover, the fact that they occurred at roughly the same time as major industrial actions in Paris reinforced the idea of a global crisis in French life. Ultimately, those who looked to a new dawn in 1919 focused not only on aggrieved consumers but also on militant workers, in particular on the massive metalworkers' strike of June. It is to this dramatic event, for many French the harbinger of revolution in 1919, that we now turn.

---

[150] The *Union des Syndicats de la Seine*, the umbrella organization of labor unions in the Paris area, supported the consumer movement but argued that it should be led by local interunion committees, not vigilance committees. This does not seem to have happened. *L'Humanité*, August 5, 1919, 1.

[151] Parisian consumer movements were unstable in two senses: they both lacked any systematic sense of organization or direction, and they also generated a broader sense of the instability of French society as a whole.

CHAPTER 6

Time, money, and revolution: the metalworkers' strike of June 1919

The Inter-union committee of Saint-Denis, after having discussed and considered the situation, has decided to transform itself into the Soviet Executive Committee and to proclaim the revolution (cries of "Long live the Soviets!") . . . the Inter-Union committee of Saint-Denis resolves to take the initiative in this revolutionary movement.

Saint-Denis, June 4, 1919.[1]

Of all the turbulent events Parisians witnessed in 1919, none more dramatically represented the revolutionary tenor of the times than the strike launched by workers in the area's metals factories. During the month of June over 160,000 metalworkers went on strike throughout Paris and its suburbs, demanding not only wage increases and the eight-hour day but also amnesty for political prisoners, a halt to French and Allied intervention in the Russian civil war, and at their most extreme the revolutionary overthrow of Clemençeau's government. Undertaken in defiance of the national metalworkers' union leadership, the spontaneous, even anarchic, character of the strike further underscored the impression, among both its proponents and its opponents, that this movement went well beyond demands for higher salaries and better working conditions. Instead, perhaps building upon the massive metalworkers' conflicts of 1918, as well as prewar anarcho-syndicalist notions of the cataclysmic general strike, the marching Parisian metalworkers of June seemed to many the very avant-garde of *la lutte finale*.[2] Finally, the fact that the strike took place in the very last month of the Paris peace negotiations, in effect ending on the same day as the signing of the peace treaty, suggested that France had at the same time conquered both the

---

[1] Archives de la Prefecture de Police [hereafter APP], BA 1386, police report of June 5, 1919.
[2] On the munitions strikes in 1918 see Kathryn Amdur, *Syndicalist Legacy: Trade Unions and Politics in Two French Cities in the Era of World War I* (Urbana: University of Illinois Press, 1986); Jean-Jacques Becker, *Les Français dans la grande guerre* (Paris: R. Laffont, 1980).

forces of German militarism and those of revolutionary anarchy. On June 28, 1919, international and social peace marched in lockstep.

The historiography of this strike, like that of the *biennio rosso* in general, has largely revolved around the question of its revolutionary character.[3] Did revolution stand on the political horizon in France in 1919, and if so did the metalworkers' strike have the potential, or the intention, to make it a reality? It certainly seemed a real possibility elsewhere in Europe. A Communist regime existed in Hungary, one had recently collapsed in Bavaria, and Germany, Austria, Italy, and Spain all seemed to tremble on the edge of insurrection. Even the British Isles and Switzerland, two bastions of bourgeois order, experienced unprecedented unrest: in Ireland the IRA was waging war against the British Black and Tans, red flags flew along the Clyde river in Glasgow, and even the peaceful Swiss seemed tempted by the Bolshevik contagion.[4] In their studies of the strike, both Bertrand Abhervé and Nicholas Papayanis emphasize the political, Marxist-inspired character of June 1919, pointing to the conflicts between the reformist leadership of the Metalworkers' Federation and the more radical ideas of rank and file Parisian metalworkers. They portray it as part of the revolutionary wave evident throughout Europe in that year, linking it to support for the Russian Revolution and hostility to Clemençeau's government in particular.[5] The more recent, and more nuanced, discussion of the metalworkers' strike by Jean-Louis Robert places the events of June in the context of the transition from war to peace, underscoring the instability of social, economic, and political life at the time, as well as the context of the broader history of the revolutionary tradition in Paris generally.[6] In spite of differences among these authors, all see the June 1919 strike as motivated to an

---

[3] Following the lead of Italian historians, I use this term to characterize the revolutionary spirit of 1919–1920. See Paolo Spriano, *The Occupation of the Factories*, translated by Gwyn Williams (London: Pluto Press, 1975); Martin Clark, *Antonio Gramsci and the Revolution that Failed* (New Haven: Yale University Press, 1977).

[4] Lindemann, *The "Red Years"*; Chris Wrigley, ed., *Challenges of Labour: Central and Western Europe, 1917–1920* (London and New York: Routledge, 1993); Michael Hopkinson, *The Irish War of Independence* (Dublin: Gill and Macmillan, 2002); Iain McLean, *The Legend of Red Clydeside* (Edinburgh: Humanities Press, 1993); David Mitchell, *1919: Red Mirage: Year of Desperate Rebellion* (London: Cape, 1970), 66–67.

[5] Bertrand Abhervé, "La grève des metallurgists parisiens de juin 1919" (Mémoire de maîtrise dissertation, Université de Paris-8, 1973); Abhervé, "Les origines de la grève des metallurgists parisiens, juin 1919," *Mouvement social*, 93 (Oct.–Dec., 1975), 75–85; Nicholas Papayanis, "Masses révolutionnaires et directions reformists: les tensions au cours des grèves des metallurgists français en 1919," *Mouvement social*, 93 (Oct.–Dec. 1975), 51–73.

[6] Jean-Louis Robert, *Les ouvriers, la patrie et la révolution: Paris 1914–1919* (Paris: Les Belles Lettres, 1995), especially 291–406.

important extent by revolutionary sentiments, if not guided by revolutionary strategies nor producing a revolutionary outcome.

This image of June 1919 as a revolution *manqué* rests essentially on a dichotomy between economic and political demands. Those who characterize the strike as insurrectional in spirit point to the willingness of many strikers to adopt slogans about political issues like the end of capitalism, the overthrow of the government, and support of the Russian Revolution; in contrast, those strikers who gave pride of place to wage demands are seen as non- or even anti-revolutionary. This dichotomy certainly dominated contemporary views of the strike and has remained largely unchallenged by historians ever since. The fact that the strike took place during (as well as contributing to) the increasingly bitter factional struggles in the French Left, struggles that ultimately split both the Socialist Party and the Confédération Générale du Travail in two, contributed to the idea that the strike pitted reformists against revolutionaries. Moreover, strikers who themselves took an insurrectional view of their movement characterized it as a rejection of economic in favor of political demands.[7] As a member of the Saint-Denis Socialist municipality argued, "the movement should not limit itself to purely economic questions, but the French proletariat should take a lesson from the benefits of contemporary revolutions and build upon the same bases the principle of social transformation."[8] In similar terms, the Socialist leader Emile Bestel declared "We will no longer limit ourselves to platonic demands. We want a regime change. Long live the revolution! Long live the Soviets!"[9]

In this chapter I contend that this dichotomy between economic and political issues, which has shaped not only views of the June 1919 strike but in general much of the historiography of labor and revolution, is fundamentally misleading.[10] Historians have long since established that material impoverishment itself does not automatically lead to revolution, that insurrection is an intrinsically political process.[11] Moreover, as Charles Tilly in

---

[7] On the history of the postwar division of the French Left see Kriegel, *Aux origines du communisme français*; Wohl, *French Communism*; Labi, *La grande division des travailleurs*; Jacques Girault and Jean-Louis Robert, *1920: le Congrès de Tours* (Paris: Messidor-Éditions Sociales, 1990).

[8] APP BA 1386, police report of June 2, 1919.   [9] APP BA 1386, police report of June 6, 1919.

[10] On the relationship between reform and revolution in modern labor movements, see for example David E. Barclay and Eric D. Weitz, eds., *Between Reform and Revolution: German Socialism and Communism from 1840 to 1990* (New York and Oxford: Berghahn Books, 1998); L. Gambone, *Revolution and Reformism: The Split Between "Moderates" and "Revolutionaries" in French Anarcho-Syndicalism* (Montreal: Red Lion Press, 1995).

[11] In particular, the revisionist school of the history of the French Revolution has long contended this. See Steven Kaplan, *Farewell, Revolution: Disputed Legacies; France, 1789–1989* (Ithaca NY: Cornell University Press, 1995); Eric Hobsbawm, *Echoes of the Marseillaise: Two Centuries Look Back on the French Revolution* (London: Verso, 1990).

particular has demonstrated, proponents of radical change can't just rely on misery and alienation but must also be able to mobilize social and political resources to attain their goals.[12] However, the dichotomy between material goals and political mobilization at times obscures the ways in which individuals and groups conceived of the former in political terms. In other words, economic and political demands are in many cases complementary rather than opposed. For example, the February 1917 revolution in Russia toppled the Tsarist regime, but it began as a women's marketplace riot over the cost of bread.[13] Concern over the cost and availability of goods did not so much lead to political consciousness as embody it.

Throughout this study I have argued that consumer consciousness and behavior in Paris during the era of World War I did not just engage in politics but frequently looked toward fundamental transformations of the political order, and that the revolutionary tenor of the immediate postwar period owed much to conflicts over consumption. In considering the history of the June 1919 Paris metalworkers' strike I move from a study of specific consumer behaviors and attitudes to an analysis of how grievances over the cost of basic goods shaped not only industrial action but revolutionary activism in general. Workers are also consumers, of course, and their needs for cheap bread and affordable housing often motivate industrial militancy. In making the case that frustrated consumerism not only helped prompt the June 1919 strike but underlay much of its radicalism I emphasize three themes. First, Parisian metalworkers, and many Parisians in general, felt that wage increases alone could not improve living conditions because they would only prompt price increases, so that therefore the solution to *la vie chère* had to be a political one. Second, like the Paris Commune half a century earlier June 1919 represented the blending of consumer grievances with the politics of urban space and society. Third, the inability of both reformists and revolutionaries to grasp and creatively mobilize this interaction between material and political grievances lay at the root of the failure of the movement. A "consumerist" reading of this strike thus offers important insights into the prospects of and hindrances to revolutionary change in postwar Paris.

[12] Charles Tilly, *Regimes and Repertoires* (University of Chicago Press, 2006); Joe Foweraker, *Theorizing Social Movements* (London and Boulder CO: Pluto Press, 1995).

[13] Barbara Alpern Engel, "Not by bread alone: subsistence riots in Russia during World War I," *Journal of Modern History*, 69/4 (December, 1997), 696–721. On women in the Russian Revolution, see also Elizabeth Wood, *The Baba and the Comrade: Gender and Politics in Revolutionary Russia* (Bloomington: Indiana University Press, 1997); Jane McDermid and Anna Hillyar, *Midwives of the Revolution: Female Bolsheviks and Women Workers in 1917* (Athens: Ohio University Press, 1999).

As in the preceding two chapters, differences of race and gender did not figure overtly in the metalworkers' strike, but rather played a muted and contextual role. The strike took place during the exclusion of women and colonial subjects from the Paris labor force and the metals industry in particular. As we shall see, the concerns of women workers received little attention from the strikers, and there are no mentions of colonial labor. Yet as I shall argue below the very fact that the strike was gendered male ultimately worked to its disadvantage, especially in comparison with the dressmakers' strike of 1917. At the same time the heavily suburban character of the strike confirmed the exclusion of Parisian labor from the metropolitan center that I noted in Chapter 4, further suggesting parallels with the process of colonial exclusion so apparent in 1919 in general. Nuances of race and gender called forth images of the man with the knife between his teeth and the barbarians at the gates of civilization. They thus contributed to the revolutionary aura of the June metalworkers' strike.

TIME VS. MONEY

In an important study Gary Cross has argued that one of the key themes of modern labor history, and of political economy in general, is the choice between time and money. As he and other scholars have observed, during the twentieth century workers in industrial and postindustrial democracies generally chose to earn more money, using that money to buy more consumer goods, rather than to work less and enjoy more leisure time. Whereas popular purchasing power expanded enormously over the course of the century, the eight-hour workday has remained standard for more than seventy years. This argument is not without flaws: it tends to leave unexplored, for example, the ways in which "work" and "leisure" have been constructed as opposites. Nonetheless, it constitutes a very useful way of approaching the intersections of consumerism and popular culture, and the politics of both.[14]

The year 1919 was a seminal one in the history of this choice. If the Bolshevik Revolution represented the greatest achievement and symbol of the radical Left in Europe immediately after the Armistice, the achievement of the eight-hour day played the same role for reformist socialism and organized labor. In 1919 much of Europe adopted this reform, similar to

---

[14] Gary Cross, *Time and Money: The Making of Consumer Culture* (London: Routledge, 1993). See also Juliet Schor, *The Overworked American: The Unexpected Decline of Leisure in America* (New York: Basic Books, 1991).

the largely successful push for votes for women at the same time. Both became symbols of the recompense owed to the ordinary peoples of Europe for their struggles and sacrifices during World War I.[15] Yet as is so often the case, when it came to enacting the eight-hour law, in France and elsewhere, the devil lay in the details. One particularly agonizing detail was the impact of shorter working hours on wages. Should workers who worked fewer hours also earn less money? This was particularly an issue for those employed on piece rates, but in general the question of productivity was central to the debate over the eight-hour day. Should those working the eight-hour day compensate for their shorter hours by greater productivity and intensity of labor, should they simply be paid higher salaries, or should they earn less money for less time? In short, should the eight-hour day force workers to choose between time and money?

We have already encountered this issue in Chapter 1. In 1917 striking dressmakers in Paris demanded a cost of living allowance so as not to lose wages by working shorter hours. A similar conundrum lay at the heart of industrial militancy in 1919, not just for the metalworkers' strike in June but also for many other labor actions that year. Yet a combination of factors, including the end of the war, the passage of national legislation enacting the eight-hour day, and the continued increase in the high cost of living in spite of the Armistice, rendered this issue all the more momentous. Much of the radicalism of the metalworkers' strike in Paris derived from the refusal of these workers to choose between time and money, insisting instead that they had a right to both short hours and high wages. On the face of it this seemed like a simple material demand, a question of income, not politics or revolution. However, as we shall see this rejection of the choice between time and money split the national Metalworkers' Federation and opened the door to the radical demands of Parisian activists. Like the dressmakers' strike of 1917, the movement of June 1919 combined an insistence on very basic material desires with awareness that the solution to those desires was at least in part political.

The movement for the eight-hour day both had a long history and also operated on a global scale. The idea of a day divided equally between work, leisure and family time, and sleep had been a goal of labor

---

[15] Gary Cross, *A Quest for Time: The Reduction of Work in Britain and France, 1840–1940* (Berkeley: University of California Press, 1989); Patrick Fridenson and Bénédicte Reynaud, eds., *La France et le temps de travail (1814–2004)* (Paris: Odile Jacob, 2004); David R. Roediger and Philip S. Foner, *Our Own Time: A History of American Labor and the Working Day* (New York: Greenwood Press, 1989); Robert Whaples, "Winning the eight-hour day, 1909–1919," *Journal of Economic History*, 50/2 (June, 1990), 393–406.

movements in Europe and America since the mid nineteenth century. Both the First and Second Internationals had adopted it as a major rallying cry; a year after its founding, the Second International had called upon national unions around the world to demonstrate for the eight-hour day on May Day 1890. But, as with the campaigns for votes for women, it took the dual impact of war and revolution to make the eight-hour day a reality. While embraced by many reformists in labor and government, for a variety of reasons, it was revolutionaries who first and foremost implemented the reduction of work time. The new Soviet Union became the first country to enact the eight-hour day, in 1917, followed by Finland, Norway, and revolutionary Germany a year later. By December 1918 the movement had spread throughout much of insurgent eastern Europe as well as provoking massive strikes in Switzerland. In February 1919 workers throughout Italy struck for the eight-hour day, and by the end of the year the governments of Spain, Portugal, Switzerland, Sweden, and the Netherlands had all passed eight-hour-day legislation. In 1918–1919 the eight-hour-day movement thus represented both the demand for reform and the threat of world revolution.[16]

This dialectic of reform and revolution also structured the debate over the eight-hour day in France. In December 1918 the Confédération Générale du Travail made the eight-hour day a central demand of its national program, and pressured the government to move speedily on the issue. Largely as a result, in January 1919 President Georges Clemenceau, certainly no friend of organized labor, established a commission to draft a law on the reduction of the length of the workday. This commission, composed of representatives of management, labor, and the national legislature, worked for over a month to produce a bill it submitted to the Chamber of Deputies at the beginning of April. Not all agreed with the proposed law: business representatives in particular felt the law would hurt industrial recovery, while some unions wanted more restrictions on overtime. Workers agreed to the bill in large part because the final version promised that they would not suffer pay cuts as a result of shorter hours. Employers, in contrast, accepted the bill largely out of fear of the political consequences of refusing. The specter of the general strikes for the eight-hour day that occurred in Glasgow and Switzerland in January 1919, plus the threats made by CGT leaders to take to the streets on May Day if their demands were not met, caused the law to win passage in record time. On April 23, 1919, only eight days after it had been introduced for debate, legislators in both the Chamber

---

[16] Cross, *Quest.*

and the Senate voted unanimously to make the eight-hour day the law of the land. Faced with the threat of revolution, the French government was willing to offer the promise of reform.[17]

But as of April 1919 the eight-hour day was little more than a promise. The law enacted the principle of the eight-hour day, but left it to individual industries to negotiate the specific terms of its application. For example, it wasn't clear whether the eight-hour day meant a forty-eight-hour week (eight hours a day Monday through Saturday) or *la semaine anglaise*, a forty-four-hour week with a half day on Saturdays. For industries with work schedules that varied seasonally, such as the garment industry and construction, it was unclear whether the eight-hour standard would be applied uniformly throughout the year or else vary according to the pace of work. Another issue was productivity and the pace of work. Some industrialists felt that the eight-hour day would only make sense if accompanied with increased workplace rationalization, a more intensive pace of labor. Many industrial reformers, both in business and in the unions, had followed Taylorist ideas of workplace science during the war, and felt that a more modernized workplace was key to the success of the new workday. Others, however, opposed Taylorism as an assault upon the autonomy of the skilled worker, and as an increase of exploitation in general. In order to ensure passage of the law, the CGT leadership had accepted, even embraced, the principle of scientific management in 1919, arguing that increased productivity was the best guarantee of both higher wages and shorter hours. Not all CGT members found this compromise acceptable.[18]

Finally, the issue of wages loomed especially large for many French workers in 1919. The CGT had won the concession that the eight-hour day should not lead to wage cuts, but again this was a matter of principle. In particular, it was not clear what would happen to those many workers who were paid by the amount they produced rather than the time they worked. Unless employers agreed to increase piece rates, shortened work hours would result either in lower earnings or an increased pace of labor. In addition, those workers who had won cost of living allowances during the war, or hoped to win them in 1919, had to contend with the possibility of forfeiting them under the new system. Given the continued increases in the

---

[17] *Ibid.*
[18] George G. Humphreys, *Taylorism in France, 1904–1920: The Impact of Scientific Management on Factory Relations and Society* (New York: Garland, 1986); Kenneth Tucker, *French Revolutionary Syndicalism and the Public Sphere* (Cambridge University Press, 1996).

prices of basic goods, the question of how to implement the eight-hour-day law became inescapably tangled up with the crisis of *la vie chère*.[19]

For these reasons, far from calming industrial discontent, the passage of the eight-hour law contributed to a sharp spike in strike activity during May and June.[20] As we have seen, the May Day riots in Paris produced violent clashes with the police and an atmosphere of near-insurrection. More generally, in the hope of pressuring employers to accept interpretations of the eight-hour-day law most favorable to them, a number of Parisian unions staged walkouts. The two central issues in most cases were time and money: on the one hand, a demand for the forty-four-hour English week, on the other hand, a desire to maintain salary levels and/or the cost of living increase. At the beginning of May garment workers in Paris went on strike, a conflict that would last for over a month. Their union addressed two essential demands to employers: "1. Application of the eight hour day, with rest time on Saturday afternoon, in all workplaces; 2. Incorporation of the cost of living allowance into general wages."[21] Parisian bank employees and cobblers also went on strike, making essentially the same demands, in May. In general, whereas strikers failed to win the English week, settling instead for eight-hour days six days a week, they did have some luck in winning their wage demands. The agreement signed between Parisian shoe manufacturers and workers made this explicit.

> In conformity with Article 2 of the law of April 23, 1919, the reduction of work-time should not result in any diminution of wages paid as of the application of this agreement.
>
> Consequently, salaries fixed by the day, by the week or by the month, based on a 60 hour week, currently paid for 55 hours, shall be maintained for 48 hours . . .
>
> *Cost of living allowances* will continue to be paid at current rates. No modifications can be made to these rates without the previous agreement of the contracting parties [emphasis in the original].[22]

Both garment workers and bank employees ultimately made similar settlements, ceding their demands for increased leisure in exchange for maintaining their salary levels in spite of the reduction of hours. Concerned above all with upholding high levels of production, Parisian employers in 1919 seem to have been more inclined to accept higher wages than shorter hours.

---

[19] Abhervé, "La grève," chapter 3.
[20] For the period May–July 1919 some 300,000 workers went on strike in France, compared to roughly 520,000 for the entire period 1915–1918. Jean-Paul Brunet, *Saint-Denis la ville rouge, 1890–1939* (Paris: Hachette, 1980), 377; Papayanis, "Masses révolutionnaires," 52.
[21] *L'Humanité*, May 6, 1919, 1. [22] *L'Humanité*, May 16, 1919, 4.

This survey of Parisian labor's reaction to the passage of the eight-hour-day law complicates the general idea that in the twentieth century workers in industrial democracies generally chose money over time. In general Parisian workers wanted both: many did opt for more money over more time in 1919, but only because they were given little choice by employers. Moreover, at issue in the period immediately after the war was not significantly increasing one's purchasing power but rather avoiding a major decline in one's income. The specific focus on cost of living allowances constituted a direct response to the seemingly runaway inflation of the period. They reflected the fear that wage increases by themselves could not ensure an acceptable standard of living, that classic industrial militancy alone was an inadequate protection against the ravages of *la vie chère*.

The turbulence of the spring of 1919 in Paris thus suggests a more nuanced perspective on the relationship between reformism and revolution. On the surface it is easy to conclude that issues like the length of the workday and cost of living allowances did not seriously threaten the capitalist status quo; certainly employers seemed willing enough to make such concessions in this period, if only to prevent the spread of the revolutionary contagion from the East. Yet, as the story of the metalworkers' strike will make clear, many Parisian workers did not see reforms like the eight-hour day as opposed to the dream of revolution, but rather an integral part of it. The idea that ensuring a decent standard of living for working people required a fundamental rupture in the economy, society, and politics of France united the struggle for cost of living allowances with support for the Bolshevik Revolution in Russia and its replication at home. The threat posed to working-class incomes by the debate over the application of the eight-hour-day law meant that insurgent consumerism would play a major role in the radicalism of June 1919.[23]

TOWARD THE METALWORKERS' STRIKE

A central reason for the revolutionary spirit of the 1919 metalworkers' strike in Paris was the increasingly bitter division between pro- and antiwar factions in the French Left. The split, part of the broader break between

[23] James Cronin, "Labor insurgency and class formation: comparative perspectives on the crisis of 1917–1920 in Europe," in James Cronin and Carmen Sirianni, eds., *Work, Community, and Power: The Experience of Labor in Europe and America, 1900–1925* (Philadelphia: Temple University Press, 1983), 20–48; Temma Kaplan, *Red City, Blue Period: Social Movements in Picasso's Barcelona* (Berkeley: University of California Press, 1992); Roberto Bianchi, *Pace, pane, terra: il 1919 in Italia* (Roma: Odradek, 2006).

reformist and revolutionary socialists across Europe that created modern Communism, began during the war years.[24] Some members of the socialist and union Left never accepted the *Union Sacrée* during the war, and as early as 1915 demonstrated their opposition by traveling to the antiwar international conference in Zimmerwald, Switzerland. The growing war weariness and rise of industrial unrest in France in 1917 transformed this spirit of opposition into a mass-based movement, so that by the time the Bolsheviks seized power in Russia both the Socialist Party and the CGT had substantial *minoritaire* antiwar factions. The Bolshevik Revolution itself had a mixed impact on the antiwar Left in France: while for the far Left the Brest-Litovsk treaty summed up the idea of revolutionary defeatism and an immediate end to the war, for most French Socialists and workers it represented a betrayal of France, thus linking Bolshevism with German militarism.[25] The end of the war resolved this problem for many, so by 1919 the antiwar minority increasingly embraced Moscow's call for world revolution.[26] As one French union declared in 1919, "The War is dead. Long live the war."[27]

Metalworkers stood at the heart of these conflicts. By the early twentieth century they had carved out a reputation as one of the most militant groups of workers in France. The national Metalworkers' Federation had taken the lead during the war in opposing the *Union Sacrée* and demanding peace rather than victory. Alphonse Merrheim, the general secretary of the Federation, had attended the Zimmerwald conference in 1915 and in general been active as one of the early leaders of the *minoritaires* in the CGT. The Federation had grown spectacularly during the last years of the war: from a membership of only 18,000 in 1916 it had ballooned to 200,000 by the spring of 1919. Many of these new members had joined as a result of the munitions strikes in 1917 and 1918, and usually supported the antiwar Left. The Parisian metalworkers' union in particular, already a standard bearer of the antiwar movement, came to symbolize the restiveness and war weariness of French labor in general.[28]

The growth of unions in the metals industry took place at the same time as the increased presence of women and colonial workers, in a way that

[24] On the postwar division of the European Left see Lindemann, *The "Red Years"*; Gruber, *International Communism*.
[25] Hence the term "Boche-vik," a play on words linking the derogatory term for German with Bolshevism.
[26] Kriegel, *Aux origines du communisme français*; Wohl, *French Communism*.
[27] Cited in Denis Brogan, *The Development of Modern France*, 2 vols., vol. II: *The Shadow of War; World War I; Between the Two Wars* (Gloucester: Peter Smith, 1970), 558.
[28] Nicholas Papayanis, *Alphonse Merrheim: The Emergence of Reformism in Revolutionary Syndicalism* (Dordrecht and Boston MA: M. Nijhoff, 1985).

reflected the differences between the two groups. Whereas few if any colonial subjects joined unions in France during this period, organized labor did have some success in recruiting women. In Paris in particular, the Metalworkers' Federation succeeded in increasing its female membership by launching a new union for both men and women, the Syndicat des Ouvriers et Ouvrières de la Seine. By the middle of 1917 this union raised the female share of unionized metalworkers in Paris to 30 percent, roughly the same as women's share of the industry's workforce in general. Moreover, the *munitionnettes* often led strikes in the metals industry during 1917 and 1918. In spite of this, discourses of industrial militancy in 1919 generally, as we have seen, excluded women rather than embracing their contributions to working-class activism. One of the great ironies of the June metalworkers' strike, and of industrial activism during 1919 in general, is that it should reach a fever pitch at the same time as the industry lost some of its most militant members.[29]

By the beginning of 1919 the conflict between majority and minority in the French Left was sharper than ever, but the situation in the Metalworkers' Federation had shifted. By July 1918 Alphonse Merrheim had reached an agreement with the majoritaire leader of the CGT, Léon Jouhaux, which led him to abandon the antiwar faction. Historians like Nicholas Papayanis have attributed this shift to factors such as fear of state repression of radical antiwar unions, and the combination of Brest-Litovsk and the German offensives of the summer of 1918. For whatever reasons, Merrheim succeeded in leading the Metalworkers' Federation, the second largest in the CGT, back into the ranks of the reformist majority.[30] However, the Paris metalworkers' union, by far the largest in the Federation, remained firmly attached to an increasingly revolutionary vision of union activism. This split within the Metalworkers' Federation, its image of the nation versus Paris that once again recalled 1871, was a key factor in the outbreak and outcome of the June 1919 strike.

On April 17, 1919, a week before the passage of the national law, the Metalworkers' Federation signed an agreement with the metals employers' organization (*Union des Industries Métallurgiques et Minières*) establishing the eight-hour day in the French metals industry. On the face of it this was a major achievement for organized labor in France, one that in fact paved the

[29] Laura Lee Downs, *Manufacturing Inequality: Gender Division in the French and British Metalworking Industries, 1914–1939* (Ithaca NY: Cornell University Press, 1995), 121–146.
[30] Papayanis, "Masses révolutionnaires."

road for the eight-hour-day law. Yet upon closer inspection some problems emerged. For example, traditionally the ten-hour workday had included time for breaks, getting dressed, and washing up – the new agreement viewed such time as external to the eight-hour day. The agreement also mandated the forty-eight-hour week, instead of the forty-four-hour English week that many workers wanted. The question of wage structures was, however, the most significant. As with the national eight-hour law, the accord maintained current salaries in spite of the shortening of the workday. However, this only applied to workers employed by the hour or day. In contrast, the law did not revise piece rates upward to compensate for the reduction in time, specifying that "In principle piece-work rates in francs will not be automatically modified by the application of the eight-hour day."[31]

Why should workers and their unions agree to cutting their own wages during a time when the prices of basic goods seemed to increase day by day? As far as both employers and the national leadership of the CGT were concerned, the answer lay in increased productivity. During the war Léon Jouhaux and other national labor leaders had embraced ideas of rationalization and Taylorism, seeing in a more modern and efficient workplace the key to a better standard of living for French workers.[32] In trying to pressure French employers and legislators to accept the eight-hour day in 1919, union leaders used a combination of sticks and carrots: while they threatened the use of widespread strikes, even revolution, they also promised acceptance of industrial rationalization to ensure continued profitability. As Jouhaux himself stated at the beginning of April 1919, "The eight-hour day ... should mark the point of departure for industrial modernization ... Thus, once more, the social consequences of working-class demands will lead to a revolutionary transformation."[33] For piece-rate workers, therefore, while wages might drop initially, more scientific management would ultimately make them more productive, benefiting everyone.

The major problem with this strategy was one that typified debates over industrial rationalization as a whole. As historians have noted, the phenomenon of scientific management of industry in France during the early twentieth century was virtually all talk and no action. Only a few firms,

---

[31] *L'Union des Métaux*, June–July 1919, cited in Bertrand Abhervé, "Les origines," 80.

[32] See John Horne, *Labour at War: France and Britain, 1914–1918* (New York: Oxford University Press, 1991); Patrick Fridenson, ed., *The French Home Front, 1914–1918* (Oxford: Berg, 1992).

[33] Cited in Abhervé, "Les origines," 80.

notably Andre Citroen's Paris automobile factory, even attempted it in any significant manner, and Citroen's failure exemplified the hazards facing such a strategy.[34] Most employers were simply not convinced that Taylorist strategies, which required substantial investment, would pay off. In particular, the small size of most metals factories in France made rationalization a pipe dream.[35] This was especially true in the Paris area: most metals workshops in the city were artisanal in scale, rarely counting more than 50 employees.[36] Such firms had neither the desire nor the wherewithal to invest in up-to-date machinery to boost productivity. Given this, the main strategy for increasing production was rather to intensify the pace of work: workers might work fewer hours, but they would work more time during each hour. Consequently, for many metalworkers in Paris and its suburbs, the eight-hour-day agreement negotiated between the Metalworkers' Federation and representatives of industry seemed to promise lower wages, a harder workday, or a combination of the two.

Such a prospect by itself would probably have caused tensions between the national Metalworkers' Federation and the Parisian metalworkers' unions. Another problem was the failure of the national federation to consult any of its members or local unions before signing the agreement. The rush to cement an accord before May Day largely explained the failure of both sides to consult their constituents. In addition, the ideological contrast between a *majoritaire* national union and the strongly *minoritaire* unions of the Department of the Seine constituted a further source of conflict. For all these reasons, many Parisian metalworkers' unions reacted to the April 17 agreement with undisguised hostility. As one union organizer noted, "When we saw this document . . . we realized that we had been cheated. We were stupefied."[37]

The April 17 agreement had to be ratified locally before becoming official. In order to arrange for this in the Paris area Merrheim and the national metalworkers' leadership set up an Entente Committee (EC) composed of six members, three from metalworkers' unions and three from the automobile and aviation union in the Paris area. The EC quickly drew up its own, more radical program for implementing the eight-hour day. Not only did it

[34] Sylvie Schweitzer, *Des engrenages à la chaine: les usines Citroen 1915–1935* (Presses Universitaires de Lyon, 1982).

[35] Humphreys, *Taylorism in France*; see also Gerd Hardach, "Industrial mobilization in 1914–1918: production, planning, and ideology," in Fridenson, ed., *The French Home Front*.

[36] Abhervé, "La grève," 35; Michael Torigian, *Every Factory a Fortress: The French Labor Movement in the Age of Ford and Hitler* (Athens: Ohio University Press, 1999).

[37] Cited in Abhervé, "Les origines," 77.

call for the English week and stricter regulation of factory conditions but it also demanded a universal minimum wage for the industry. Unlike the April 17 agreement, satisfaction of this demand would have given a substantial wage increase to all metalworkers, including those paid by the piece.[38] Although historians like Annie Kriegel have pointed to the radical nature of the EC and viewed these demands as an attempt to provoke a revolutionary strike, it is also quite likely that the EC's program simply reflected rank and file discontent with the impact of inflation on their standard of living.[39] More importantly, the fact that the main difference between moderate and radical unionists seemed to be not hours or politics but rather wages and compensation underscores the connection between material conditions and revolutionary activism in the spring of 1919.

Not surprisingly, employers preferred to continue negotiating with the national Federation rather than deal with the EC, and the wisdom of doing so became evident on May 24, when the Federation signed a second agreement with them. This new agreement did secure the 44-hour week for metalworkers, but the salary provisions remained unchanged from the first accord. This new agreement effectively cut the ground out from under the EC, further poisoning relations between organized metalworkers in Paris and the national Federation, and laying the ground for the June strike.[40] The agreement specified that the eight-hour-day provisions would be implemented on June 1, 1919; the national Federation had signaled its willingness to consider a general strike of the industry if this deadline wasn't met.[41] The signing of the May 24th accord, however, led many metalworkers in Paris to the conclusion that the Federation was not serious and that they would have to take matters into their own hands.

The result was a series of wildcat strikes in the Paris area during the last week of May. Like garment workers and bank employees, many metalworkers in the Department of the Seine had already reacted to the passage of the eight-hour-day law by demanding its immediate enactment on favorable terms. For example, 100 metalworkers in a factory in Saint-Denis went on strike for two weeks, from May 10 to May 22, demanding both a salary increase and the eight-hour day. At the same time, 250 airplane mechanics at a factory in Puteaux struck for the eight-hour day. Both strikes were successful.[42] After May 24 more metalworkers went on strike, often in the

---

[38] Abhervé, "La grève," chapter 4.   [39] Kriegel, *Aux origines du communisme français*, 300–301.
[40] Abhervé, "La grève," chapter 4.
[41] Archives Nationales [hereafter AN] F7 13367, police report of May 12, 1919.
[42] *Statistique des grèves pour 1919–1920* (Paris: Imprimerie nationale, 1922), 180–181, 216–217.

belief that the Federation could or would no longer defend their interests, and that direct action was the only remaining solution. A major strike broke out at the Panhard factory in Paris on May 26, and by the 27th several thousand metalworkers had walked off the job at factories throughout the area.[43] At a meeting of the mechanics' union in Ivry on May 30, a metalworkers' union activist named Dumercq declared that: "The ameliorations we have won are only palliatives; the next reforms to be won are the nationalization of the railroads, of the mines, and of the Insurance industry, which only serves to make the fortune of a few capitalists at the expense of the proletarians."[44] Dumercq went on to praise the Russian Revolution and to attack Allied intervention in the Russian civil war.

Many metalworkers and union activists at the time, and several historians since, felt that this was not a good time for a strike, that the industry employers were actually looking to provoke one in order to tame the radical Left and assert greater control over the labor process in their factories. In April 1919, the Citroen plant had used the pretext of a strike to fire many workers no longer needed for wartime production, and some union activists feared that other employers would use a strike similarly.[45] Given the increasing effervescence in many metals' factories in Paris and its suburbs, and the June 1 deadline for implementing the eight-hour-day agreement, however, many metalworkers felt they had no choice but to go on strike. On Saturday May 31, the EC met and agreed to declare an industry-wide strike in Paris and its suburbs on Monday June 2. The next day, Sunday June 1, representatives of all the individual metals' unions in the Department of the Seine met, and overwhelmingly agreed to join the strike the next day.

It bears remembering that the decision to strike took place in the context of the widespread demobilization of women and colonial subjects from the industry. If metalworkers feared losing their jobs in the spring of 1919, they had concrete examples of that prospect close to hand. Striking metalworkers did at times call for the firing of women from the industry, although they were more likely to demand equal wages for them (so they wouldn't undercut male wages). At the same time they did not at all protest the firing of colonial subjects. As Jean-Louis Robert has noted, concerns that the use of foreign labor would result in greater unemployment were especially pronounced in 1919, and colonial workers seem to have been the

---

[43] *Ibid.*, 220–221. [44] AN F7 13367, police report of May 30, 1919.
[45] AN F7 13367, police reports of April 9 and April 25, 1919.

most affected by such fears.[46] The radicalism of the Parisian metalworkers thus blended both a rejection and an embrace of the segmentation of the labor market, both an egalitarian impulse and a desire for race and gender privilege. This unstable and at times contradictory set of attitudes meshed well with the generally unstable character of the looming metalworkers' strike.

Although the outbreak of the Paris metalworkers' strike occurred in reaction both to negotiations over the eight-hour day and to tensions between the majority and minority factions in the CGT, at the heart of it lay increasing discontent over *la vie chère*. The fact that the Metalworkers' Federation and representatives of the metals industry were able to reach an agreement that even included the 44-hour week, rejected by most other employers at the time, but did not reflect the substantial wage increases demanded by the EC, underscores the centrality of remuneration at a time when workers saw their salaries eroded by inflation. As Bertrand Abhervé has noted, the members of the EC were closer to the rank and file metalworkers in Paris than were Merrheim and the other leaders of the Federation, and thus more aware of the tremendous concern caused by the sharp rise in the prices of basic goods in the capital and its suburbs.[47] Yet even Léon Jouhaux, convinced *majoritaire* and secretary general of the CGT, recognized that "the causes of this 'turbulence' are especially the high cost of living and the employers' slowness in transforming the structure of labor."[48] Although observers would focus on the "political" demands made by the strikers as indicators of the movement's revolutionary quality, in actual fact the unrest caused by anger over the high cost of foods and other basic goods took the lead in pushing it in a radical direction.[49]

A GENERAL STRIKE OF PARISIAN METALWORKERS

In Paris, metalworkers and mechanics are also on strike. They are not asking for the eight-hour day. They have it already. They are asking that the eight-hour day not result in a salary reduction.[50]

---

[46] Jean-Louis Robert, "Ouvriers et mouvement ouvrier parisiens pendant la grande guerre et l'immédiate après-guerre" (Doctorat d'Etat thesis, Université de Paris-1, 1989), 419.

[47] Abhervé, "La grève," chapter 4.   [48] AN F7 13576, police report of June 5, 1919.

[49] The fact that women and colonial workers were also paid less, at a time when the cost of living loomed so centrally in working-class activism, also underscores the significance of race and gender distinctions in 1919.

[50] *L'Humanité*, June 2, 1919, 1.

The strike began on Monday, June 2, at 9 a.m. The EC had transformed itself into the (more or less) official strike committee the previous evening, and those workers who joined the walkout for the most part acknowledged its authority. Initially the strike was far more successful than anyone, including the members of the EC and the leaders of the Federation, had foreseen. By the end of the first day some 100,000 metalworkers had joined the strike throughout Paris and its suburbs, and that number rose to 165,000 by the end of the next day.[51] This was impressive not only because of the opposition of the national Federation to the strike but also because of the low rate of unionization of the industry in the Paris area. Together the metalworkers' unions of the Department of the Seine only counted some 10,000 members at the beginning of June: this number rose to 70,000 during the strike.[52] In spite of the small number of union members and activists, in June 1919 the overwhelming majority of metalworkers in the Paris area joined the strike. The movement was strongest in the largest factories, all of which were paralyzed. The giant Renault works in Boulogne and the Citroen factory in the fifteenth *arrondissement* of Paris had both already witnessed significant labor unrest before June, and were quickly deserted at the start of the strike.[53] But the strike also emptied most small workshops throughout the city and its suburbs. Roving bands of strikers circulated throughout the area, trying to persuade (or in some cases force) the undecided to join the movement. They even succeeded in getting some workers in factories whose owners had already signed agreements with the unions to walk out on strike anyway (Illustration 6.1).[54] At a time when France was technically still in a state of war, the largest center of munitions production in the country effectively ceased to function.

More than the demands formulated by the strike committee, the very turbulence of the June movement led many, both favorable and opposed, to see in it an attempt at revolution. Most of the strikers had little or no experience with unions and had little desire to obey union discipline or strategy. Observers noted the presence of many former soldiers, people who wanted immediate results and had little patience with the niceties of labor organizing. In describing a protest meeting on June 2, one police agent reported that "A recently demobilized member of the audience, clothed in uniform, announced that he had been organizing factory walkouts since the

---

[51] Abhervé, "La grève," chapter 5; Papayanis, "Masses révolutionnaires," 56.
[52] Abhervé, "La grève," chapter 9; AN F7 13576, police report of July 9, 1919.
[53] Robert, *Les ouvriers, la patrie et la Révolution*, 346–350.
[54] AN F7 13576, police report of June 5, 1919.

6.1 Metalworkers on strike in Billancourt, June 1919

morning. He argued that in addition to their wage demands the strikers should demand the cessation of the expedition in Russia, complete and total amnesty for all those condemned by the Councils of War, immediate and complete demobilization, and the promise of amnesty for the mutineers of the Black Sea Fleet."[55] While relatively little violence took place during the strike, especially compared to the events of May Day, strikers harassed those who didn't join the movement, and also at times attacked union leaders as ineffective at best, traitors to the working class at worst.

Day after day, the committee rooms of the various union organizations were invaded by excited mobs, who treated the leaders to all manner of abuse and even, on one occasion, carried them off bodily to be exposed in public to the insults of an infuriated crowd.[56]

During the first week of the strike in particular, strikers held daily mass meetings throughout the Paris area, meetings marked by both large

[55] AN F7 13367, police report of June 3, 1919. In general, meeting participants rejected such appeals, insisting on the more corporative nature of the strike. See also AN F7 13367, police report of June 2, 1919.
[56] Cited in Wohl, *French Communism*, 137.

attendance and loud enthusiasm. Some 1,800 strikers attended a meeting on the afternoon of the first day of the strike at the municipal theater of Saint-Denis, the northern suburb which would, as I shall discuss in greater detail below, emerge as the center of revolutionary activism in June. One speaker, after warning those present against the machinations of *agents provocateurs* working for the employers and the government, went on to recommend the creation of Soviet councils: "if their creation is realized we will be able to pay Clemençeau back (applause)." The anarchist Emile Bestel spoke next, similarly portraying the strike as a key moment in the revolutionary struggle.

We will not budge . . . on our demand for the application of the eight hour day without any forfeit [of wages] as well as the maintenance of current wage levels . . . However, we should also take a more ideal view of our movement, because tomorrow our comrades in Paris mass transport and perhaps even the railway workers will make common cause with us to demand their right to a living and to attempt a social transformation.

Let us turn our eyes toward revolutionary Russia, and let us try to establish the salutary Soviet regime here at home.[57]

Bestel's vision of a strike that went well beyond the metals industry was not just a revolutionary fantasy. The working-class unrest that had begun earlier in the spring continued to increase in June, so that by the second week of the month much of the city seemed to be on strike. Whereas in May some 215,000 workers went on strike in France, the figure for June was over half a million.[58] The garment workers of Paris were already on strike, and their walkout continued until the end of the first week of June. Pharmacy workers, goldsmiths, laundresses, and other groups also staged strikes during that month. At the height of the movement well over 250,000 workers had walked off the job in the Department of the Seine.[59]

Aside from the metalworkers' movement, the most dramatic strike to hit Paris in June 1919 was the massive job action staged by the transportation union. Few workplace actions have a greater impact on urban life than a strike staged by bus drivers and subway conductors, which has the power to bring life in twentieth-century cities to a grinding halt (Illustration 6.2).[60] On June 3, a day after the metalworkers struck, some 6,000 tram and subway conductors began their own job action, like so many others

---

[57] APP BA 1386, police report of June 2, 1919. Bestel's speech was greeted by lively applause from the 1,800 people present in the audience.
[58] Wohl, *French Communism*, 137.   [59] *Le Petit Parisien*, June 3, 1919, 2; Brunet, *Saint-Denis*, 377.
[60] Michael Marmo, *More Profile than Courage: The New York City Transit Strike of 1966* (Albany: State University of New York Press, 1990).

6.2 A tramway car stopped by striking transport workers, boulevard Voltaire, June 1919

demanding wage increases to compensate for the high cost of living. That morning Parisians woke up to a city without mass transit:

Since yesterday morning the strike has been general. The North–South [tramway line] has completely closed its stations. In the Metro, only a few cars circulated on lines 1, 3, 4, and 8, driven exclusively by engineers employed by the Company.

These trains, which arrived a half hour apart and which only stopped at the major transfer stations, were certainly far from able to satisfy the normally intense needs for travel by subway.

Taking advantage of being freed from working underground, some 10,000 strikers and their families staged a combination of picnic and union meeting in the Bois de Boulogne, vowing to stand firm in support of the strike.[61]

The large number and variety of strikes that accompanied the metal-workers' movement in June 1919 led some strikers and observers to believe that this could be the beginning of a general strike, one that might take a revolutionary turn. Could it be that the old anarcho-syndicalist romantic vision of the general strike might finally become a reality in the year after the

[61] *L'Humanité*, June 4, 1919, 1.

Armistice? To an important extent, the possibility of realizing this vision depended upon the attitude of French railway workers. Similar to the metalworkers, while the Paris railway workers' unions strongly supported the CGT minority, the national railway workers' federation, led by Bidegaray, belonged to the *majoritaire* faction and opposed joining the metalworkers' strike. On June 6 some 12,000 railway workers of the Department of the Seine held a mass meeting in Paris to debate the issue. One faction led by the anarchist Henri Sirolle presented a resolution calling for an immediate sympathy strike, but this was opposed by *minoritaire* leader (and future head of the Communist Confédération Générale du Travail Unitaire) Gaston Monmousseau, who argued for a political statement that opposed Allied intervention in the Soviet civil war but did not commit the union to a strike. Monmousseau's resolution passed: although many Parisian railway workers sympathized with the strike, especially its radical ideas about social transformation (shouts of "Long live the immediate general strike! Long live the Revolution!" continually interrupted the speakers) their failure to join in the strike movement effectively prevented it from becoming a general strike of all Parisian labor, much less the *lutte finale* of which so many revolutionaries had dreamed.[62]

Nonetheless, the aura of revolution persisted for many of the strikers in June, as well as for many who observed the tumultuous nature of the movement and read the inflammatory language issued by many of the strike committees. Many employers concluded that the strikers wanted nothing less than the overthrow of capitalism, and used the radicalism of the movement to justify their resistance to it.[63] The national government was also concerned that it was facing a potential insurrection: not only did it mobilize soldiers and students to help run the trams and subways during the transportation strike, but also (mindful of the chaos of May Day) massed some 17,000 troops in the Department of the Seine by the end of the first week of the strike to ensure public order.[64] At the same time, many on the French Left who observed the strike felt that Paris might be about to experience its own Red October. Writing in the pages of *La vie ouvrière*, the revolutionary syndicalist leader Pierre Monatte said:

Where are we going? Where are we going? From discontent to discontent, from strike to strike, from a semi-economic and semi-political strike to a purely political

---

[62] Robert, *Les ouvriers, la patrie et la Révolution*, 394–395; *Le Figaro*, June 7, 1919, 1.

[63] Brunet, *Saint-Denis*, 215–216; APP BA 1386, police report of June 10, 1919; AN F7 13367, police report of May 31, 1919.

[64] Brunet, *Saint-Denis*, 222; APP BA 1386, police report of June 11, 1919.

strike. We're going straight to the bankruptcy of the bourgeoisie, that is, to the Revolution.[65]

How can one explain, in a nation preparing to celebrate victory after over four long years of war, this eruption of revolutionary sentiment? Contemporary observers and historians have generally advanced two explanations: the challenge to the capitalist world order posed by the Russian Revolution, and the material difficulties confronting many Parisian workers. Certainly the Bolshevik regime enjoyed tremendous popularity among Left-wing workers and union activists in the spring and summer of 1919, all the more so in that the war against Germany seemed to have given way to a capitalist crusade against the infant Soviet Union.[66] Moreover, in 1919 world revolution seemed at least possible, even likely for some. Why then should Paris, traditional capital of revolution, lag behind in such tumultuous times? As Emile Bestel declared at the beginning of the strike, "Bourgeois society has failed. Let us now turn our eyes toward the revolutions in the East, forward for the victory of the international proletariat."[67]

At the same time, victory over Germany had not brought better times for working-class families. The conversion from wartime production to a peacetime economy brought widespread unemployment in the metals industry and others tied to the military effort. As we have seen, women and foreign, especially colonial, laborers bore the brunt of these sacrifices, yet all had to contend with the possibility of losing their jobs. At the same time the sharp increases in the price of basic goods continued to rise during the first half of the year: if one uses a figure of 100 for 1914, the index of inflation had risen to 238 in January 1919, 242 in February, and 252 in June.[68] In short, the war might be won, but times were still hard and the specter of the world revolution beckoned.[69]

---

[65] Cited in Wohl, *French Communism*, 137.

[66] Kriegel, *Aux origines du communisme français*, 248–267. See also Hélène Iswolsky, "The Russian Revolution seen from Paris," *Russian Review*, 26/2 (April, 1967), 153–163; Thomas A. Peake, "Jacques Sadoul and the Russian Intervention question, 1919," *Russian Review*, 32/1 (January, 1973), 54–63; Claude Willard, "La connaissance de la révolution russe et l'expérience soviétique par le mouvement ouvrier français en 1918–1919," *Cahiers de l'Institut Maurice Thorez*, 12–13 (1975).

[67] APP BA 1386, police report of June 2, 1919.

[68] Abhervé, "Les origines," 78; AN F7 13656, police report of April 4, 1919; AN F7 13958, letter of September 4, 1919.

[69] "Everywhere the working masses protest against the domination of capitalism. In Italy, in England, in France these masses must use all possible means to prevent the governments of the Entente continuing their intervention against the Russian and Hungarian workers' revolutions." APP BA 1386, police report of June 4, 1919.

What we need to explain more thoroughly is the connection between such specific material concerns and the lure of revolutionary ideology. The coexistence of the two in June 1919 gave the strike an inchoate, schizoid appearance; as Robert Wohl has observed, "the heterogeneous coalition of revolutionaries, reformists, and angry masses responded to different stimuli. A quick reform pushed through the Chamber, a concession on ages, an hour chopped from the workday, and the strike that yesterday seemed to constitute an embryo of social revolution dissolved into thin air."[70] Yet this description neglects the fact that many metalworkers and other strikers in June 1919 saw the standard of living and calls for revolution as intimately linked. Rhetorical references to Red October often went together with anger over inflation and its effects upon salaries and workers' standard of living.[71] For many workers, both government and employers had demonstrated their inability to control the cost of living, so that only more extreme measures could ultimately protect the working-class consumer.

Many directed their anger against the employers, feeling that the high salaries they might grant with one hand they took back in the form of higher prices with the other. At a strike meeting in suburban Aubervilliers, a union representative declared that "I hope that we will be able to make all the potentates of metallurgy understand that the metalworking proletariat has had enough of these starvation wages."[72] Another speaker, Tirand of the locksmiths' union, went farther. Addressing 800 strikers at a meeting in Pavillons-sous-Bois, he claimed "We've had enough of producing for the exploiters . . . the proletarian is emerging from his torpor. He is fighting to obtain a bit of bread for himself and his family, and the wages he is asking for are inferior to the cost of living . . . The red dawn that we see is the same one rising in the East, which should bring a change of regime for all the workers and realize our ideal."[73]

At the same time, strikers directed their anger against the government, blaming it both for supporting the metals employers and for not doing anything about *la vie chère*. State experiments with rationing and price controls of basic goods, especially food and housing, during the war had in effect politicized consumption. In the spring and summer of 1919 it was not yet certain that public authorities would end these controls; many workers (and others) continued to hold the government primarily responsible for what seemed to be runaway inflation. In exhorting 2,000 strikers in the

---

[70] Wohl, *French Communism*, 121.   [71] Brunet, *Saint-Denis*, 328–334.
[72] BA 1386, police report of June 10, 1919.   [73] APP BA 1386, police report of June 16, 1919.

eastern suburbs to take a revolutionary view of the movement, Tommasi of the automobile and aviation union declared:

it is not banal satisfactions relative to the application of the eight-hour day and wage increases that can satisfy workers today. More is necessary: we must break the chains of slavery; the proletariat must liberate itself definitively from the employers and the bourgeoisie in general. [The orator then emphasized] the impotence of the Government and of the Parliament to stop the rise in the cost of living.[74]

Or, in the words of another strike leader, "A revolution is necessary and it's got to come, because the public authorities aren't doing anything to solve the high cost of living."[75]

In short, many workers trying to improve or simply maintain their standard of living were quite willing to go on strike to do so, yet also concluded that wage increases by themselves could not solve the problem. In an important article, James Cronin has argued that the roots of working-class insurgency during the *biennio rosso* lay in the failure of state intervention in the war economy. State controls over basic goods led many Parisians of all types to see the government as ultimately responsible for their living standards, and to conclude that the decline of those living standards caused by *la vie chère* could only be resolved politically, at their most extreme by a fundamental change of regime. I would argue that both the successes as well as the failures led to this conclusion: people expected more of government precisely because it had done so much during the war. While many leaders and rank and file members of the June movement saw material demands and revolutionary ideology as opposed, they also felt that only revolution could guarantee a decent standard of living for the Parisian metalworker. In this reading of the situation, far from representing the reformist aspect of the movement, the desire to ensure decent access to basic consumer goods itself helped to fuel the insurgent spirit of the 1919 metalworkers' strike.[76]

REVOLT IN THE SUBURBS AND THE COMMUNE OF SAINT-DENIS

The bourgeoisie thought it had killed the Commune in 1871, but today Saint-Denis intends to revive it stronger than ever.[77]

---

[74] AN F7 13367, police report of June 22, 1919.   [75] AN F7 13367, police report of June 17, 1919.

[76] James Cronin, "Labor insurgency and class formation: comparative perspectives on the crisis of 1917–1920 in Europe," in James Cronin and Carmen Sirianni, eds., *Work, Community, and Power: The Experience of Labor in Europe and America, 1900–1925* (Philadelphia: Temple University Press, 1983), 20–48.

[77] Gaston Philippe, Mayor of Saint-Denis. See APP BA 1386, police report of June 5, 1919.

A look at the urban geography of the metalworkers' strike also illustrates its revolutionary character. In particular, much like the Paris Commune of 1871, the image of the strike as insurgency reflected not only material demands and insurrectional slogans, but also urban issues. As Jean-Louis Robert has pointed out, June 1919 was a series of decentralized job actions rather than a unified strike movement. The wildcat character of the strike and the diverse nature of the metals industry in the Department of the Seine allowed different interpretations of tactics and goals to flourish during June. As we shall see, the suburbs of Paris in particular emerged as the rampart of radicalism and the symbol of the strikers' demands for a new day. More than anyplace else, the city of Saint-Denis emerged as the reddest *commune* in the Paris area, symbolizing the revolutionary potential of the movement as a whole.

One of the most popular legends about the early history of Paris concerns the life and death of Saint Denis, Bishop of Paris during the third century AD. Sent from Italy to convert the heathen Gauls to Christianity, Denis' active and successful proselytizing evidently aroused the anger of the local Druid priests. According to the legend, around the year 250 they captured Denis and executed him on top of the highest hill near Paris, chopping off his head. Denis' saga did not end there, however: the story goes that after his execution his body stood back up, picking up his severed head, and walked north two miles (preaching all the way) until it collapsed once and for all. The site of his execution was named Mound of the Martyrs, or Montmartre. His final resting place took his name, Saint-Denis, and on the spot where he fell Christian faithful built a shrine. In the thirteenth century the Church transformed this shrine into the Basilica of Saint-Denis, down to the present day the necropolis of the kings and queens of France.[78]

In June 1919 the spirit of revolution seemed to replicate the mythic journey of Saint Denis, leaving Montmartre (and Paris in general) to resettle in the town that bears his name. During the late nineteenth century Montmartre had symbolized everything revolutionary about Parisian life, in both politics and aesthetics. The picturesque neighborhood gave birth not only to Impressionism but also to the Paris Commune.[79] By the end of World War I, however, the avant-garde, both cultural and political, had moved elsewhere. By 1919 Montparnasse had become the new center of the

---

[78] Jean-Marie Le Gall, *Le mythe de Saint Denis: entre renaissance et révolution* (Seyssell: Champ Vallon, 2007).
[79] Gérald Dittmar, *Montmartre, de la République à la Commune* (Paris: Dittmar, 2007); Louis Chevalier, *Montmartre du plaisir et du crime* (Paris: R. Laffont, 1980).

city's literary and artistic bohemia. Neither did it represent the heart of the revolutionary Left the way it had half a century earlier. The fact that Georges Clemençeau, who in 1870 had been elected mayor of Montmartre by the Radical party, now embodied the status quo in France was perhaps the most obvious example of this transition.

Nothing better symbolized the new face of Montmartre than the Basilica of Sacré Coeur. As is well known, legitimist forces planned the new church as an expiation of the sins of the Commune, linking the radical Left in France to the heathen priests who had martyred Saint Denis on the same spot. In spite of ferocious opposition by the local artists and intelligentsia, the new basilica slowly arose during the glory years of fin-de-siècle Montmartre, a white church looming disapprovingly over a red neighborhood. It was formally consecrated on October 16, 1919, now representing not just the martyrdom of the Commune but also the nation's suffering during World War I. Sacré Coeur has since become the ultimate symbol of Montmartre, the centerpiece of numerous faux Impressionist paintings and postcards of the area. In this way as well, therefore, it continues to represent the end of the community's revolutionary traditions.[80]

One should not make too much of this contrast: Montmartre remained a working-class neighborhood in the early twentieth century and, as we saw in the previous chapter, still had its periods of popular activism. Nonetheless, by 1919 the Paris suburbs had become the center of urban marginality and revolutionary politics that Montmartre had once represented. As historians of modern Paris have demonstrated, by the early twentieth century the suburban communities of the Department of the Seine had become the center not just of industry but also of working-class community in the Paris area.[81] This became a key factor in the June metalworkers' strike, which was in many ways the first suburban uprising in modern Paris. The idea that the suburbs threatened the well-being and civilization of the urban center, representing the barbarians at the gate, has a long history in France. At the same time, as the uprisings of November 2005 have demonstrated, new associations of the suburbs with multiculturalism, disaffected youth, and

---

[80] Jacquest Benoist, *Le Sacré-Coeur de Montmartre* (Paris: Éditions Ouvrières, 1992); Raymond Jonas, *France and the Cult of the Sacred Heart: An Epic Tale for Modern Times* (Berkeley: University of California Press, 2000).

[81] On the Paris suburbs in the early twentieth century see, among others, Brunet, *Saint-Denis*; Jean Bastié, *La croissance de la banlieue parisienne* (Paris: Presses Universitaires de France, 1964); Tyler Stovall, *The Rise of the Paris Red Belt* (Berkeley: University of California Press, 1990); Annie Fourcaut, ed., *Un siècle de banlieue parisienne, 1859–1964: guide de recherché* (Paris: Harmattan, 1988); Jean-Paul Brunet, ed., *Immigration, vie politique et populisme en banlieue parisienne, fin XIXe–XXe siècles* (Paris: Harmattan, 1995).

Islamic fundamentalism have revived the idea of the urban frontier as a zone of political danger, indeed insurrection.[82] Although it affected many parts of the city of Paris as well, the June 1919 metalworkers' strike had its greatest impact in the suburbs, sites of the largest metals factories and working-class communities. The fact that the strike represented not just proletarian discontent but also the menace of *la banlieue* underscored its revolutionary character.[83]

This was all the more true because the most radical factions of the strike, those who most consistently called for insurrection and cited the Russian Revolution as a model to emulate, arose in the suburbs. In particular Saint-Denis became the epicenter of the revolutionary Left during the strike. In that community, one of the largest and most industrialized suburbs of Paris, the city's inter-union council, the various strike committees, and the municipality worked together not only to support the strike but also to give it the most maximalist orientation possible, and to try to impose that orientation upon the movement as a whole. In this sense, as we shall discuss in more detail shortly, the "Soviet of Saint-Denis" was the true heir of the Paris Commune. It was only fitting, perhaps, that in an era when thrones were toppling all across Europe, the specter of revolution in France should manifest itself in the city known as the burial ground of kings.

The suburban orientation of the strike, and in particular its most radical elements, reflected the strength of community networks and the relative weakness of union organization. A generation of labor historians has shown how strikes are often as much community events as workplace and professional movements, and the very instability of June both mirrored and allowed the emergence of local perspectives and concerns.[84] At the same time, however, this suburban focus derived in large part from the failure of the unions to control (or even understand) the movement. This was true not only of the national Metalworkers' Federation, but also of much of the local union infrastructure. In decreeing the strike the EC had anticipated neither its scope nor its turbulence, and was in no way prepared for it. Not only did far more workers go on strike than expected, but their insistence on

---

[82] Tyler Stovall, "From red belt to black belt: race, class, and urban marginality in twentieth century Paris," in Sue Peabody and Tyler Stovall, eds., *The Color of Liberty: Histories of Race in France* (Durham NC: Duke University Press, 2003); Gilles Kepel, *Les banlieues d'Islam: naissance d'une religion en France* (Paris: Seuil, 1987); Paul Silverstein, *Algeria in France: Transpolitics, Race, and Nation* (Bloomington: Indiana University Press, 2004).

[83] On the suburbs as a symbol of danger and marginality see John H. Merriman, *The Margins of City Life: Explorations on the French Urban Frontier, 1815–1851* (New York: Oxford University Press, 1991).

[84] See David Brody, "Reconciling the old labor history and the new," *Pacific Historical Review*, 62/1 (February, 1993), 1–18.

political demands also disconcerted the leadership. Moreover, once the strike began the members of the EC realized what a weak position the strikers were in, to the extent that many believed industry had in fact provoked the conflict in order to destroy or at least weaken the Paris unions.[85] As of June 2 the EC had not undertaken even basic preparations for the conflict: as one report noted, "Instead of first making reasonably sure of being able to finance it [the metalworkers' strike], like any other enterprise, the syndicate was from the beginning calling for aid. For this and other current strikes the Union of the Syndicates of the Seine had been maintaining soup kitchens, having credit at the cooperative stores, to which an indebtedness was run up of "several hundred thousand francs."[86]

For a variety of reasons, the June 1919 strike quickly devolved into a series of local actions based on neighborhood and community. Since most of the strikers had never belonged to a union before, they had little or no experience of what to expect from union leaders during a strike, so that they were less likely to look to the union hall for guidance. Since employers had responded to the movement with a lockout, even large factories could not serve as gathering places for strikers. In their place, municipalities, especially those controlled by the Left, could offer meeting halls as well as providing soup kitchens and other services for those on strike. At the same time, the very success of the strike movement in general contributed to its balkanization. The transport workers' walkout, which brought much of Paris to a halt during the first two weeks of June, also made it difficult for strike leaders to coordinate their activities throughout the Department of the Seine. It tended to reinforce the *esprit de clocher*, so much a part of traditional life in Paris, so that the metalworkers' movement came to resemble less one big strike and more a series of local actions scattered throughout Paris and its suburbs. At a meeting of the Inter-union committee of the Seine on June 6, Hyacinthe Dubreuil of the Metalworkers' Federation summed up the situation:

The extent and the importance of the movement, the lack of means of transportation make things difficult for the metals union organizers, who find it impossible to travel to the strike meetings.

These meetings are invaded by people without authority who transform this professional and demand-oriented movement into an extra-union and political movement ... In Ivry, in Puteaux, in Saint-Denis, this situation has taken a

---

[85] AN F7 13576, police report of June 5, 1919.
[86] The Commission on Foreign Inquiry of the National Civic Federation, *The Labor Situation in Great Britain and France* (New York: E. P. Dutton, 1919), 239.

particularly aggressive character. There is no more strike committee, no more unions, but [only] local committees.[87]

The fact that Dubreuil emphasized suburban communities as symbols of the disorderly nature of the strike was no accident. Just as the suburbs represented the antithesis of orderly urban space in general, so in June 1919 did they incarnate the unstable and diffuse nature of working-class activism. Not only did many of the most militant and radical strikers come from the suburbs, but in general they dominated the strike's mobilization of urban geography. In a statistical analysis Jean-Louis Robert has demonstrated that no less than 98 percent of all the demonstrations associated with the metalworkers' strike took place in the suburbs, not the city of Paris.[88] This represented a sharp reversal from the riots of May Day: whereas in May workers had in effect invaded the city in a claim to urban space, in June they essentially abandoned it. If May represented the expulsion of working-class politics from the heart of the city, June confirmed its success. From this perspective, whereas Paris represented a hostile foreign environment, the city that had beaten and expelled the May Day demonstrators, the suburbs, especially those with Leftist municipal governments, represented home.[89] Frequently unable to get to the capital because of the transportation strike, workers instead demonstrated where they lived. The following description of a metalworkers' demonstration in the northeastern suburbs seems to typify the role of suburban public space during the strike.

The strikers of the northern and northeastern suburbs, numbering about 20,000, marched behind banners indicating the establishments where they worked. They arrived at the city hall of Pré-Saint-Gervais in parade formation, then went up Chateau Rouge hill to the porte Brunet, where the demonstration was supposed to disband. It was a very orderly parade, there were no incidents, no shouts, no revolutionary emblems. A few people sang the *Internationale*.[90]

A few points stand out in this brief description. The demonstration was both very large and very peaceful: in contrast to the prevailing images of both the strike and the suburbs in general, order reigned. Yet it was not the order of the status quo: people did sing the *Internationale*, combining revolutionary conviction with a sense of discipline and self-mastery. The other notable characteristic of the demonstration was its route. The city hall of the small suburb of Pré-Saint-Gervais serves as a rallying point,

---

[87] AN F7 13576, police report of June 6, 1919.
[88] Robert, *Les ouvriers, la patrie et la Révolution*, 334.   [89] *Ibid.*, 335–338.
[90] APP BA 1386, police report of June 4, 1919. See also a similar description of a demonstration of 15,000 strikers at Aubervilliers City Hall, *ibid.*

symbolizing the central role played by suburban municipalities during the strike. Moreover, the demonstration ended at the porte Brunet, one of the gates linking Paris and its suburbs: the city was a place where workers did not belong. To an important extent the strike unfolded on the margins of Parisian urban space: in doing so it demarcated the city not only spatially but also temporally. As Paris gentrified inexorably during the twentieth century it gradually became a place where working people, especially working-class youth, traveled in search of amusement before going home to the suburbs. The abandonment of the city by working-class politics in the contemporary era had its symbolic beginning in June 1919.[91]

Of all the varied suburban communities ringing Paris in 1919, Saint-Denis quickly emerged as the center of the strike movement and of its revolutionary faction in particular. Jean-Paul Brunet has called Saint-Denis "the French Manchester," and in the early twentieth century the city was the very model of industrial suburbia. During the nineteenth century the community had industrialized rapidly, engulfing the charming little town center with its basilica and creating a swath of factories that stretched southward to the city walls of Paris. The modern industrial suburb so quickly submerged the provincial small town that as late as the end of the nineteenth century one could still find milk cows and sheep placidly grazing in the shadow of blast-furnace towers. By 1919 Saint-Denis had some 75,000 inhabitants, largely working class, making it the biggest single suburb in the Department of the Seine.[92]

The Socialist Party had won control of the Saint-Denis city government for the first time in 1892, and they returned to power in 1912, and elected Gaston Philippe mayor. Philippe's administration governed the city throughout the war and in 1919 would take the lead in ranging the municipality solidly in support of the striking metalworkers. The strike itself had an immediate, dramatic impact on the city. At the giant Delaunay-Belleville factory, one of the largest in the region with 3,300 workers, not a single person showed up on Monday June 2, and other local factories reported similar situations.[93] Some 12,000 workers in Saint-Denis joined the strike during the first week, and overwhelmingly they

[91] On the gentrification of Paris in the twentieth century, see Anthony Sutcliffe, *The Autumn of Central Paris: The Defeat of Town Planning 1850–1970* (London: Edward Arnold, 1970); Norma Evenson, *Paris: A Century of Change* (New Haven CT: Yale University Press, 1979). For a general overview see Colin Jones, *Paris: Biography of a City* (New York: Viking, 2005).

[92] Jean-Paul Brunet, *Saint-Denis la ville rouge: socialisme et communisme en banlieue ouvrière, 1890–1939* (Paris: Hachette, 1980), 15–33.

[93] APP BA 1386, police report of June 3, 1919.

looked to the Socialist municipality not only to help them win but also to express their goals and lead the movement.

And Gaston Philippe and the city council did not disappoint them. Speaking to a crowd of 1,800 strikers at the municipal theater on the first day of the strike, Philippe promised that:

the municipality would put all the foodstuffs it possessed at the disposition of the strikers in order to enable them to fight until they won complete satisfaction . . . the French proletariat should not remain indifferent [to the Russian and German revolutions]; it must itself also shake off the yoke of the capitalist regime and loudly proclaim its total emancipation.

The bourgeois class . . . is bankrupt, the Government that rules us cannot resolve our financial problems and thus demonstrates its impotence.

The French proletariat must therefore join with the universal proletariat to make its own revolution.[94]

Throughout the strike, and especially during its first tumultuous week, Saint-Denis' Socialist municipal officials frequently addressed strike meetings, not only promising material and moral support, but also underscoring the revolutionary character of the movement.[95]

The other major working-class institution in Saint-Denis that took the lead in organizing the June strike was the city's Inter-union committee, the representative of all local affiliates of the CGT. In a situation in which not only the national Metalworkers' Federation but also the EC seemed unwilling or unable to lead the strike, Inter-union committees throughout the Paris area, especially in the industrial suburbs, stepped in to fill the gap. They varied widely in their effectiveness and in their political orientation; that of Saint-Denis seems to have been one of the most organized and most radical in the Department of the Seine.

There are 26 Inter-union committees in the Paris region, but the majority of them have never given proof of any vitality. That of St.-Denis, in contrast, has always been notable for its great activity . . . The Inter-union committee of St.-Denis was particularly active during the war and instead of limiting itself to the role defined for it by the Union of Syndicats [of the Seine], it has thrown itself resolutely into revolutionary political action, guided in this by PHILIPPE, mayor of St.-Denis . . .

Therefore, since the beginnings of the current movement the Inter-union committee of St.-Denis has organized a series of meetings for local strikers.

In all these meetings, the speakers have competed with each other to see who could use the most violent terms, recommending a revolution on the model of

[94] APP BA 1386, police report of June 2, 1919.
[95] APP BA 1386, police reports of June 4, 5, 6, and 7, 1919.

Russia, boasting about the soviet regime and preaching the adoption of hard-line communism.[96]

At roughly the same time Léon Jouhaux informed a meeting of the Union of Syndicats of the Seine that "I have received letters from Inter-union committees … [in] Puteaux, Suresnes and Courbevoie that demand the intervention of the CGT, that declare that the true goal of the strike is a revolution that should oust the Government and proclaim the general strike. The committee of Saint-Denis writes in the same terms, adding that the CGT should take the place of Clemenceau."[97]

It was the Inter-union committee of Saint-Denis that sent shock waves across France on June 4 by proclaiming that the revolution had triumphed in the city and that it was converting itself into a council of soviets.[98] After dropping this bombshell in front of a wildly enthusiastic crowd of over 2,500 people, Pothion of the committee went on to call upon all Inter-union committees throughout France to demand that the CGT seize power from the government. Such inflammatory language prompted the Minister of the Interior to call in Mayor Philippe for a meeting, and President Clemenceau began moving troops into the Saint-Denis area. The speeches of June 4 in particular established Saint-Denis as the heart of the metal-workers' strike and symbol of its revolutionary potential. If a new Paris Commune were to arise, it would clearly be here.[99]

In voicing such incendiary statements, the members of both the municipality and the Inter-union committee not only articulated their own hopes for a new day but also responded to the excitement and desires of thousands of working people in their city. For the first weeks of June, at least, Saint-Denis seemed gripped by revolutionary fervor. Not only was the walkout almost universally supported in the city's metal factories, but it soon turned into a general strike of Dionysian workers: by June 6, 16,000 had joined the movement, usually without or against the leadership of local unions. Rallies of thousands of strikers took place virtually every day, and many joined demonstrations proclaiming their support for the movement in the streets of the city. On June 5, for example, a large group of strikers led by Socialists Bourreau and Bestel marched down the rue de Paris, flying the red banner of the Inter-union committee. At several points they stopped trucks carrying soldiers, calling upon those inside not to fire upon them but instead to join with them in the overthrow of Clemenceau's government.[100]

---

[96] APP BA 1386, police report of June 4, 1919.   [97] AN F7 13576, police report of June 6, 1919.
[98] See the quotation that opens this chapter.   [99] Brunet, *Saint-Denis*, 217–218.
[100] APP BA 1386, police report of June 5, 1919.

The next day, another demonstration took place after a meeting that had attracted 8,000 strikers:

At the end of the meeting [5 p.m.] the strikers formed a cortege which circulated through the streets of the city singing the *Internationale*.

At the head of it marched PHILIPPE, BOUREAU, delegates of the strike committee, and a group of about twenty soldiers, including a sergeant of the 155th heavy artillery regiment, carrying a red flag upon which was written the words "Interunion committee of Saint-Denis".

The parade marched to the square in front of City Hall.

The soldiers then entered the building, appearing at the windows waving red flags and booing CLEMENCEAU.

The national flag, which is always flown from City Hall, was taken down but put back up a few seconds later.

One striker named LONGUET sang the last two couplets of the *Internationale* from the balcony of City Hall, and the demonstrators sang the chorus along with him. PHILIPPE thanked the strikers for their calm and asked them to maintain this attitude. He then asked them to continue the strike.

At 5.30 the strikers dispersed without incident.[101]

In both demonstrations, the prominence given to incidents of fraternization with soldiers betrayed both police fears and strikers' hopes of parallels with the beginnings of the Commune as well as with contemporary revolutions going on throughout Europe.[102]

As Jean-Paul Brunet has pointed out, for all the revolutionary bravado of many local leaders in Saint-Denis, the political leaders of the city took care not to go too far in tweaking the Tiger's tail. They never took any steps, for example, to challenge the police or to gather arms for the strikers. Rather, they often seemed to be negotiating delicately between the overheated ardor of the crowds they addressed and the powers of the state that surrounded them. Philippe and the other leaders were well aware that the police had numerous spies attending the strike meetings in the city, and realized that they could only go so far in channeling the spirit of revolutionary Petrograd. When the mayor met with Minister of the Interior Pams, he assured him that the strike was revolutionary in the sense of transcending capitalism, not in the sense of bloody insurrection in the streets. If Philippe and other leaders of the Saint-Denis Left took inspiration from the Paris Commune in 1919, they also remained well aware of its

---

[101] APP BA 1386, police report of June 6, 1919.
[102] On the fraternization of soldiers during the Russian Revolution, see Allan K. Wildman, *The End of the Russian Imperial Army: The Old Army and the Soldiers' Revolt* (Princeton University Press, 1980).

fate and were not prepared to subject their constituents to a similar outcome.[103]

Nonetheless Saint-Denis, and the suburbs in general, constituted the heart of the revolutionary vision of June 1919. Throughout the course of the strike suburban activists spoke most forcefully in favor of pushing the movement to extremes, of challenging and ultimately overthrowing the economic and political status quo. This was true even though not all suburbs were as radical as Saint-Denis, and some of the outer *arrondissements* of Paris (notably the twelfth, thirteenth, and twentieth) also proclaimed an attachment to the far Left. In Boulogne, for example, site of the giant Renault auto works, strikers formed a Red Guard on June 13 to support the strikers against both the police and the leaders of the CGT.[104] Even in Aubervilliers, home to a large chemicals industry and one of the least militant of the Paris suburbs, strikers at times took extremist positions.

> At the end of the meeting which took place this morning . . . in Aubervilliers, the 2,000 striking metalworkers present were given two ballots, one inscribed "Corporative" the other "Social". It was explained to them that the first option meant that the strike should have corporative improvements as a goal, whereas the other meant revolution. Only 800 people voted and the social program won by 40 votes.[105]

In addition to voicing moral support for the strike, suburban officials also took concrete actions to render aid to strikers in their communities. Most importantly, they ran a series of soup kitchens (*soupes populaires*) to help individuals and families who had suddenly lost their means of support. Given the impromptu nature of the strike, there was no strike fund to pay participants. The Union of Syndicates of the Seine contributed to these programs, as did the national Metalworkers' Federation, individual unions, and cooperatives, but they were frequently run under the auspices of local strike committees or socialist municipalities.[106] Activists sometimes used this charitable work as a way of marshaling support for the movement. In Saint-Denis, for example, strikers approached businessmen in the city asking for donations for the soup kitchens and threatening boycotts of those who refused. They also pressured non-socialist suburban municipalities to

---

[103] Brunet, *Saint-Denis*, 217–218; APP BA 1386, police report of June 7, 1919. It is worth noting that after his meeting with Pams, Philippe played little further public role in the strike. APP BA 1386, police report of June 28, 1919.

[104] Robert, *Les ouvriers, la patrie et la Révolution*, 343–350.

[105] APP BA 1386, police report of June 25, 1919. For another example of the paradoxical idea of voting on revolution at the time, see Spriano, *Occupation of the Factories*.

[106] APP BA 1386, police report of June 13, 1919.

donate funds.[107] In the absence of strong centralized direction, these soup kitchens reinforced, both in Paris and in suburban communities, the extremely local nature of the strike.

Ultimately, for a variety of reasons the Paris Commune did not reappear in 1919. Nonetheless, the geography of the June movement made it clear that the tradition of working-class radicalism it represented had not disappeared entirely, but rather moved beyond the city limits into suburbia. This shift had both advantages and disadvantages for would-be revolutionaries. In the suburbs, activists could rely on socialist municipalities as well as local union committees that proved forthcoming in both material and moral support of the metalworkers' strike. At the same time, their distance from the city center meant that their actions had relatively less impact and received less notice. The riots of May Day, which took place in the heart of the city, got a lot more publicity than did the demonstrations of June. Two themes that would resurface continually in the history of French labor during the twentieth century, militancy and isolation, became evident in the suburban strikes of June 1919.[108]

GENERAL STRIKE, INTERNATIONAL STRIKE,
AND DEFEAT

By the end of the first week of June those who regarded the metalworkers' strike as the first step toward revolution had some grounds for optimism. Not only had the walkout succeeded beyond all reasonable expectations in attracting the mass of Parisian metalworkers, but many if not most of those who joined the movement enthusiastically supported explicitly political slogans and goals. Yet in order to make the revolution one first had to win the strike, and the movement faced significant challenges in reaching that goal. Not for nothing had the national metalworkers' leadership argued that the time was not right for a major strike. For both tactical and ideological reasons, the Left wing of the movement believed it could only succeed if it went beyond the metalworkers of Paris and became a national, even international, struggle. That this had already happened in some suburban communities provided a model for the expansion of the movement. Ultimately, however, radical activists failed to transform the

---

[107] APP BA 1386, police report of June 13, 1919.
[108] See on this theme Gérard Noiriel, *Les ouvriers dans la société française, XIXe–XXe siècle* (Paris: Seuil, 1986); Roger Magraw, *A History of the French Working Class* (Cambridge MA: Blackwell, 1992).

turbulence of June 1919 into a national movement, and this failure led directly to the defeat of the strike.

Four major challenges confronted the striking metalworkers in June. First, the employers of the metals industry were united in opposition to the movement, and dead set against making any concessions to it. Some, especially owners of small and medium-sized firms, did accept some of the strikers' demands. The massive size of the walkout and the incendiary language of many participants led some employers to fear that revolution was indeed nigh. Yet, as it soon became clear that the strike would be essentially peaceful and that the forces of order remained in control of the situation, employer resistance hardened. Moreover, in general the metals industry was in a good position to resist a strike. Not only was unemployment high in 1919 but many employers, faced with the need to plan for reconversion to peacetime needs, were not at all averse to a temporary halt in production, especially since shortages of primary materials and the disorganization of transportation networks hindered their ability to make and sell their products. As John Horne has pointed out, some large employers also anticipated that a work stoppage would enable them to retool their factories with more up-to-date (and labor-saving) machinery.[109]

Second, the strike was not popular among the public as a whole. Even though many Parisians, not just metalworkers, joined the June movement, many more saw it as annoying at best, evil and treasonous at worst. It is interesting to compare public reactions to the 1919 strike with attitudes to the garment workers' strike of 1917. In the latter case, even though the strike occurred during the middle of the war, the overwhelmingly female participants were able to portray themselves as victimized consumers and mothers trying to feed their children. Moreover, the peaceful, indeed celebratory nature of the strike's demonstrations in the city won over many Parisians to their cause. In contrast, the metalworkers' strike seemed to represent disorder and revolution; the frequent references to soviets linked the movement with a Bolshevik Revolution deeply unpopular among many in France thanks to its associations with Brest-Litovsk and defeatism. The revolutionary tenor of much of the strike's discourse overshadowed the strikers' concerns with consumer issues, even though the two were closely linked. Moreover, many Parisians considered the prospect of an anarchic strike in the capital while the German delegation was there to

---

[109] Horne, *Labour at War*; Joshua Cole, "The transition to peace, 1918–1919," in Winter and Robert, *Capital Cities at War*.

negotiate the peace treaty to be a national embarrassment.[110] Finally, it is ironic, given that one of the strikers' main political demands was the more rapid demobilization of French soldiers, that some should accuse the strike of actually retarding the return of the *poilus* to their homes and families. For a variety of reasons, therefore, the strikers of June 1919 failed to garner the broad public approval needed to ensure the success of the strike, let alone transform it into something more fundamental.[111]

Gender played a role in public perceptions of the metalworkers' strike, as the above comparison suggests, and the gendered nature of the movement shaped and limited its revolutionary image. Not only did men completely dominate the strike, they staged it at a time when large numbers of women were being summarily dismissed from the metals industry. The strikers' attitudes toward women workers were complex. On the one hand, some saw the presence of women in the industry as a symbol of the de-skilling and rationalization they were trying to prevent. Strikers at the Citroen works in April 1919 went so far as to demand the firing of women workers, for example.[112] On the other hand, strike committees in June overwhelmingly included in their demands to employers the principle of equal pay for men and women. At a strike meeting in Paris on June 4, one striker presented the demands of women in the industry for a pay raise for women as well as the English week.[113] Yet in general few women spoke at strike meetings, and their specific concerns received little attention. More generally, the perception of the strike as concerned with the factory and politics rather than home and *la vie chère* corresponded to a distinction between dangerous men and oppressed women, one that worked to the disadvantage of the striking metalworkers.[114]

Third, the strike movement remained largely limited to the Department of the Seine. Given the widespread nature of the strike in Paris and its suburbs during the first week of June, many strikers hoped that it would soon become a national movement. On June 3, miners did go on strike in

---

[110] As one appeal to the strikers noted, "Parisians, the peace is not yet signed." *Le Petit Parisien*, June 6, 1919, 1.

[111] Writing in the pages of *La Victoire* Gustave Hervé, former militant anarcho-syndicalist turned ultra-patriot, wrote "At the moment when the victorious Republic is dictating the peace, a peace of justice no matter what people say, a peace of right, a Wilsonian peace, to the aggressors who killed 1,600,000 of our people and ravaged ten of our departments, our working class, as if taken by a spirit of madness, has undertaken strikes that, at the present hour, risk sabotaging the victory so dearly acquired . . . One could truly say that our Parisian working class wants to make us taste the rule of the sabre for a fourth time." Cited in *Le Figaro*, June 6, 1919, 2.

[112] AN F7 13367, police report of April 9, 1919.   [113] APP BA 1386, police report of June 4, 1919.

[114] See Downs, *Manufacturing Inequality*.

northern France, and demonstrations also occurred in port cities like Toulon and Brest when sailors protested against sending materials on French ships to the White armies in Russia.[115] One persistent rumor suggested that soldiers in Toulouse had revolted and formed a soviet in the city.[116] Yet in general the provinces remained quiet, so much so that 40 percent of all the strike days lost in France during 1919 occurred in the Department of the Seine.[117] During the second week of the strike the national CGT leadership promised to stage a 24-hour general strike on June 16 to support the miners' and sailors' unions, but failed to follow up on this, so that only the miners walked out on that day.[118] Even more than in 1871, therefore, in 1919 the possibilities of revolution in Paris failed to stir the rest of the country, leaving the national capital isolated and alone.

Fourth, and by far most important, the failure to win over the national leadership of the Metalworkers' Federation and of the CGT in general ultimately doomed the June 1919 strike. The spontaneous character of the strike was both a source of strength and of weakness. It gave the movement a dynamic character that went beyond traditional union actions, and prompted an unprecedented level of mass participation in an industry known for its low unionization rates. At the same time, the reticence if not outright opposition of many union leaders to the strike, or at least to its more radical positions, made it extremely difficult for strikers to transform their enthusiasm into something more enduring. The national leadership devoted most of its efforts during June to attempts to direct the strike into productive channels, and to use its militancy to win concessions from metals employers. To a certain extent they succeeded, but often at the cost of outraging the rank and file strikers who accused them of betraying the movement. As a result, after the revolutionary optimism of the first weeks the strike ended in an atmosphere of disillusionment and mutual recriminations.[119]

As noted above, Alphonse Merrheim and the national Metalworkers' Federation played no role in initiating the strike, and throughout June took no leadership role in directing it. At the same time, the EC quickly became disillusioned with the course of the strike, especially its revolutionary character. Having initially launched the movement in defiance of the national union leadership, the EC soon repented and began to work closely

[115] Brunet, *Saint-Denis*, 221.   [116] APP BA 1386, police report of June 5, 1919.
[117] Robert, *Les ouvriers, la patrie et la Révolution*, 399.   [118] Brunet, *Saint-Denis*, 224.
[119] This was a major issue for discussion at the special congress of the national Metalworkers' Federation held in September. See *Fédération des ouvriers sur métaux, Congrès extraordinaire des 10, 11, 12 et 13 septembre 1919, Rapport moral*. See also Papayanis, "Masses révolutionnaires," 62–73; AN F7 13367, police reports of June 22, July 17, July 20, and August 30, 1919.

with the Federation.[120] Both followed a strategy of negotiating with industry representatives while at the same time keeping the partisans of a more political strike at bay. On June 3 the EC met with representatives of the metals employers and the Minister of Labor, and agreed to negotiations on the basis of the April 17 and May 24 agreements. These lasted for about a week, but foundered over the refusal of employers to accept the EC's demands for higher wages and cost of living allowances.[121] When the EC met on June 9 it passed a motion to continue the strike on a strictly economic basis. In response, the Inter-union committee of Saint-Denis put forth a counter-resolution emphasizing the strike as an episode in the broader class struggle. The EC rejected this motion and succeeded in convincing many strike committees to follow its advice. However, others continued to assert their political and revolutionary interpretation of the movement, so that by the second week of June the EC was clearly no longer the leader of a unified metalworkers' strike. Instead, the movement became even more fragmented.[122]

New negotiations began on June 12, accompanied by increased public attacks by employers on the strikers as not only overpaid but also responsible for slowing down demobilization and the conclusion of the peace negotiations. Industry representatives even hired airplanes to drop leaflets explaining their position onto the square in front of Notre Dame and other places throughout the city.[123] At the same time the CGT leadership clearly proclaimed its rejection of any general strike in support of the metalworkers, a position reinforced by the decision of the Paris transport workers to end their strike on June 16 without obtaining a wage increase. In speaking to strikers' meetings, EC leaders appealed to them to give the negotiations a chance. Speaking in Aubervilliers on June 16, Dumercq asked his listeners to "Have faith in your union leaders and follow their advice. Our demands should not deviate from the issue of our corporate interests."[124]

Not surprisingly, such advice was not at all to the liking of the revolutionary Left, which continued to push for a more political strike. The next day a meeting of 1,200 strikers in Saint-Denis condemned the strategy of the national leadership.

[120] AN F7 13576, police report of June 5, 1919.
[121] Robert, *Les ouvriers, la patrie et la Révolution*, 295–296.
[122] *Ibid.*, 297; Papayanis, "Masses révolutionnaires," 60–61.
[123] *Le Petit Parisien*, June 13, 1919; APP BA 1386, police report of June 15, 1919.
[124] APP BA 1386, police report of June 16, 1919.

[Emile] BESTEL charged the leaders of the CGT with no longer representing the aspirations of the working class and playing the game of the Government during the present movement.

The meeting passed a resolution declaring that the union councils meeting tonight should oust the directors of the Metals Entente Committee . . . and orient the strike in a revolutionary direction.[125]

The meeting of local strike committees that took place that night saw renewed conflict between moderate and revolutionary forces leading to a compromise resolution that maintained the economic orientation of the strike but left open the possibility of a broader general strike if the national Federation approved.[126] This was not enough for the radicals: led by the Inter-union committee of Saint-Denis, they went on to found their own Action Committee to wrest control from the EC and reaffirm the political nature of the strike.[127]

Given the clear support among the mass of strikers enjoyed by the Left, the leaders of the EC and the national Federation looked for ways to defuse the conflict by making concessions on the issue of a possible general strike. On June 21 the Federation signed a compromise agreement with employers that did grant cost of living allowances and some other wage demands. As far as the union leadership was concerned, this should end the strike, bringing concrete gains to Parisian metalworkers. In order to prevent the repudiation of the agreement by strikers, as had happened with those of April and May, Merrheim agreed to the principle of a national general strike for political goals: amnesty for political prisoners, rapid demobilization of soldiers, and an end to Allied intervention in Russia. However, the strike had to be approved by the Interfederal Cartel, the organization of all the major Federations of the CGT.[128]

In its meeting in Paris on June 25, the Interfederal Cartel rejected once and for all engaging the CGT in a general strike to support the metalworkers, arguing that such a broad movement was not appropriate for a strike about economic demands.[129] The Cartel thus attacked the idea of a revolutionary strike on two grounds, both rejecting the political desires of many strikers and refusing to engage in the extension of the movement that might render a revolutionary outcome possible. For the leaders of both the CGT and the Parisian strikers, the decision of the Interfederal Cartel clearly

---

[125] APP BA 1386, police report of June 17, 1919.   [126] APP BA 1386, police report of June 19, 1919.
[127] APP BA 1386, police report of June 21, 1919.
[128] Abhervé, "La grève," 139–140; Robert, *Les ouvriers, la patrie et la Révolution*, 298–299; AN F7 13367, police reports of June 22 and June 23, 1919.
[129] AN F7 13576, police report of June 26, 1919.

spelled the doom of the revolutionary dream. As one speaker noted in a mass meeting held in Saint-Denis the next day, "This morning the strike committee, after having learned of the declaration of the Interfederal Cartel, has considered the situation in a cold light. Together with you we recognize that we have been shamefully ridiculed by the representatives of the big federations. We are not abandoning our ideas of social transformation, but we are obliged today to only discuss corporate issues."[130]

In contrast, many of the striking metalworkers simply refused to go along with the Cartel's decision and abandon their view of the strike. Strikers throughout the Paris area greeted the decision with a palpable sense of outrage, condemning the CGT leaders as traitors and even threatening violent retribution. On June 26 a delegation of strikers from the twentieth *arrondissement* marched to CGT headquarters to demand an explanation; about thirty of them grabbed a CGT staff member and forced him to meet with them.[131] By the next day the situation in Paris had gotten even more tense, as a police report noted:

Yesterday ... an extraordinary animation could be observed at the *Maison des Syndicats* [CGT headquarters in Paris].

The leaders of the CGT were meeting in JOUHAUX's office when they were informed that after a meeting organized in Pré-Saint-Gervais by striking metalworkers, 10,000 demonstrators were en route to "BURN DOWN THE CGT AND KICK OUT ALL THE UNION LEADERS" ...

Numerous young people, newly come to the organization, would not pardon the Cartel and the CGT for what they called their "treason." They have decided to resort to violence on this or that leader; some of them even want to burn down the CGT and the Stock Exchange.[132]

In trying to avoid such reactions from the strikers, the Cartel had tossed a bone to the partisans of political action. While opposed to turning the metalworkers' strike into a revolutionary movement, the CGT leadership was willing to consider action to protest certain political issues, notably Allied intervention in Russia. Moreover, such a movement could assume an international dimension. During the spring of 1919 socialists and union activists in Britain, France, and Italy had discussed the prospect of joint action against foreign involvement in the Soviet civil war.[133] On June 25, partly in compensation for its refusal to countenance a general strike in France, the Cartel did approve in theory the idea of a 24-hour general strike

---

[130] APP BA 1386, police report of June 26, 1919. [131] AN F7 13576, police report of June 27, 1919.
[132] AN F7 13576, police report of June 28, 1919. Nothing actually happened to CGT headquarters, but the leadership did place guards there overnight.
[133] Wohl, *French Communism*, 138.

in all three countries, directed both against Allied intervention vs. the Bolsheviks and also against the high cost of living, to take place in July. The linking of these two issues arose out of a complex series of negotiations in each country, but it underscored once again how revolutionary politics and concern over material conditions could at least coexist. As the union made clear, the question of inflation lay at the heart of the movement. A CGT manifesto about the proposed strike issued in early July stated that:

The workers of France, using the tool of the international resolution, will make their demonstration address the imperious necessity to remedy the situation created by the cost of living, by creating new sources of consumption, and by inaugurating tough economic policies . . .
  The demonstration of July 21 will be a formidable warning, because of the work stoppage it will provoke for 24 hours in our country, and will have the following meaning:
  Rapid demobilization without restrictions; reestablishment of constitutional liberties; full and entire amnesty; cessation of all intervention in Russia.
  But in addition and above all it will also call for:
  War against the high cost of living by any means necessary! [emphases in the original][134]

One can read this statement in two ways. On the one hand, it showcases the desire of the CGT's majority faction to emphasize corporate demands while at the same time incorporating issues that were political, if not necessarily revolutionary. On the other, the decision to address these issues in the context of an international general strike, and the association between political issues and militant anger over the cost of living, suggested the potentially revolutionary character of the latter. Moreover, including the question of *la vie chère* in the proposed general strike showed that its importance went far beyond Paris. In the first week of July, for example, widespread food rioting broke out in Florence, Livorno, and Palermo, leading to the establishment of soviets across the country and forcing the national government to enact widespread price cuts for basic goods.[135] In Italy, much more than in France, it seemed that the cost of living issue could lead directly to insurrection.[136]

CGT leaders used the prospect of this international protest to argue that Parisian metalworkers may have suffered a setback but that the struggle had merely shifted to new terrain. Speaking before a group of strikers in Aubervilliers on June 29, EC leader Dumercq declared that:

[134] *Le Petit Parisien*, July 4, 1919, 3.
[135] *Le Petit Parisien*, July 7, 1919, 3; Maier, *Recasting Bourgeois Europe*, 117.
[136] See on this point Bianchi, *Pace, pane, terra*.

the resumption of work does not mean the definitive abandonment of our demands ... We will still need you next month, when in full accord with the proletarians of England and of Italy we will decree a general strike. I hope that you will respond in great numbers to our appeal. The strike that you have just under-taken is the first big step made by the metalworkers. It will help show the way for the great events to come.[137]

Yet international strike or not, the Cartel's decision to reject a general strike signaled the end of the movement, and everyone knew it. Many strikers, convinced the cause was lost, began filtering back to work. On June 27 metals employers announced they would end the lockout on the 30th on the basis of the June 21 agreement. The next day the EC called for a return to work on the last day of the month.[138] The Left held meetings to protest the decision, including one in Pré-Saint-Gervais that attracted 8,000 strikers, but was not able to offer any concrete plans to save the strike. Over the next few days, as people all over France celebrated the signing of the treaty in Versailles and the final end of World War I, metalworkers returned in defeat to their jobs. Only 50,000 remained on strike by June 30, and by July 4 the movement was effectively over.[139] Dreams of revolution might survive in Paris, but clearly the prospect of reviving the Commune in 1919 had failed.

The metalworkers' strike of June 1919 had much in common with the consumer protests that erupted in the city during the same year. Like them, it arose as a popular movement outside the confines of traditional labor organizations, with an unstable, even anarchic quality that reflected and contributed to the turbulent character of the era. Like them, it combined a concern about *la vie chère* with a belief in radical, even revolutionary solutions to current problems. Like them, it took place in a period that was redefining questions of gender and race in ways that at times shaped its profile and outcome. Finally, like the movements around housing and food costs, the metalworkers' strike was an intensely local phenomenon, one that both relied upon neighborhood and community, and at the same time challenged the spatial organization of power in Paris. Not only its "political" demands but, more importantly, its very structure, the fact that it blurred the bounds between labor and politics, between production and consumption, made it a revolutionary movement.

Whatever its implications, in the short term the strike failed. Not only did workers return to the job without guarantees that they would be granted the terms of the contract negotiated by the national Federation, but many

---

[137] APP BA 1386, police report of June 29, 1919.
[138] *Ibid.*; see also police reports of June 27 and June 28.   [139] Abhervé, "La grève," chapter 7.

were fired for taking part in the walkout. Citroen alone fired two-thirds of those who joined the strike.[140] The 24-hour international general strike proposed for July 21 also failed.[141] On July 20 the CGT leadership suddenly cancelled the event, after having been promised by Clemençeau that he would move to meet their demands about amnesty, the pace of demobilization, and the high cost of living.[142] Moreover, when the CGT did stage a major general strike in May 1920, Parisian metalworkers remained largely aloof from the movement, which in its own turn proved a disaster.[143] More than any other event, the failure of the 1919 metalworkers' strike demonstrated the inability of French activists to translate postwar consumer discontent into a frontal challenge to capitalism.

At the same time, however, the strike underscored the political and insurgent nature of consumption in 1919. A great paradox of the movement was the tendency of both participants and commentators to draw a sharp line between "economic" and "political" demands, when in fact the former had a great deal to do with the latter. Discontent over *la vie chère* was probably the key factor in prompting thousands of metalworkers to demand revolution in June 1919. The failure to realize the political implications of this fact, a failure shared by both majoritaire and minoritaire factions of the French Left, both doomed the movement and illustrated the limits of revolutionary thinking in France at the end of the war. It is worth noting, for example, that even though the strike failed its militancy did push employers to grant cost of living allowances in their final offer on June 21, after much resistance. The end of the strike came at the same time as the end of a twilight period that combined war and peace; even though the movement to regulate the cost of food would arise later, the end of June marked the beginning of the postwar era and the effective end of the possible concatenation of war and revolution.

---

[140] *Ibid.*   [141] AN F7 13367, police reports of July 17, 1919, July 20, 1919.
[142] Wohl, *French Communism*, 138–139.
[143] AN F7 13275, police reports of May 6, 1920, May 7, 1920, and May 15, 1920.

Conclusion: legacies

In our own time it has become customary to write the history of working-class struggles and social movements in terms of failure. Not only did workers in Europe, America, and throughout the world stop short of entering the Promised Land of socialist equality, they also proved unable in many instances to maintain any significant class identity in general, succumbing to the temptations of individual upward mobility instead. Worst of all, those socialist movements that did assume rule either turned to dictatorship and lost popular legitimacy (and ultimately power) or else abandoned the quest for working-class empowerment. From Stalin's Russia to the China of Deng Xiao-Peng, the failures of socialism litter the landscape of twentieth-century history.[1]

So run the standard narratives of working-class identity, politics, and revolution in the modern era. In analyzing Parisian labor in 1919, this study has departed from this template in a number of respects. It has focused less on the failure (or success) of revolutionary politics and more on the reasons for their existence in the first place. Along those lines, it has devoted most of its attention to the micro-politics of working-class struggles, seeking to understand how questions of daily existence came to assume a political dimension. Perhaps most important, it has attempted to use this potentially revolutionary movement as a way of illustrating broader changes in Parisian working-class life, highlighting less what did not happen and more what did. Workers in Paris may not have taken the revolutionary path in 1919, but neither did they return to prewar social and political traditions, tracing instead the outlines of new roads into a new century.

In the few remaining pages of this study I should like to first sum up my major conclusions about Paris in 1919, then consider the legacies of these events for the twentieth century as a whole. What can one year tell us about the history of several decades? What lessons about "ordinary" times can we

---

[1] James Scott, *Seeing Like a State: How Certain Schemes to Improve the Human Condition Have Failed* (New Haven: Yale University Press, 1998).

draw from analyzing an extraordinary period, or for that matter did the tempestuous nature of the *biennio rosso* contribute to a certain view of the twentieth century in general as unsettled? More concretely, I wish to explore how the central themes of this study played out in Parisian and French life beyond 1919, and their implications for our understanding of the contemporary era. These themes did not develop in simple linear fashion, nor were they necessarily present at the same time in the same ways. Yet whereas I do not regard 1919 as a turning point in the classic sense of the phrase, considering its main components strikes me as a useful way of coming to grips with the legacy of a century that so recently retreated into the past.

Was 1919 a revolutionary year in Paris? No and yes. No, most obviously, because no successful revolution took place; instead the Third Republic lumbered on to become the Methuselah of French democratic regimes, finally dying as it was born in the throes of military defeat. No, also, because unlike in much of the rest of Europe no realistic prospect of the revolutionary overthrow of the established order ever existed. But in another sense 1919 did assume a revolutionary character, because so many Parisians believed revolution was possible and because more than a few tried to make it happen. It was revolutionary also in the multiple crises that erupted in a variety of interlocking aspects of working-class life, and in particular in the politicization of the everyday which those crises highlighted. Finally, it was revolutionary precisely because Paris in 1919 lay at the interstices of a world in turmoil, so that one could easily extrapolate from local to global upheaval, and vice versa.

In examining the revolutionary character of this year I have focused upon three primary themes, worth restating here: the politicization of consumer life; the instability of working-class identity; and the intense, unprecedented interaction of global and local politics. Before 1914 the Third Republic had for the most part pursued policies of non-intervention in the consumer economy, instead giving market forces pride of place in setting prices and supplies. While certainly not absolute, this emphasis on liberal political economy had the support of powerful groups in French politics and society. By suspending these principles, World War I made the French state responsible and thus accountable for providing basic material goods. Such goods, especially food and housing, thus became sites of political conflict, and came to symbolize at a micro-political level broader struggles that the spirit of wartime unity had in part driven underground. With the war's end, attempts to terminate state control of commodity pricing and supply prompted a series of spontaneous consumer movements that tried (sometimes successfully, sometimes not) to maintain public regulation of the consumer sphere and to impose popular sovereignty over the world of goods. Such struggles drew in large numbers of women, both challenging and reaffirming the traditional gendered structures of working-class social movements, and contributed significantly to the sense of revolutionary disarray in Paris after the Armistice. Moreover, consumer concerns lent themselves readily to revolutionary politics in 1919. Because many workers observed that strikes for higher wages were useless in an era of rampant inflation, they therefore concluded that the solution to *la vie chère* must be a political one, and if the government could not control the situation, then one must control the government. As the June 1919 metalworkers' strike made clear, in these conditions a desire for material improvements and for a fundamental transformation of the social and political order could go hand in hand.

The local popular struggles in Paris mirrored and interacted with global politics in 1919. As the site of the peace negotiations that ended World War I, the French capital not only hosted the (temporarily) successful attempt to resolve the European conflicts that produced the war, but also witnessed the birth of the two central world struggles of the new century, between capitalism and Communism, and between imperial centers and colonized peripheries. Much of the spectacular nature of Parisian working-class politics in 1919 derived from and resonated with this larger context, as the demonstrations of both May Day and Bastille Day made clear. Public urban space became a physical metaphor for a divided world; in particular, the contrast between city and suburb reflected differences between East and West, North and South. The end of the metalworkers' strike, the single most important challenge to the Parisian status quo in 1919, on virtually the same day as the signing of the Treaty of Versailles, definitively underscored these parallels. Not just diplomats and politicians, but also working-class Parisians enjoyed a position astride the world's stage in the year after the Armistice. In that year, the local and the transnational moved to similar rhythms.

The instability of the world order so evident in 1919 corresponded to the instability of working-class identity in the French capital. In particular, the most dramatic local manifestation of the transnational was postcolonial, the debate over the use and exclusion from France of colonial labor after the Armistice. Both the Paris peace conference and the Parisian working class sought to rebuild a sense of postwar normality by excluding the colonial Other in 1919, and in doing so both inadvertently highlighted faultlines that would become increasingly contested during the twentieth century. At the same time, conflicts over the role of working women in postwar industry showed how contemporary uncertainties about gender as a whole had the power to shape and reshape class identities and definitions. Should one view women as producers, consumers, or a combination of the two, and more generally how did gender and class articulate each other in the aftermath of World War I? Finally, the very diversity of Parisian labor, and the shifting balance between urban and suburban spaces, challenged established notions of what it meant to be a worker in modern France. A snapshot of a city and a world in flux, the instability of 1919 spoke to a sense of unmoored conventions and unbounded possibilities, including revolution itself.

For many in Paris, France, and beyond, therefore, 1919 seemed a revolutionary year, not just because of the many radical movements that surfaced then but also because of this sense that a transformation of the world was indeed possible. A comparison with the other year of the *biennio rosso*, 1920, illustrates this point. In two important respects 1920 has taken precedence over 1919 in the history of the French Left. Not only did the CGT stage the largest general strike ever to take place in France up till then, but the end of the year witnessed the permanent split in the political Left and the birth of the French Communist Party. At first glance one could easily conclude that the greatest challenges to the established order arose in 1920, not the year before. Yet upon closer inspection 1920 revealed the limits of revolutionary activism much more than its potential. The general strike of May 1920 arose above all in response to the increasing successes of the antiwar and revolutionary minority faction in the CGT; as a result, the national union leadership established neither clear goals nor a viable strategy for the movement. Although hundreds of thousands heeded the strike call, many others (including most Parisian metalworkers) stayed home. Faced with the firm opposition of the government, the strike collapsed in total defeat after three weeks. The consequences were catastrophic for organized labor in France: the CGT saw its membership tumble from 2.5 million at the beginning of 1920 to less than 600,000 a year later.[2]

Similarly, as Annie Kriegel has argued, the founding of the French Communist Party underscored the weakness of revolution in France, not its strength. When French Socialists voted massively to affiliate with the Communist Third International at the Congress of Tours in December 1920, they did so in the context of a Leftist movement reeling from a series of defeats.[3] Not only was the union movement in full retreat, but in November 1919 French voters had elected the most conservative government in half a

---

[2] Wohl, *French Communism*, 165; Adrian Jones, "The French railway strikes of January–May 1920: new syndicalist ideas and emergent communism," *French Historical Studies*, 12/4 (Autumn, 1982), 508–540.
[3] Annie Kriegel, *Aux origines du communisme français* (Paris: Flammarion, 1970); Kriegel, *Le Congrès de Tours, decembre 1920: naissance du Parti communiste français* (Paris: R. Julliard, 1964); Jean Fréville, *La nuit finit à Tours: naissance du Parti communiste français* (Paris: Éditions Sociales, 1970).

century.[4] In contrast the Soviet Union had won its battle for survival, and was thus in a moral position to give lessons on insurrection to a country that had long regarded itself as the homeland of revolution. At Tours, therefore, the French Left vainly attempted to revive the dying revolutionary hopes of the *biennio rosso* by adopting a new political model far removed from its own traditions, one that would take another generation to bear fruit. In 1920, therefore, the two most powerful tropes of the prewar revolutionary Left, the general strike and the Socialist Party, both conclusively demonstrated their inability to change the world.[5]

The year 1920 demonstrated the failure of the attempts to institutionalize the revolutionary *élan* so prevalent in 1919. In particular, not only did the spontaneous social and strike movements of 1919 prove unsustainable, but activists did not succeed (or often even imagine) trying to coordinate them in a multifaceted challenge to the established order. Nonetheless, for much of 1919 one could still believe in revolution, because turmoil seemed the rule in so many spheres of Parisian life. The fact that such hopes (or fears) soon proved groundless does not lessen their immediate impact or historical significance. For a brief period of time at the end of "the war to end all wars" many Parisians felt a new world was in the making, and aspects of working-class life lent credence to such beliefs. In the final pages of this study I shall explore what this exceptional span of a few months would mean for the new century.

If revolution did not happen, what did? The year 1919 constituted a key moment in the transformation of working-class life and politics in not only Paris but France as a whole. It illustrated the subtle, complex interactions of old traditions and new conditions, its very instability casting in bold relief some central themes that would characterize French labor for decades to come. Looking both backward to the nineteenth century and forward to the twentieth, this singular year heralded the advent of a new French working class.

Central to this was a new type of diversity. Throughout this study I have contended that a key aspect of working-class life in Paris was its heterogeneous quality. In one sense, of course, such diversity among the popular classes of France was not new at all. As Eugene Weber and other historians of the modernization of France have demonstrated, the rise of a coherent national

---

[4] The phenomenon of a revolutionary year culminating in a Right-wing electoral backlash provides a parallel between France in 1919 and both France and the United States in 1968.

[5] Again, this corresponds closely to the model outlined in Frances Fox Piven and Richard Cloward, *Poor People's Movements: Why They Succeed, How They Fail* (New York: Vintage, 1979).

identity depended in many ways on flattening out and homogenizing local and regional cultures.[6] To a certain extent Paris in 1919 continued to reflect this traditional heterogeneity: its many resemblances to the Paris Commune and its failure to achieve a national consensus highlighted this.

At the same time, though, one can catch glimpses of a new type of diversity, one that interacted with national and even global contexts. Much more than the Commune, 1919 created a powerful, permanent sense of connectedness with the world far beyond the Department of the Seine. The French capital was still traditional enough to permit the June metalworkers' strike to devolve into a series of local, even neighborhood movements. Yet if Saint-Denis in the end stopped short of an 1871-style insurrection, this was in large part because of local leaders' awareness of the futility of acting without national support. The tremendous occupational, ethnic, and local diversity of the Parisian working class survived, but the turbulence of the immediate postwar era underscored a much stronger sense of belonging to a national (and ultimately global) community of labor.[7]

Gender and race played key roles in this new sense of diversity. Parisian working women played a central role in the events of 1919 in two respects: the process of demobilizing them from wartime industry, and their massive involvement in the consumer struggles of that year.[8] For women, 1919 looked both backward and forward. It recalled the struggles around moral economy of the *ancien régime*, and at the same time anticipated new images of working-class women after 1945, when images of woman as the angel of the new consumer economy seemed to displace the idea of women as producers.[9] Similarly for men, 1919 illustrated key themes in the relationship between masculinity and labor in the coming century. As an important new body of literature has made clear, the French state heavily promoted paternal images of masculinity, what Laura Levine Frader has called the "male breadwinner

---

[6] Eugene Weber, *Peasants into Frenchmen* (Stanford University Press, 1976); Roger Price, *The Modernization of Rural France* (New York: St. Martin's Press, 1983); Caroline Ford, *Creating the Nation in Provincial France: Religion and Political Identity in Brittany* (Princeton University Press, 1993).

[7] Herrick Chapman, Mark Kesselman, and Martin Schain, eds., *A Century of Organized Labor in France: A Union Movement for the Twenty First Century?* (New York: St. Martin's Press, 1998); Roger Magraw, *A History of the French Working Class* (Oxford: Blackwell, 1992).

[8] Charles Sowerwine, *Sisters or Citizens? Women and Socialism in France since 1876* (Cambridge University Press, 1982); Sylvie Schweitzer, *Les femmes ont toujours travaillé: une histoire de leur métiers, XIXe et XXe siècles* (Paris: Jacob, 2002); Louise A. Tilly and Joan Scott, *Women, Work, and Family* (New York: Holt, Rinehart, and Winston, 1978).

[9] Claire Duchen, "Occupation housewife: the domestic ideal in 1950s France," *French Cultural Studies*, 2/4 (1991), 1–13; Victoria de Grazia and Ellen Furlough, eds., *The Sex of Things: Gender and Consumption in Historical Perspective* (Berkeley: University of California Press, 1996); Maggie Andrews and Mary M. Talbot, eds., *All the World and Her Husband: Women in Twentieth Century Consumer Culture* (London: Cassell, 2000).

ideal."[10] While the expulsion of women from heavy industry in 1919 seemed to uphold this idea, the fact that women quickly reentered into the Parisian and national labor force, going on to increase substantially their participation in heavy industry compared to the period before 1914, revealed its tenuous character. In general, 1919 called into question the gendered nature of labor that arose during the late nineteenth century, exposing the many different ways in which women and men created working-class communities. Debates about gender and working-class identity ultimately raised the question of the relationship between work and "leisure," production and consumption, for working Parisians in general. The year 1919 placed issues of gender on the table and in one way or another they would remain there for the decades to come.

Similarly, the controversies over colonial labor anticipated the new salience of racial difference during the twentieth century. The forced departure of war workers from the colonies in 1919 seemed to restore the traditional ethnic composition of Parisian labor, but in fact this process created an illusion of racial homogeneity. One impact was to de-racialize in large part (but not entirely) European foreigners, who after World War I found themselves much more welcome in France than before. At the same time it set a pattern for the expulsion of the racial Other that would resurface, far more tragically, with the deportation of foreign Jews to the death camps of the 1940s.[11] The year 1919 established whiteness as one characteristic of working-class identity in France, yet also demonstrated the artificial nature of such a construct; the parallel between the repatriation of colonial workers and a new emphasis on wage labor in the colonies themselves underscored the racially segmented character of French labor, and indeed of greater France as a whole.[12]

---

[10] Laura Levine Frader, *Breadwinners and Citizens: Gender in the Making of the French Social Model* (Durham NC: Duke University Press, 2008); Kristen Stromberg Childers, *Fathers, Families, and the State in France, 1914–1945* (Ithaca NY: Cornell University Press, 2003); Rachel Fuchs, *Contested Paternity: Constructing Families in Modern France* (Baltimore MD: Johns Hopkins University Press, 2008).

[11] Vicki Caron, *Uneasy Asylum: France and the Jewish Refugee Crisis* (Stanford University Press, 1999); Susan Zucotti, *The Holocaust, the French, and the Jews* (Lincoln: University of Nebraska Press, 1999). In general, 1919 represented a period of transition for Jews in France. As Paula Hyman has noted, after the anti-Semitic upsurge of the Dreyfus Affair, World War I brought a new level of acceptance and tolerance for French Jews, who (like their co-religionnaires in Germany) made enormous sacrifices for the war effort. At the same time, the beginnings of large-scale Jewish immigration to France, especially to Paris, in the early 1920s would provide the context for the new anti-Semitism of the 1930s and the genocidal policies of the 1940s. While anti-Semitism certainly existed in Paris in 1919, it did not play a significant role in public affairs. However, it was significant for the future that the famous anti-Semitic tract, *The Protocols of the Elders of Zion*, was first published in French translation in 1919. Paula Hyman, *From Dreyfus to Vichy: The Remaking of French Jewry, 1906–1939* (New York: Columbia University Press, 1979); Pierre Birnbaum, *"La France aux Français": histoire des haines nationalistes* (Paris: Seuil, 2006).

[12] On colonial and postcolonial whiteness, see Michael G. Vann, "White City on the Red River: race, power, and culture in French colonial Hanoi, 1872–1954" (Ph.D. dissertation, University of California, Santa Cruz, 1999); Elisa Camiscioli, "Producing citizens, reproducing the 'French race':

Finally, 1919 heralded a new relationship between working-class militancy and the state in modern France. Although a broad social and political consensus called for public authorities to abandon wartime protections for labor, working-class mobilization around a variety of issues forestalled its complete victory, ensuring that the legacy of the interventionist state would endure. At the same time, 1919 conclusively buried the prewar anarcho-syndicalist tradition. In their decentralized and spontaneous character the strikes and consumer movements of 1919 had much in common with the ideals of revolutionary anarcho-syndicalism. Yet they consistently appealed for public intervention rather than the destruction of the state as a whole. The immediate postwar era thus confirmed the politicization of everyday life created by World War I, demonstrating that its legacy would continue well into peacetime. The creation of the French Communist Party the following year, a new political formation that emphasized the capture of the state rather than its destruction, owed more than a little to the social and political turmoil of 1919.[13]

While it underscored the importance of the state, 1919 reaffirmed traditions of spontaneous working-class activism, recasting them in a new guise for a new century. While it recalled many aspects of the Paris Commune, one must equally consider 1919 the predecessor of May and June 1968.[14] Like those of 1919, the working-class revolts of May had a spontaneous, anarchic character at odds with the union and political leadership of the French Left: as in 1919, the revolutionary character of the year was less a concerted effort to overthrow the state and more a polyvalent and unstable series of insurgent movements. Like that in 1919, the May 1968 movement brought a new level of attention to the condition of women and the problems faced by immigrant workers and racial minorities.

Finally, the working-class unrest in 1968 also recalled that of 1919 in that it too revolved to a significant extent around consumer issues. The largest general strike in French history occurred during a period of unprecedented working-class affluence, a fact that seemed surprising and paradoxical to observers at the time. In an important study, Michael Seidman has argued that French labor in 1968 was much more concerned with material and

immigration, demography, pronatalism in early twentieth century France," *Gender and History*, 13 (November, 2001), 593–621; Alfred J. Lopez, ed., *Postcolonial Whiteness: A Critical Reader on Race and Empire* (Albany: State University of New York Press, 2005).

[13] Janet Horne, *A Social Laboratory for Modern France: The Musée Social and the Rise of the Welfare State* (Durham NC: Duke University Press, 2002); Paul V. Dutton, *Origins of the French Welfare State: The Struggle for Social Reform in France, 1914–1947* (Cambridge University Press, 2002).

[14] On the workers' revolt in 1968 see Xavier Vigna, *L'insubordination ouvrière dans les années 68: essai d'histoire politique des usines* (Presses Universitaires de Rennes, 2007).

consumer issues than with making revolution.[15] However, I would suggest that, just as in the case of 1919, it is sometimes hard to separate the two, and that much of the drama of May 1968 arose from the desires and dissatisfactions produced by consumer society. If the instability and multifaceted character of social and labor movements typified the revolutionary character of 1919, 1968 demonstrated that this tradition lived on well into the late twentieth century.

To answer the question posed at the beginning of this section, 1919 played an instrumental role in the rise of a French working class both more unified and more internally variegated than before, one that preserved the dream of revolution but adapted it to the new face of state power in the early twentieth century. In the short term, 1919 and the *biennio rosso* failed to emulate the Russian Revolution in Paris, a failure that substantially weakened French labor unions and politics during the 1920s. If one takes a longer view, however, one can glimpse the outlines of a new class formation that blended the traditional militancy of the male Parisian skilled worker with the consumer concerns of women into a synthesis capable of forging a national labor consensus. Ultimately, the mixture of social identity and political activism so evident in Paris in 1919 would provide a crucial legacy for what it meant to be a worker in France.

The social and political movements discussed in this book have an importance that goes far beyond a year in the life of the French capital. Consumerism and politics, gender and race, and the interaction of local and global forces all appear time and time again in the annals of the modern era as key determinants of both state policy and everyday life. My investigation of Paris in 1919 has been driven by a belief in the larger significance of these themes, so it is only fitting that I end this story by considering what contributions a microhistory can make to understanding them.

One of the consequences of the end of the twentieth century has been attempts by historians to make sense of that era as a whole, to tease out central principles and developments. For many, consumerism has emerged as one of those defining aspects of modernity, even postmodernity.[16] Recently two leading consumer historians (whose work in general this study has relied on heavily) have published major accounts of the history of consumerism in

---

[15] Michael Seidman, *The Imaginary Revolution: Parisian Students and Workers in 1968* (New York: Berghahn, 2004).

[16] See, for example, Susan Strasser, Charles McGovern, and Matthias Judt, eds., *Getting and Spending: European and American Consumer Societies in the Twentieth Century* (New York: Cambridge University Press, 1998); Lawrence B. Glickman, ed., *Consumer Society in American History: A Reader* (Ithaca NY: Cornell University Press, 1999).

the contemporary era. Both Gary Cross and Victoria de Grazia argue that American-style consumerism was the dominant material and ideological force of the twentieth century.[17] Their research is wide-ranging, their arguments fascinating and in many cases compelling. De Grazia and Cross both ground their work in post-Cold War triumphalist narratives of American power, reading the collapse of the Soviet Union at the end of the century back into an explanation of that century's history in general. Cross portrays consumerism as the one successful ideology of the modern era, deployed by advocates of ever-increasing plenty and market capitalism to define the essence of what it means to be American. De Grazia sees American consumerism as a successful, "irresistible" empire (again, in comparison with the failures of other modern empires) whose products and moral values have not only conquered but been eagerly embraced by Europeans. Both tend to conceive of consumerism as a belief system directed by business elites with the goal of expanding markets, and both tend to oppose a consumerist embrace of the value of things with an ascetic rejection of materialism.[18]

The studies of Cross and de Grazia conclusively establish the central significance of consumerism in the making of the contemporary world. While both authors are clearly aware of the many different political meanings of the desire for goods, they nonetheless both subscribe to a teleological narrative that privileges market capitalist visions of consumerism. Neither, and this is true of much of the historical literature on consumerism, grapples with the relationship between consumer dissatisfaction and radical political change.[19] Yet as we have seen in the case of Paris in 1919, frustrated consumerism and revolutionary ideas can go hand in hand. It is, for example, a truism of consumer studies that consumerism can subvert radical movements by commodifying them: examples, such as blue jeans or organic foods, are legion.[20] However, this is only half of the story; it is also true that cultural and social

---

[17] Victoria de Grazia, *Irresistible Empire: America's Advance through Twentieth-Century Europe* (Cambridge MA: Harvard University Press, 2005); Gary Cross, *An All-Consuming Century: Why Commercialism Won in Modern America* (New York: Columbia University Press, 2002).

[18] For another example of a major work on modern consumerism by a prominent historian, one that pays more attention to non-hegemonic uses of consumer culture, see Lizabeth Cohen, *A Consumer's Republic: The Politics of Mass Consumption in Postwar America* (New York: Knopf, 2003).

[19] For examples of works that do, see Ellen Furlough and Carl Strikwerda, eds., *Consumers Against Capitalism? Consumer Cooperation in Europe, North America, and Japan, 1840–1990* (Lanham MD: Rowman and Littlefield, 1999); Dana Frank, *Purchasing Power: Consumer Organizing, Gender, and the Seattle Labor Movement, 1919–1929* (Cambridge University Press, 1994); Michele Micheletti, *Political Virtue and Shopping: Individualism, Consumerism, and Collective Action* (New York: Palgrave Macmillan, 2003); Luc Bihl, *Une histoire du mouvement consommateur: mille ans de luttes* (Paris: Aubier, 1984).

[20] Thomas Frank, *The Conquest of Cool: Business Culture, Counterculture and the Rise of Hip Consumerism* (University of Chicago Press, 1997); Joseph Heath, *Nation of Rebels: Why Counterculture Became Consumer Culture* (New York: Harper Business, 2004).

movements continually find ways of subverting dominant ideologies through the use of consumer goods. To give one example from recent history, during the 1992 urban uprisings that struck Los Angeles and many other American cities in the wake of the beating of Rodney King, the PayLess drug-store chain ran ads saying "Hurry down to PayLess before the bargains are all gone!", even as looters were pillaging its branches throughout southern California.[21]

One can find a similarly dialogic relationship between consumerism and resistance in the popular culture of interwar Paris. In *The French in Love and War* Charles Rearick has chronicled the interaction of working-class identity and commercial culture in the aftermath of World War I. He shows how the idea of the *petit peuple* achieved prominence in popular songs, plays, and movies, and how the producers of commercial entertainments often strove to depoliticize such images. At the same time, however, the importance of workers as consumers limited this process of cooptation, ensuring the centrality of working people to interwar Parisian culture. In particular, the "little guy" came to represent Paris and France as a whole; the process of transforming ideas of national unity to foreground working-class experience, which I describe in Chapter 1, persisted during the years after the Armistice, returning in full force during the Popular Front. The working-class struggles of 1919 thus left an important legacy for the popular culture of twentieth-century Paris.[22]

Such an analysis complements rather than challenges the studies of Victoria de Grazia and Gary Cross, counterposing resistance and hegemony. I contend that consumer resistance has its own history, one that has elaborated and continues to elaborate alternatives to market capitalism and the American Way. As Michel de Certeau has argued, consumerism is less the application of hegemony and more a dialogic process of negotiation between producers, marketers, and consumers.[23] Moreover, I suggest that no study of consumerism is complete without a consideration of this dimension, which plays a significant role in shaping consumer culture in general. Ultimately, individuals and communities inscribe the goods they desire, buy, and use with many different meanings often radically different from or even opposed to the ideas inscribed upon them by those who sell them.

---

[21] Jen Nessel, "Fax from LA: images of the surreal city," *The Nation*, June 1, 1992, 746–748.
[22] Charles Rearick, *The French in Love and War: Popular Culture in the Era of the World Wars* (New Haven and London: Yale University Press, 1997). For a contrary view, one that contends that interwar commercial culture portrayed workers negatively, see Joelle Neulander, *Programming National Identity: The Culture of Radio in Interwar France* (Baton Rouge: Louisiana State University Press, 2009).
[23] Michel de Certeau, *The Practice of Everyday Life*, ed. Luce Giard (Minneapolis: University of Minnesota Press, 1998). See also Mark Poster, "The question of agency: Michel de Certeau and the history of consumerism," *Diacritics*, 22/2 (Summer, 1992), 94–107.

The contemporary history of the welfare state provides another perspective on the politics of consumer resistance.[24] Consumerist market capitalism and the expansion of social welfare benefits in Europe after 1945 often appear to arise from fundamentally different conceptions of society. Yet in actual fact welfarist provisions like guaranteed employment, health care, and state pensions went a long way toward making the postwar explosion of consumerism possible: one was much more likely to buy a car or refrigerator on credit if one didn't have to worry about being fired. From this viewpoint, the many popular movements that have arisen in Europe recently in response to state attempts to restrict welfare state benefits should be considered consumer movements, struggles to ensure certain popular standards of living.[25] The idea of the consumer citizen thus has multiple meanings: not only does it speak to business attempts to substitute commercial choice for political participation, it also refers to popular beliefs in the connection between adequate standards of living and democracy itself.[26]

Paris in 1919 thus provides an excellent example of the micro-politics of popular consumption and consumer resistance. It also illustrates the value of postcolonial and transnational approaches to modern French history. The universalist ideal, the belief that the core values of the French Revolution constitute a beacon of enlightenment to all the peoples of the world, has been a staple of the political culture of modern France. This ideal has proved both fruitful and problematic; the paradox of a nation with a specific national culture that also viewed that culture as defining civilization for all has created both the triumphs and the tragedies of the civilizing mission.[27] The history of France in the twentieth century has in large part been one in which the relationship between the nation and the world changed from an emphasis on the export of French power and culture overseas to a new level of the import of global influences into the Hexagon. Both the rise of Americanization as a political and cultural phenomenon and the presence of new postcolonial populations on national soil in the era after 1945 underscored this new

[24] François Ewald, *L'état providence* (Paris: B. Grasset, 1986).
[25] Jet Bussemaker, ed., *Citizenship and Welfare State Reform in Europe* (New York and London: Routledge, 1999); Vicente Navarro, ed., *Neoliberalism, Globalization, and Inequalities: Consequences for Health and Quality of Life* (Amityville NY: Baywood, 2007).
[26] De Grazia, *Irresistible Empire*, 336–375; Lisa Tiersten, *Marianne in the Market: Envisioning Consumer Society in Fin-de-Siècle France* (Berkeley: University of California Press, 2001), 185–236.
[27] Alice Conklin, *A Mission to Civilize: The Republican Idea of Empire in France and West Africa* (Stanford University Press, 1997); Roger Celestin and Eliane Dal Molin, *France from 1851 to the Present: Universalism in Crisis* (New York: Palgrave Macmillan, 2007).

openness to foreign influences, and their new significance in shaping French culture and identity.[28]

Paris in 1919 stood at a crucial intersection of France's relationship to the wider world. Never again in the twentieth century would the city be so central to global affairs. As the Bastille Day victory march demonstrated graphically, France represented not just a victorious power in 1919 but indeed the center of the struggle for liberty and civilization. Yet at the same time the 1919 Paris peace conference did not represent France dictating its terms to the world; rather it showcased conflicts between other powers ultimately greater than itself, so that Paris also represented the relative weakness of the nation and the advent of the dominant powers of the new century, the United States and the Soviet Union. In a similar vein Paris in 1919 illustrated both the apex of French and European overseas empires, and the forces that would bring about their demise. Moreover, the expulsion of colonial labor constituted an ultimately vain rejection of postcolonialism, one that only underscored the racial context of class and national identity in the metropole. All the conflicts of a world in turmoil ran through Paris in 1919, illustrating both the reasons for and the limits of the universalist ideal.

Yet Paris was not just a stage for others: rather I contend life in the city was changed by its interaction with global forces. One cannot fully grasp the history of the French capital in this period without confronting the context of world events. The influence of the Russian Bolsheviks and their revolution upon the French Left in this period is of course well known. Events like May Day and the June metalworkers' strike, especially in Saint-Denis, mimicked and replicated the global contest between the forces of Wilson and Lenin. However, the global struggle between North and South, empire and anti-colonial nationalism, also shaped the life of Paris in 1919. Not only did the expulsion of colonial labor parallel the silencing of anti-imperialist voices during the peace negotiations, but the increasingly sharp contrast between city and suburb, most evident during the metalworkers' strike, replicated that between metropole and colony on a transnational scale. World politics marched through the streets of Paris in 1919, and those streets in turn gave concrete form to the desires and fears of hundreds of millions throughout the world.

In this respect also, 1919 provided a powerful legacy for twentieth-century France. Both transnational and postcolonial influences returned in a big way during World War II: not only did American troops help liberate the nation,

---

[28] Kristin Ross, *Fast Cars, Clean Bodies: Decolonization and the Reordering of French Culture* (Cambridge MA: MIT Press, 1995).

but a majority of the "Free French" troops in fact came from the colonies, where Charles de Gaulle scored his first successes as leader of the Resistance.[29] What World War I began, World War II made permanent. As Kristin Ross has demonstrated, Americanization and decolonization together shaped the 1950s in France, and contemporary French identity has remained indebted to these influences.[30] At the dawn of the twenty-first century disputes about "immigration" and race dominate the nation's social and political landscape. Moreover, commentators at times portray France as once again a key battleground in what Samuel Huntington has termed the clash of civilizations, between the West and integralist Islam.[31] During the 2005 uprisings in France, one newspaper referred to the Paris suburbs as "Fallujah-sur-Seine."[32] Nearly a century after 1919, the conflicts of the world again run through the French capital.

The importance of these themes, and their salience for the history of the twentieth century in general, underscore my earlier contention that 1919 is important less as a turning point in history and more as a year illustrating the outlines of the contemporary era. Its very turbulence metaphorically anticipated the upheavals of the decades to come, both the outlines of some of the principal conflicts and the interactions between high and mass politics, global and local contexts, that would characterize them. In this sense, too, this study represents a micro-history, encapsulating in miniature a much broader tale. In the year after the Armistice, the French capital brought together, illustrated, and transformed all the tensions of a world balanced between war and peace, and in doing so fundamentally reshaped the identity of the working people who have always constituted the city's heart and soul. A remarkable year for a remarkable city, 1919 affirmed at the dawn of the contemporary era the unique status of Paris as a window on the world, a city whose local life, more than at any other time in its history, was the story of humanity.

In the end, this study suggests an alternative type of revolution in the twentieth century. Like their epochal predecessor in 1789, the Russian, Chinese, and other great upheavals of the twentieth century combined the

[29] Driss Maghraoui, "Moroccan colonial troops: history, memory and the culture of French colonialism" (Ph.D. dissertation, University of California, Santa Cruz, 2000); Charles Onana, *1940–1945: Noirs, Blancs, Beurs: libérateurs de la France* (Paris: Duboiris, 2006); Martin Thomas, *The French Empire at War, 1940–1945* (Manchester University Press, 1998). As historians have recently learned, colonial troops were deliberately excluded from the liberation of Paris in 1944, paralleling their exclusion from France in 1919.

[30] Ross, *Fast Cars*.

[31] Olivier Roy, *La laïcité face à l'Islam* (Paris: Stock, 2005); Gilles Kepel, *Les banlieues d'Islam: naissance d'une religion en France* (Paris: Seuil, 1987); Joan Scott, *The Politics of the Veil* (Princeton University Press, 2007).

[32] *The Weekly Standard*, November 3, 2005.

traumas of war with a fierce desire to remake the world and a drive for modernization. They occurred in relatively underdeveloped societies, politically and economically, and they registered their greatest successes (and ultimately greatest failures) in dragging and kicking their peoples to the forefront of historical progress. For the leaders of these world historical movements, the seizure of state power was a means not just to social transformation but equally to material empowerment.[33]

Paris in 1919 represents something different, a revolutionary moment that did not succeed in overthrowing the established political order but nonetheless illustrated profound changes in different levels of society. It occurred in an advanced society, economically, socially, and politically, and in a nation strained by the trials of total war but nonetheless victorious. If the Soviet revolution symbolized the rush to modernization, Paris after the Armistice had about it a whiff of the postmodern, signaled by its mixture of labor and consumer concerns, the dominance of turbulence rather than ideological teleology, its complex rethinking of identity and identities, and its negotiations of boundaries and diasporas. Like 1968 (and what has become known as "the sixties" in general), it pushed the limits of both workplace and consumer life, complicating and calling into question demarcations between the two.[34]

For a more recent example of this, one need only turn to the riots that convulsed the suburbs of Paris and other French cities in November 2005. The suburban uprisings of that year underscored the tensions produced by the changing nature of French society at the beginning of the twenty-first century, in particular representing a challenge to standard notions of French identity from the postcolonial periphery. At the same time the riots involved a significant level of consumer discontent, symbolized by the specter of thousands of burning cars torched by disaffected suburban youth. Like the metalworkers' strike of June 1919, the riots of November 2005 were overwhelmingly suburban; unlike it, they succeeded in mobilizing participants on a national level. Followed by a major student uprising in Paris in the spring of 2006, the events of 2005 made it clear that the revolutionary tradition of the French capital remained a living tradition.[35]

[33] The historiography of revolution is of course immense. See, for example, Theda Skocpol, *States and Social Revolutions: A Comparative Analysis of France, Russia, and China* (Cambridge University Press, 1979); David Close and Carl Bridge, eds., *Revolution: A History of the Idea* (London: Croom Helm, 1985).
[34] Herbert Marcuse, *The New Left and the 1960s*, ed. Douglas Kellner (London: Routledge, 2005); David Caute, *The Year of the Barricades: A Journey through 1968* (New York: Harper and Row, 1988); Bernard Gourbin, *L'esprit des années 60* (Le Coudray-Macouard: Cheminements, 2006).
[35] Laurent Mucchielli and Véronique Le Goaziou, eds., *Quand les banlieues brûlent . . .: retour sur les émeutes de novembre 2005* (Paris: La Découverte, 2007); Clémentine Autain *et al.*, *Banlieue, lendemains de révolte* (Paris: La Dispute et Regards, 2006).

It is in this reading of revolution that one can ultimately challenge the narrative of working-class failure noted at the start of this chapter. Such a narrative is not only empirical but also political, tending to validate elite agendas and the forces of contemporary capitalist globalization: if resistance failed in the past, it has no utility for the present or future.[36] In contrast, one can point to some very real achievements of the social movements of postwar Paris. Activists successfully maintained rent control, making a very real difference in the lives of many Parisians and slowing the gentrification of the city.[37] More generally, they demonstrated that the state could be a force for popular empowerment as well as official repression, and that dominant liberal narratives could be successfully contested. To take seriously a rejection of the hard-and-fast dichotomy between reform and revolution ultimately means acknowledging that for many Parisians such concrete accomplishments were indeed revolutionary. Above all, the revolutionary turmoil of 1919 underscored the multivalent character of political activism and the ability of women and men from many different walks of life to become the subjects of history. Such successes may not constitute a revolution in the classic sense, but they made a tremendous difference to the lives of Parisians at the time, and to their sons and daughters in the future. To accentuate the positive here at the end is not to neglect the many failures of 1919, failures this book has outlined in depth. Rather, it is to underscore the importance of the transformative vision in human affairs, a vision of a better world that suffused the upheavals of Paris in 1919, and which constitutes their most important legacy for our time.[38]

---

[36] See on this point the remarks of Donald Reid discussed by Kristin Ross in her *May '68 and Its Afterlives* (University of Chicago Press, 2002), 131.

[37] On the persistence of working-class culture and politics in twentieth-century Paris see Rosemary Wakeman, *The Heroic City: Paris, 1945–1958* (University of Chicago Press, 2009).

[38] Mike Haynes and Jim Wolfreys, eds., *History and Revolution: Refuting Revisionism* (London and New York: Verso, 2007).

Bibliography

ARCHIVES

ARCHIVES NATIONALES, PARIS: CARTONS

94 AP 135, 140 – Albert Thomas papers, on colonial labor

F7 13015 – police reports, Union des Syndicats de la Seine, 1919

F7 13617 – reports on conditions in war plants

FN 23 199 – press clippings on food riots in Paris, 1919

F7 13356 – police reports, demobilization of women workers in war plants, Paris, 1919

F7 13619 – reports on colonial workers and French workers

F7 13366 – Parisian war plants, women's strikes, 1917

F 14 11331, 11334 – reports on colonial labor

F7 13367 – surveillance of war factories, 1915–1919

F7 13273 – May Day, Paris, 1919

F7 13755 – Parisian renters' unions, 1919–1921

F7 13771 – police reports on metalworkers' congress, Lyon, September 1919

F 22 2565 – Ministry of Labor, 1919

F 23 188 – cost of living in Paris, 1917–1919

F7 13576 – Confédération Générale du Travail, 1918–1919

F7 13656, 13658 – police reports, strikes, Paris, 1919

F7 13958 – government programs on cost of living, 1915–1924

F7 13275 – 1920 general strike

F12 8023, 8024 – working-class agitation, 1918

F12 8036 – press clippings on the eight-hour day, 1919

ARCHIVES NATIONALES, SECTION D'OUTRE-MER, AIX-EN-PROVENCE: CARTONS

SLOTFOM 10/2–5 – Indochinese soldiers and workers

1/8 – postal censorship of colonial workers' correspondence, 1916–1924
Direction de Services Militaires, cartons 5, 6 – correspondence from Colonial Ministry, 1916–1918

SERVICES HISTORIQUES DE L'ARMÉE DE TERRE, VINCENNES: CARTONS

7 N 997 – colonial labor in France, 1916–1918
7 N 985 – police reports on civilian morale in Paris, 1917
7 N 144 – Colonial Labor Service (SOTC) correspondence, 1916–1917
7 N 1001 – postal censorship, colonial labor, 1916–1918
6 N 149 – postal censorship, colonial, 1917–1918
6 N 270 – statistics on North Africans in France, 1918–1919
7 N 435 – recruitment of North African labor, 1915
5 N 134 – recruitment of Chinese labor, Truptil Mission, 1915
17 N 157 – SOTC and colonial labor, 1917–1918
7 N 949 – Postal Censorship Commission

BIBLIOTHÈQUE MARGUERITE DURAND, PARIS: PRESS CLIPPING FILE ON 1917 DRESSMAKERS' STRIKE

ARCHIVES DE LA PRÉFECTURE DE POLICE DE PARIS: CARTONS:

BA 1376 – dressmakers' strikes, 1917–1918
BA 1407, 1408 – strikes in Paris, May–July, 1919
BA 1587, 1588 – physiognomy of Paris, 1919
BA 1639, 67 – confidential bulletin on civilian morale, 1917–1919
BA 1386 – police reports, metalworkers' strike, Paris, 1919
BA 860–862 – wartime censorship of theatrical performances in Paris
BA 1614 – popular mood of Parisian population, 1917–1921
Registre du Commisariat de Police, eleventh *arrondissement*, 1919

BIBLIOTHÈQUE ADMINISTRATIVE DE LA VILLE DE PARIS

Conseil Municipal de Paris, *Procès-Verbaux*, 1914–1919
Conseil Général de la Seine, *Procès-Verbaux*, 1919

ARCHIVES DÉPARTEMENTALES DE PARIS

Listes nominatives du recensement, D2M8
article 152 (1921) – Boulogne;

article 250 (1926) – eleventh *arrondissement*, Paris
article 266 (1926) – thirteenth *arrondissement*, Paris
article 167 (1921) – Drancy

NEWSPAPERS AND PERIODICALS

L'Avenir
L'Echo de Paris
Le Figaro
La France Libre
La Gazette des Tribunaux
La Grande Revue
L'Humanité
L'Information ouvrière et sociale
L'Intransigeant
Le Journal
Journal Officiel de la République Française
La Lanterne
Le Matin
Le Petit Journal
Le Petit Parisien
Revue Internationale du Travail
Le Temps
La Victoire
La Voix Ouvrière

OTHER PUBLISHED PRIMARY SOURCES

Abensour, Léon, "Le problème de la démobilisation féminine," *La Grande Revue* (January, 1919)

Adam, H. Pearl, *Paris Sees It Through: A Diary, 1914–1919* (New York and London: Hodder and Stoughton, 1919)

Annuaire de la cooperation (Paris: Fédération Nationale des Coops de Consommation, 1920)

Annuaire statistique de la ville de Paris, 1923–4 (Paris: Société anonyme de publications périodiques, 1927)

Auge-Laribé, Michel, *Agriculture in France during the War* (New Haven: Yale University Press, 1927)

Azzano, Laurent, *Mes joyeuses années au faubourg* (Paris: France-Empire, 1985)

Barthas, Louis, *Les cahiers de guerre de Louis Barthas, tonnelier, 1914–1919* (Paris: Maspero, 1978)

Benjamin, Walter, "Paris, the capital of the nineteenth century" (1935), in Steiner, *Walter Benjamin*

Bertillon, Jacques, *De la fréquence des principales causes de décès à Paris pendant la seconde moitié du XIXe siècle et notamment pendant la période 1886–1905* (Paris: Imprimerie Municipale, 1906)

Blanc, Edouard, *La ceinture rouge* (Paris: Éditions Spes, 1927)

Bonnefond, M., "Les colonies de bicoques de la region parisienne," *La vie urbaine*, 25, 26 (1925)

Bouvier, Jeanne, *Mes mémoires ou 59 années d'activité industrielle, sociale et intellectuelle d'une ouvrière 1876–1935* (Paris: La Découverte/Maspero, 1983)

"My memoirs; or, fifty-nine years of industrial, social, and intellectual activity by a working woman, 1876–1935," in Traugott, *The French Worker*.

Brogan, Denis, *The Development of Modern France*, 2 vols., vol. ii: *The Shadow of War; World War I; Between the Two Wars* (Gloucester MA: Peter Smith, 1970)

Bulletin du Ministère du Travail, 1919

Collin, Charles, *Silhouettes de lotissements* (Paris: Bloud & Gay, 1931)

The Commission on Foreign Inquiry of the National Civic Federation, *The Labor Situation in Great Britain and France* (New York: E. P. Dutton, 1919)

De Beauvoir, Simone, *Memoirs of a Dutiful Daughter* (New York: Harper Perennial, 2005)

Deletang, Louise, *Journal d'une ouvrière parisienne pendant la guerre* (Paris: Éditions Eugène Figuière, 1935)

Département de la Seine, *Rapport rélatif à la crise du logement* (Paris: Imprimerie Municipale, 1921)

Didion, J., *Les salaries étrangers en France* (Paris: M. Giard, 1911)

Dos Passos, John, *1919* (New York: Harcourt, Brace, and Co., 1932)

Mr. Wilson's War (Garden City NY: Doubleday, 1962)

Three Soldiers (Boston: Houghton Mifflin, 1921)

Duclos, Jacques, *Mémoires* (Paris: Fayard, 1968)

Fédération des ouvriers sur métaux, *Congrès extraordinaire des 10, 11, 12 et 13 septembre 1919, Rapport moral*

Fender, François-Xavier, *La crise du bâtiment dans la region parisienne* (Paris: Librairie du Recueil Sirey, 1935)

Frezouls, Paul, *Les ouvriers étrangers en France* (Montpellier: G. Fermin, 1909)

George, David Lloyd, *Memoirs of the Peace Conference* (New Haven: Yale University Press, 1939)

Grant, Marjorie, *Verdun Days in Paris* (London: W. Collins Sons, 1918)

Gurney, Peter, *Co-operative Culture and the Politics of Consumption in England, 1870–1930* (Manchester University Press, 1996)

Hammerstrand, Nils, "The housing problem in Paris," *Journal of the American Institute of Architects* (February, 1920), 88–89

Hamp, Pierre, *La France, pays ouvrier* (Paris: Nouvelle revue française, 1916)

Henrey, Mrs. Robert, *The Little Madeleine* (New York: E. P. Dutton, 1953)

House, Edward, *What Really Happened at Paris: The Story of the Peace Conference, 1918–1919* (New York: C. Scribner's Sons, 1921)

Huber, Michel, "Quarante années de la Statistique générale de la France: 1896–1936," *Journal de la Société de Statistique de Paris* (1937)

Leyret, Henri, *En plein faubourg, moeurs ouvrières* (Paris: Charpentier-Fasquelle, 1895)

Michaud, René, *J'avais vingt ans: un jeune ouvrier au début du siècle* (Paris: Éditions Syndicalistes, 1967)

Nogaro, Bertrand and Lucien Weil, *La main-d'oeuvre etrangère et colonial pendant la guerre* (Paris: Presses Universitaires de France, 1926)

Norbert, Gomar, *L'émigration algérienne en France* (Paris: Presses Universitaires de France, 1931)

d'Ormesson, Wladimir, *Le problème des lotissements* (Paris: Éditions Spes, 1928)

Pasquet, Louis, *Immigration et la main-d'oeuvre étrangère en France* (Paris: Rieder, 1927)

Pinot, Pierre, *Food Supply in France during the War* (New Haven: Yale University Press, 1927)

Sellier, Henri, *La crise du logement et l'intervention publique en matière d'habitation populaire dans l'agglomération parisienne* (Paris: Éditions de l'office public d'habitations à bon marché du département de la Seine, 1921)

Sellier, Henri, A. Bruggeman, and Marcel Poëte, *Paris pendant la guerre* (Paris: Presses Universitaires de France, 1926)

Servière, J., "La peine des femmes," *L'Information ouvrière et sociale* (May 5, 1918)

Seymour, Charles, *Letters from the Paris Peace Conference* (New Haven: Yale University Press, 1965)

Statistique Générale de France, *Résultats statistiques du recensement générale de la population* (Paris: Imprimerie nationale, 1925)

Statistique des grèves pour 1919–1920 (Paris: Imprimerie nationale, 1922)

Thorez, Maurice, *Fils du peuple* (Paris: Éditions sociales, 1970)

Valdour, Jacques, (pseud.), *Ateliers et taudis de la banlieue de Paris* (Paris: Éditions Spes, 1923)

   Le faubourg (Paris: Éditions Spes, 1925)

   Ouvriers parisiens d'après guerre (Paris: Arthur Rousseau, 1921)

de Vincennes, Jean, *Le bon dieu dans le bled* (Paris: G. Beauchesne, 1929)

Zaîontchkovsky, A., *Les Alliés contre la Russie avant, pendant et après la guerre mondiale (faits et documents)* (Paris: A. Delpuech, 1926)

SECONDARY SOURCES

Aaron, Michele, *Spectatorship: The Power of Looking On* (London and New York: Wallflower, 2007)

Abad, Reynald, *Le Grande Marché: l'approvisionnement alimentaire de Paris sous l'ancien régime* (Paris: Fayard, 2002)

Abel, Richard, *French Cinema: The First Wave, 1915–1929* (Princeton University Press, 1984)

Abhervé, Bertrand, "La grève des métalluristes parisiens de juin 1919" (*mémoire de maîtrise* thesis, Université de Paris-8, 1973)

"Les origines de la grève des métallurgists parisiens, juin 1919," *Mouvement social,* 93 (October–December, 1975), 75–85

Accampo, Elinor, *Industrialization, Family Life, and Class Relations in Saint-Chamond, 1815–1914* (Berkeley: University of California Press, 1989)

Agamben, Giorgio, *The Coming Community,* translated by Michael Hardt (Minneapolis: University of Minnesota Press, 1993)

Ambler, Charles, "Alcohol, racial segregation, and popular politics in northern Rhodesia," *Journal of African History,* 31/2 (1990)

Amdur, Kathryn, *Syndicalist Legacy: Trade Unions and Politics in Two French Cities in the Era of World War I* (Urbana: University of Illinois Press, 1986)

Andrew, Edward, "Class in itself and class against capital: Karl Marx and his classifiers," *Canadian Journal of Political Science/Revue canadienne de science politique,* 16/3 (September, 1983), 577–584

Andrews, Maggie and Mary M. Talbot, eds., *All the World and Her Husband: Women in Twentieth Century Consumer Culture* (London: Cassell, 2000)

Appadurai, Arjun, *Modernity at Large: Cultural Dimensions of Globalization* (Minneapolis: University of Minnesota Press, 1996)

Apter, Emily, "French colonial studies and postcolonial theory," *SubStance,* 76–77 (1995)

Archer-Shaw, Petrine, *Negrophilia: Avant-Garde Paris and Black Culture in the 1920s* (New York: Thames and Hudson, 2000)

Ariès, Philippe, *Histoire des populations françaises et leurs attitudes devant la vie depuis le XVIIIe siècle* (Paris: Éditions du Seuil, 1948)

Arthur, Susan B., "Unfinished projects: decolonization and the philosophy of Jean-Paul Sartre" (Ph.D. dissertation, University of California, Berkeley, 2004)

Atkins, Peter J., *et al.,* *Food and the City in Europe since 1800* (Burlington VT: Ashgate, 2007)

Audoin-Rouzeau, Stéphane, *Men at War, 1914–1918: National Sentiment and Trench Journalism in France during the First World War,* translated by Helen McPhail (Providence RI: Berg, 1992)

Auslander, Leora, *Taste and Power: Furnishing Modern France* (Berkeley: University of California Press, 1996)

Autain, Clémentine, *et al.,* *Banlieue, lendemains de révolte* (Paris: La Dispute et Régards, 2006)

Bacchetta, Paola and Margaret Power, eds, *Right-wing Women: From Conservatives to Extremists around the World* (New York: Routledge, 2002)

Bancel, Nicolas and Pascal Blanchard, "From colonial to postcolonial: reflections on the colonial debate in France," in Forsdick and Murphy, *Postcolonial Thought in the French-Speaking World.*

Barbeau, Arthur E. and Florette Henri, *The Unknown Soldiers: Black American Troops in World War I* (Philadelphia: Temple University Press, 1974)

Barclay, David E. and Eric D. Weitz, eds., *Between Reform and Revolution: German Socialism and Communism from 1840 to 1990* (New York and Oxford: Berghahn Books, 1998)

Barman, Genevieve and Nicole Dulioust, "Les années françaises de Deng Xiaoping (1920–1925)," *Vingtième Siècle,* 20 (1988)

Bastié, Jean, *La croissance de la banlieue parisienne* (Paris: Presses Universitaires de France, 1964)

Bauman, Zygmunt, "Exit *homo politicus,* enter *homo consumens,*" in Kate Soper and Frank Trentmann, *Citizenship and Consumption.*

Beaudu, Edouard, *et al., Histoire du music-hall* (Paris: Éditions de Paris, 1954)

Becker, Jean-Jacques, *1914: comment les français sont entrés dans la guerre* (Paris: Presses de la Fondation Nationale de Science Politique, 1977)

　Les français dans la grande guerre (Paris: R. Laffont, 1980)

　The Great War and the French People, translated by Arnold Pomerans (New York: Berg, 1985)

Becker, Jean-Jacques and Annie Kriegel, *1914, la guerre et le mouvement ouvrier français* (Paris: Armand Colin, 1964)

Becker, Jean-Jacques and Serge Berstein, *Histoire de l'anticommunisme,* vol. 1: *1917–1940* (Paris: Olivier Urban, 1987)

Bédarida, François, *et al., Pour une histoire de la statistique* (Paris: Institut National de la Statistique et des Etudes Economiques, 1976)

Beik, William, *Urban Protest in 17th Century France: The Culture of Retribution* (Cambridge University Press, 1997)

Bell, Daniel, *The End of Ideology: On the Exhaustion of Political Ideas in the Fifties: With "The Resumption of History in the New Century"* (Cambridge MA: Harvard University Press, 2000)

Bellamy, Richard and Darrow Schechter, *Gramsci and the Italian State* (New York: St. Martin's Press, 1993)

Benoist, Jacques, *Le Sacré-Coeur de Montmartre* (Paris: Éditions ouvrières, 1992)

Benstock, Shari, *Women of the Left Bank, 1900–1940* (Austin: University of Texas Press, 1986)

Berger, John, "The nature of mass demonstrations," *New Society,* May 23, 1968

Berlanstein, Lenard R., *Big Business and Industrial Conflict in Nineteenth-Century France* (Berkeley: University of California Press, 1991)

　The Working People of Paris, 1871–1914 (Baltimore: Johns Hopkins University Press, 1984)

Berlanstein, Lenard R., ed., *Rethinking Labor History* (Urbana: University of Illinois Press, 1993)

Berliner, Brett, *Ambivalent Desire: The Exotic Black Other in France* (Amherst: University of Massachusetts Press, 2002)

Berry, David, *A History of the French Anarchist Movement, 1917 to 1945* (Westport CT: Greenwood Press, 2002)

Bertrand, Charles, ed., *Revolutionary Situations in Europe, 1917–1922: Germany, Italy, Austria-Hungary* (Montreal: Interuniversity Centre for European Studies, 1977)

Betts, Raymond, *Tricouleur: The French Overseas Empire* (London: Gordon & Cremonesi, 1978)

Bianchi, Roberto, *Pace, pane, terra: il 1919 in Italia* (Rome: Odradek, 2006)

Bihl, Lucien, *Une histoire du mouvement consommateur: mille ans de luttes* (Paris: Aubier, 1984)

Bird, Stewart, *et al.*, *Solidarity Forever: An Oral History of the IWW* (Chicago: Lake View Press, 1985)

Birnbaum, Pierre, *"La France aux Français": histoire des haines nationalistes* (Paris: Seuil, 2006)

Blake, Jody, *La Tumulte Noir: Modernist Art and Popular Entertainment in Jazz-Age Paris* (University Park: Pennsylvania State University Press, 1999)

Blanchard, Pacal, Nicolas Bancel, and Sandrine Lemaire, eds., *La fracture coloniale: la société française au prisme de l'héritage colonial* (Paris: La Découverte, 2005)

Bohstedt, John, "Gender, household and community politics: women in English riots," *Past and Present*, 120 (August, 1988)

Bonnell, Victoria E., ed., *The Russian Worker: Life and Labor under the Tsarist Regime* (Berkeley: University of California Press, 1983)

Bonzon, Thierry and Belinda Davis, "Feeding the cities," in Winter and Robert, *Capital Cities at War*.

Borge, Jacques and Nicolas Viasnoff, *Archives de Paris* (Paris: Balland, 1981)

Bournon, Fernand, *Paris-Atlas illustré* (Paris: Larousse, 1989)

Bouton, Cynthia, *The Flour War: Gender, Class, and Community in Late Ancien Régime French Society* (University Park PA: Pennsylvania State University Press, 1993)

"Gendered behavior in subsistence riots: the French flour war of 1775," *Journal of Social History*, 23/4 (Summer, 1990)

Braudel, Fernand, *The Identity of France*, 2 vols., translated by Sian Reynolds (New York: HarperCollins, 1988–1990)

Breen, T. H., *The Marketplace of Revolution: How Consumer Politics Shaped American Independence* (Oxford University Press, 2004)

Brody, David, "Reconciling the old labor history and the new," *Pacific Historical Review*, 62/1 (February, 1993), 1–18.

Brooke, Stephen, "Gender and working class identity in Britain during the 1950s," *Journal of Social History*, 34/4 (Summer, 2001), 773–795

Brown, Doug, ed., *Thorstein Veblen in the Twenty First Century: A Commemoration of "The Theory of the Leisure Class," 1899–1999* (Cheltenham: Edward Elgar, 1998)

Brown, Jacqueline Nassy, *Dropping Anchor, Setting Sail: Geographies of Race in Black Liverpool* (Princeton University Press, 2005)

Bruckner, Pascal, *La tyrannie de la pénitence* (Paris: Grasset, 2006)

Brunet, Jean-Paul, *Police contre FLN: le drame d'octobre 1961* (Paris: Flammarion, 1999)

Saint-Denis la ville rouge: socialisme et communisme en banlieue ouvrière, 1890–1939 (Paris: Hachette, 1980)

Brunet, Jean-Paul, ed., *Immigration, vie politique et populisme en banlieue parisienne, fin XIXe–XXe siècles* (Paris: L'Harmattan, 1995)

Burgmann, Verity, "From syndicalism to Seattle: class and the politics of identity," *International Labor and Working Class History*, 67 (Spring, 2005)

Burke, Timothy, *Lifebuoy Men, Lux Women: Commodification, Consumption, and Cleanliness in Modern Zimbabwe* (Durham NC: Duke University Press, 1996)

Burnett, John, ed., *The Annals of Labour: Autobiographies of British Working-Class People, 1820–1920* (Bloomington: Indiana University Press, 1974)

Bussemaker, Jet, ed., *Citizenship and Welfare State Reform in Europe* (New York and London: Routledge, 1999)

Butsch, Richard, ed., *For Fun and Profit: The Transformation of Leisure into Consumption* (Philadelphia: Temple University Press, 1990)

Cabanes, Bruno, *La victoire endeuillé: la sortie de guerre des soldats français 1918–1920* (Paris: Seuil, 2004)

Calhoun, Craig, "'New social movements' of the early nineteenth century," *Social Science History*, 17/3 (Fall, 1993)

Callahan, Michael D., *A Sacred Trust: The League of Nations and Africa, 1929–1946* (Brighton: Sussex Academic Press, 2004)

Camiscioli, Elisa, "Producing citizens, reproducing the 'French race': immigration, demography, pronatalism in early twentieth century France," *Gender and History*, 13 (November, 2001), 593–621
  Reproducing the French Race: Immigration, Intimacy, and Embodiment in the Early Twentieth Century (Durham NC: Duke University Press, 2009)

Caron, Vicki, *Uneasy Asylum: France and the Jewish Refugee Crisis* (Stanford University Press, 1999)

Casalis, Laura, ed., *Parisian Fashion, from the "Journal des dames et des modes,"* translated by John Shepley (New York: Rizzoli, 1979–1980)

Castarède, Jean, *Histoire du luxe en France: des origines à nos jours* (Paris: Eyrolles, 2007)

Caute, David, *The Year of the Barricades: A Journey through 1968* (New York: Harper and Row, 1988)

Celestin, Roger and Eliane Dal Molin, *France from 1851 to the Present: Universalism in Crisis* (New York: Palgrave Macmillan, 2007)

Celik, Zeynep, *Urban Forms and Colonial Confrontations: Algiers under French Rule* (Berkeley: University of California Press, 1997)

Chadwick, Whitney and Tirza True Latimer, eds., *The Modern Woman Revisited* (New Brunswick: Rutgers University Press, 2003)

Chapman, Herrick and Laura Frader, eds., *Race in France: Interdisciplinary Perspectives on the Politics of Difference* (New York: Berghahn Books, 2004)

Chapman, Herrick, Mark Kesselman, and Martin Schain, eds., *A Century of Organized Labor in France: A Union Movement for the Twenty First Century?* (New York: St. Martin's Press, 1998)

Charle, Christophe, *Le siècle de la presse, 1830–1939* (Paris: Seuil, 2004)

Charles, Jacques, *Cent ans de music-hall* (Paris: Jeheber, 1956)

Chartier, Roger, "Texts, symbols and Frenchness," *Journal of Modern History*, 57 (1985)

Charvet, Marie, *Les fortifications de Paris: de l'hygiène à l'urbanisme, 1880–1919* (Rennes: Presses Universitaires de Rennes, 2005)

Chevalier, Louis, "La formation de la population parisienne au 19e siècle," *Cahiers de l'Institut National des Études Démographiques*, 10 (1950)
  Laboring Classes and Dangerous Classes in Paris during the First Half of the Nineteenth Century, translated by Frank Jellinek (Princeton University Press, 1973)
  Montmartre du plaisir et du crime (Paris: R. Laffont, 1980)
Chiesa, Lorenzo, *Subjectivity and Otherness: A Philosophical Reading of Lacan* (Cambridge MA: MIT Press, 2007)
Childers, Kristin Stromberg, *Fathers, Families, and the State in France, 1914–1945* (Ithaca NY: Cornell University Press, 2003)
Clark, Martin, *Antonio Gramsci and the Revolution That Failed* (New Haven: Yale University Press, 1977)
Clarke, John, "Pessimism versus populism: the problematic politics of popular culture," in Butsch, *For Fun and Profit*
Close, David and Carl Bridge, eds., *Revolution: A History of the Idea* (London: Croom Helm, 1985)
Clozier, René, *La Gare du Nord* (Paris: J.-B. Bailliere et fils, 1940)
Coats, A. W., "Contrary moralities: plebs, paternalists and political economists," *Past and Present*, 54 (February, 1972)
Coetzee, Frans and Marilyn Shevin-Coetzee, eds., *Authority, Identity, and the Social History of the Great War* (Providence: Berghahn Books, 1995)
Coffin, Judith, *The Politics of Women's Work: The Paris Garment Trades, 1759–1915* (Princeton University Press, 1996)
Cohen, Jean, "Rethinking social movements," *Berkeley Journal of Sociology*, 28 (1983)
Cohen, Lizabeth, *A Consumer's Republic: The Politics of Mass Consumption in Postwar America* (New York: Knopf, 2003)
  Making a New Deal: Industrial Workers in Chicago, 1919–1931 (Cambridge University Press, 1990)
Cole, Joshua, *The Power of Large Numbers: Population, Politics, and Gender in Nineteenth Century France* (Ithaca NY: Cornell University Press, 2000)
  "Remembering the Battle of Paris, 17 October 1961, in French and Algerian Memory," *French Politics, Culture, and Society*, 21/3 (Fall, 2003)
  "The transition to peace, 1918–1919," in Winter and Robert, *Capital Cities at War*.
Coles, Anthony James, "The moral economy of the crowd: some twentieth-century food riots," *Journal of British Studies*, 18/1 (Fall, 1978)
Collinet, Michel, *Essai sur la condition ouvrière* (Paris: Éditions ouvrières, 1951)
Collins, Patricia Hill, "It's all in the family: intersections of gender, race, and nation," *Hypatia*, 13/3 (Summer, 1998)
Conklin, Alice, *A Mission to Civilize: The Republican Idea of Empire in France and West Africa* (Stanford University Press, 1997)
Contee, Clarence G., "DuBois, the NAACP, and the Pan-African Congress of 1919," *Journal of Negro History*, 57/1 (January, 1972), 13–28

Cooper, Frederick, *Colonialism in Question: Theory, Knowledge, History* (Berkeley: University of California Press, 2005)

"Conflict and connection: rethinking colonial African history," *American Historical Review*, 99/5 (December, 1994)

Corbin, Alain, ed., *La Barricade* (Paris: Presses Universitaires de la Sorbonne, 1997)

Corlett, William, *Community without Unity: A Politics of Derridian Extravagance* (Durham NC: Duke University Press, 1993)

Coste, Michel, "Les métallos: une generation de pionniers de la proche banlieue parisienne," in Magri and Topalov, *Villes ouvrières.*

Crane, Diana, *Fashion and its Social Agendas: Class, Gender, and Identity in Clothing* (University of Chicago Press, 2000)

Crary, Jonathan, *Techniques of the Observer: On Vision and Modernity in the Nineteenth Century* (Cambridge MA: Harvard University Press, 1990)

Crenshaw, Kimberle, "Mapping the margins: intersectionality, identity politics, and violence against women of color," *Stanford Law Review*, 43/6 (1991)

Critchlow, Donald T., *Phyllis Schlafly and Grassroots Conservatism: A Woman's Crusade* (Princeton University Press, 2005)

Cronin, James, "Labor insurgency and class formation: comparative perspectives on the crisis of 1917–1920 in Europe," in Cronin and Sirianni, *Work, Community, and Power.*

"Rethinking the legacy of labor," in Cronin and Sirianni, *Work, Community, and Power.*

Cronin, James and Carmen Sirianni, eds., *Work, Community, and Power: The Experience of Labor in Europe and America, 1900–1925* (Philadelphia: Temple University Press, 1983)

Cross, Gary, *An All-Consuming Century: Why Commercialism Won in Modern America* (New York: Columbia University Press, 2002)

"Consumer history and dilemmas of working-class history," *Labor History Review*, 62/3 (1997)

Immigrant Workers in Industrial France (Philadelphia: Temple University Press, 1983)

A Quest for Time: The Reduction of Work in Britain and France, 1840–1940 (Berkeley: University of California Press, 1989)

Time and Money: The Making of Consumer Culture (London: Routledge, 1993)

Crowston, Claire, *Fabricating Women: The Seamstresses of Old Regime France, 1675–1791* (Durham NC: Duke University Press, 2001)

Crush, Jonathan and Charles Ambler, eds., *Liquor and Labor in Southern Africa* (Athens: Ohio University Press, 1992)

D'Anieri, Paul, *et al.*, "New social movements in historical perspective," *Comparative Politics* (July, 1990)

Darmon, Pierre, *Vivre à Paris pendant la Grande Guerre* (Paris: Fayard, 2002)

Darnton, Robert, *The Great Cat Massacre and Other Episodes in French Cultural History* (New York: Vintage, 1984)

The Kiss of Lamourette: Reflections in Cultural History (New York: Norton, 1990)

"The symbolic element in history," *Journal of Modern History*, 58 (1986)

Darrow, Margaret H., *French Women and the First World War: War Stories of the Home Front* (Oxford and New York: Berg, 2000)

Daumard, Adeline, *La bourgeoisie parisienne de 1815 à 1848* (Paris: Albin Michel, 1996)

Daumas, Maurice and Jacques Payen, eds., *Evolution de la géographie industrielle de Paris et sa proche banlieue au XIXe siècle* (Paris: Centre de documentation d'histoire des techniques, 1976)

Davis, Belinda J., *Home Fires Burning: Food, Politics, and Everyday Life in World War I Berlin* (Chapel Hill: University of North Carolina Press, 2000)

Davis, Mike, *City of Quartz: Excavating the Future in Los Angeles* (London and New York: Verso, 2006)

Davis, Susan, *Parades and Power: Street Theatre in 19th Century Philadelphia* (Philadelphia PA: Temple University Press, 1986)

De Beauvoir, Simone, *The Second Sex* (New York: Vintage, 1952)

De Certeau, Michel, *The Practice of Everyday Life*, ed. Luce Giard (Minneapolis: University of Minnesota Press, 1998)

De Grazia, Victoria, "Beyond time and money," *International Labor and Working Class History*, 43 (Spring, 1993), 24–30

"Empowering women as citizen-consumers," in de Grazia and Furlough, *The Sex of Things*.

Irresistible Empire: America's Advance through Twentieth Century Europe (Cambridge MA: Harvard University Press, 2005)

De Grazia, Victoria and Ellen Furlough, eds., *The Sex of Things: Gender and Consumption in Historical Perspective* (Berkeley: University of California Press, 1996)

de Jean, Joan, *The Essence of Style: How the French Invented High Fashion, Fine Food, Chic Cafés, Style, Sophistication, and Glamour* (New York: Free Press, 2005)

de Jouvenel, Bertrand, *No Vacancies* (New York: New York Foundation for Economic Education, 1948)

Debord, Guy, *The Society of the Spectacle* (Detroit: Black and Red Press, 1983)

Deeb, Maurice, *Party Politics in Egypt: The Wafd and Its Rivals, 1919–1939* (London: Ithaca Press, 1979)

Delatour, Yvonne, "Le travail des femmes, 1914–1918," *Francia*, 2 (1974)

Delon, Pierre, *Les employés: un siècle de lutte* (Paris: Éditions sociales, 1969)

Derrida, Jacques, *Of Grammatology*, translated by Gayatri Chakravorty Spivak (Baltimore: Johns Hopkins University Press, 1976)

Dewitte, Patrick, *Les mouvements nègres en France, 1919–1939* (Paris: L'Harmattan, 1985)

Dittmar, Gérald, *Montmartre de la République à la Commune* (Paris: Dittmar, 2007)

Dommanget, Maurice, *Histoire du premier mai* (Paris: Éditions de la Tete des Feuilles, 1972)

Donadey, Anne, "'Y'a bon Banania': ethics and cultural criticism in the colonial context," *French Cultural Studies*, 11/31 (2000)

Downs, Laura Lee, *Manufacturing Inequality: Gender Division in the French and British Metalworking Industries, 1914–1939* (Ithaca: Cornell University Press, 1995)

Draper, Alfred, *Amritsar: The Massacre That Ended the Raj* (London: Cassell, 1981)

D'Souza, Aruna and Tom McDonough, eds., *The Invisible Flâneuse? Gender, Public Space and Visual Culture in Nineteenth Century Paris* (Manchester University Press, 2006)

Dubusset, M., F. Thébaud, and C. Vincent, "Les munitionnettes de la Seine," in Patrick Fridenson, ed., *1914–1918: l'autre front* (Paris: Éditions Ouvrières, 1977)

Duchen, Claire, "Occupation housewife: the domestic ideal in 1950s France," *French Cultural Studies*, 2/4 (1991), 1–13

Dutton, Paul V., *Origins of the French Welfare State: The Struggle for Social Reform in France, 1914–1947* (Cambridge University Press, 2002)

Duyvendak, Jan Willem, *The Power of Politics: New Social Movements in France* (Boulder CO: Westview Press, 1995)

Dyer, Colin, *Population and Society in Twentieth Century France* (London: Hodder and Stoughton, 1978)

"Women's strikes and the politics of popular egalitarianism in France, 1916–18," in Berlanstein, *Rethinking Labor History*.

Eder, Klaus, *The New Politics of Class: Social Movements and Cultural Dynamics in Advanced Societies* (London: Sage, 1993)

Edwards, Stewart, *The Paris Commune, 1871* (London: Eyre and Spottiswoode, 1971)

Ehrenreich, Barbara and John, *Long March, Short Spring: The Student Uprising at Home and Abroad* (New York: Monthly Review Press, 1969)

Einaudi, Jean-Luc, *La bataille de Paris: 17 Octobre 1961* (Paris: Seuil, 1991)

Eley, Geoff, "Is all the world a text? From social history to the history of society two decades later," in Gabrielle M. Spiegel, *Practicing History*.

Engel, Barbara Alpern, "Not by bread alone: subsistence riots in Russia during World War I," *Journal of Modern History*, 69/4 (December, 1997), 696–721

Evans, Sara M., *Personal Politics: The Roots of Women's Liberation in the Civil Rights Movement and the New Left* (New York: Random House, 1979)

Evenson, Norma, *Paris: A Century of Change, 1878–1978* (New Haven: Yale University Press, 1979)

Ewald, François, *L'état providence* (Paris: B. Grasset, 1986)

Ewen, Stuart and Elizabeth, *Channels of Desire: Mass Images and the Shaping of American Consciousness* (New York: McGraw Hill, 1982)

Ezra, Elizabeth, *The Colonial Unconscious: Race and Culture in Interwar France* (Ithaca NY: Cornell University Press, 2000)

Fainsod, Merle, *International Socialism and the World War* (New York: Octagon Books, 1966)

Fanon, Frantz, *Black Skin, White Masks* (New York: Grove Press, 1967)

Faure, Alain, "A l'aube des transport de masse: les 'trains ouvriers' de la banlieue de Paris," *Revue d'histoire moderne et contemporaine*, 40/2 (April–June, 1993)

"Nous travaillons 10 heures par jour, plus le chemin," in Magri and Topalov, *Villes ouvrières.*

Paris careme-prenant: du carnaval à part au XIXe siècle (Paris: Hachette, 1978)

Favre, Mireille, "Un milieu porteur de modernisation: travailleurs et tirailleurs Vietnamiens en France pendant la première guerre mondiale" (thesis, École nationale des Chartes, 1986)

Fay, Peter Ward, *The Opium War, 1840–1842* (Chapel Hill: University of North Carolina Press, 1998)

Featherstone, Mike, Scott Lash, and Roland Robertson, eds., *Global Modernities* (London: Sage Publications, 1995)

Ferro, Marc, *Cinéma et histoire* (Paris: Denoel, 1977)

Fine, Martin, "Albert Thomas: a reformer's vision of modernization, 1914–1932," *Journal of Contemporary History*, 12 (1977)

Fitzpatrick, Sheila, *The Russian Revolution, 1917–1932* (Oxford University Press, 1994)

Flandrin, Jean-Louis and Massimo Montanari, eds., *Histoire de l'alimentation* (Paris: Fayard, 1996)

Flonneau, Jean-Marie, "Crise de vie chère et mouvement syndical 1910–1914," *Mouvement Social* (July–September, 1970)

Ford, Caroline, *Creating the Nation in Provincial France: Religion and Political Identity in Brittany* (Princeton University Press, 1993)

Forsdick, Charles and David Murphy, eds., *Postcolonial Thought in the French-Speaking World* (Liverpool University Press, 2009)

Fourcaut, Annie, *Banlieue rouge, 1920–1960* (Paris: Éditions Autrement, 1992)

Bobigny, banlieue rouge (Paris: Éditions Ouvrières, 1986)

Femmes à l'usine en France dans l'entre deux guerres (Paris: Maspero, 1982)

Un siècle de banlieue parisienne, 1859–1964: guide de recherche (Paris: L'Harmattan, 1988)

Foweraker, Joe, *Theorizing Social Movements* (London and Boulder CO: Pluto Press, 1995)

Frader, Laura L. *Breadwinners and Citizens: Gender in the Making of the French Social Model* (Durham NC: Duke University Press, 2008)

Frader, Laura L. and Sonya Rose, eds., *Gender and Class in Modern Europe* (Ithaca NY: Cornell University Press, 1996)

Frank, Dana, *Purchasing Power: Consumer Organizing, Gender, and the Seattle Labor Movement, 1919–1929* (New York: Cambridge University Press, 1994)

Frank, Thomas, *The Conquest of Cool: Business Culture, Counterculture and the Rise of Hip Consumerism* (University of Chicago Press, 1997)

Fraser, Steven and Josh Freeman, eds., *Audacious Democracy: Labor, Intellectuals, and the Social Reconstruction of America* (Boston: Houghton Mifflin, 1997)

Fréville, Jean, *La nuit finit à Tours: naissance du Parti communiste français* (Paris: Éditions sociales, 1970)

Fridenson, Patrick, ed., *1914–1918: l'autre front* (Paris: Éditions Ouvrières, 1977)

The French Home Front, 1914–1918, translated by Bruce Little (Providence RI and Oxford: Berg, 1992)

Histoire des usines Rénault (Paris: Seuil, 1972)

"The impact of the war on French workers," in Wall and Winter, *The Upheaval of War*.

Fridenson, Patrick and Bénédicte Reynaud, eds., *La France et le temps de travail (1814–2004)* (Paris: Odile Jacob, 2004)

Frisch, Michael H. and Daniel J. Walkowitz, eds., *Working Class America: Essays on Labor, Community, and American Society* (Urbana: University of Illinois Press, 1982)

Fromkin, David, *A Peace to End All Peace: The Fall of the Ottoman Empire and the Creation of the Modern Middle East* (New York: Avon Books, 1990)

Fryer, David, *The Intervention of the Other: Ethical Subjectivity in Levinas and Lacan* (New York: Other Press, 2004)

Fuchs, Rachel, *Contested Paternity: Constructing Families in Modern France* (Baltimore MD: Johns Hopkins University Press, 2008)

   Poor and Pregnant in Paris: Strategies for Survival in the Nineteenth Century (New Brunswick NJ: Rutgers University Press, 1992)

Fukuyama, Francis, *The End of History and the Last Man* (New York: Bard, 1998)

Furlough, Ellen, *Consumer Cooperation in France: The Politics of Consumption 1834–1930* (Ithaca NY: Cornell University Press, 1991)

Furlough, Ellen and Carl Strikwerda, eds., *Consumers against Capitalism? Consumer Cooperation in Europe, North America, and Japan, 1840–1990* (Lanham MD: Rowman and Littlefield, 1999)

Fussell, Paul, *The Great War and Modern Memory* (New York: Oxford University Press, 2000)

   Uniforms: Why We Are What We Wear (Boston: Houghton Mifflin, 2002)

Gaillard, Jeanne, *Communes de province, Commune de Paris* (Paris: Flammarion, 1971)

   Paris, la ville 1852–1870 (Paris: L'Harmattan, 1997)

Gallagher, Catherine and Stephen Greenblatt, *Practicing New Historicism* (University of Chicago Press, 2000)

Gambone, L., *Revolution and Reformism: The Split between "Moderates" and "Revolutionaries" in French Anarcho-Syndicalism* (Montreal: Red Lion Press, 1995)

Gasnault, François, *Guinguettes et lorettes: bals publics à Paris au XIXe siècle* (Paris: Aubier, 1986)

Geertz, Clifford, *Negara: The Theatre State in 19th Century Bali* (Princeton University Press, 1980)

Genovese, Elizabeth Fox, "The many faces of moral economy: a contribution to the debate," *Past and Present*, 58 (February, 1973)

George, Pierre, *Études sur la banlieue: essays méthodologiques* (Paris: A. Colin, 1950)

Gilroy, Paul, *The Black Atlantic: Modernity and Double Consciousness* (Cambridge MA: Harvard University Press, 1993)

Giltin, Todd, "The Rise of Identity Politics," *Dissent* (Spring, 1993)

   The Sixties: Years of Hope, Days of Rage (New York: Bantam, 1993)

Girault, Jacques and Jean-Louis Robert, *1920: le Congrès de Tours* (Paris: Messidor-Éditions Sociales, 1990)

Girault, Jacques, ed., *Sur l'implantation du parti communiste français dans l'entre-deux-guerres* (Paris: Éditions Sociales, 1977)

    La Commune et Bordeaux (Paris: Éditions Sociales, 1971)

Glickman, Lawrence B., ed., *Consumer Society in American History: A Reader* (Ithaca NY: Cornell University Press, 1999)

Goldberg, Harvey, *The Life of Jean Jaurès: A Biography of the Great French Socialist and Intellectual* (Madison: University of Wisconsin Press, 1962)

Gourbin, Bernard, *L'esprit des années 60* (Le Coudray-Macouard: Cheminements, 2006)

Gras, Christian, *Alfred Rosmer et le mouvement révolutionnaire international* (Paris: Maspero, 1971)

Grayzel, Susan, *Women's Identities at War: Gender, Motherhood, and Politics in Britain and France during the First World War* (Chapel Hill: University of North Carolina Press, 1999)

Green, Nancy L., *The Pletzl of Paris: Jewish Immigrant Workers in the Belle Epoque* (New York: Holmes and Meier, 1986)

    "Quartier et travail: les immigrés juifs dans le Marais et derrière les machines à coudre, 1900–1939," in Magri and Topalov, *Villes ouvrières.*

    Ready-to-Wear, Ready-to-Work: A Century of Industry and Immigrants in Paris and New York (Durham NC: Duke University Press, 1997)

Greenberg, Louis, *Sisters of Liberty: Marseille, Lyon, Paris, and the Reaction to a Centralized State, 1868–1871* (Cambridge MA: Harvard University Press, 1971)

Gruber, Helmut, ed., *International Communism in the Era of Lenin: A Documentary History* (Ithaca NY: Cornell University Press, 1967)

Guerrand, Roger-Henri, *L'aventure du métropolitain* (Paris: Éditions de la Découverte, 1986)

    Le logement populaire en France (Paris: École nationale supérieure des beaux arts, 1983)

    Les origines du logement social en France (Paris: Éditions ouvrières, 1967)

Gullickson, Gay, *Spinners and Weavers of Auffray: Rural Industry and the Sexual Division of Labor in a French Village, 1750–1850* (Cambridge University Press, 1986)

Haine, W. Scott, "The development of leisure and the transformation of working-class adolescence, Paris 1830–1940," *Journal of Family History*, 17/4 (1992)

Hall, John, ed., *Reworking Class* (Ithaca: Cornell University Press, 1997)

Hall, Stuart and Tony Jefferson, eds., *Resistance through Ritual: Youth Subcultures in Post War Britain* (London: Hutchinson, 1976)

Hanagan, Michael and Marcel van der Linden, eds., "New approaches to global labor history," special edition of *International Labor and Working Class History*, 66 (Fall, 2004)

Hanna, Martha, *Your Death Would Be Mine: Paul and Marie Pireaud in the Great War* (Cambridge MA: Harvard University Press, 2006)

Hanson, Paul, "The 'vie chère' riots of 1911: traditional protests in modern garb," *Journal of Social History*, 21/3 (Spring, 1988)

Hardach, Gerd, "Industrial mobilization in 1914–1918: production, planning, and ideology," in Fridenson, *The French Home Front*

Hargreaves, Alec, *Immigration, "Race" and Ethnicity in Contemporary France* (London and New York: Routledge, 1995)

Hargreaves, Alec and Mark Mckinney, eds., *Post-Colonial Cultures in France* (London and New York: Routledge, 1997)

Harvey, David, *Consciousness and the Urban Experience: Studies in the History and Theory of Capitalist Urbanization* (Baltimore: Johns Hopkins University Press, 1985)

Paris, Capital of Modernity (New York: Routledge, 2003)

Social Justice and the City (London: Arnold, 1973)

Hausser, Elisabeth, *Paris au jour le jour: les événements vu par la presse, 1900–1919* (Paris: Les Éditions de Minuit, 1968)

Haynes, Mike and Jim Wolfreys, eds., *History and Revolution: Refuting Revisionism* (London and New York: Verso, 2007)

Healy, Maureen, *Vienna and the Fall of the Hapsburg Empire: Total War and Everyday Life in World War I* (Cambridge University Press, 2004)

Heath, Joseph, *Nation of Rebels: Why Counterculture Became Consumer Culture* (New York: Harper Business, 2004)

Hebdige, Dick, *Subculture: The Meaning of Style* (London: Methuen, 1979)

Hennebique, Alain, "Albert Thomas and the war industries," in Fridenson, *The French Home Front*

Hilton, Matthew, *Consumerism in Twentieth Century Britain: The Search for a Historical Movement* (Cambridge University Press, 2003)

Hine, Darlene Clark and Jacqueline McLeod, eds., *Crossing Boundaries: Comparative History of Black People in Diaspora* (Bloomington: Indiana University Press, 1999)

Hobsbawm, Eric, *Echoes of the Marseillaise: Two Centuries Look Back on the French Revolution* (London: Verso, 1990)

"Identity politics and the Left," in Fraser and Freeman, *Audacious Democracy*

Holt, Tom, "Marking: race, race-making, and writing of history," *American Historical Review*, 106/1 (February, 1995), 1–20

Hopkinson, Michael, *The Irish War of Independence* (Dublin: Gill and Macmillan, 2002)

Horkheimer, Max and Theodor Adorno, *Dialectic of Enlightenment* (London: Allen Lane, 1973)

Horne, Janet, *A Social Laboratory for Modern France: The Musée Social and the Rise of the Welfare State* (Durham NC: Duke University Press, 2002)

Horne, John, "The Comité d'Action (CGT-Parti Socialiste) and the origins of wartime labor reformism (1914–1916)," in Fridenson, *The French Home Front*

"Démobilisations culturelles après la Grande Guerre," *14–18 Aujourd'hui*, Éditions Noesis (Paris, May 2002)

"Immigrant workers in France during World War I," *French Historical Studies*, 14/1 (Spring, 1985)

Labour at War: France and Britain, 1914–1918 (Oxford University Press, 1991)

House, Jim and Neil MacMaster, *Paris, 1961: Algerians, State Terror, and Memory* (New York: Oxford University Press, 2006)

Huang, Ray, *1587: A Year of No Significance: The Ming Dynasty in Decline* (New Haven: Yale University Press, 1981)

Huber, Michel, *La population de la France, son évolution et ses perspectives* (Paris: Hachette, 1937)

Hughes, Alex, *Heterographies: Sexual Difference in French Autobiography* (Oxford: Berg, 1999)

Humphreys, George G., *Taylorism in France, 1904–1920: The Impact of Scientific Management on Factory Relations and Society* (New York: Garland, 1986)

Hunt, Lynn, ed., *The New Cultural History* (Berkeley: University of California Press, 1989)

Hyman, Paula, *From Dreyfus to Vichy: The Remaking of French Jewry, 1906–1959* (New York: Columbia University Press, 1979)

Ignatiev, Noel, *How the Irish Became White* (New York: Routledge, 1995)

Iriye, Akira, "The internationalization of history," *American Historical Review*, 94/1 (February, 1989), 1–10

Iswolsky, Hélène, "The Russian Revolution seen from Paris," *Russian Review*, 26/2 (April, 1967), 153–163

Jackson, Jeffrey, *Making Jazz French: Music and Modern Life in Interwar Paris* (Durham NC: Duke University Press, 2003)

Jackson, Julian, *The Popular Front in France* (Cambridge University Press, 1988)

Jacobson, Matthew Frye, *Whiteness of a Different Color: European Immigrants and the Alchemy of Race* (Cambridge MA: Harvard University Press, 1998)

Jacquemet, Gérard, *Belleville au XIXe siècle* (Paris: J. Touzot, 1984)

Jay, Martin, *Songs of Experience: Modern American and European Variations on a Universal Theme* (Berkeley: University of California Press, 2005)

Jonas, Raymond, *France and the Cult of the Sacred Heart: An Epic Tale for Modern Times* (Berkeley: University of California Press, 2000)

Jones, Adrian, "The French railway strikes of January–May 1920: new syndicalist ideas and emergent communism," *French Historical Studies*, 12/4 (Autumn, 1982), 508–540

Jones, Colin, *Paris: Biography of a City* (New York: Viking, 2005)

Jones, Gareth Stedman, *Languages of Class: Studies in English Working Class History 1832–1982* (Cambridge University Press, 1983)

Joseph, Nathan, *Uniforms and Nonuniforms: Communication through Clothing* (Westport CT: Greenwood Press, 1986)

Joyce, Patrick, *Visions of the People: Industrial England and the Question of Class, 1840–1914* (Cambridge University Press, 1991)

Julliard, Jacques, *Autonomie ouvrière: études sur le syndicalisme d'action directe* (Paris: Gallimard/Le Seuil, 1988)

Kaplan, Steven L., *The Bakers of Paris and the Bread Question, 1700–1775* (Durham NC: Duke University Press, 1996)

Bread, Politics, and Political Economy in the Reign of Louis XV, 2 vols. (The Hague: Martinus Nijhoff, 1976)

Farewell, Revolution: Disputed Legacies; France, 1789–1989 (Ithaca NY: Cornell University Press, 1995)

Good Bread is Back: A Contemporary History of French Bread, the Way it is Made, and Those who Make it (Durham NC: Duke University Press, 2006)

Provisioning Paris: Merchants and Millers in the Grain and Flour Trade during the Eighteenth Century (Ithaca NY: Cornell University Press, 1984)

Kaplan, Temma, "Female consciousness and collective action: the case of Barcelona, 1910–1918," *Signs*, 7/2 (Winter, 1981)

Red City, Blue Period: Social Movements in Picasso's Barcelona (Berkeley: University of California Press, 1992)

Kaspi, André and Antoine Marès, *Le Paris des étrangers, 1919–1939* (Paris: Imprimerie nationale, 1992)

Keene, Jennifer D., *Doughboys, World War I, and the Remaking of American Culture* (Baltimore: Johns Hopkins University Press, 2001)

Kemp, Tom, *The French Economy, 1913–1939* (London: Longman, 1972)

Kepel, Gilles, *Les banlieues d'Islam: naissance d'une religion en France* (Paris: Seuil, 1987)

Keylor, William, ed., *The Legacy of the Great War: Peacemaking, 1919* (Boston: Houghton Mifflin, 1998)

Kivilu, Sabakinu, "Pauvreté et misère: éléments pour une économie politique des pillages," *Canadian Journal of African Studies*, 33/2–3 (1999), 448–482

Klingaman, William, *1919: The Year Our World Began* (New York: St. Martin's Press, 1987)

Kriegel, Annie, *Aux origines du communisme français: contribution à l'histoire du mouvement ouvrier français* (Paris: Flammarion, 1970)

Le Congrès de Tours, décembre 1920: naissance du Parti communiste français (Paris: R. Julliard, 1964)

Kuisel, Richard, *Capitalism and the State in Modern France* (Cambridge University Press, 1981)

Kurlansky, Mark, *1968: The Year That Rocked the World* (New York: Random House, 2005)

Labi, Maurice, *La grande division des travailleurs* (Paris: Éditions ouvrières, 1964)

Lacouture, Jean, *Ho Chi Minh, A Political Biography* (New York: Random House, 1968)

Larana, E., *et al.*, *New Social Movements: From Ideology to Identity* (Philadelphia: Temple University Press, 1994)

Lears, T. J. Jackson, ed., *The Culture of Consumption: Critical Essays in American History, 1880–1980* (New York: Pantheon, 1983)

Lebovics, Herman, *Bringing the Empire Back Home: France in the Global Age* (Durham NC: Duke University Press, 2004)

True France: The Wars over Cultural Identity, 1900–1945 (Ithaca NY: Cornell University Press, 1992)

Le Bras, Hervé, ed., *L'invention des populations: biologie, ideologie et politique* (Paris: Odile Jacob, 2000)

Le Gall, Jean-Marie, *Le mythe de Saint Denis: entre renaissance et révolution* (Seysell: Champ Vallon, 2007)

Lehning, James R., *The Melodramatic Thread: Spectacle and Political Culture in Modern France* (Bloomington: Indiana University Press, 2007)

Lejeune, Philippe, *L'autobiographie en France* (Paris: A. Colin, 1998)

Leveque, Jean-Jacques, *Vie et histoire du 13ème arrondissement* (Paris: Hervas, 1987)

Levin, Miriam R., *When the Eiffel Tower Was New: French Visions of Progress at the Centennial of the Revolution* (Amherst: University of Massachusetts Press, 1989)

Levinas, Emmanuel, *Humanism of the Other*, translated by Nidra Poller (Urbana: University of Illinois Press, 2003)

Lévy, Alma, *et al.*, *Des filles comme les autres: au-delà du foulard* (Paris: La Découverte, 2004)

Lewis, Mary Dewhurst, *The Boundaries of the Republic: Migrant Rights and the Limits of Universalism in France, 1918–1940* (Stanford University Press, 2007)
"Une théorie raciale des valeurs? Démobilisation des travailleurs immigrés et mobilisation des stereotypes à la fin de la Grande Guerre," translated by Sandrine Bertaux, in Le Bras, *L'invention des populations*

Liddle, Peter H., ed., *Home Fires and Foreign Fields: British Social and Military Experience in the First World War* (London: Brassey's Defence Publishers, 1985)

Lidtke, Vernon, *The Alternative Culture: Socialist Labor in Imperial Germany* (Oxford University Press, 1985)

Lindemann, Albert S., *The "Red Years": European Socialism versus Bolshevism, 1919–1921* (Berkeley: University of California Press, 1974)

Link, Arthur, *Woodrow Wilson: War, Revolution, and Peace* (Arlington Heights IL: Harlan Davidson, 1979)

Liu, Tessie, *The Weaver's Knot: The Contradictions of Class Struggle and Family Solidarity in Western France, 1750–1914* (Ithaca NY: Cornell University Press, 1994)

Lopez, Alfred J., ed., *Postcolonial Whiteness: A Critical Reader on Race and Empire* (Albany: State University of New York Press, 2005)

Lorcerie, Françoise, *La politisation du voile: l'affaire en France, en Europe et dans le monde* (Paris: Harmattan, 2005)

MacMaster, Neil, *Colonial Migrants and Racism: Algerians in France, 1900–1962* (New York: St. Martin's Press, 1997)

MacMillan, Margaret, *Paris 1919: Six Months that Changed the World* (New York: Random House, 2002)

Maghraoui, Driss, "Moroccan colonial troops: history, memory and the culture of French colonialism" (Ph.D. dissertation, University of California, Santa Cruz, 2000)

Maginnis, John, "The Big Parade: Paris – 1919," *Laurels*, 55/2 (Fall, 1984), 80–82

Magraw, Roger, *A History of the French Working Class* (Cambridge MA: Blackwell, 1992)

"Paris, 1917–1920: labour protest and popular politics," in Chris Wrigley, *Challenges of Labour*, 136–140

Magri, Susanna, "Housing," in Winter and Robert, *Capital Cities at War*

"Les locataires se syndiquent," in Quillot and Guerrand, *Cents ans d'habitat social*

"Le mouvement des locataires à Paris et dans sa banlieue, 1919–1925," *Mouvement social*, 137 (October–December, 1986)

La politique du logement et besoins en main-d'oeuvre (Paris: Centre de sociologie urbaine, 1972)

"Les propriétaires, les locataires, la loi. Jalons pour une analyse sociologique des rapports de location, Paris 1850–1920," *Revue française de sociologie*, 37/3 (July–September, 1996)

Magri, Susanna and Christian Topalov, eds., *Villes ouvrières, 1900–1950* (Paris: L'Harmattan, 1989)

Maier, Charles, *Recasting Bourgeois Europe: Stabilization in France, Germany and Italy in the Decade of World War I* (Princeton University Press, 1975)

Manela, Erez, *The Wilsonian Moment: Self-Determination and the International Origins of Anticolonial Nationalism* (New York: Oxford University Press, 2007)

Mann, Charles C., *1491: New Revelations of the Americas before Columbus* (New York: Vintage, 2006)

Marcus, Sharon, *Apartment Stories: City and Home in Nineteenth Century Paris and London* (Berkeley: University of California Press, 1999)

Marcuse, Herbert, *The New Left and the 1960s*, ed. Douglas Kellner (London: Routledge, 2005)

One-Dimensional Man: Studies in the Ideology of Advanced Industrial Society (Boston MA: Beacon Press, 1964)

Marmo, Michael, *More Profile than Courage: The New York City Transit Strike of 1966* (Albany: State University of New York Press, 1990)

Martell, Edward, ed., *Who Was Who Among English and European Authors, 1931–1949* (Detroit: Gale Research Company, 1978)

Martin, Laurent, *La presse écrite en France au XXe siècle* (Paris: Librairie Générale Française, 2005)

Marx, Karl, *The Eighteenth Brumaire of Louis Bonaparte* (New York: International Publishers, 1963)

Mayer, Arno, "The lower middle class as a historical problem," *Journal of Modern History*, 47/3 (1975)

The Persistence of the Old Regime: Europe to the Great War (New York: Pantheon, 1981)

The Politics and Diplomacy of Peacemaking: Containment and Counterrevolution at Versailles, 1918–1919 (New York: Knopf, 1967)

Wilson vs. Lenin: Political Origins of the New Diplomacy (Cleveland: World Publishing Company, 1959)

Mayeur, Jean and Madeleine Rebérioux, *The Third Republic from Its Origins to the Great War, 1871–1914* (Cambridge University Press, 1984)

Maza, Sarah, *The Myth of the French Bourgeoisie: An Essay on the Social Imaginary, 1750–1850* (Cambridge MA: Harvard University Press, 2003)

Mazower, Mark, *Dark Continent: Europe's Twentieth Century* (New York: Vintage, 2000)

McBride, Theresa, "A woman's world: department stores and the evolution of women's employment, 1870–1920," *French Historical Studies*, 10 (1978), 664–683

McClintock, Anne, "The angel of progress: pitfalls of the term 'post-colonialism,'" *Social Text*, 31/32 (1992)

Imperial Leather: Race, Gender, and Sexuality in the Colonial Context (New York: Routledge, 1995)

McDermid, Jane and Anna Hillyard, *Midwives of the Revolution: Female Bolsheviks and Women Workers in 1917* (Athens: Ohio University Press, 1999)

McKendrick, Neil, *et al.*, *The Birth of a Consumer Society: The Commercialization of Eighteenth-Century England* (Bloomington: Indiana University Press, 1982)

McLean, Iain, *The Legend of Red Clydeside* (Edinburgh: Humanities Press, 1993)

McMillan, James F., *Housewife or Harlot: The Place of Women in French Society, 1870–1940* (New York: St. Martin's Press, 1981)

Melucci, Alberto A., "A strange kind of newness: what's new in new social movements?" in Larana, *New Social Movements*

Merriman, John, *The Margins of City Life: Explorations on the French Urban Frontier, 1815–1851* (Oxford University Press, 1991)

Meusy, Jean-Jacques, ed., *La Bellevilloise (1877–1939): une page de l'histoire de la coopération et du mouvement ouvrier français* (Paris: Créaphis, 2001)

Meyer, Alain and Christine Moissinac, *Représentations sociales et littéraires: centre et périphérie, Paris 1908–1939* (Paris: IAURIF, 1979)

Meynier, G., "Les Algériens en France, 1914–1918," *Revue d'Histoire maghrébine*, 5 (1976)

Miami Theory Collective, ed., *Community at Loose Ends* (Minneapolis: University of Minnesota Press, 1991)

Micheletti, Michele, *Political Virtue and Shopping: Individualism, Consumerism, and Collective Action* (New York: Palgrave Macmillan, 2003)

Miller, Michael, *The Bon Marché: Bourgeois Culture and the Department Store, 1896–1920* (Princeton University Press, 1981)

Mintz, Sidney W., *Sweetness and Power: The Place of Sugar in Modern History* (New York: Penguin, 1985)

Mitchell, Barbara, *The Practical Revolutionaries: A New Interpretation of the French Anarchosyndicalists* (New York: Greenwood Press, 1987)

Mitchell, David J., *1919: Red Mirage: Year of Desperate Rebellion* (London: Cape, 1970)

Miyoshi, Masao, "A borderless world? From colonialism to transnationalism and the decline of the nation-state," *Critical Inquiry*, 19/4 (Summer, 1993)

Modood, Tariq and Pnina Werbner, eds., *The Politics of Multiculturalism in the New Europe: Racism, Identity, and Community* (London: Zed Books, 1997)

Monjauvis, Lucien, *Jean-Pierre Timbaud* (Paris: Éditions sociales, 1971)

Mucchielli, Laurent and Véronique Le Goaziou, eds., *Quand les banlieues brûlent . . .: retour sur les émeutes de novembre 2005* (Paris: La Découverte, 2007)

Nair, Janaki, "Contending ideologies? The Mass Awakener's Union and the Congress in Mysore, 1936–1942," *Social Scientist*, 22/7–8 (July, 1994)

Nancy, Jean-Luc, *La communauté désoeuvrée* (Paris: Bourgeois, 1986)

Navarro, Vicente, ed., *Neoliberalism, Globalization, and Inequalities: Consequences for Health and Quality of Life* (Amityville NY: Baywood Pub., 2007)

Nessel, Jan, "Fax from LA: images of the surreal city," *The Nation*, June 1, 1992, 746–748

Neulander, Joelle, *Programming National Identity: The Culture of Radio in Interwar France* (Baton Rouge: Louisiana State University Press, 2009)

Newton, Judith, Mary Ryan, and Judith Walkowitz, eds., *Sex and Class in Women's History* (Boston MA: Routledge and Kegan Paul, 1983)

Noiriel, Gérard, "Les espaces de l'immigration ouvrière," in Magri and Topalov, *Villes ouvrières*.

    Gens d'ici venus d'ailleurs: la France de l'immigration, 1900 à nos jours (Paris: Chêne, 2004)

    Les ouvriers dans la société française, XIXe–XXe siècle (Paris: Seuil, 1986)

Nolan, Mary, *Visions of Modernity: American Business and the Modernization of Germany* (New York: Oxford University Press, 1994)

Nora, Pierre, *Realms of Memory: Rethinking the French Past*, 3 vols., translated by Arthur Goldhammer (New York: Columbia University Press, 1996)

Nord, Philip, *Paris Shopkeepers and the Politics of Resentment* (Princeton University Press, 1986)

    "The welfare state in France, 1870–1914," *French Historical Studies*, 13/1 (Spring, 1994)

Nye, Robert A., *Masculinity and Male Codes of Honor in Modern France* (Oxford University Press, 1993)

Onana, Charles, *1940–1945: Noirs, Blancs, Beurs: libérateurs de la France* (Paris: Duboiris, 2006)

Ozouf, Mona, *Festivals and the French Revolution*, translated by Alan Sheridan (Cambridge MA: Harvard University Press, 1988)

Papayanis, Nicholas, *Alphonse Merrheim: The Emergence of Reformism in Revolutionary Syndicalism* (Dordrecht and Boston MA: M. Nijhoff, 1985)

    "Masses révolutionnaires et directions reformistes: les tensions au cours des grèves des metallurgistes français en 1919," *Mouvement social*, 93 (October–December, 1975), 51–73

Patterson, Tiffany Ruby and Robin D. G. Kelley, "Unfinished migrations: reflections on the African diaspora and the making of the modern world," *African Studies Review*, 43/1 (April, 2000)

Peabody, Sue and Tyler Stovall, eds., *The Color of Liberty: Histories of Race in France* (Durham NC: Duke University Press, 2003)

Peake, Thomas A., "Jacques Sadoul and the Russian intervention question, 1919," *Russian Review*, 32/1 (January, 1973), 54–63

Peiss, Kathy, "Making up, making over: cosmetics, consumer culture, and women's identity," in de Grazia and Furlough, *The Sex of Things*

Pérez, Louis A., *On Becoming Cuban: Identity, Nationality, and Culture* (Chapel Hill: University of North Carolina Press, 1999)

Perrot, Michelle, "The First of May 1890 in France: the birth of a working class ritual," in Thane, *et al.*, *The Power of the Past*

"Les rapports entre ouvriers français et étrangers (1871–1893)," *Bulletin de la Société d'histoire moderne*, 12/15–16 (1960)

Perrot, Philippe, *Fashioning the Bourgeoisie: A History of Clothing in the Nineteenth Century*, translated by Richard Bienvenu (Princeton University Press, 1994)

Le luxe: une richesse entre faste et confort, XVIIIe–XIXe siècle (Paris: Seuil, 1995)

Peru, Jean-Jacques, "Du village à la cité ouvrière, Drancy, 1896–1936" (Mémoire de maîtrise thesis, Université de Paris-1, 1977–1978)

Petonnet, Colette, *On est tous dans le brouillard: ethnologie des banlieues* (Paris: Galilée, 1980)

Petrini, Carlo, *Slow Food: The Case for Taste*, translated by William McCuaig (New York: Columbia University Press, 2004)

Pichado, Nelson A., "New social movements: a critical review," *Annual Review of Sociology*, 23 (1997)

Pinkney, David, *Napoleon III and the Rebuilding of Paris* (Princeton University Press, 1958)

Pipes, Richard, *Russia under the Bolshevik Regime: Lenin and the Birth of the Bolshevik State* (New York: Vintage, 1994)

Piven, Frances Fox and Richard Cloward, *Poor People's Movements: Why They Succeed, How They Fail* (New York: Vintage, 1979)

Polasky, Janet L., *The Democratic Socialism of Emile Vandervelde: Between Reform and Revolution* (Oxford and Providence RI: Berg, 1995)

Pollan, Michael, *The Omnivore's Dilemma: A Natural History of Four Meals* (New York: Penguin, 2007)

Pomeranz, Kenneth, *The Great Divergence: Europe, China, and the Making of the Modern World Economy* (Princeton University Press, 2000)

Popkin, Jeremy D., *History, Historians and Autobiography* (University of Chicago Press, 2005)

Poster, Mark, "The question of agency: Michel de Certeau and the history of consumerism," *Diacritics*, 22/2 (Summer, 1992), 94–107

Price, Roger, *The Modernization of Rural France* (New York: St. Martin's Press, 1983)

Quillot, Roger and Roger-Henri Guerrand, *Cents ans d'habitat social: une utopie réaliste* (Paris: A. Michel, 1989)

Raison-Jourde, Françoise, *La colonie auvergnate de Paris au XIXe siècle* (Paris: Ville de Paris, 1976)

Rajsfus, Maurice, *Drancy: un camp de concentration très ordinaire* (Paris: J'ai lu, 2004)

Rancière, Jacques, "The myth of the artisan: critical reflections on a category of social history," *International Labor and Working Class History*, 24 (Fall, 1983)
La nuit des prolétaires (Paris: Fayard, 1981)

Rappaport, Erika, *Shopping for Pleasure: Women in the Making of London's West End* (Princeton University Press, 2000)

Read, Anthony, *A World on Fire: 1919 and the Battle with Bolshevism* (New York and London: W. W. Norton & Co., 2008)

Rearick, Charles, *The French in Love and War: Popular Culture in the Era of the World Wars* (New Haven and London: Yale University Press, 1997)
Pleasures of the Belle Epoque (New Haven: Yale University Press, 1985)

Reid, Donald, *Paris Sewers and Sewermen: Realities and Representations* (Cambridge MA: Harvard University Press, 1991)
"Reflections on labor history and language," in Berlanstein, *Rethinking Labor History*

Ribeiro, Aileen, *Fashion in the French Revolution* (New York: Holmes and Meier, 1988)

Rich, Jeremy, *A Workman Is Worthy of His Meat: Food and Colonialism in the Gabon Estuary* (Lincoln: University of Nebraska Press, 2007)

Richards, Eric, "The last Scottish food riots," *Past and Present*, Supplement, 6 (1982)

Rifkin, Adrian, *Street Noises: Parisian Pleasure, 1900–1940* (Manchester University Press, 1993)

Robert, Jean-Louis, "La Bellevilloise dans la tourmente de la Grande Guerre," in Meusy, *La Bellevilloise*
"La CGT et la famille ouvrière, 1914–1918," *Mouvement social*, 116 (July–September, 1981)
"Cooperatives and the Labor Movement in Paris during the Great War," in Fridenson, *The French Home Front*
"Ouvriers et mouvement ouvrier parisiens pendant la grande guerre et l'immédiate après-guerre" (Doctorat d' État thesis, Université de Paris-1, 1989)
Les ouvriers, la Patrie et la Révolution: Paris 1914–1919 (Paris: Annales Littéraires de l'Université de Besançon/Les Belles Lettres, 1995)
La scission syndicale de 1921 (Paris: Publications de la Sorbonne, 1980)

Roberts, Mary-Louise, *Civilization without Sexes: Reconstructing Gender in Postwar France, 1917–1927* (University of Chicago Press, 1994)
"Samson and Delilah revisited: the politics of fashion in 1920s Paris," in Chadwick and Latimer, *The Modern Woman Revisited*

Robertson, Roland, "Glocalization: time-space and homogeneity-heterogeneity," in Featherstone *et al.*, *Global Modernities*

Roche, Daniel, *La culture des apparences: histoire du vêtement au XVIIe et XVIIIe siècles* (Paris: Fayard, 1989)

Roediger, David, *The Wages of Whiteness: Race and the Making of the American Working Class* (London: Verso, 2007)

Working Toward Whiteness: How America's Immigrants Became White: The Strange Journey from Ellis Island to the Suburbs (New York: Basic Books, 2005)

Roediger, David R. and Philip S. Foner, *Our Own Time: A History of American Labor and the Working Day* (New York: Greenwood Press, 1989)

Root, H. L., "Politiques frumentaires et violence collective en Europe moderne," *Annales E.S.C.*, 45/1 (January–March, 1990)

Rosanvallon, Pierre, *L'État en France* (Paris: Seuil, 1990)

Rosenberg, Clifford, *Policing Paris: The Origins of Modern Immigration Control between the Wars* (Ithaca NY: Cornell University Press, 2006)

Rosenfeld, Michael J., "Celebration, politics, selective looting and riots: a micro level study of the Bulls Riot of 1992 in Chicago," *Social Problems*, 44/4 (November, 1997), 483–502

Rosenzweig, Roy, *Eight Hours for What We will: Workers and Leisure in an Industrial City, 1870–1920* (New York: Cambridge University Press, 1983)

Rosmer, Alfred, *Le mouvement ouvrier pendant la guerre*, 2 vols. (Paris: Librairie du Travail, 1936–1956)

Ross, Kristin, *Fast Cars, Clean Bodies: Decolonization and the Reordering of French Culture* (Cambridge MA: MIT Press, 1995)

May '68 and Its Afterlives (University of Chicago Press, 2002)

Rossel, Andre, *Premier Mai: 90 ans de lutte populaire dans le monde* (Paris: Éditions de la Courtille, 1977)

Roy, Olivier, *La laïcité face à l'Islam* (Paris: Stock, 2005)

Rudé, Georges, "La taxation populaire de mai 1775 à Paris et dans la region parisienne," *Annales historiques de la Révolution Française*, 143 (April–June, 1956)

"La taxation populaire de mai 1775 en Picardie en Normandie et dans Le Beauvaisis," *Annales historiques de la Révolution Française*, 165 (July–September, 1961)

Ryan, Mary, "The American parade: representations of the nineteenth-century social order," in Hunt, *The New Cultural History*

Said, Edward, *Orientalism* (New York: Vintage, 1994)

Sallée, André and Philippe Chauveau, *Music-hall et café-concert* (Paris: Bordas, 1985)

Sang-gyo, An, *The Nature and Spirit of Korea: The March First Independence Movement versus Japanese Colonization* (Seoul: Korean Publishing Co., n.d.)

Sanson, Rosemonde, *Les 14 juillet, fête et conscience nationale, 1789–1975* (Paris: Flammarion, 1976)

Sartre, Jean-Paul, "Le Tiers Monde commence en banlieue," *Situations VIII* (Paris: Gallimard, 1972)

Sasges, Gerard, "The alcohol regime in Indochina 1897–1933" (Ph.D. dissertation, University of California, Berkeley, 2006)

Sauvy, Alfred, *Histoire économique de la France entre les deux guerres*, 4 vols. (Paris: Fayard, 1965–1975)

"Statistique générale et Service national des statistiques de 1919 à 1944," *Journal de la Société de statistique de Paris* (1975)

Schneider, William, *Quality and Quantity: The Quest for Biological Regeneration in Twentieth Century France* (New York: Cambridge University Press, 1990)

Schor, Juliet, *The Overworked American: The Unexpected Decline of Leisure in America* (New York: Basic Books, 1991)

Schwartz, Vanessa, *Spectacular Realities: Early Mass Culture in Fin-de-siècle Paris* (Berkeley: University of California Press, 1999)

Schweitzer, Sylvie, *Des engrenages à la chaine: les usines Citroen, 1915–1935* (Presses Universitaires de Lyon, 1982)

   Les femmes ont toujours travaillé: une histoire de leurs métiers, XIXe et XXe siècle (Paris: Jacob, 2002)

Scott, James, *The Moral Economy of the Peasant: Rebellion and Subsistence in Southeast Asia* (New Haven: Yale University Press, 1976)

   Seeing like a State: How Certain Schemes to Improve the Human Condition Have Failed (New Haven: Yale University Press, 1998)

   Weapons of the Weak: Everyday Forms of Peasant Resistance (New Haven: Yale University Press, 1985)

Scott, Joan, "The evidence of experience," *Critical Inquiry*, 17/4 (Summer, 1991)

   Gender and the Politics of History (New York: Columbia University Press, 1988)

   The Politics of the Veil (Princeton University Press, 2007)

Segalen, Martine, "L'esprit de famille à Nanterre," *Vingtième siècle*, 14 (April–June, 1987)

Seidman, Michael, *The Imaginary Revolution: Parisian Students and Workers in 1968* (New York: Berghahn, 2004)

   Workers Against Work: Labor in Paris and Barcelona During the Popular Front (Berkeley: University of California Press, 1991)

Sewell, William H., *Logics of History: Social Theory and Social Transformation* (University of Chicago Press, 2005)

Shapiro, Anne-Louise, *Housing the Poor of Paris* (Madison: University of Wisconsin Press, 1984)

Sharpe, William and Leonard Wallock, eds., *Visions of the Modern City* (New York: Proceedings of the Heyman Center for the Humanities, Columbia University, 1986)

Shattuck, Roger, *The Banquet Years: The Origins of the Avant-Garde in France, 1885 to World War I* (New York: Vintage, 1968)

Shovlin, John, *The Political Economy of Virtue: Luxury, Patriotism, and the Origins of the French Revolution* (Ithaca: Cornell University Press, 2006)

Sibeud, Emmanuelle, "Post-colonial et Colonial Studies: enjeux et débat," *Revue d'Histoire Moderne et Contemporaine*, 51 (2004)

Silverman, Debora, *Art Nouveau in Fin-de-Siècle France* (Berkeley: University of California Press, 1989)

Silverstein, Paul, *Algeria in France: Transpolitics, Race, and Nation* (Bloomington: Indiana University Press, 2004)

Sinanoglou, I., "Frenchmen, the revolutionary heritage and the Russian Revolution," *International History Review*, 2/4 (October, 1980)

Sirkus, Judith, *Sexing the Citizen: Morality and Masculinity in France, 1870–1920* (Ithaca: Cornell University Press, 2006)

Skocpol, Theda, *States and Social Revolutions: A Comparative Analysis of France, Russia, and China* (Cambridge University Press, 1979)

Smith, Bonnie G., *Confessions of a Concierge: Madame Lucie's History of Twentieth Century France* (New Haven: Yale University Press, 1985)

The Gender of History: Men, Women, and Historical Practice (Cambridge MA: Harvard University Press, 2000)

Smith, Leonard V., "Masculinity, memory, and the French First World War novel: Henri Barbusse and Roland Dorgelès," in Coetzee and Coetzee, *Authority, Identity, and the Social History of the Great War*

Smith, Sidonie and Julia Watson, *Reading Autobiography: A Guide for Interpreting Life Narratives* (Minneapolis: University of Minnesota Press, 2001)

Smith, Timothy B., *Creating the Welfare State in France, 1880–1940* (Montreal: McGill-Queen's University Press, 2003)

Sohn, Anne-Marie, *"Sois un homme!": la construction de la masculinité au XIXe siècle* (Paris: Seuil, 2009)

Soper, Kate and Frank Trentmann, eds., *Citizenship and Consumption* (Basingstoke and New York: Palgrave Macmillan, 2008)

Sowerine, Charles, *Sisters or Citizens? Women and Socialism in France since 1876* (Cambridge University Press, 1982)

Sperber, Jonathan, *The European Revolutions, 1848–1851* (New York: Cambridge University Press, 2005)

Spiegel, Gabrielle M., ed., *Practicing History: New Directions in Historical Writing After the Linguistic Turn* (New York: Routledge, 2005)

Spriano, Paolo, *The Occupation of the Factories: Italy 1920*, translated by Gwyn Williams (London: Pluto, 1975)

Stallybrass, Peter and Allon White, *The Politics and Poetics of Transgression* (Ithaca: Cornell University Press, 1986)

Stearns, Peter, *Consumerism in World History: The Global Transformation of Desire* (New York: Routledge, 2001)

Revolutionary Syndicalism and French Labor: A Cause Without Rebels (New Brunswick: Rutgers University Press, 1971)

Steedman, Carolyn Kay, *Landscape for a Good Woman: A Story of Two Lives* (New Brunswick: Rutgers University Press, 1986)

Steele, Valerie, *Paris Fashion: A Cultural History* (New York: Oxford University Press, 1988)

Steiner, Uwe, ed., *Walter Benjamin: An Introduction to His Work and Thought*, translated by Michael Winkler (University of Chicago Press, 2010)

Stone, Judith F., *The Search for Social Peace: Reform Legislation in France, 1890–1914* (Albany: State University of New York Press, 1985)

Stora, Benjamin, "Les Algériens dans le Paris de l'entre-deux-guerres," in Kaspi and Marès, *Le Paris des étrangers*

Stovall, Tyler, "Colour-blind France? Colonial workers during the First World War," *Race and Class*, 35/2 (October–December, 1993)

"From red belt to black belt: race, class, and urban marginality in Paris," in Peabody and Stovall, *The Color of Liberty*

"Love, labor, and race: colonial men and white women in France during the Great War," in Stovall and Van Den Abbeele, *French Civilization and Its Discontents*

"National identity and shifting imperial frontiers: whiteness and the exclusion of colonial labor after World War I," *Representations*, 84/1 (2003)

The Rise of the Paris Red Belt (Berkeley: University of California Press, 1990)

"*Sous les toits de Paris*: the working class and the Paris housing crisis, 1914–1924," *Proceedings of the Annual Meeting of the Western Society for French History*, 14 (1987)

Stovall, Tyler and Georges Van Den Abbeele, eds., *French Civilization and Its Discontents: Nationalism, Colonialism, Race* (Lanham MD: Lexington Books, 2003)

Strasser, Susan, Charles McGovern, and Matthias Judt, eds., *Getting and Spending: European and American Consumer Societies in the Twentieth Century* (New York: Cambridge University Press, 1998)

Sussman, Warren, *Culture as History: The Transformation of American Society in the Twentieth Century* (New York: Pantheon, 1984)

Sutcliffe, Anthony, *The Autumn of Central Paris: The Defeat of Town Planning 1850–1970* (London: Edward Arnold, 1970)

Sweeney, Regina Marie, *Singing Our Way to Victory: French Cultural Politics and Music during the Great War* (Middletown CT: Wesleyan University Press, 2001)

Tester, Keith, ed., *The Flaneur* (London and New York: Routledge, 1994)

Thane, Pat, Geoffrey Crossick, and Roderick Floud, eds., *The Power of the Past* (Cambridge University Press, 1977)

Thébaud, Françoise, *La femme au temps de la guerre de 14* (Paris: Éditions Stock, 1986)

Thelen, David, "The nation and beyond: transnational perspectives on United States history," *Journal of American History*, 86/3 (December, 1999), 965–975

Thomas, Martin, *The French Empire at War, 1940–1945* (Manchester University Press, 1998)

Thompson, E. P., *Customs in Common* (New York: New Press, 1993)

The Making of the English Working Class (London: V. Gollancz, 1963)

"The moral economy of the English crowd in the eighteenth century," *Past and Present*, 50 (February, 1971)

Thompson, J. M., *Russia, Bolshevism, and the Versailles Peace* (Princeton University Press, 1966)

Thompson, Willie, *The Left in History: Revolution and Reform in Twentieth Century Politics* (London: Pluto, 1997)

Tiersten, Lisa, *Marianne in the Market: Envisioning Consumer Society in Fin-de-Siècle France* (Berkeley: University of California Press, 2001)

Tilly, Charles, *The Contentious French* (Cambridge MA: Belknap Press, 1986)

"Food supply and public order in modern Europe," in C. Tilly, *The Formation of National States*

Regimes and Repertoires (Chicago: University of Chicago Press, 2006)

Tilly, Charles, ed., *The Formation of National States in Western Europe* (Princeton University Press, 1975)

Tilly, Louise, "The food riot as a form of political conflict in France," *Journal of Interdisciplinary History*, 2/1 (Summer, 1971)

Tilly, Louise and Joan Scott, *Women, Work, and Family* (New York: Holt, Rinehart, and Winston, 1978)

Todd, Emmanuel, *The Making of Modern France: Ideology, Politics, and Culture* (Oxford: Basil Blackwell, 1991)

Topalov, Christian, *Le logement en France: histoire d'une marchandise impossible* (Paris: Presses de la Fondation nationale des sciences politiques, 1987)

Torigian, Michael, *Every Factory a Fortress: The French Labor Movement in the Age of Ford and Hitler* (Athens: Ohio University Press, 1999)

Touraine, Alain, *L'evolution du travail ouvrier aux usines Renault* (Paris: Centre Nationale de la Récherche Scientifique, 1955)

The Voice and the Eye: An Analysis of Social Movements (Cambridge University Press, 2003)

Trang, Gaspard Thu, *Ho Chi Minh à Paris, 1917–1923* (Paris: L'Harmattan, 1992)

Traugott, Mark, "Barricades as repertoire: continuities and discontinuities in the history of French contention," *Social Science History*, 17/2 (Summer, 1993)

Traugott, Mark, ed., *The French Worker: Autobiographies from the Early Industrial Era* (Berkeley: University of California Press, 1993)

Trentmann, Frank, "Beyond consumerism: new historical perspectives on consumption," *Journal of Contemporary History*, 39/3 (July, 2004)

Trentmann, Frank and Flemming Just, *Food and Conflict in Europe in the Age of the Two World Wars* (New York: Palgrave Macmillan, 2006)

Tucker, Kenneth, *French Revolutionary Syndicalism and the Public Sphere* (Cambridge University Press, 1996)

Van der Linden, Marcel, "Transnationalizing American labor history," *Journal of American History*, 86/3 (December, 1999)

Van Der Stegen, "Les chinois en France, 1915–1925" (Mémoire de maîtrise thesis, Université de Paris X, 1974)

Vanier, Henriette, *La mode et ses métiers: frivolités et luttes des classes, 1830–1870* (Paris: A. Colin, 1960)

Vann, Michael G., "White City on the Red River: race, power, and culture in French colonial Hanoi, 1872–1954" (Ph.D. dissertation, University of California, Santa Cruz, 1999)

Veblen, Thorstein, *Theory of the Leisure Class: An Economic Study of Institutions* (New York: Macmillan, 1899)

Vidalenc, Jean, "La main-d'oeuvre étrangère en France et la première guerre mondiale (1901–1926)," *Francia*, 2 (1974)

Vigna, Xavier, *L'insubordination ouvrière dans les années 68: essai d'histoire politique des usines* (Presses Universitaires de Rennes, 2007)

Waites, Bernard, "The government of the Home Front and the 'moral economy' of the working class," in Liddle, *Home Fires and Foreign Fields*

Wakeman, Rosemary, *The Heroic City: Paris, 1945–1958* (University of Chicago Press, 2009)

Wall, Richard and Jay Winter, eds., *The Upheaval of War* (Cambridge University Press, 1988)

Walton, Whitney, *France at the Crystal Palace: Bourgeois Taste and Artisan Manufacture in the Nineteenth Century* (Berkeley: University of California Press, 1992)

Walworth, A., *Wilson and His Peacemakers: American Diplomacy at the Paris Peace Conference* (New York: Norton, 1986)

Warnod, Andre, *Les bals de Paris* (Paris: Les Éditions G. Crès, 1922)

Watts, Sydney, *Meat Matters: Butchers, Politics, and Market Culture in Eighteenth Century Paris* (University of Rochester Press, 2006)

Weber, Caroline, *Queen of Fashion: What Marie Antoinette Wore to the Revolution* (New York: Henry Holt, 2006)

Weber, Eugene, *Peasants into Frenchmen* (Stanford University Press, 1976)

Weiss, John, "Origins of the French welfare state: Poor Relief in the Third Republic, 1871–1914," *French Historical Studies*, 13 (Spring, 1983)

Whaples, Robert, "Winning the eight-hour day, 1909–1919," *Journal of Economic History*, 50/2 (June, 1990), 393–406

Wilder, Gary, *The French Imperial Nation-State: Negritude and Colonial Humanism between the Wars* (University of Chicago Press, 2005)

Wildman, Allan K., *The End of the Russian Imperial Army: The Old Army and the Soldiers' Revolt* (Princeton University Press, 1980)

Willard, Claude, "La connaissance de la revolution russe et l'expérience sovietique par le mouvement ouvrier français en 1918–1919," *Cahiers de l'institut Maurice Thorez* (1975), 12–13

Williams, Dwayne E., "Rethinking the African diaspora: a comparative look at race and identity in a transatlantic community," in Hine and McLeod, *Crossing Boundaries*

Williams, Gwyn, *Proletarian Order: Antonio Gramsci, Factory Councils, and the Origins of Italian Communism, 1911–1921* (London: Pluto, 1975)

Williams, Linda, *Viewing Positions* (New Brunswick: Rutgers University Press, 1994)

Williams, Raymond, *Culture and Society* (New York: Columbia University Press, 1960)

Willmott, Peter and Michael Young, *Family and Class in a London Suburb* (London: Routledge and Kegan Paul, 1960)

Winter, Jay, Geoffrey Parker, and Mary R. Habeck, eds., *The Great War and the Twentieth Century* (New Haven: Yale University Press, 2000)

Winter, Jay and Jean-Louis Robert, eds., *Capital Cities at War: Paris, London, Berlin, 1914–1919* (Cambridge University Press, 1997)

Wishnia, Judith, *The Proletarianization of the Fonctionnaires: Civil Service Workers and the Labor Movement under the Third Republic* (Baton Rouge: Louisiana State University Press, 1990)

Wohl, Robert, *French Communism in the Making* (Stanford University Press, 1966)

Wood, Elizabeth, *The Baba and the Comrade: Gender and Politics in Revolutionary Russia* (Bloomington: Indiana University Press, 1997)

Wrigley, Chris, ed., *Challenges of Labour: Central and Western Europe, 1917–1920* (London and New York: Routledge, 1993)

Wrigley, Richard, *The Politics of Appearances: Representations of Dress in Revolutionary France* (Oxford: Berg, 2002)

Young, Robert, *White Mythologies: Writing History and the West* (London and New York: Routledge, 2004)

Zdatny, Steven, *The Politics of Survival: Artisans in Twentieth Century France* (New York: Oxford University Press, 1990)

Zucotti, Susan, *The Holocaust, the French, and the Jews* (Lincoln: University of Nebraska Press, 1999)

Zylberberg-Hocquard, Marie-Hélène, *Femmes et féminisme dans le mouvement ouvrier français* (Paris: Éditions ouvrières, 1981)

Index

Adam, H. Pearl, 34, 49, 103, 151, 158, 166, 168, 176
automobile as luxury, 11, 68–69, 75, 76

barricades
  description of battle, 164
  establishment of, 77, 78
  heightened level of intra-class as well as inter-class conflict, 105
  representing integration of working people into an undifferentiated mass culture, 179
  treaty afterwards, 174
  urban public space, effect on, 155
basic consumer goods
  all classes bought, symbol of unity, 27
  class conflict, 27
  cross-class alliances over high cost, 27
  "national" or "victory" commodities
    creation and purpose of, 72–74
    dissatisfaction with, 73–74
  policy of *laissez-faire*, 71
  politicization of everyday commodities, 181, 190, 290
  revolutionary movement, heart of, 182
  shortages as basis for revolution, 76–77
  see also clothing, food
Basilica of Sacré Coeur, 264
Bastille Day celebrations compared to May Day, 156–157, 172–174, 175–180
Boulogne-Billancourt suburban municipality, *see* working-class identity
Bouvier, Jeanne, 61
bread
  bakers' wartime behavior as excessive, 29, 68
  ban on specialty breads, 52–53, 56, 68, 72
  creation of "national" commodity, 72–74
  daily struggle, 27
  ingredients restrictions, 72
  "national" or "victory" loaf, 72, 73
  price control, 51, 52
  rationing, 71

restrictions as provoking revolution, 76
shortages and hoarding, 51
symbol of class conflict and lack of commitment to war effort, 53
symbol of diets and politics, 51
symbol of social and economic difference, 51
wartime Paris, in, 51–53

cell phones, 75
Clemençeau, Georges, 103, 146, 158, 160, 161, 164, 166, 238, 239, 244, 257, 264, 270, 271, 282
clothing
  attitude toward, 33, 57
  dressmakers' strikes of 1917, 57, 58
  elite consumerism, 58
  French Revolution, 32
  gender shaped views of food and clothing in contrasting ways, 35–36
  increased elegance of lower class, 59–60
  men and women distinguished, 35
  Muslim women, 33
  political history (link between politics, clothing, and the nation), 32–35
  shaped consumer culture, 27
  standardization of clothing and taste, 59
  symbolized mass discontent, 58
  uniform as social distinction, 35
  uniforms worn by soldiers, 33
  see also fashion/garment industry
coal shortage, 66, 68, 219, 228
consumer movement
  base of upsurge in tenant activism, 199
  basic consumer goods at heart of, 182
  central themes, 184
  contrasting wartime and postwar economic policies, 191
  cooperatives movement, 191, 226–227
  demobilizing the consumer economy, 190–193

CPSIA information can be obtained
at www.ICGtesting.com
Printed in the USA
LVHW02s1731060718
582932LV00014B/349/P